D0871882

Advances in the Evolutionary Synthesis of Intelligent Agents

Advances in the Evolutionary Synthesis of Intelligent Agents

edited by Mukesh Patel, Vasant Honavar, Karthik Balakrishnan

A Bradford Book
The MIT Press
Cambridge, Massachusetts
London, England

Library of Congress Cataloging-in-Publication Data

Patel, Mukesh.
  Advances in the evolutionary synthesis of intelligent agents / Mukesh Patel, Vasant Honavar, Karthik Balakrishnan
    p.   cm.
  "A Bradford Book."
  Includes bibliographical references and index.
  ISBN 0-262-16201-6 (hc. : alk. paper)
  1. Intelligent agents (computer software). 2. Evolutionary programming (Computer science). I. Honavar, Vasant, 1960-. II. Balakrishnan, Karthik, 1970- . III. Title.

QA76.76.I58 P78   2001
006.3—dc21   00-052691

To my parents and Leonard Uhr – my mentor and friend.

Vasant Honavar

To the truly wonderful women in my life – my wife, my mother, and my sisters.

Karthik Balakrishnan

Contents

Contributors

Karthik Balakrishnan
Decision Analytics Group
Obongo Inc.
Redwood City, USA
balak_k@yahoo.com

Egbert Boers
Artificial Intelligence Group
National Aerospace Laboratory
Amsterdam, The Netherlands
boers@nlr.nl

Brian Carse
Faculty of Engineering
University of the West of England
Bristol, UK
Brian.Carse@uwe.ac.uk

Frederick Crabbe IV
Computer Science Department
University of California
Los Angeles, USA
cardo@cs.ucla.edu

Melania Degeratu
Program in Applied Mathematical
and Computational Sciences
University of Iowa
Iowa City, USA
mdegerat@math.uiowa.edu

Michael Dyer
Computer Science Department
University of California
Los Angeles, USA
dyer@cs.ucla.edu

Dario Floreano
Department of Computer Science
Swiss Federal Institute of Technology
Lausanne, Switzerland
Dario.Floreano@epfl.ch

Terence Fogarty
Department of Computer Studies
Napier University
Edinburgh, UK
tcf@dcs.napier.ac.uk

Frederic Gruau
Laboaratoire d'Informatique
Robotique et Microelectronique de
Montpellier
Montpellier, France
gruau@lirmm.fr

Vasant Honavar
Department of Computer Science
Iowa State University
Ames, USA
honavar@cs.iastate.edu

Yong Liu
Computer Science Division
Electrotechnical Laboratory
Ibaraki, Japan
yliu@etl.go.jp

Bruce MacLennan
Computer Science Department
University of Tennessee
Knoxville, USA
MacLennan@cs.utk.edu

Thilo Mahnig
RWCP Theoretical Foundation
GMD Laboratory
Sankt Augustin, Germany
thilo.mahnig@gmd.de

Filippo Menczer
Department of Management Sciences
University of Iowa
Iowa City, USA
filippo-menczer@uiowa.edu

J. J. Merelo
Departamento de Electrónica y
Tecnología de los Computadores
Universidad de Granada
Granada, Spain
jmerelo@kal-el.ugr.es

Olivier Michel
LAMI
Swiss Federal Institute of Technology
Lausanne, Switzerland
Olivier.Michel@epfl.ch

Risto Miikkulainen
Department of Computer Sciences
The University of Texas at Austin
Austin, USA
risto@cs.utexas.edu

Francesco Mondada
K-Team SA
Switzerland
mondada@k-team.com

F. Moran
Departamento de Bioquimica y
Biología MolecularI
Universidad Complutense de Madrid
Madrid, Spain
fmoran@solea.quim.ucm.es

David Moriarty
Information Sciences Institute
University of Southern California
Marina del Rey, USA
moriarty@isi.edu

Heinz Muehlenbein
RWCP Theoretical Foundation
GMD Laboratory
Sankt Augustin, Germany
muehlenbein@gmd.de

Stefano Nolfi
Institute of Psychology
C.N.R.
Rome, Italy
nolfi@ip.rm.cnr.it

Domenico Parisi
Institute of Psychology
C.N.R.
Rome, Italy
parisi@ip.rm.cnr.it

Mukesh Patel
Applitech Solution Limited
Ahmedabad, India
mukesh@applitechsolution.com

A. Prieto
Departamento de Electrónica y
Tecnología de los Computadores
Universidad de Granada
Granada, Spain

Ida Sprinkhuizen-Kuyper
Computer Science Department
Universiteit Maastricht
Maastricht, The Netherlands
kuyper@cs.unimaas.nl

William Street
Department of Management Sciences
University of Iowa
Iowa City, USA
nick-street@uiowa.edu

John Sullivan
Faculty of Engineering
University of the West of England
Bristol, UK
John.Sullivan@uwe.ac.uk

Xin Yao
School of Computer Science
The University of Birmingham
Birmingham, UK
x.yao@cs.bham.ac.uk

Preface

The emergence of Artificial Intelligence and Cognitive Sciences concerned with understanding and modeling intelligent systems, both natural and synthetic, is perhaps one of the most significant intellectual developments of the twentieth century.

From the earliest writings of India and Greece, understanding minds and brains has been a fundamental problem in philosophy. The invention of the digital computer in the 1940s made this a central concern of computer scientists. Among the first uses of the digital computer, in the 1950s, was the development of computer programs to model perception, reasoning, learning, and evolution. Ensuing developments in the theory of computation, design and analysis of algorithms and the synthesis of programmable information processing systems, provided a new set of tools with which to study appropriately embodied minds and brains – both natural as well as artificial – through the analysis, design, and evaluation of computers and programs that exhibit aspects of intelligent behavior.

This systems approach to understanding intelligent behavior has been driven largely by the working hypothesis of Artificial Intelligence, which simply states that *thought processes can be modeled by computation or information processing*. The philosophical roots of this hypothesis can be traced at least as far back as the attempts of Helmholtz, Leibnitz, and Boole to explain thought processes in terms of mechanical (or in modern terms, algorithmic or computational) processes. The advent of molecular biology, heralded by the discovery of genetic code, has ushered in a similar information processing approach to the study of living systems. This has resulted in the emergence of computational molecular biology, synthetic biology (or artificial life), and related disciplines, which are driven by the working hypothesis that *life processes can be modeled and/or understood by computation or information processing*.

Systems whose information processing structures are fully programmed to their last detail, despite being viewed as the *ideal* in many areas of computer science and engineering, are extremely difficult to design for all but the simplest and the most routine of applications. The designers of such systems have to be able to anticipate in advance all possible contingencies such a system could ever encounter, and program appropriate procedures to deal with each of them. Dynamic, open, real-world world environments call for *adaptive and learning systems* that are equipped with processes that allow them to modify their behavior, as needed, by changing their information processing structures. Long-term collective survival in changing environments calls for systems that can *evolve*. Biological intelligence has emerged over the millennia and depends crucially on evolution and learning – or rather, it is hard to conceive of a God so intelligent and yet so stupid, so mundane at detail yet so brilliant at the fantastic, as to – like a watchmaker – tediously craft each living creature to its last detail.

Cognitive and information structures and processes, embodied in living systems, offer us impressive existence proofs of many highly effective designs for adaptive, flexible, and creative biological intelligent agents. They are also a great source of ideas for designing artificially intelligent agents. Against this background, this book explores some of the central problems in artificial intelligence, cognitive science, and synthetic biology, namely the modeling of information structures and processes that create and adapt intelligent agents through evolution and learning.

Work on this book began in 1995 when two of us (Vasant Honavar and Mukesh Patel) independently started efforts to put together edited volumes on evolutionary approaches to the synthesis of intelligent systems. When we became aware of each other's work, it seemed logical to pool the efforts and produce a single edited volume. With encouragement from Harry Stanton of MIT press, we invited a team of authors to contribute chapters covering various aspects of evolutionary synthesis of intelligent systems. The original target date for publication of the book was late 1997. However, the sad demise of Harry Stanton interfered with this plan. Fortunately, Doug Sery, who inherited the project in 1998, was very supportive of the project and determined to see it through.

Karthik Balakrishnan joined the team in 1998. Honavar and Patel are grateful to Balakrishnan for taking over a large portion of the effort of putting together this volume between 1998 and 2000. During this period, all of the contributed chapters went through several rounds of reviews and revisions. The final product is the result of the collective work of the authors of the various chapters and the three editors.

The chapters included in this volume represent recent advances in evolutionary approaches to the synthesis of intelligent software agents and intelligent artifacts for a variety of applications. The chapters may be broadly divided into four categories. The first set of chapters demonstrates the raw power of evolution in determining effective solutions to complex tasks such as walking behaviors for 8-legged robots, evolution of meaningful communication in a population of agents, addressing of multi-objective tradeoffs inherent in the design of accurate and compact codebook vectors for vector quantization, and the design of effective box-pushing robot behaviors. The second set of chapters explores mechanisms to make evolutionary design *scalable*, largely through the use of biologically inspired *development* mechanisms. These include a recipe-like genetic coding based on L-systems (inspired by DNA coding of amino acids) and models of artificial neurogenesis (cell differentiation, division, migration, axonal growth, guidance, target recognition, etc.).

The third set of chapters largely deals with equivalents of *ontogenetic learning*, which encompass the use of powerful local learning algorithms to quickly improve and explore the promising solutions discovered by the underlying evolutionary search. These include gradient-descent based learning of radial-basis function network architectures designed by evolution, different flavors of Hebbian adaptation of evolved neural architectures, and the evolution of learning parameters and rules for second-order neural network architectures. The final set of chapters extends the principle of evolutionary search along novel and useful directions. These include the use of *local selection* as a powerful yet computationally inexpensive alternative to the more popular global selection schemes (e.g., proportional, tournament, etc.), *symbiotic evolution* for evolving and exploiting cooperating blocks (or units) of the neural network solution, treating the evolved population as an *ensemble of solutions* and exploiting the population diversity to produce enhanced and robust solutions, and developing a theoretically sound alternate interpretation of evolutionary search that operates over search distributions rather than recombination/crossover.

A summary of the key contributions of each chapter follows.

Evolutionary Synthesis of Complex Agent Programs

In Chapter 1, Balakrishnan and Honavar introduce the powerful agent synthesis paradigms of evolution and learning. Drawing inspiration from biological processes at work in the design of varied, and in many instances unique, adaptations of life forms, the authors present evolutionary synthesis of artificial neural networks as a computationally efficient approach for the exploration of useful, efficient, and perhaps even *intelligent* behaviors in artificial automata. Most important, the authors present a formal characterization of *properties* of genetic representations of neural architectures.

In Chapter 2, Gruau and Quatramaran address a challenging problem of evolving *walking gaits* for an 8-legged robot. This task is particularly difficult because the leg-controller must not only move the individual legs, but also coordinate them appropriately to ensure that the robot is balanced and stable. Using a genetic representation based on *cellular encoding*, they evolve programs for transforming a graph and decoding it into a neural network. Perhaps the greatest benefit of this graph-grammar encoding scheme is its ability to evolve *reusable modules* or *subnetworks*, an aspect of critical importance in the control of the 8-legged robot. This encoding is used to evolve the architecture of the neurocontroller, along with the weights, the number of input and output units, as well as the *type* of units (*temporal* for duration of movement sequence and *spatial* for intensity of movement). The authors propose and use an *interactive approach*, calling for human intervention in identifying and promoting the emergence and adaptation of specific *regularities*. They achieve this by visually monitoring the evolutionary process and rewarding potentially promising features by increasing their fitness evaluations. The authors claim that this *semi-supervised* approach works well, requiring far fewer evolutionary generations to evolve acceptable behaviors than pure evolutionary search. They present a number of interesting walking behaviors that evolved, including *wavewalk* – moving one leg at a time, and the true *quadripod gait* – moving four legs at a time.

MacLennan presents an extremely interesting application of evolution in Chapter 3. He considers the evolution of meaningful communication in agent populations. In the first set of experiments, he arms the agents with *finite state machines* (FSMs) (which are computationally equivalent to a restricted class of neural networks), capable of reading *single symbols* and communicating/writing single symbols in return. The agents are rewarded for recognizing and responding with correct symbols. Using a *direct encoding* scheme to represent the transition tables of the FSMs, he demonstrates interesting results in the evolution of communication in this agent population. He shows that the evolved agents appear to communicate meaningfully using single symbols, and to some extent, pairs of symbols exhibiting rudimentary syntax. Owing to the limitations of FSMs, primarily their inability to *generalize*, MacLennan and his students also explore the use of simple feed-forward neural network structures for communication. In these experiments, they evolve the network architecture and use back-propagation to train the network. Again they demonstrate the evolution of meaningful communication, although the results are characteristically different from those using FSMs.

In Chapter 4, Merelo et al. adopt an evolutionary approach to address an important consideration in unsupervised classification problems. Unsupervised classifiers or clustering algorithms must not only discover compact, well-defined groups of patterns in the data, but also deliver the correct number of groups/clusters. This is a difficult multi-objective optimization problem with few practical algorithmic solutions. The common approach is to fix the number of desired clusters *a priori* as in the popular k-means algorithm. Vector Quantization (VQ) is a classification technique in which a set of labeled vectors, called the *codebook*, are given, and classification of an input is performed by identifying the codebook vector that matches it best. However, in order to use VQ, one needs the codebook to be specified. Kohonen's Learning Vector Quantization (LVQ) is an approach that can *learn* codebooks from a set of initial vectors. However, even with this approach, the size of the codebook needs to be set in advance. But how does one know what the size should be? Merelo et al. use an evolutionary approach to design the codebook, optimizing accuracy, distortion, and size. This multi-objective optimization leads to codebook designs that are smaller and more accurate than those obtained with LVQ, and contain fewer weights than back-propagation trained neural networks of similar accuracy. The authors demonstrate the power and utility of this approach in separating a set of Gaussian non-overlapping clusters and breast cancer diagnosis.

In Chapter 5, Balakrishnan and Honavar address the evolution of effective box-pushing behaviors. They use a multi-level, variable-length genetic representation that possesses many of the properties described in Chapter 1. Using this mechanism, they evolve both feed-forward and recurrent neuro-controllers for a heavily constrained box-pushing task. They analyze the evolved networks to clearly demonstrate the mechanism by which successful box-pushing behaviors emerge, leading to critical insights into the nature of the task in general, and the ability of evolution to deal effectively with the imposed constraints in particular. Through a variety of experiments the authors highlight the role of *memory* in effective box-pushing behaviors, and show how evolution tailors the designs to match (and surmount) constraints. The authors also discuss the evolution of robot sensory systems, and present empirical results in the co-evolution and co-adaptation of robot sensory and neural systems. They show that evolution often discovers sensory system designs that employ minimal numbers of sensors. Further, they also show that evolution can be trusted to discover robust controllers when the task environment is noisy.

Evolution and Development of Agent Programs

Although evolution is a powerful and adaptive search technique, its application is often limited owing to the immense computational effort involved in searching complex solution spaces. Local or environment guided search can often help alleviate this problem by quickly exploring promising areas identified by the evolutionary mechanism. Many authors have explored such combinations of evolutionary and local search, with much success. One such local mechanism is inspired by developmental and molecular biology. This deals with the notion of *development*, which can be crudely defined as *adaptation that is a result of an interaction between genetically inherited information and environmental influences*. Development is usually associated with determining the *phenotype* from the *genotype*, possibly influenced by environmental factors, as is evidenced in the following three chapters.

In Chapter 6, Boers and Sprinkhuizen-Kuyper present a novel genetic representation for neural network architectures that is inspired by DNA coding of amino acids. This representation or coding mechanism can be thought of as a *recipe* for creating a neural network rather than its direct *blueprint*. This powerful and novel coding is a graph grammar based directly on the parallel string rewriting mechanism of L-systems, where each genotype contains a set of production rules, which when decoded produces the corresponding phenotype (or neural network). The primary benefit of this coding mechanism is its scalability in coding potentially large neural network structures. In addition, such grammar based representations also easily handle and foster the emergence of *modular designs*. The authors present results on the evolution of modular architectures for the famous *what-where* task. They also present an enhancement of the development process that constructively adds modules and units to the decoded network, and address its implications for exploiting the Baldwin effect in the Darwinian evolution framework.

Drawing inspiration from developmental and molecular biology, Michel presents a model of *artificial neurogenesis* in Chapter 7. He uses this procedure to evolve and develop dynamical recurrent neural networks to control mobile robot behaviors such as maze traversal and obstacle avoidance. His model of neurogenesis, based on protein synthesis regulation, includes artificial specifications of processes such as cell differentiation, division, migration, axonal growth, guidance, and target recognition. In addition, the linear threshold function units that are evolved are also adapted using simple Hebbian learning techniques. The preliminary results obtained using this approach offer much promise for the design of large, modular neural networks. The author presents examples of interesting behaviors evolved using this approach for the robot Khepera. Michel also discusses issues involved in the transfer of robot behaviors evolved in simulation, to real robots.

In Chapter 8, Parisi and Nolfi present a comprehensive view of the role of development in the evolutionary synthesis of neural networks. In their view, development is any change in the individual that is genetically *trig-*

gered/influenced. Using this broad definition, they summarize their considerable research in various aspects of development, including self-teaching networks, a model of neurogenesis (axonal growth process), self-directed learning, a model of temporal development with genetic information expressed at different *ages* of the individual, etc. Self-directed learning is demonstrated using an architecture wherein the neural network learns to predict the sensory consequences of the movements of the agent. The authors show that this ability endows the agents with more effective behaviors. Self-teaching networks contain two subnetworks; one produces the behavioral responses of the agent, while the other produces a teaching or supervisory input used to adapt the first subnetwork. The authors also experiment with individuals that are cognizant of their age, allowing adaptation of behaviors with age. The authors demonstrate and discuss results of these different developmental techniques in the context of agent behaviors such as foraging (food finding), wall/obstacle avoidance, goal approaching, etc. In most cases they use *a priori* fixed neural network architectures and a simple direct encoding to evolve the weights of the network.

Enhancing Evolutionary Search Through Local Learning

In addition to the use of recipe-like genetic codings that develop into neural architectures under the influence of environmental factors, other, more powerful local search algorithms can also be used in conjunction with evolutionary search. The following chapters present examples of the use of such learning techniques to further shape the solutions discovered by evolution.

In Chapter 9, Carse et al. address the design of radial basis function (RBF) neural networks using a hybrid approach that involves the use of evolution to discover optimal network architectures (number of hidden units, radial basis function centers and widths, etc.) and a gradient-descent based learning algorithm for tuning the connection weights. The authors introduce two interesting notions in the chapter – a novel crossover operator that identifies *similar units* no matter where they appear on the genotype, and a scaling of training epochs that assigns fewer training cycles to networks in the early stages of evolution, and progressively more as evolution advances. The rationale behind the former idea is to make evolutionary search more efficient by handling the *competing conventions/permutations* problem (where the exact same phenotype has multiple genetic representations), while the latter is inspired by the fact that networks in early stages of evolution are perhaps not architecturally close to ideal, and hence little effort need be wasted in training them. The idea thus is to discover the optimal structure first and then fine tune it. The authors use variable length genotypes, with a direct encoding of the network architecture. They show that this approach produces relatively small yet accurate RBF networks on a number of problems, including the Mackey-Glass chaotic time series prediction problem.

In Chapter 10, Floreano et al. investigate chase-escape behaviors co-evolving in a framework of two miniature mobile robots, a predator with a vision system and a faster prey with only proximity sensors. Both robots are controlled using recurrent neural networks evolved in a competitive co-evolutionary setting. Inspired by the thesis that unpredictable and dynamic environments require the *evolution of adaptivity*, the authors explore mechanisms that produce solutions capable of coping with changing environments. This becomes particularly critical in co-evolving populations owing to the phenomenon known as the *Red Queen Effect*. In such situations, adaptive traits evolved by one species are often annulled by the evolution of counteractive traits in a competing species, thereby producing *dynamic fitness landscapes*. In order to evolve agent designs that can cope with such dynamic and unpredictable changes, the authors explore three broad approaches – (1) maintaining diversity in evolving populations, (2) preferentially selecting genotypes whose mutant neighbors are different but equally viable, and (3) incorporating mechanisms of ontogenetic adaptation. The authors use a direct encoding representation to evolve weights within *a priori* fixed network architectures, and in later experiments, noise levels and parameters for Hebbian learning. They present results of interesting evolved chase-escape behaviors.

Crabbe and Dyer, in Chapter 11, present a flexible neural network architecture that can learn to approach and/or avoid multiple goals in dynamic environments. Artificial agents endowed with this architecture, called MAX-SON (max-based second order network), learn spatial navigation tasks faster than other reinforcement-based learning approaches such as Q-learning. The learning architecture employs two subnetworks – a second-order policy network that generates agent actions in response to sensory inputs, and a first-order value network that produces reinforcement signals to adapt the policy networks. Of particular importance are two thresholds, θ_1 and θ_2, that control the response of the agent to sudden sensory changes or fluctuations. The authors demonstrate the emergence of effective behaviors for agents seeking food and drink and avoiding poisons. The final set of experiments demonstrates the ability of this approach in producing agents driven by *internal goals*, i.e., agents seek food or water only when they are hungry or thirsty, respectively. The authors use an evolutionary approach to determine optimal settings for the thresholds, which strongly influence the learning rules of the agents. They also present results in evolving portions of the learning rules themselves.

Novel Extensions and Interpretations of Evolutionary Search

Although evolutionary algorithms have proven themselves to be efficient and effective heuristic search techniques, their applicability is often limited owing to a few drawbacks such as the phenomenon of *premature convergence*, lack of concrete theoretical underpinnings, etc. This has prompted researchers to extend or interpret evolutionary search mechanism in novel and useful ways. The final set of chapters in this compilation extend basic evolutionary search along interesting and useful dimensions.

In Chapter 12, Menczer et al. present an interesting variation of evolutionary algorithms, namely, *local selection*. Their algorithm ELSA (Evolutionary Local Selection Algorithm) creates and maintains diversity in the population by placing *geographic* constraints on evolutionary search. In their approach, individuals/agents in the population compete for finite environmental resources, with similar agents obtaining less energy than dissimilar ones. Agents accumulating more than a certain fixed threshold of energy reproduce via mutation, while agents with no energy die. This environment-mediated crowding leads to diverse populations containing heterogeneous individuals. Such heterogeneity is a must for certain kinds of cover or Pareto optimization problems. For example, on problems with multi-criterion or expensive fitness functions, ELSA can quickly find a set of solutions using a simplified fitness function. Some other technique can then be used to compare these solutions to pick the right one. Using a direct encoding of feed-forward neural networks, the authors demonstrate the power of ELSA on a number of application domains, including evolution of sensors and adaptive behaviors, design of realistic ecological models, web-information browsing agents, and feature selection for classification tasks.

Moriarty and Miikkulainen present the SANE (Symbiotic, Adaptive Neuro-Evolution) approach in Chapter 13. The SANE approach differs from conventional evolution of neural architectures in that each individual in the population is a neuron rather than a neural network. In the fitness evaluation phase, pools of neurons are randomly drawn from the population to construct neural networks, which are then evaluated on the target task. The fitness of the resulting neural network is then distributed among the component neurons. Evolution thus favors neurons that can cooperate with each other. This approach supports heterogeneity by maintaining a diverse set of neurons, since neurons *specialize* to search different areas of the solution space. This leads to immediate benefits in the prevention of premature convergence. The authors use a direct encoding scheme that consists of *label-weight* pairs. They use this encoding to evolve the architecture and weights of feedforward networks. They demonstrate the utility of this approach on two interesting tasks – as a value ordering method in scheduling an auto assembly line, and as a filter for minimax search in an Othello playing program. The authors find that SANE easily optimizes sophisticated evaluation functions.

In Chapter 14, Yao and Liu use an Evolutionary Programming (EP) approach to evolving both single neural networks as well as ensembles. They introduce two key notions in this chapter – a set of mutation operators that can be sequentially applied to produce parsimonious networks, and an ensemble interpretation of evolved populations. Using a direct encoding representation, the authors evolve the architecture and weight of feed-forward networks for applications such as medical diagnosis, credit card assessment, and the Mackey-Glass chaotic time-series analysis. The evolved networks are trained using the back-propagation algorithm. The authors use a Lamarckian learning framework wherein the learned weights and architectures are inherited by offspring. Of particular interest is the authors' treatment of final evolved populations. They regard the final population of neural networks as an ensemble, and combine the outputs from different individuals using mechanisms such as voting and averaging. Since diversity often exists in evolved populations, this ensemble treatment produces results that are often better than the best single network in the population.

Muehlenbein and Mahnig develop a sound theoretical analysis of genetic algorithms in Chapter 15. Using results from classical population genetics and statistics, they show that genetic search can be closely approximated by a new search algorithm called the Univariate Marginal Distribution Algorithm (UMDA), which operates over probability distributions instead of recombinations of strings. To make UMDA tractable, the authors develop another variation of the algorithm that works with factorized probability distributions, an algorithm called Factorized Distribution Algorithm (FDA). The appropriate factorizations are determined from the data by mapping probability distributions to Bayesian networks. The authors demonstrate applications of this approach in the synthesis of programs via probabilistic trees and the synthesis of neural trees. Although synthesis of complex neural networks is currently outside the scope of this work, options exist for resolving this issue. The authors feel this can be done either by extending Bayesian networks to application domains of neural networks, or by restricting the structure of neural networks to be handled by Bayesian networks. This work is particularly interesting owing to the sound theoretical underpinnings.

Acknowledgments

We would like to thank all the authors whose contributions made this book a reality. We are grateful to Dr. Harry Stanton for his vision and enthusiastic encouragement during the early stages. He is sorely missed by those who had the good fortune to have known him. The project owes a great deal to Doug Sery who stepped in and saw project through to its completion after Harry's demise. Without his patience, unrelenting support, and understanding, it is unlikely that this volume would have been completed. We would like to acknowledge the able assistance provided by editorial and production staff of MIT press at all stages of production of this book.

We are grateful to United States National Science Foundation, the Department of Defense, the National Institute of Health, the European Engineering and Physical Sciences Research Council, and other funding agencies for their support of research and education in Cognitive, Biological, and Computer and Information Sciences in general, and the research presented in this book in particular.

Honavar is indebted to the Computer Science department at Iowa State University for its support of this project. He is also grateful to the School of Computer Science, the Robotics Institute, the Center for Automated Learning and Discovery, and the Center for Neural Basis for Cognition at Carnegie Mellon University where some of the work on this book was completed during his sabbatical in 1998.

Balakrishnan would like to thank the Department of Computer Science at Iowa State University, Allstate Research and Planning Center, and Obongo Inc., for providing the resources and support for this project. He is also grateful to IBM for providing a research Fellowship that made some of this work possible.

We are indebted to our students, teachers, colleagues, family, and friends from whom we have learned a great deal over the years.

Honavar is indebted to Leonard Uhr for introducing him to research in artificial intelligence and being a wonderful mentor and friend. He has benefited and learned from interactions with members of the artificial intelligence, neural computing, evolutionary computing, machine learning, intelligent agents, cognitive science, complex adaptive systems, computational biology, and neuroscience communities (at one time or another) at the University of Wisconsin-Madison (especially Gregg Oden, Jude Shavlik, Charles Dyer, Larry Travis, Lola Lopes, David Finton, Matt Zeidenberg, Jose Cavazos, Peter Sandon, Roland Chin and Josh Chover), Iowa State University (especially Rajesh Parekh, Chun-Hsien Chen, Karthik Balakrishnan, Jihoon Yang, Armin Mikler, Rushi Bhatt, Adrian Silvescu, Doina Caragea, Drena Dobbs, Jack Lutz, Gavin Naylor, Codrin Nichitiu, Olivier Bousquet, John Mayfield, Philip Haydon, Dan Voytas, Pat Schnable, Giora Slutzki, Leigh Tesfatsion, Di Cook, Don Sakaguchi, Srdija Jeftinija, Les Miller, David Fernandez-Baca, James McCalley, Johnny Wong, Mok-dong Chung, and Vadim Kirillov), and elsewhere (especially Tom Mitchell, Pat Langley, David Touretzky, Lee Giles, Ron Sun, Massimo Negrotti, David Goldberg, David Fogel, Wolfgang Banzaf, and John Koza).

Patel would like to extend particular thanks to Ben du Boulay (at Sussex University), Marco Colombetti (at Politechnico di Milano) and Brendon McGonigle (at Edinburgh University) – each in their own way played a significant role in helping him conceive and realize the idea of such a collection of papers.

Balakrishnan is deeply indebted to his family for their love and support all through his life. In particular, he would like to extend a special note of gratitude to his parents Shantha and R Balakrishnan, his wife Usha Nandini, and his sisters Usha and Sandhya, for always being there for him. He would also like to thank Vasant Honavar for being his research mentor. Balakrishnan is indebted to numerous teachers, friends and colleagues, from whom he has learned much. He would especially like to thank Dan Ashlock, Albert Baker, Rushi Bhatt, Olivier Bousquet, Chun-Hsien Chen, Veronica Dark, Dario Floreano, David Juedes, Filippo Menczer, Armin Mikler, Rajesh Parekh, William Robinson, Leigh Tesfatsion, Noe Tuason, Johnny Wong, and Jihoon Yang.

Last but not the least, we are indebted to the artificial intelligence, neural computing, evolutionary computing, synthetic biology, computational biology, and cognitive science research communities at large whose work has directly or indirectly helped shape the theme and contents of this book.

Karthik Balakrishnan   Redwood City, USA
Vasant Honavar   Ames, USA
Mukesh Patel   Ahmedabad, India

1 Evolutionary and Neural Synthesis of Intelligent Agents

Karthik Balakrishnan and Vasant Honavar

1.1 Introduction

From its very inception in the late 1950s and early 1960s, the field of Artificial Intelligence, has concerned itself with the analysis and synthesis of *intelligent agents*. Although there is no universally accepted definition of intelligence, for our purposes here, we treat any software or hardware entity as an intelligent agent, provided it demonstrates behaviors that would be characterized as *intelligent* if performed by normal human beings under similar circumstances. This generic definition of agency applies to robots, software systems for pattern classification and prediction, and recent advances in mobile software systems (softbots) for information gathering, data mining, and electronic commerce. The design and development of such agents is a topic of considerable ongoing research and draws on advances in a variety of disciplines including artificial intelligence, robotics, cognitive systems, design of algorithms, control systems, electrical and mechanical engineering, programming languages, computer networks, distributed computing, databases, programming languages, statistical analysis and modeling, etc.

In very simplistic terms, an agent may be defined as an entity that *perceives* its environment through *sensors* and *acts* upon it through its *effectors* [76]. However, for the agents to be useful, they must also be capable of *interpreting perceptions*, *reasoning*, and choosing actions *autonomously* and in ways suited to achieving their intended *goals*. Since the agents are often expected to operate reliably in unknown, partially known, and dynamic environments, they must also possess mechanisms to *learn* and *adapt* their behaviors through their interactions with their environments. In addition, in some cases, we may also require the agents to be *mobile* and move or access different places or parts of their operating environments. Finally, we may expect the agents to be *persistent*, *rational*, etc., and to work in groups, which requires them to *collaborate* and *communicate* [76, 87, 60].

It can be seen that this definition of agents applies to robots that occupy and operate in physical environments, software systems for evaluation and optimization, *softbots* that inhabit the electronic worlds defined by computers and computer networks, and even *animals* (or biological agents) that cohabit this planet. Robots have been used in a wide variety of application scenarios like geo, space, and underwater exploration, material handling and delivery, security patrolling, control applications in hazardous environments like chemical plants and nuclear reactors, etc., [14, 18, 90, 62]. Intelligent software systems have been extensively used as automated tools for diagnosis, evaluation, analysis and optimization. Softbots are being increasingly used for information gathering and retrieval, data mining, e-commerce, news, mail and information filtering, etc., [7].

In general, an agent can be characterized by two elements: its *program* and its *architecture*. The agent program is a mapping that determines the actions of the agent in response to its sensory inputs, while architecture refers to the computing and physical medium on which this agent program is executed [76]. For example, a *mail filtering agent* might be programmed in a language such as C++ and executed on a computer, or a robot might be programmed to move about and collect empty soda cans using its *gripper arm*. Thus, the architecture of the agent, to a large extent, determines the *kinds* of things the agent is capable of doing, while the program determines *what* the agent does at any given instance of time. In addition to these two elements, the agent *environment* governs the kinds of tasks or behaviors that are within the scope of any agent operating in that environment. For instance, if there are no soda cans in the robot's environment, the can collecting behavior is of no practical use.

Given a particular agent environment the question then is, how can we design agents with the necessary behaviors and abilities to solve a given task (or a set of tasks)?

The field of Artificial Intelligence (AI) has long concerned itself with the design, development, and deployment of intelligent agents for a variety of practical, real-world applications [73, 86, 81, 76]. A number of tools and techniques have been developed for synthesizing such agent programs (e.g., expert systems, logical and probabilistic inference techniques, case-based reasoning systems, etc.) [73, 24, 40, 17, 16, 76].

However, designing programs using most of these approaches requires considerable knowledge of the application domain being addressed by the agent. This process of *knowledge extraction* (also called knowledge engineering) is often difficult either owing to the lack of precise knowledge of the domain (e.g., medical diagnosis) or the inability to procure knowledge owing to other limitations (e.g., detailed environmental characteristics of, say, planet Saturn). We thus require agent design mechanisms that work either with little domain-specific knowledge or allow the agent to acquire the desired information through its own experiences. This has led to considerable development of the field of *machine learning* (ML), which provides a variety of modes and methods for *automatic synthesis* of agent programs [35, 36, 44, 74, 58].

1.2 Design of Biological Agents

Among the processes of natural adaptation responsible for the design of biological agents (animals), probably the most crucial is that of *evolution*, which excels in producing agents designed to overcome the constraints and limitations imposed by their environments. For example, *flashlight fish (photoblepharon palpebratus)*, inhabits deep-waters where there is little surface light. However, this is not really a problem since evolution has equipped these creatures with *active vision* systems. These fishes produce and emit their own light, and use it to detect obstacles, prey, etc. This vision system is unlike any seen on surface-dwelling organisms [27].

Apart from evolution, *learning* is another biological process that allows animals to successfully adapt to their environments. For instance, animals learn to respond to specific stimuli (*conditioning*) and ignore others (*habituation*), recognize objects and places, communicate, engage in species-specific behaviors, etc., [51, 23, 27, 52]. Intelligent behavior in animals emerges as a result of interaction between the information processing structures possessed by the animal and the environments that they inhabit. For instance, it is well known that marine turtles (e.g., *Chelonia mydas*) lay their eggs on tropical beaches (e.g., Ascension Island in the Atlantic ocean). When the eggs hatch, the young automatically crawl to the water without any kind of parental supervision. They appear to be genetically programmed to interpret cues emanating from large bodies of water or patches of sky over them [27]. Animals are also capable of learning features of specific environments that they inhabit during their lifetime. For instance, rodents have the ability to learn and successfully navigate through complex mazes [82, 61].

These processes of natural adaptation, namely, evolution and learning, play a significant role in shaping the behaviors of biological agents. They differ from each other in some significant aspects including the spatio-temporal scales at which they operate. While learning operates on individuals, evolution works over entire populations (or species). Further, learning operates during the lifetime of the individual and is presumably aided by long lifespans, while evolution works over generations, well beyond an individual's effective lifespan [1].

Despite these apparent differences, evolution and learning work synergistically to produce animals capable of surviving and functioning in diverse environments. While the architectures of biological agents (e.g., digestive, respiratory, nervous, immune, and reproductive systems) are shaped by evolution, the agent programs (e.g., behaviors like foraging, feeding, grooming, sleeping, escape, etc.) are affected and altered by both evolutionary and learning phenomena. In such cases, evolution produces the *innate* (or genetically programmed) behaviors which are then modified and contoured to the animal's experiences in the specific environment to which it is exposed. Thus, by equipping the agents with good designs and instincts, evolution allows them to survive sufficiently long to learn the behaviors appropriate for the environment in question.

Although the processes of evolution and learning are reasonably well detailed, there are still many gaps to be filled before a complete understanding of such processes can be claimed. Ongoing research in the neurosciences, cognitive psychology, animal behavior, genetics, etc., is providing new insights into the exact nature of the mechanisms employed by these processes: the structures they require and the functions they compute. This has led to many new hypotheses and theories of such mechanisms. *Computational modeling* efforts complement such research endeavors by providing valuable tools for *testing* theories and hypotheses in controlled, simulated environments. Such modeling efforts can potentially identify and suggest avenues of further research that can help fill in the gaps in current human understanding of the modeled processes [10].

As outlined in the previous sections, the enterprise of designing agents has to take into account three key aspects: the nature of the environment, agent architecture, and agent program. The primary focus of this book is on evolutionary synthesis of intelligent agents with a secondary focus on the use of learning mechanisms to enhance agent designs. The chapters that follow consider the design of agent programs using processes that are loosely modeled after biological evolution. They explore several alternative architectures and paradigms for intelligent agent architectures including *artificial neural networks*. They provide several examples of successful use of evolutionary and neural approaches to the synthesis of agent architectures and agent programs.

1.3   Agent Programs

As we mentioned earlier, the agent *program* is primarily responsible for the behavior of the agent or robot in a given environment. The agent program determines the sensory inputs available to the agent at any given moment in time, processes the inputs in ways suited to the goals (or functionalities) of the agent, and determines appropriate agent actions to be performed.

In order to be used in practice, these programs have to be *encoded* within the agents using an appropriate *language* and the agents must possess mechanisms to *interpret* and *execute* them. Some of the earliest programs were realized using *circuits and control systems* that directly sensed input events, processed them via appropriate *transfer functions*, and directly controlled the output behaviors of the robot [46]. Examples of such representations include systems used in the control of industrial robots, robotic arms, etc. [2]. However, these approaches require the transfer function to be known and appropriately implemented, which is often difficult in practice. In addition, these control mechanisms are rather inflexible and reprogramming the robot for a different behavior or task may entail extensive changes.

The advent of computers and their ability to be effectively *reprogrammed*, opened up entirely new possibilities in the design of agent programs for modern-day robots and software agents. In these cases, the agent programs are written in some computer language (e.g., C++, Java, LISP), and executed by the computer. The program receives the necessary inputs from the agent sensors, processes them appropriately to determine the actions to be performed, and controls the agent actuators to realize the intended behaviors. The sensors and actuators may be physical (as in the case of robots) or virtual (as in the case of most software agents). The behavior of the agent can be changed by changing the agent program associated with it.

The question then is, how can we develop agent programs that will enable the agent to exhibit the desired behaviors?

Designing Control Programs for Agent Behaviors

Many contemporary agents make use of programs that are *manually* developed. This is a daunting task, given the fact that the agent-environment interactions exhibit a host of a priori unknown or unpredictable effects. In addition, complex agent behaviors often involve tradeoffs between multiple competing alternatives. For example, suppose a robot has the task of clearing a room by pushing boxes to the walls. Let us also assume that the robot has limited sensing ranges that prevent it from observing the contents of the entire room and it does not have any means to remember the positions of boxes it has observed in the past. Suppose this robot currently observes two boxes. Which one should it approach and push? This decision is critical as it directly affects the subsequent behaviors of the robot. We may program the robot to approach the closer of the two boxes, but can we be sure that such a decision made at the local level will indeed lead to any kind of globally optimal behavior? Manually designing control programs to effectively address such competing alternatives is an equally challenging proposition.

We thus need approaches to *automate* the synthesis of scalable, robust, flexible, and adaptive agent programs for a variety of practical applications. In recent years two kinds of automatic design approaches have met with much success: *discovery* and *learning*. Approaches belonging to the former category typically include some mechanism to *search* the space of agent programs in the hope of finding or discovering a good one. Each program found during this search is evaluated in environments that are representative of those that are expected to be encountered by the agent and the best ones are retained. Some discovery approaches (e.g., evolutionary search) use these evaluations to *guide* or *focus* the search procedure, making the process more efficient. The latter category includes approaches that allow the robot behaviors to be modified based on the experiences of the agent, i.e., the robot *learns* the correct behaviors based on its experience in the environment.

In the remainder of this chapter we will introduce two paradigms that aid in the automatic synthesis of agent programs. Artificial neural networks, finite state automata, rule-based production systems, Lambda Calculus, etc., offer alternative computational models for the design of agent programs. As shown by the pioneering work of Turing, Church, Post, Markov, and others, they are all essentially equivalent in terms of the class of information processing operations that they can realize [83, 56, 47]. However, in practice, each paradigm has its own advantages and disadvantages in the context of specific applications. It is therefore not at all uncommon to use hybrid models that integrate and exploit the advantages of multiple paradigms in synergistic and complementary ways [38, 80, 26]. In what follows, we focus primarily on evolutionary synthesis of neural architectures for intelligent agents. However, many of the same issues arise in the automated synthesis of agents with other information processing architectures as well (e.g., rule-based systems).

1.4 Artificial Neural Networks as Agent Programs

Artificial neural networks offer an attractive paradigm of computation for the synthesis of agent programs for a variety of reasons including their potential for *massively parallel computation*, *robustness* in the presence of noise, *resilience* to the failure of components, and amenability to *adaptation* and *learning* via the modification of computational structures, among others.

What are Artificial Neural Networks?

Artificial neural networks are models of computation that are inspired by, and loosely based on, the nervous systems in biological organisms. They are conventionally modeled as massively parallel networks of simple computing elements, called *units*, that are connected together by *adaptive links* called *weights*, as shown in Figure 1.1. Each unit in the network computes some simple function of its inputs (called the *activation function*) and propagates its outputs to other units to which it happens to be connected. A number of activation functions are used in practice, the most common ones being the *threshold*, *linear*, *sigmoid*, and *radial-basis* functions. The weights associated with a unit represent the strength of the synapses between the corresponding units, as will be explained shortly. Each unit is also assumed to be associated with a special weight, called the *threshold* or *bias*, that is assumed to be connected to a constant source of +1 (or a -1). This threshold or bias serves to modulate the firing properties of the corresponding unit and is a critical component in the design of these networks.

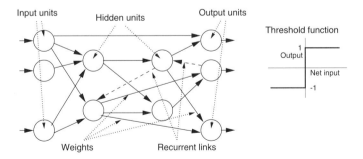

Figure 1.1
Artificial neural network (left) and the bipolar threshold activation function (right).

The input to an n-input (including the bias) unit is typically represented by a pattern vector $\mathbf{X} \in \mathcal{R}^n$ or in the case of binary patterns, by a binary vector $\mathbf{X} \in [0, 1]^n$. The weights associated with an n-input unit i are typically represented by an n-dimensional weight vector $\mathbf{W}_i \in \mathcal{R}^n$. By popular convention, the first element of the weight vector usually represents the threshold (or bias). The input activation of a unit i, represented by A_i, in response to a pattern $\mathbf{X}$ on its input links is usually given by the vector dot product: $A_i = \mathbf{W}_i.\mathbf{X}$. The output of the unit is a function of A_i and is dictated by the activation function chosen. For example, the *bipolar threshold* activation function, shown in Figure 1.1, produces: $O_i = 1$ if $A_i = \mathbf{W}_i.\mathbf{X} \geq 0$ and $O_i = -1$ otherwise.

Units in the network that receive input directly from the environment are referred to as *input units*, while the units that provide the environment with the results of network computations are called *output units*. In conventional neural network terminology, the set of input and output units are said to reside in *input* and *output layers*. In addition to these kinds of units, the networks can also have other units that aid in the network computations but do not have a direct interface to or from the external environment. Such units are referred to as *hidden units*. Often, the hidden units critically determine the kinds of mappings or computations the networks are capable of performing.

In a typical neural network the activations are propagated as follows. At any given instance of time, the input *pattern* is applied to the input units of the network. These input activations are then propagated to the units that are connected to these input units, and the activations of these second layer units are computed. Now the activations of these units are propagated via their output links to other units, and this process continues until the activations reach the units in the output layer. Once the computations of the output layer units are complete (or in the case of recurrent networks the network activity stabilizes), the resulting firing pattern across the output layer units is said to be the output of the network in response to the corresponding input pattern. Thus, in a typical neural network, activations enter the input units, propagate through links and hidden units, and produce an activation in the units of the output layer.

A wide variety of artificial neural networks have been studied in the literature. Apart from differences stemming from the activation functions used, neural networks can also be distinguished based on their topological organization. For instance, networks can be single-layered or multi-layered; sparsely connected or completely connected; strictly layered or arbitrarily connected; composed of homogeneous or heterogeneous computing elements, etc. Perhaps the most important architectural (and hence functional) distinction is between networks that are simply *feed-forward* (where their connectivity graph does not contain any directed cycles) and *recurrent* (where the networks contain feedback loops). Feed-forward networks can be trained via a host of simple learning algorithms and have found widespread use in pattern recognition, function interpolation, and system modeling applications. In contrast to feed-forward networks, recurrent networks have the ability to remember and use past network activations through the use of recurrent (or feedback) links. These networks have thus found natural applications in domains involving temporal dependencies, for instance, in sequence learning, speech recognition, motion control in robots, etc. For further details regarding artificial neural networks and their rather chequered history, the reader is referred to any of a number of excellent texts [15, 32, 45, 22, 43, 31, 74].

Design of Artificial Neural Networks

As may be inferred, the input-output mapping realized by an artificial neural network is a function of the numbers of units, the functions they compute, the topology of their connectivity, the strength of their connections (weights), the control algorithm for propagating activations through the network, etc., [35]. Thus, to create a neural network with a desired input-output mapping, one has to appropriately design these different components of the network. Not surprisingly, *network synthesis* of this sort is an extremely difficult task because the different components of the network and their interactions are often very complex and hard to characterize accurately.

Much of the research on neural network synthesis has focused on algorithms that modify the weights within an otherwise fixed network architecture [22]. This essentially entails a search for a setting of the weights that endows the network with the desired input-output behavior. For example, in a network used in classification applications we desire weights that will allow the network to correctly classify all (or most of) the samples in the training set. Since this is fundamentally an *optimization* problem, a variety of optimization methods (gradient-descent, simulated annealing, etc.) can be used to determine the weights. Most of the popular learning algorithms use some form of error-guided search (e.g., changing each modifiable parameter in the direction of the negative gradient of a suitably defined error measure with respect to the parameter of interest). A number of such learning algorithms have been developed, both for *supervised* learning (where the desired outputs of the network are specified by an external teacher) and *unsupervised* learning (where the network learns to classify, categorize, or self-organize without external supervision). For details regarding these learning paradigms, the reader is referred to [22, 43, 30, 74].

Although a number of techiniques have been developed to adapt the weights within a given neural network, the design of the neural architecture still poses a few problems. Conventional approaches often rely on human experience, intuition, and rules-of-thumb to determine the network architectures. In recent years, a number of *constructive* and *destructive* algorithms have been developed, that aid in the design of neural network architectures. While constructive algorithms incrementally build network architectures one unit (or one module) at a time [34, 37, 63, 89], destructive algorithms allow arbitrary networks to be pruned one unit (or one module) at a time. Thus, not only do these approaches synthesize network architectures, but also entertain the possibility of discovering *compact* (or minimal) networks. A number of such constructive and destructive learning algorithms have been developed, each offering its own characteristic bias.

In addition to these approaches, *evolutionary algorithms* (to be descibed shortly) have also been used to search the space of neural architectures for near-optimal designs (see [5] for a bibliography). This evolutionary approach to the design of neural network architectures forms the core of this compilation.

1.5   Evolutionary Algorithms

Evolutionary algorithms, loosely inspired by biological evolutionary processes, have gained considerable popularity as tools for searching vast, complex, deceptive, and multimodal search spaces [33, 25, 57]. Following the metaphor of biological evolution, these algorithms work with populations of individuals, where each individual represents a point in the space being searched. Viewed as a search for a *solution* to a problem, each individual then represents (or encodes) a solution to the problem on hand. As with biological evolutionary systems, each individual is characterized by a *genetic representation* or *genetic encoding*, which typically consists of an arrangement of *genes* (usually in a string form). These genes take on values called *alleles*, from a suitably defined domain of values. This genetic representation is referred to as the *genotype* in biology. The actual individual, in our case a solution, is referred to as the *phenotype*. As in biological evolutionary processes, phenotypes in artificial evolution are produced from genotypes through a process of *decoding* and *development*, as shown in Figure 1.2. Thus, while a human being corresponds to a phenotype, his/her chromosomes correspond to the genotype. The processes of nurture, growth, learning, etc., then correspond to the decoding/developmental processes the transform the genotype into a phenotype.

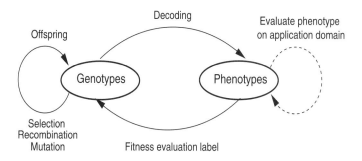

Figure 1.2
The functioning of an evolutionary algorithm.

In artificial evolution (also referred to as simulated evolution), solutions represented by the phenotypes are evaluated based on the target problem for which solutions are being sought. This evaluation of the phenotypes assigns differential fitness labels to the corresponding genotypes. Processes akin to natural selection then preferentially choose genotypes of higher fitness to participate in probabilistically more numbers of matings. These matings between chosen individuals leads to offsprings that derive their genetic material from their parents via artificial genetic operators that roughly correspond to the biological operators of *recombination* and *mutation*. These artificial genetic operators are popularly referred to as *crossover* and *mutation*. The offspring genotypes are then decoded into phenotypes and the process repeats itself. Over many generations the processes of selection, crossover, and mutation, gradually lead to populations containing genotypes that correspond to high fitness phenotypes. This general procedure, perhaps with minor variations, is at the heart of most evolutionary systems.

The literature broadly distinguishes between four different classes of evolutionary approaches: *genetic algorithms*, *genetic programming*, *evolutionary programming*, and *evolutionary strategies*. While genetic algorithms typically use *binary* (or bit) strings to represent genotypes [33, 25], genetic programming evolves *programs* in some given *language* [42]. Both these paradigms perform evolutionary search via genetic operators of crossover and mutation. Evolutionary programming, on the other hand, allows complex structures in the genotypes but only uses a mutation operator [20]. Evolution strategies are typically used for parameter optimization [78, 3]. They employ recombination and mutation, and also permit *self-learning* (or evolutionary adaptation) of strategy parameters (e.g., variance of the Gaussian mutations). In recent years, the distinctions between these different paradigms have become rather fuzzy with researchers borrowing from the strengths of different paradigms. For instance, we use complex data structures for representing genotypes and employ both recombination as well as mutation operators to perform the evolutionary search [4]. In this regard our approach may be described as a combination of evolutionary programming and genetic algorithms. For these reasons we prefer to use the generic term, *evolutionary algorithms*, to describe our approach to the use of artificial evolution.

As each population member represents a potential solution, evolutionary algorithms effectively perform a *population-based* search in solution space. Since this is equivalent to exploring multiple regions of the space in parallel, evolutionary algorithms are efficient search tools for vast spaces. In addition, the population-based nature of evolutionary search often helps it overcome problems associated with *local maxima*, making it very suitable for searching multi-modal spaces. Further, the genetic encoding and genetic operators can be chosen to be fairly generic, requiring the user to only specify the decoding function and the *fitness* or *evaluation* function. In most cases these functions can be specified using *little* domain-specific knowledge. Thus, one does not necessarily have to understand the intricacies of the problem in order to use an evolutionary approach to solve it.

Evolutionary Synthesis of Agent Programs

As demonstrated by several of the chapters that follow, evolutionary algorithms offer a promising approach to synthesis of agent programs (in the form of artificial neural networks, LISP programs, etc.) for a wide variety of tasks [68, 19, 71, 29, 70, 64, 72, 69, 88, 13, 53, 85, 41, 12, 48, 54, 59, 8, 50].

In such cases, evolutionary search operates in the space of agent programs, with each member of the population representing an agent *behavior*. By evaluating these behaviors on the target agent task and performing fitness-proportionate reproduction, evolution discovers agent programs that exhibit the desired behaviors.

1.6 Evolutionary Synthesis of Neural Systems

In an earlier section we alluded to the difficulty of synthesizing artificial neural networks that possess specific input-output mappings. Owing to the many
properties of evolutionary algorithms, primarily their ability to search vast,
complex, and multimodal search spaces using little domain-specific knowledge, they have found natural applications in the automatic synthesis of artificial neural networks. Several researchers have recently begun to investigate
evolutionary techniques for designing such neural architectures (see [5] for a
bibliography).

Probably the distinguishing feature of an evolutionary approach to network
synthesis is that unlike neural network learning algorithms that typically determine weights within *a priori* fixed architectures and constructive/destructive
algorithms that simply design network architectures without directly adapting
the weights, evolutionary algorithms permit *co-evolution* or *co-design* of the
network architecture as well as the weights. Evolutionary algorithm may be
easily extended to automatically adapt other parameters such as rates of mutation [79] and learning rate [77], and even the learning algorithm [9]. In addition, by appropriately modifying the fitness function, the same evolutionary
system can be used to synthesize vastly different neural networks, each satisfying different task-specific performance measures (e.g., accuracy, speed, robustness, etc.) or user-specified design constraints (e.g., compactness, numbers
of units, links and layers, fan-in/fan-out constraints, power consumption, heat
dissipation, area/volume when implemented in hardware, etc.). Evolutionary
algorithms also allow these networks to be optimized along multiple dimensions either *implicitly* [4] or *explicitly* via the use of different multi-objective
optimization approaches [21, 67, 66, 39].

An Example of Evolutionary Synthesis of Neural Networks

A number of researchers have designed evolutionary systems to synthesize
neural networks for a variety of applications. Here we will present the approach
adopted by Miller et al. (1989).

In their system, Miller et al., *encode* the topology of an N unit neural
network by a *connectivity constraint matrix* C, of dimension $N \times (N + 1)$,
as shown in Figure 1.3. Here, the first N columns specify the constraints
on the connections between the N units, and the final column codes for the
connection that corresponds to the *threshold or bias* of each unit. Each entry
C_{ij}, of the connectivity constraint matrix indicates the nature of the constraint

on the connection from unit j to unit i (or the constraint on the threshold bias of unit i if $j = N + 1$). While $C_{ij} = 0$ indicates the *absence* of a *trainable* connection between units j and i, a value of 1 signals the *presence* of such a trainable link. The rows of the matrix are concatenated to yield a bit-string of length $N \times (N + 1)$. This is the genotype in their evolutionary system.

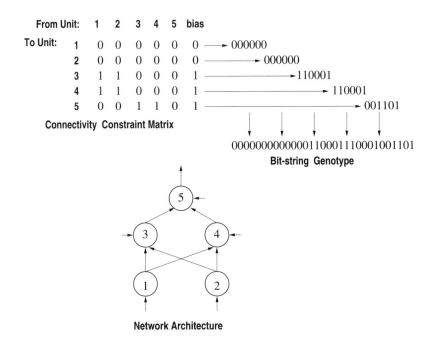

Figure 1.3
An example of an evolutionary approach to the synthesis of neural networks.

The fitness of the genotype is evaluated as follows. First, the genotype is *decoded* into the corresponding neural network (or the phenotype). This decoded network has connections (or weights) between units that have a 1 in the corresponding position in the connectivity constraint matrix (or the genotype), as explained earlier. Even though feedback connections can be specified in the genotype, they are ignored by the decoding mechanism. The system thus evolves purely feed-forward networks. Next, all the connections in the network are set to small random values and trained for a fixed number of epochs on a given set of training examples, using the *back-propagation* algorithm [75]. The *total sum squared error* ($\mathcal{E}$) of the network, at the end of the training phase, is used as the *fitness* measure, with *low* values of $\mathcal{E}$ corresponding to better performance and hence a higher fitness label for the corresponding genotype.

The system maintains a population of such genotypes (bit-strings), and uses a *fitness-proportionate* selection scheme for choosing parents for reproduction. The genetic operator *crossover* swaps rows between parents while *mutation* randomly flips bits in the genotype with some low, pre-specified probability. The researchers used this evolutionary system to design neural networks for the *XOR, four-quadrant* and *pattern-copying* problems [55].

1.7   Genetic Representations of Neural Architectures

Central to any evolutionary design system is the choice of the *genetic representation*, i.e., the encoding of genotypes and the mechanism for decoding them into phenotypes. The choice of the representation is critical since it not only dictates the kinds of phenotypes (and hence solutions) that can be generated by the system, but also determines the amount of *resources* (e.g., time, space, etc.) expended in this effort. Further, the genetic operators for the system are also defined based largely on the representation chosen. These factors contribute directly to the *efficiency* (e.g., time, space, etc.) and the *efficacy* (e.g., quality of solution found, etc.) of the evolutionary search procedure [66, 65]. Thus, a careful characterization of the properties of genetic representations as they relate to the performance of evolutionary systems, is a necessary and useful venture.

Some authors have attempted to characterize *properties* of genetic representations of neural architectures [11, 28]. However, most such characterizations have been restricted to a specification of the properties of the encoding scheme without considering in detail the associated decoding process. This is an important oversight because the decoding process not only determines the phenotypes that emerge from a given genotype, but also critically influences the resources required in the bargain. For instance, a cryptic encoding scheme might be compact from a storage perspective but might entail a decoding process that is rather involved (both in terms of time and storage space). If we were blind to the effects of the decoding process, we might be enamoured by this encoding scheme and use it as our genetic representation. This would have severe consequences on the performance of the evolutionary system.

For these reasons it is imperative that we consider the encoding and the decoding process as a closely related pair while characterizing different properties of genetic representations. Given this motivation, we have identified and precisely defined a number of key properties of genetic representations of neural architectures, taking both the encoding and the decoding processes into account [6]. However, it must be pointed out that this is only a preliminary characterization and we expect these definitions to get more refined as we examine a large variety of evolutionary systems more closely. The following section describes these properties.

Properties of Genetic Representations of Neural Architectures

In order to develop formal descriptions of properties of genetic representations, we need the following definitions.

- $\mathcal{G}_\mathcal{R}$ is the space of genotypes representable in the chosen genetic representation scheme $\mathcal{R}$. $\mathcal{G}_\mathcal{R}$ may be explicitly enumerated or implicitly specified using a grammar Γ whose language $L(\Gamma) = \mathcal{G}_\mathcal{R}$.

- $p = \mathcal{D}(g, \mathcal{E}_D)$, where $\mathcal{D}$ is the decoding function that produces the phenotype p corresponding to the genotype g possibly under the influence of the environment $\mathcal{E}_D$ (e.g., the environment may set the parameters of the decoding function). A value of λ for $\mathcal{E}_D$ denotes the lack of direct interaction between the decoding process and the environment. It should be borne in mind that $\mathcal{D}$ may be *stochastic*, with an underlying probability distribution over the space of phenotypes.

- $p_2 = \mathcal{L}(p_1, \mathcal{E}_L)$, where the learning procedure $\mathcal{L}$ generates phenotype p_2 from phenotype p_1 under the influence of the environment $\mathcal{E}_L$. The environment may provide the training examples, set the free parameters (e.g., the learning rate used by the algorithm) etc. We will use $\mathcal{L} = \lambda$ to denote the absence of any form of learning in the system. In the following discussion we will use the term *decoding function* to refer to both $\mathcal{D}$ and $\mathcal{L}$. This slight abuse of notation allows the following properties to apply to genetic representations in general, even though they are presented in the context of evolutionary design of neural architectures.

- $\mathcal{P}_\mathcal{R}$ is the space of all phenotypes that can be constructed (in principle) given a particular genetic representation scheme $\mathcal{R}$. Mathematically, $\mathcal{P}_\mathcal{R} = \{p / \exists g \in \mathcal{G}_\mathcal{R}[(p_1 = \mathcal{D}(g, \mathcal{E}_D)) \wedge (p = \mathcal{L}(p_1, \mathcal{E}_L))]$

• $\mathcal{S}$ is the set of *solution networks*, i.e., neural architectures or phenotypes that satisfy the desired performance criterion (as measured by the fitness function π) in a given environment $\mathcal{E}_\pi$. If an evolutionary system with a particular representation $\mathcal{R}$ is to successfully find solutions (even in principle), $\mathcal{S} \subseteq \mathcal{P}_\mathcal{R}$, or, at the very least, $\mathcal{S} \cap \mathcal{P}_\mathcal{R} \neq \emptyset$. In other words, there must be at least one solution network that can be constructed given the chosen representation $\mathcal{R}$.

• $\mathcal{A}$ is the set of *acceptable* or *valid* neural architectures. For instance, a network may be deemed invalid or unacceptable if it does not have any paths from the inputs to the outputs. In general, $\mathcal{A}$ may be different from $\mathcal{P}_\mathcal{R}$. However, it must be the case that $\mathcal{A} \cap \mathcal{S} \neq \emptyset$ if a particular evolutionary system is to be useful in practice.

We now identify some properties of genetic representations of neural architectures. Unless otherwise specified, we will assume the following definitions are with respect to an *a priori* fixed choice of $\mathcal{E}_D$, $\mathcal{L}$, and $\mathcal{E}_L$.

1. **Completeness:** A representation $\mathcal{R}$ is *complete* if every neural architecture in the solution set can be constructed (in principle) by the system. Formally, the following two statements are equivalent definitions of completeness.
• $(\forall s \in \mathcal{S})(\exists g \in \mathcal{G}_\mathcal{R})[(p_1 = \mathcal{D}(g, \mathcal{E}_D)) \wedge (s = \mathcal{L}(p_1, \mathcal{E}_L))]$
• $\mathcal{S} \subseteq \mathcal{P}_\mathcal{R}$
Thus, completeness demands that the representation be capable of producing all possible solutions to the problem. Often, this may be hard to satisfy and one may have to choose between *partially complete* representations. In such cases, another figure of merit called *solution density*, denoted by $\frac{|\mathcal{S} \cap \mathcal{P}_\mathcal{R}|}{|\mathcal{P}_\mathcal{R}|}$, might be useful. One would then choose representations that correspond to higher solution densities, since this implies a higher likelihood of finding solutions. It should be noted that if the solution density is very high, even a *random search* procedure will yield good solutions and one may not have much use for an evolutionary approach.

2. **Closure:** A representation $\mathcal{R}$ is *completely closed* if *every* genotype decodes to an acceptable phenotype. The following two assertions are both equivalent definitions of closure.
• $(\forall g \in \mathcal{G}_\mathcal{R})[(p_1 = \mathcal{D}(g, \mathcal{E}_D)) \wedge (\mathcal{L}(p_1, \mathcal{E}_L) \in \mathcal{A})]$
• $\mathcal{P}_\mathcal{R} \subseteq \mathcal{A}$
A representation that is not closed can be transformed into a closed system by *constraining* the decoding function, thereby preventing it from generating invalid phenotypes. Additionally, if the genetic operators are designed to have

the property of closure, then one can envision *constrained closure* wherein all genotypes do not correspond to acceptable phenotypes, however, closure is guaranteed since the system *never* generates the invalid genotypes. Closure has bearings on the *efficiency* of the evolutionary procedure as it determines the amount of effort (space, time, etc.) wasted in generating unacceptable phenotypes.

3. **Compactness:** Suppose two genotypes g_1 and g_2 both decode to the same phenotype p, then g_1 is said to be more *compact* than g_2 if g_1 occupies less *space* than g_2:

- $(p_1 = \mathcal{D}(g_1, \mathcal{E}_D)) \wedge (p = \mathcal{L}(p_1, \mathcal{E}_L)) \wedge (p_2 = \mathcal{D}(g_2, \mathcal{E}_D)) \wedge (p = \mathcal{L}(p_2, \mathcal{E}_L)) \wedge |g_1| < |g_2|$

where $|g|$ denotes the size of storage for genotype g.

This definition corresponds to *topological-compactness* defined by Gruau (1994). His definition of *functional-compactness* – which compares the genotype sizes of two phenotypes that exhibit the same behavior, can be expressed in our framework (for solution networks) as

- $(p_1 = \mathcal{D}(g_1, \mathcal{E}_D)) \wedge (\mathcal{L}(p_1, \mathcal{E}_L) \in \mathcal{S}) \wedge (p_2 = \mathcal{D}(g_2, \mathcal{E}_D)) \wedge (\mathcal{L}(p_2, \mathcal{E}_L) \in \mathcal{S}) \wedge |g_1| < |g_2|$

Compactness is a useful property as it allows us to choose genetic representations that use space more efficiently. However, compact and cryptic representations often require considerable decoding effort to produce the corresponding phenotype. This is the classic space-time tradeoff inherent in algorithm design. Hence, the benefits offered by a compact representation must be evaluated in light of the increased decoding effort before one representation can be declared preferable over another.

4. **Scalability:** Several notions of scalability are of interest. For the time being we will restrict our attention to the *change* in the *size* of the phenotype, measured in terms of the numbers of units, connections, or modules. This change in the size of the phenotype manifests itself as a change in the *size* of the encoding (space needed to store the genotype), and a corresponding change in *decoding time*. We can characterize the relationship in terms of the *asymptotic order of growth* notation commonly used in analyzing computer algorithms — $O(\cdot)$.

For instance, let $n_{N,C} \in \mathcal{A}$ be a network (phenotype) with N units and C connections (the actual connectivity pattern does not really matter in this example). We say that the representation is $O(K)$–*size-scalable with respect to units* if the addition of *one* unit to the phenotype $n_{N,C}$ requires an increase in the size of the corresponding genotype by $O(K)$, where K is some function of N and C. For instance, if a given representation is $O(N^2)$ size-scalable with respect to units,

then the addition of one unit to the phenotype increases the size of the genotype by $O(N^2)$. Size-scalability of encodings with respect to connections, modules, etc., can be similarly defined.

The representation is said to be $O(K)$– *time-scalable with respect to units* if the time taken for decoding the genotype for $n_{N+1,C}$ exceeds that used for $n_{N,C}$ by no more than $O(K)$. Similarly, time-scalability with respect to the number of connections, modules, etc., can also be defined.

Scalability is central to understanding the space-time consequences of using a particular genetic representation scheme in different contexts. In conjunction with completeness and compactness, scalability can be effectively used to characterize genetic representations.

5. **Multiplicity:** A representation $\mathcal{R}$ is said to exhibit *genotypic multiplicity* if multiple genotypes decode to an identical phenotype. In other words, the decoding function is a many to one mapping from the space of genotypes to the corresponding phenotypic space.

- $(\exists n \in \mathcal{P}_{\mathcal{R}}) \, (| \, \{g \in \mathcal{G}_{\mathcal{R}} / (p = \mathcal{D}(g, \mathcal{E}_D)) \wedge (n = \mathcal{L}(p, \mathcal{E}_L))\} \, | > 1)$

Genotypic multiplicity may result from a variety of sources including the encoding and decoding mechanisms. If a genetic representation has the property of genotypic multiplicity, it is possible that multiple genotypes decode to the same *solution* phenotype. In such cases, if the density of solutions is also high, then a large fraction of the genotypic space corresponds to potential solutions. This will make the evolutionary search procedure very effective.

A representation $\mathcal{R}$ is said to exhibit *phenotypic multiplicity* if different instances of the same genotype can decode to different phenotypes. In other words, the decoding function is a one to many mapping of genotypes into phenotypes.

- $(\exists g_1, g_2 \in \mathcal{G}_{\mathcal{R}})[(p_1 = \mathcal{D}(g_1, \mathcal{E}_D)) \wedge (n_1 = \mathcal{L}(p_1, \mathcal{E}_L))) \wedge (p_2 = \mathcal{D}(g_2, \mathcal{E}_D)) \wedge (n_2 = \mathcal{L}(p_2, \mathcal{E}_L))) \wedge (g_1 = g_2) \wedge (n_1 \neq n_2)]$

Phenotypic multiplicity may result from several factors including the effects of the environment, learning, or stochastic aspects of the decoding process. If the density of solutions is low, then the property of phenotypic multiplicity increases the possibility of decoding to a solution phenotype.

6. **Ontogenetic Plasticity:** A representation $\mathcal{R}$ exhibits *ontogenetic plasticity* if the determination of the phenotype corresponding to a given geno-

type is influenced by the environment. This may happen as a result of either environment-sensitive developmental processes (in which case $\mathcal{E}_D \neq \lambda$), or learning processes (in which case $\mathcal{L} \neq \lambda$).

Ontogenetic plasticity is a useful property for constraining or modifying the decoding process based on the dictates of the application domain. For instance, if one is evolving networks for a pattern classification problem, the search for a solution network can be dramatically enhanced by utilizing a *supervised* learning algorithm for training individual phenotypes in the population. However, if such training examples are not available to permit supervised learning, one will have to be content with a purely evolutionary search.

7. **Modularity:** Gruau's notion of *modularity* [28] is as follows: Suppose a *network* n_1 includes several instances of a subnetwork n_2 then the encoding (genotype) of n_1 is *modular* if it codes for n_2 only once, with instructions to copy it that would be understood by the decoding process. Modularity is closely tied to the existence of *organized structure* or regularity in the phenotype that can be concisely expressed in the genotype in a form that can be used by the decoding process. Other notions of modularity dealing with *functional* modules, *recursively-defined* modules etc., are also worth exploring. It can be observed that the property of modularity automatically results in more compact genetic encodings and a potential *lack* of redundancy (described below). In modular representations any change in the genotypic encoding of a module, either due to genetic influences or errors, affects all instances of the module in the phenotype. Non-modular representations, on the other hand, are resistive to such complete alterations. It is hard to decide *a priori* which scenario is better, since modular representations benefit from benign changes while non-modular representations are more robust to deleterious ones.

8. **Redundancy:** Redundancy can manifest itself at various levels and in different forms in an evolutionary system. Redundancy often contributes to the robustness of the system in the face of failure of components or processes. For instance, if the reproduction and/or decoding processes are error-prone, an evolutionary system can benefit from *genotypic redundancy* (e.g., the genotype contains redundant genes) or *decoding redundancy* (e.g., the decoding process reads the genotype more than once). If the phenotype is prone to failure of components (e.g., units, connections, sub-networks, etc.), the system can benefit from *phenotypic redundancy*. Phenotypic redundancy can be either *topological* (e.g., multiple identical units, connections, etc.) or *functional* (e.g., dissimilar units, connections, etc., that somehow impart the same function).

It is worth noting that genotypic redundancy does not necessarily imply phenotypic redundancy and vice versa (depending on the nature of the decoding process). This simply reiterates the importance of examining the entire representation (encoding as well as decoding) when defining properties of evolutionary systems. Also note that there are many ways to realize both genotypic as well as phenotypic redundancy: by replication of identical components (structural redundancy) or by replication of functionally identical units, or by building in modules or processes that can dynamically restructure themselves when faced with failure of components etc. [84].

9. **Complexity:** Complexity is perhaps one of the most important properties of any evolutionary system. However, it is rather difficult to characterize satisfactorily using any single definition. It is probably best to think of complexity using several different notions including: *structural complexity* of genotypes, *decoding complexity, computational (space/time) complexity* of each of the components of the system (including decoding of genotypes, fitness evaluation, reproduction, etc.), and perhaps even other measures inspired by *information theory* (e.g., entropy, Kolmogorov complexity, etc.) [49].

Although it is clear that one would like to use a genetic representation that leads to lower system complexities, the many interacting elements of the evolutionary system, genetic representations and their properties, and the existence of many different kinds of complexities, make it hard to arrive at *one* scalar measure that would satisfy all. Needless to say, characterization of complexity remains a subjective measure of the user's preferences and the dictates of the application problem.

This list of properties, although by no means complete, is nevertheless relevant in an operationally useful characterization of evolutionary systems in general, and the design of neural architectures in particular. Table 1.1 illustrates a characterization of the evolutionary system proposed by Miller et al., that was described in Section 1.6.

1.8 Summary

In this chapter we have introduced the evolutionary approach to the synthesis of agent programs in general, and artificial neural networks in particular. That evolution is a powerful, and more importantly, an aptly suited design approach for this undertaking, will be amply demonstrated in the chapters to follow.

Since the efficiency and efficacy of any evolutionary design system is crit-

Table 1.1
Properties of the genetic representation used by Miller et al.

Property	Satisfied?	Comments
Completeness	$\checkmark$	With respect to feed-forward networks.
Closure	$\times$	Invalid networks can result.
Topological Compactness	$\checkmark$	Determined by back-propagation.
Functional Compactness	$\checkmark$	Also possible.
Space Scalability	$\checkmark$	$O(N)$ with respect to units.
Time Scalability	$\checkmark$	$O(N)$ with respect to units.
Genotypic Multiplicity	$\times$	No genotypic multiplicity.
Phenotypic Multiplicity	$\checkmark$	Dictated by back-propagation.
Ontogenetic Plasticity	$\checkmark$	Back-propagation used for training.
Modularity	$\times$	Genotype only specifies connections.
Genotypic/Decoding Redundancy	$\times$	One gene for each connection.
Phenotypic Redundancy	$\checkmark$	Units and modules, but not connections.
Space Complexity	$\checkmark$	Dictated by genotype size.
Time Complexity	$\checkmark$	Dictated by GA and back-propagation.

ically governed by the encoding mechanism chosen for specifying the genotypes and the decoding mechanism for transforming them into phenotypes, extreme care must be taken to ensure that these two mechanisms are designed with the application problem in mind. To aid this process, in this chapter, we identified and formalized a number of properties of such genetic representations. To the extent possible, we have tried to characterize each property in precise terms. This characterization of properties of genetic representations will hopefully help in the rational choice of genetic representations for different applications.

For instance, suppose we need to design neurocontrollers for robots that have to operate in hazardous and *a priori* unknown environments. Examples of such applications include exploration of unknown terrains, nuclear waste cleanup, space exploration, etc. Since robots in such environments are required to plan and execute sequences of actions (where each action in a sequence may be dependent on previous actions performed as well as the sensory inputs), a recurrent neural network is probably needed. Further, if the system is to be used to design robots capable of functioning in different, *a priori* unknown environments, the robot controllers must have ontogenetic plasticity, i.e., the robots must be capable of learning from their experiences in the environment. The hazardous nature (e.g., in nuclear waste cleanup) or remoteness of the environment (e.g., in the case of robots used to explore distant planets) makes it desirable that the controllers operate robustly in the face of component failures etc., which calls for phenotypic redundancy of some form (e.g., duplication of units, links, or modules of the neurocontroller). In addition, implementation technology and cost considerations might impose additional constraints on the design of the controller. For instance, hardware realization using current VLSI technology would benefit from locally connected, modular networks built from simple processors. Also extended periods of autonomous operation might require designs that are efficient in terms of power consumption, etc.

In order to design a robot controller satisfying these multiple performance constraints, one might resort to an evolutionary design approach. In such cases, a number of these constraints translate into properties that we have identified in Section 1.7. Using these, one can choose an appropriate genetic representation that can be used to evolve appropriate robot behaviors. Elsewhere we have demonstrated an evolutionary approach to the synthesis of robot behaviors for a box-pushing task, where we choose a genetic representation based on the properties we have identified in this chapter [4].

The remaining chapters in this volume address fundamental concerns and demonstrate successful applications of evolutionary search in the synthesis of intelligent agent designs and behaviors. The chapters are authored by prominent researchers, each an authority in his/her area of expertise. In this sense, this compilation presents a unique snapshot of cutting-edge research from leading researchers around the world.

References

[1]D. H. Ackley and M. L. Littman. Interactions between learning and evolution. In *Proceedings of the Second International Conference on Artificial Life*, pages 487–509, 1991.

[2]D. Anand and R. Zmood. *Introduction to Control Systems*. Butterworth-Heinemann, Oxford, 1995.

[3]T. Bäck, G. Rudolph, and H.-P. Schwefel. Evolutionary programming and evolution strategies: Similarities and differences. In *Proceedings of the Second Annual Conference on Evolutionary Programming*, pages 11–22. 1993.

[4]K. Balakrishnan. *Biologically Inspired Computational Structures and Processes for Autonomous Agents and Robots*. PhD thesis, Department Of Computer Science, Iowa State University, Ames, IA, 1998.

[5]K. Balakrishnan and V. Honavar. Evolutionary design of neural architectures — a preliminary taxonomy and guide to literature. Technical Report CS TR 95-01, Department of Computer Science, Iowa State University, Ames, IA, 1995.

[6]K. Balakrishnan and V. Honavar. Properties of genetic representations of neural architectures. In *Proceedings of the World Congress on Neural Networks*, pages 807–813, 1995.

[7]J. Bradshaw, editor. *Software Agents*. MIT Press, Cambridge, MA, 1997.

[8]F. Cecconi, F. Menczer, and R. Belew. Maturation and evolution of imitative learning in artificial organisms. *Adaptive Behavior*, 4(1):179–198, 1995.

[9]D. J. Chalmers. The evolution of learning: An experiment in genetic connectionism. In

Proceedings of the 1990 Connectionist Models Summer School, pages 81–90, 1990.

[10]P. Churchland and T. Sejnowski. *The Computational Brain*. MIT Press, Cambridge, MA, 1992.

[11]R. Collins and D. Jefferson. An artificial neural network representation for artificial organisms. In *Proceedings of the Conference on Parallel Problem Solving from Nature*, pages 259–263, 1990.

[12]R. Collins and D. Jefferson. Antfarm: Towards simulated evolution. In *Proceedings of the Second International Conference on Artificial Life*, pages 579–601, 1991.

[13]M. Colombetti and M. Dorigo. Learning to control an autonomous robot by distributed genetic algorithms. In *From Animals to Animats 2: Proceedings of the Second International Conference on Simulation of Adaptive Behavior*, 1992.

[14]I. Cox and G. Wilfong, editors. *Autonomous Robot Vehicles*. Springer-Verlag, New York, NY, 1990.

[15]J. Dayhoff. *Neural Network Architectures: An Introduction*. Van Nostrand Reinhold, New York, 1990.

[16]T. Dean, J. Allen, and Y. Aloimonos. *Artificial Intelligence - Theory and Practice*. Benjamin Cummings, Redwood City, CA, 1995.

[17]J. Durkin. *Expert Systems – Design and Development*. Macmillan, New York, NY, 1994.

[18]H. Everett. *Sensors for Mobile Robots: Theory and Application*. A. K. Peters Ltd, Wellesley, MA, 1995.

[19]D. Floreano and F. Mondada. Automatic creation of an autonomous agent: Genetic evolution of a neural-network driven robot. In *from Animals to Animats 3: Proceedings of the Third International Conference on Simulation of Adaptive Behavior*, pages 421–430, 1994.

[20]D. Fogel. Asymptotic convergence properties of genetic algorithms and evolutionary programming: Analysis and experiments. *Cybernetics and Systems: An International Journal*, 25:389–407, 1994.

[21]C. Fonseca and P. Fleming. An overview of evolutionary algorithms in multi-objective optimization. *Evolutionary Computation*, 3(1):1–16, 1995.

[22]S. Gallant. *Neural Network Learning and Expert Systems*. MIT Press, Cambridge, MA, 1993.

[23]C. Gallistel. *The Organization of Learning*. MIT Press, Cambridge, MA, 1990.

[24]M. Ginsberg. *Essentials of Artificial Intelligence*. Morgan Kaufmann, San Mateo, CA, 1993.

[25]D. Goldberg. *Genetic Algorithms in Search, Optimization, and Machine Learning*. Addison Wesley, Reading, MA, 1989.

[26]S. Goonatilake and S. Khebbal, editors. *Intelligent Hybrid Systems*. John Wiley, West Sussex, UK, 1995.

[27]J. Grier and T. Burk. *Biology of Animal Behavior*. Mosley-Year Book, New York, NY, 2 edition, 1992.

[28]F. Gruau. Genetic micro programming of neural networks. In K. Kinnear, editor, *Advances in Genetic Programming*. MIT Press, Cambridge, MA, 1994.

[29]I. Harvey, P. Husbands, and D. Cliff. Seeing the light: Artificial evolution, real vision. In *From Animals to Animats 3: Proceedings of the Third International Conference on Simulation of Adaptive Behavior*, 1994.

[30]M. H. Hassoun. *Fundamentals of Artificial Neural Networks*. MIT Press, Cambridge, MA, 1995.

[31]S. Haykin. *Neural Networks*. Macmillan, New York, NY, 1994.

[32]J. Hertz, A. Krogh, and R. Palmer. *Introduction to the Theory of Neural Computation*. Addison Wesley, Redwood City, CA, 1991.

[33]J. Holland. *Adaptation in Natural and Artificial Systems*. The University of Michigan Press,

Ann Arbor, 1975.

[34]V. Honavar. *Generative Learning Structures and Processes for Generalized Connectionist Networks*. PhD thesis, Department of Computer Science, University of Wisconsin, Madison, WI, 1990.

[35]V. Honavar. Toward learning systems that integrate different strategies and representations. In V. Honavar and L. Uhr, editors, *Artificial Intelligence and Neural Networks: Steps Toward Principled Integration*, pages 561–580. Academic Press, San Diego, CA, 1994.

[36]V. Honavar. Intelligent agents. In J. Williams and K. Sochats, editors, *Encyclopedia of Information Technology*. Marcel Dekker, New York, NY, 1998.

[37]V. Honavar and L. Uhr. Generative learning structures and processes for generalized connectionist networks. *Information Sciences*, 70:75–108, 1993.

[38]V. Honavar and L. Uhr, editors. *Artificial Intelligence and Neural Networks – Steps toward Principled Integration*. Academic Press, San Diego, CA, 1994.

[39]J. Horn and N. Nafpliotis. Multiobjetive optimization using the niched pareto genetic algorithm. Illigal technical report 93005, University of Illinois, Urbana-Champaign, IL, 1993.

[40]J. Kolodner. *Case-Based Reasoning*. Morgan Kaufmann, San Mateo, CA, 1993.

[41]J. Koza. Genetic evolution and co-evolution of computer programs. In *Proceedings of the Second International Conference on Artificial Life*, pages 603–629, 1991.

[42]J. R. Koza. *Genetic Programming: On the Programming of Computers by Means of Natural Selection*. MIT Press, Cambridge, MA, 1992.

[43]S. Y. Kung. *Digital Neural Networks*. Prentice Hall, New York, NY, 1993.

[44]P. Langley. *Elements of Machine Learning*. Morgan Kauffman, San Mateo, CA, 1995.

[45]D. Levine. *Introduction to Neural and Cognitive Modeling*. Lawrence Earlbaum Associates, Hillsdale, NJ, 1991.

[46]F. Lewis, C. Abdallah, and D. Dawson, editors. *Control of Robot Manipulators*. Macmillan, New York, NY, 1993.

[47]H. Lewis and C. Papadimitriou. *Elements of the Theory of Computation*. Prentice Hall, Englewood Cliffs, NJ, 1981.

[48]M. Lewis, A. Fagg, and A. Sodium. Genetic programming approach to the construction of a neural network for control of a walking robot. In *Proceedings of the IEEE International Conference on Robotics and Automation*, 1992.

[49]M. Li and P. Vitanyi. *An Introduction to Kolmogorov Complexity and Its Applications*. Springer-Verlag, New York, NY, 1997.

[50]H. Lund, J. Hallam, and W.-P. Lee. Evolving robot morphology. In *Proceedings of IEEE Fourth International Conference on Evolutionary Computation*, 1997.

[51]N. Mackintosh. *Conditioning and Associative Learning*. Clarendon, New York, NY, 1983.

[52]D. McFarland. *Animal Behavior*. Longman Scientific and Technical, Essex, England, 1993.

[53]F. Menczer and R. Belew. Evolving sensors in environments of controlled complexity. In *Proceedings of the Fourth International Conference on Artificial Life*, 1994.

[54]O. Miglino, K. Nafasi, and C. Taylor. Selection for wandering behavior in a small robot. *Artificial Life*, 2(1):101–116, 1994.

[55]G. Miller, P. Todd, and S. Hegde. Designing neural networks using genetic algorithms. In *Proceedings of the Third International Conference on Genetic Algorithms*, pages 379–384, 1989.

[56]M. Minsky. *Computation: Finite and Infinite Machines*. Prentice Hall, Englewood Cliffs, NJ, 1967.

[57]M. Mitchell. *An Introduction to Genetic Algorithms*. MIT Press, Cambridge, MA, 1996.

[58]T. Mitchell. *Machine Learning*. McGraw Hill, New York, NY, 1997.

[59]S. Nolfi, J. Elman, and D. Parisi. Learning and evolution in neural networks. *Adaptive*

Behavior, 3(1):5–28, 1994.

[60]H. Nwana. Software agents: An overview. *Knowledge Engineering Review*, 11(3), 1996.

[61]J. O'Keefe and L. Nadel. *The Hippocampus as a Cognitive Map*. Clarendon, Oxford, UK, 1978.

[62]O. Omidvar and P. van der Smagt, editors. *Neural Systems for Robotics*. Academic Press, San Diego, CA, 1997.

[63]R. Parekh. *Constructive learning: Inducing grammars and neural networks*. PhD thesis, Department of Computer Science, Iowa State University, Ames, IA, 1998.

[64]M. Patel. Concept formation: A complex adaptive approach. *Theoria*, (20):89–108, 1994.

[65]M. Patel. Situation assessment and adaptive learning: Theoretical and experimental issues. In *Proceedings of the Second International Round-Table on Abstract Intelligent Agents*, 1994.

[66]M. Patel. Constraints on task and search complexity in ga+nn models of learning and adaptive behaviour. In T. Fogarty, editor, *Evolutionary Computing 2*, pages 200–224. Springer-Verlag, Berlin, 1995.

[67]M. Patel. Heuristic constraints on search complexity for multi-modal non-optimal models. In *IEEE International Conference on Evolutionary Computation*, 1995.

[68]M. Patel, M. Colombetti, and M. Dorigo. Evolutionary learning for intelligent automation: A case study. *Journal of Intelligent Automation and Soft Computing*, 1(1):29–42, 1995.

[69]M. Patel and M. Dorigo. Adaptive learning of a robot arm. In *Selected Papers from AISB Workshop on Evolutionary Computation*, pages 180–194, 1994.

[70]M. Patel and V. Maniezzo. Nn's and ga's: Evolving co-operative behaviour in adaptive learning agents. In *IEEE World Congress on Computational Intelligence*, 1994.

[71]C. Reynolds. Evolution of corridor following behavior in a noisy world. In *From Animals to Animats 3: Proceedings of the Third International Conference on Simulation of Adaptive Behavior*, 1994.

[72]C. Reynolds. Evolution of obstacle avoidance behavior: Using noise to promote robust solutions. In K. Kinnear, editor, *Advances in Genetic Programming*. MIT Press, Cambridge, MA, 1994.

[73]E. Rich and K. Knight. *Aritificial Intelligence*. McGraw Hill, New York, NY, 1991.

[74]B. Ripley. *Pattern Recognition and Neural Networks*. Cambridge University Press, New York, NY, 1996.

[75]D. E. Rumelhart and J. L. McClelland, editors. *Parallel Distributed Processing, Vol I-II*. MIT Press, Cambridge, MA, 1986.

[76]S. Russell and P. Norvig. *Artificial Intelligence - A Modern Approach*. Prentice Hall, Englewood Cliffs, NJ, 1995.

[77]R. Salomon. Improved convergence rate of back-propagation with dynamic adaptation of the learning rate. In *Proceedings of the First International Conference on Parallel Problem Solving from Nature*, pages 269–273, 1991.

[78]H.-P. Schwefel, editor. *Numerical Optimization of Computer Models*. John Wiley, Chichester, UK, 1981.

[79]H.-P. Schwefel. Collective phenomena in evolutionary systems. In *Proceedings of 31st Annual Meeting of the International Society for General System Research*, pages 1025–1033, 1987.

[80]R. Sun and L. Bookman, editors. *Computational Architectures Integrating Symbolic and Neural Processes*. Kluwer Academic, New York, NY, 1994.

[81]S. L. Tanimoto. *Elements of Artificial Intelligence Using Common Lisp*. Computer Science Press, New York, NY, 1995.

[82]E. Tolman. Cognitive maps in rats and men. *Psychological Review*, 55:189–208, 1948.

[83]L. Uhr and V. Honavar. Introduction. In V. Honavar and L. Uhr, editors, *Artificial*

Intelligence and Neural Networks: Steps Toward Principled Integration. Academic Press, San Diego, CA, 1994.

[84]J. von Neumann. Probabilistic logics and the synthesis of reliable organisms from unreliable components. In C. Shannon and J. McCarthy, editors, *Automata Studies*, pages 43–98. Princeton University Press, Princeton, NJ, 1956.

[85]J. Walker. Evolution of simple virtual robots using genetic algorithms. Master's thesis, Department of Mechanical Engineering, Iowa State University, Ames, IA, 1995.

[86]P. Winston. *Artificial Intelligence*. Addison Wesley, New York, NY, 1992.

[87]M. Wooldridge and N. Jennings. Intelligent agents: Theory and practice. *Knowledge Engineering Review*, 10(2):115–152, 1995.

[88]B. Yamauchi and R. Beer. Integrating reactive, sequential, and learning behavior using dynamical neural networks. In *From Animals to Animats 3: Proceedings of the Third International Conference on Simulation of Adaptive Behavior*, pages 382–391, 1994.

[89]J. Yang, R. Parekh, and V. Honavar. DistAl: An inter-pattern distance-based constructive learning algorithm. In *Proceedings of the International Joint Conference on Neural Networks*, Anchorage, Alaska, 1998. To appear.

[90]A. Zalzala and A. Morris, editors. *Neural Networks for Robotic Control: Theory and Applications*. Ellis Horwood, New York, NY, 1996.

2 Cellular Encoding for Interactive Evolutionary Robotics

Frédéric Gruau and Kameel Quatramaran

This work reports experiments in interactive evolutionary robotics. The goal is to evolve an Artificial Neural Network (ANN) to control the locomotion of an 8-legged robot. The ANNs are encoded using a cellular developmental process called cellular encoding. In a previous work similar experiments have been carried on successfully on a simulated robot. They took however around 1,000,000 different ANN evaluations. In this work the fitness is determined on a real robot, and no more than a few hundreds evaluations can be performed. Various ideas were implemented so as to decrease the required number of evaluations from 1,000,000 to 200. First we used cell cloning and link typing. Second we did as many things as possible interactively: interactive problem decomposition, interactive syntactic constraints, interactive fitness. More precisely: 1- A modular design was chosen where a controller for an individual leg, with a precise neuronal interface was developed. 2- Syntactic constraints were used to promote useful building blocks and impose an 8-fold symmetry. 3- We determined the fitness interactively by hand. We can reward features that would otherwise be very difficult to locate automatically. Interactive evolutionary robotics turns out to be quite successful, in the first bug-free run a global locomotion controller that is faster than a programmed controller could be evolved.

2.1 Introduction

The Motivation for Interactive Evolutionary Algorithm

In [93] Dave Cliff, Inman Harvey and Phil Husbands from the University of Sussex lay down a chart for the development of cognitive architectures, or control systems, for situated autonomous agent. They claim that the design by hand of control systems capable of complex sensorimotor processing is likely to become prohibitively difficult as the complexity increases, and they advocate the use of Evolutionary Algorithm (EA) to evolve recurrent dynamic neural networks as a potentially efficient engineering method. Our goal is to try to present a concrete proof of this claim by showing an example of big (> 16 units) control system generated using EA. The difference between our work and what we call the "Sussex" approach is that we consider EAs as only one element of the ANN design process. An engineering method is something which is used to help problem solving, that may be combined with any additional symbolic knowledge one can have about a given problem. We would never expect EAs to do everything from scratch. Our view is that EA should be used interactively in the process of ANN design, but not as a magic wand that will solve all the problems. In contrast with this point of view, Cliff Harvey and Husband seem to rely more on EAs. In [93] they use a direct coding of the ANN. They find ANN without particular regularities, although they acknowledge the fact that a coding which could generate repeated structure would be more appropriate. The advantage of the Sussex approach is that it is pure machine learning, without human intervention. In contrast, we use EA interactively in the ANN design. This is similar to supervised machine learning.

How Do We Supervise the Evolutionary Algorithm?

The key element that enables us to help the EAs with symbolic knowledge is the way we encode ANNs. What is coded is a developmental process: how a cell divides and divides again and generates a graph of interconnected cells that finally become an ANN. The development is coded on a tree. We help the EA by providing syntactic constraints, a "grammar" which restrict the number of possible trees to those having the right syntax. This is similar to program in C needing to satisfy the C-syntax. Syntactic constraints impose a prior probability on the distribution of ANN. One advantage of our approach is that we are able to study the structure of our ANN, identify some regularities, and help the emergence of them by choosing the appropriate syntactic constraints. We don't want to use neurons in a sort of densely connected neural soup, a sort of raw computational power which has to be shaped by evolutionary computation. Instead we want a sparsely connected structure, with hierarchy and symmetries, where it is possible to analyze what's going on just by looking at the architecture. We think one needs a lot of faith to believe that EAs can quickly generate complex highly structured ANNs, from scratch. Perhaps nature has proven it is possible, but it took a lot of time and a huge number of individuals. Our approach is to use symbolic knowledge whenever it is easy and simple. By symbolic we mean things which can be expressed by syntactic constraints which are formally BNF grammars. By easy we mean symmetries that anybody can perceive. We see symbols as a general format that can define the symmetries of the problem or decompose a problem into sub-problems, or else provide building blocks. The discovery of such things is time-expensive to automate with evolutionary computation, but easily perceived by the human eye. Any non-scientific person can point out the symmetries of the 8-legged robot, and thus build the "symmetry format". We view Evolutionary Computation of ANN as a "design amplifier" that can "ground" this symmetry format on the real world. This is may be another way to address the well known symbol grounding problem.

The Challenge of This Work

It is possible to automate problem decomposition and symmetry detection. First of all we should say that we still do automatic problem decomposition in this work, the EA automatically decomposes the problem of generating 8 coupled oscillators, into the problem of generating a singleton, and putting together copies of it. However we give some information about the decom-position, since we provide the number 8. In [95] we show that the EA could alone decompose the 6-legged locomotion problem into the sub-problem of generating a sub-ANN for controlling one leg and put together six copies of the sub-ANN. There we did not give the number 6. We also needed a powerful IPSC860 32 processor parallel machine, and over 1,000,000 evaluations. We are now working with a real robot, and each fitness evaluation takes a few min-utes, and is done by hand. The challenge of this paper was to solve the same problem with only a few hundred evaluations. At the outset, this did not seem promising. Four ideas made it possible:

- We enhanced the developmental process by adding cellular cloning and link typing,
- Using syntactic constraints, we forced three cloning divisions at the root of the cellular code, so as to be sure than an 8-fold symmetric network would develop.
- Each leg has two degrees of freedom, and two output units are needed to control them. We first evolved a leg controller to reduce those two outputs to a single output commanding the forward stroke and the return stroke. This way the problem is simplified to the task of generating 8 coupled oscillators.
- We determined the fitness by hand. We visually monitored the EA so as to reward any potentially interesting feature that would otherwise had been very difficult to detect automatically. We steer the EA starting from generating easy oscillatory behavior, and then evolving the leg coupling.

The paper presents what is cellular encoding, cell cloning and link typing, how we use syntactic constraints, experiments done with only one leg, and then

with all the legs. Automatically generated drawing represent different ANN
that were found at different stages of the evolution. We discuss the behavior
of the robot, and try to explain it based on an analysis on the architecture,
whenever possible. The description tries to render how it feels to breed robots.

2.2   Review of Cellular Encoding

Cellular encoding is a language for local graph transformations that controls
the division of cells which grow into an Artificial Neural Network (ANN) [94].
Other kind of developmental process have been proposed in the literature, a
good review can be found in [98]. Many schemes have been proposed with
partly the goal of modeling biological reality. Cellular encoding has been
created with the sole purpose of computer problem solving, and its efficiency
has been shown on a range of different problem, a review can be found in [96].
We explain the basic version of Cellular Encoding in this section, as shown in
figure 2.1. A cell has an input site and an output site and can be linked to other
cells with directed and ordered links. A cell or a link also possesses a list of
internal registers that represent local memory. The registers are initialized with
a default value, and are duplicated when a cell division occurs. The registers
contain neuron attributes such as weights and the threshold value. The graph
transformations can be classified into cell divisions and modifications of cell
and link registers.

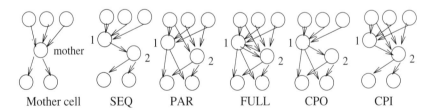

Figure 2.1
Illustration of main type of division: SEQ, PAR, FULL, CPO, CPI.

A cell division replaces one cell called the parent cell by two cells called
child cells. A cell division must specify how the two child cells will be linked.
For practical purposes, we give a name to each graph transformation; these
names in turn are manipulated by the genetic algorithm. In the *sequential*
division denoted SEQ the first child cell inherits the input links, the second child

cell inherits the output links and the first child cell is connected to the second child cell. In the *parallel* division denoted PAR both child cells inherit both the input and output links from the parent cell. Hence, each link is duplicated. The child cells are not connected. In general, a particular cell division is specified by indicating for each child cell which link is inherited from the mother cell. The FULL division is the sequential and the parallel division combined. All the links are duplicated, and the two child cells are interconnected with two links, one for each direction. This division can generate completely connected sub-ANNs. The CPO division (CoPy Output) is a sequential division, plus the output links are duplicated in both child cells. Similarly, the CPI division (CoPy Input) is a sequential division, plus the input links are duplicated. Before describing the instructions used to modify cell registers it is useful to describe how an ANN unit performs a computation. The default value of the weights is 1, and the bias is 0. The default transfer function is the identity. Each neuron computes the weighted sum of its inputs, applies the transfer function to obtain s, and updates the activity a using the equation $a = a+(s-a)/\tau$ where τ is the time constant of the neuron. See the figures 2.5, 2.10, and 2.12 for examples of neural networks. The ANNs computation is performed with integers; the activity is coded using 12 bits so that 4096 corresponds to activity 1. The instruction SBIAS x sets the bias to $x/4096$. The instruction DELTAT sets the time constant of the neuron. SACT sets the initial activity of the neuron. The instruction STEP (resp LINEAR) sets the transfer function to the clipped linear function between -1 and $+1$ (resp to the identity function). The instruction PI sets the sigmoid to multiply all its input together. The WEIGHT instruction is used to modify link registers. It has k integer parameters, each one specifying a real number in floating point notation: the real is equal to the integer between -255 and 256 divided by 256. The parameters are used to set the k weights of the first input links. If a neuron happens to have more than k input links, the weights of the supernumerary input links will be set by default to the value 256 (i.e., $\frac{256}{256} = 1$).

The cellular code is a *grammar-tree* with nodes labeled by names of graph transformations. Each cell carries a duplicate copy of the grammar tree and has an internal register called a reading head that points to a particular position of the grammar tree. At each step of development, each cell executes the graph transformation pointed to by its reading head and then advances the reading head to the left or to the right subtree. After cells terminate development they lose their reading-heads and become neurons.

The order in which cells execute graph transformations is determined as follows: once a cell has executed its graph transformation, it enters a First In First Out (FIFO) queue. The next cell to execute is the head of the FIFO queue. If the cell divides, the child which reads the left subtree enters the FIFO queue first. This order of execution tries to model what would happen if cells were active in parallel. It ensures that a cell cannot be active twice while another cell has not been active at all. The WAIT instruction makes a cell wait for a specified number of steps, and makes it possible to also encode a particular order of execution.

We also used the control program symbol PROGN. The program symbol PROGN has an arbitrary number of subtrees, and all the subtrees are executed one after the other, starting from the subtree number one.

Consider a control problem where the number of control variables is n and the number of sensors is p. We want to solve this control problem using an ANN with p input units and n output units. There are two possibilities to generate those I/O units. The first method is to impose the I/O units using appropriate syntactic constraints. At the beginning of the development the initial graph of cells consists of p input units connected to a reading cell which is connected to n output units. The input and output units do not read any code, they are fixed during all the development. In effective these cells are pointers or place-holders for the inputs and outputs. The initial reading cell reads at the root of the grammar tree. It will divide according to what it reads and generate all the cells that will eventually generate the final decoded ANN. The second method that we often prefer to use, is to have the EA find itself the right number of I/O units. The development starts with a single cell connected to the input pointer cell and the output pointer cell. At the end of the development, the input (resp. output) units are those which are connected to the input (resp. output) pointer cell. We let the evolutionary algorithm find the right number of input and output unit, by putting a term in the fitness to reward networks that have a correct number of I/O units. The problem with the first method is that we can easily generate an ANN where all the output units output the same signals, and all the inputs are just systematically summed in a weighted sum. The second method works usually better, because the EA is forced to generate a specific cellular code for each I/O unit, that will specify how it is to be connected to the rest of the ANN, and with which weights. To implement the second method we will use the instruction BLOC which blocs the development of a cell until all its input neurons are neurons, and the instruction TESTIO which compares the number of inputs to a specified integer value, and sets a flag accordingly. The flag is later used to compute the fitness.

Last, the instruction CYC is used to add a recurrent link to a unit, from the output site to the input site. That unit can then perform other divisions, duplicate the recurrent link, and generates recurrent connections everywhere.

2.3   Enhancement of Cellular Encoding

We had to enhance cellular encoding with cloning division, and the use of types. We also implemented another way to obtain recurrent links. All these new elements are reported in this section.

The cloning operation is really easy to implement and is done by encapsulating a division instruction into a PROGN instruction. After the division, the two child cells only modify some registers and cut some links, then they simply go to execute the next instruction of the PROGN, and since they both execute the same instruction, it generates a highly symmetric ANN. Figure 2.2 presents a simple example of cloning.

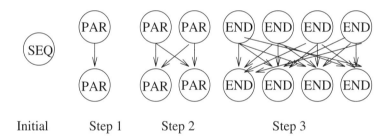

| Initial | Step 1 | Step 2 | Step 3 |

Figure 2.2
The cloning operation, the above ANN is developed from the code
PROGN(SEQ)(PAR)(PAR)(END) which contains three clone division. The development takes three steps, one for each clone.

The instruction that we are now presenting has a version for the input unit which ends with the letter 'I' and one for the output units which ends with the letter 'O'. We are now going to use another link register called the *type* register, which will be initialized when a link is created between two child cells, and that is later used to select links for cutting, reversing, or setting the weight. We also introduce two sets of generic instructions – one to select links, and another one to set the link register.

The instructions beginning with 'C' and continuing by the name of a register r are used to select links. This instruction selects the links whose register is equal to the value of the argument. For example CTYPEI(1) selects all the input links for which the type register is equal to 1. There is another register called NEW which is a flag that is set each time a new link is created between two child cells, or a recurrent link is added. CNEWO(1) selects all the newly created links, going out of the output site.

The instructions beginning with 'S' and continuing by the name of a register are used to set the value of a register, in some previously selected links. For example the sequence PROGN(CNEWI(1))(STYPEI(2)) sets the type register of newly created links from the input site, to the value 2. In this work, we only use this instruction for the weights, and for the type.

We also use the instruction RESTRICTI and RESTRICTO which has two arguments x and d_x. It is used to reduce a list of preselected links. Let say there are 10 input links whose type is 2. We can select the 5th and the 6th using the sequence PROGN(CTYPEI (2))(RESTRICTI(5)(2)).

The type register together with the select and the set instructions can be used to encode the connections from the neurons to the input and output pointer cell. Those connections are crucial, since they determine which are the input and the output units. Using type registers, we can let each neuron individually encode whether it is or it is not an input or an output unit. We assign two different types, say 0 and 1, to the link that links the ancestor cell to respectively the input pointer cell and the output pointer cell. We ensure that each time a cell divide, the links get duplicated, so that at the near end of the development, all the cells are connected to both the input and the output pointer cell. But then we ensure that each cell can potentially cut the links whose type are 0 or 1. In other words, if a cell wants to be an input unit, it just does nothing, but if it does not want, then it has to cut its input link of type 0.

Last, we use another instruction to add recurrent links. The instructions REVERSEI and REVERSEO duplicates a previously selected link from cell a to cell b, and changes the direction of the duplicate, making it go from cell b to cell a.

2.4   Syntactic Constraints

We used a BNF grammar as a general technique to specify both a subset of syntactically correct grammar-trees and the underlying data structure. The default data structure is a tree. When the data structure is not a tree, it can be a *list, set* or *integer.* By using syntactic constraints on the trees produced by the BNF grammar, a recursive nonterminal of the type *tree* can be associated with a range that specifies a lower and upper bound on the number of recursive rewritings. In our experiments, this is used to set a lower bound m and an upper bound M on the number of neurons in the final neural network architecture. For the *list* and *set* data structure we set a range for the number of elements in these structures. For the *integer* data structure we set a lower bound and an upper bound of a random integer value. The *list* and *set* data structures are described by a set of subtrees called the "*elements*." The *list* data structure is used to store a vector of subtrees. Each of the subtrees is derived using one of the elements. Two subtrees may be derived using the same element. The *set* data structure is like the *list* data structure, except that each of the subtrees must be derived using a different element. So for example, the rule

$$< A >::= (list[2..2]of(0)(1))$$

generates the trees ((0)(0)), ((0)(1)), ((1)(0)), ((1)(1). The rule

$$< A >::= (set[2..2]of(0)(1))$$

generates only the trees ((0)(1)) and ((1)(0)).

Figure 2.3 shows a simple example of syntactic constraints used to restrict the space of possible solutions.

```
<nn>[0..8]; <axiom> ::=   <nn>

<nn>   ::= (  PAR(<nn>)(<nn>)  )
            |  (   CPO(<nn>)(<nn>)  )
            |  (  SEQ  (<nn>)(<nn>)  )
            |  (   <attribute>  )

<attribute> ::=
            (PROGN : set[0..4] of
               (WEIGHT: list[8..8] of
                  (integer[-255..+255]))
               (DELTAT(integer[1..+40]))
               (SBIAS(integer[-4096..+4096]))
               (STEP)  )
```

Figure 2.3
Tutorial example of syntactic constraints

The nonterminal <nn> is recursive. It can be rewritten recursively between 0 and 8 times. Each time is it rewritten recursively, it generates a division and adds a new ANN unit. Thus the final number of ANN units will be between 1 and 9. Note that in this particular case, the size of the ANN is proportional to the size of the genome, therefore constraints of the grammar in figure 2.3 which controls the size of genome, results directly in constraints on ANN growth which controls the ANN size.

The nonterminal <attribute> is used to implement a subset of four possible specializations of the ANN units. The first 8 weights can be set to values between -1 and $+1$. The time constant can be set to a value that ranges from 1 to 40, and the bias is set to a value between -1 and $+1$. The transfer function can be set to the STEP function instead of the default transfer function. Since the lower bound on the *set* range is 0, there can be 0 specializations generated, in which case the ANN unit will compute the sum of its inputs and apply the identity function. Because the upper bound on the *set* is 4, all the 4 specializations can be generated. In this case, the neuron will make a weighted sum, subtract the bias, and apply the clipped linear function. If the lower and the upper bound had both been 1, then exactly one and only one of the features would be operational. This can be used to select an instruction with a given probability. For example, the sequence PROGN: set [1..1] of (WAIT) (WAIT) (WAIT) (CYC) generates a recurrent link with a probability of 0.25.

Crossover.   Crossover must be implemented such that two cellular codes that are syntactically correct produce an offspring that is also syntactically correct (i.e. that can be parsed by the BNF grammar). Each terminal of a grammar tree has a primary type. The primary label of a terminal is the name of the nonterminal that generated it. Crossover with another tree may occur only if the two root symbols of the subtrees being exchanged have the same primary label. This simple mechanism ensures the closure of the crossover operator with respect to the syntactic constraints.

Crossover between two *trees* is the classic crossover used in Genetic Programming as advocated by Koza [99], where two subtrees are exchanged. Crossover between two *integers* is disabled. Crossover between two *lists*, or two *sets* is implemented like crossover between bit strings, since the underlying arrangement of all these data structures is a string.

Mutation.   To mutate one node of a tree labeled by a terminal t, we replace the subtree beginning at this node by a single node labeled with the nonterminal parent of t. Then we rewrite the tree using the BNF grammar. To mutate a *list, set* or *array* data structure, we randomly add or suppress an element.

To mutate an integer, we add a random value uniformly distributed between $\pm max(2, (M - n)/8)$. M and m are the upper and lower bounds of the specified integer range.

Each time an offspring is created, all the nodes are mutated with a small probability. For *tree*, *list* and *set* nodes the mutation rate is 0.05, while for the *integer* node it is 0.5. Those probability may be reset at run time of the EA.

2.5   The Leg Controller

The Challenge

The leg does a *power stroke* when it pushes on the ground to pull the body forward, and the `return stroke` when it lifts the leg and takes it forward. The challenge in this first experiment was to build a good leg controller, one that does not drag the leg on the return stroke, and that starts to push on the ground right at the beginning of the power stroke. The ANN had one single input. The input of 4096 on the input unit must trigger the power stroke, and the input of 0 must trigger the return stroke. This implies the right scheduling of four different actions: when exactly the neuron responsible for lifting and swinging, actually lifts up and down, or swings forwards and backwards.

General Setting

The command of return stroke or power stroke was hand generated during the genetic run, so as to be able to reproduce the movement whenever and as many times as desired. The EA used 20 individuals, the fitness was given according to a set of features: the highest and the lowest leg position had to be correct, the movement of the leg must start exactly when the signal is received, there must not be dragging of the leg on the return stroke, so the leg must first be lifted and then brought forward. Second the leg must rest on the floor at once on the power stroke, therefore the leg must be first put on the floor and then moved backward. Each of these features determined a range of fitness; the ranges were chosen in such a way that for all the features that were checked, the intersection of the ranges was not empty. The fitness was then adjusted according to a subjective judgement. The ranges evolved during the run, so as to fit the evolution. The EA was run around 30 generations. Fitness evaluation is much quicker than with the complete locomotion controller, because we have to watch the leg moving for only a very short period of time to be able to assess the performance, That is how we did up to six hundred evaluations.

Syntactic Constraints Used for the Leg Controller

We now comment on the syntactic constraints used in this run, which are
described in figure 2.4.

```
<nn>[6..20]; begin <axiom> ::= (LABEL
  (SEQ (WAIT) (PAR
        (<nn>)
       (PROGN
          (PAR)
          (PAR(PAR(PAR(WAIT)(WAIT)))(WAIT))(PAR(WAIT)(PAR(WAIT)(PAR(WAIT)
             (WAIT)) )) ) ) ) ) )

<nn> ::=    (SEQ(<nn>)(<nn>))
        |  (PAR(<nn>)(<nn>))
        |  (SHARI1(<nn>)(<nn>))
        |  (CPI(<nn>)(<nn>))
        |  (CPO(<nn>)(<nn>))
        |  (FULL(<nn>)(<nn>))
        |  (<tunit>)
     |  (<sunit>)

<tunit> ::= (PROGN  (STEP)
                (PROGN : set[1..3] of
                  ( DELTAT (integer[1..40]))
                ( WEIGHT: list[8..8] of ( integer[-256..+256]) )
                ( SBIAS  (integer[-4096..+4096])) )   )


<sunit> ::= (PROGN
                (LINEAR)
                (PROGN : set[2..2] of
                ( WEIGHT: list[8..8] of ( integer[-1024..+1024]) )
                ( SBIAS  (integer[-4096..+4096])) )   )
```

Figure 2.4
Syntactic constraints used for the leg controller

We did not use link typing or clone instructions for the leg controller,
the ideas to use them came to us when we began to tackle the problem of
evolving the whole locomotion controller. The non terminal <nn> generates
one neuron, each time it is rewritten, since it can be rewritten between 6
and 20 times, the number of neurons will be between 7 and 21. The division
instructions are classic, except for the SHARI1 where the input links are shared
between the two child cells, the first child gets the first input, and the second
child gets the other inputs. The ANN begins by generating 14 fake output units

using parallel division (one clone and 7 normal). Those units reproduce the input signal. In this way, we can compare the movement on the leg whose controller is evolved, with the raw signal that moves the 7 other legs. The non-terminal <nn> is rewritten between 6 and 20 times, and finally the neuron specializes either as a temporal unit (non-terminal <t-unit>) or as a spatial unit (non-terminal <s-unit>.) The temporal units have a threshold sigmoid and a time constant that is genetically determined. They are used to introduce a delay in a signal, and the spatial units have a linear sigmoid, and a bias that is genetically determined. They are used to translate and multiply a signal by genetically specified constants. Those two types of units are the building blocks needed to generate a fixed length sequence of signals of different intensities and duration. The duration is controlled by the temporal units, and the intensity by the spatial units.

Explanation of the Solutions

Figure 2.5 presents the leg controller found by the Evolutionary Algorithm, together with four different settings of the activities inside the ANN, and the corresponding leg positions.

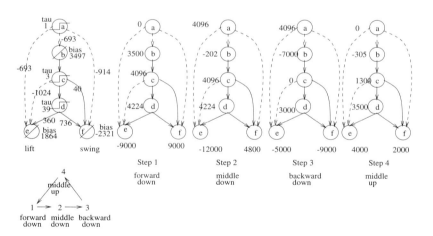

Figure 2.5
The leg controller, and four different settings of the activities inside the ANN, together with the corresponding leg positions. The default values are not represented. The default weight is 256, the default bias is 0, and the default time constant is 3. The diagonal line means the linear sigmoid, the stair case means the step function sigmoid.

Figure 2.6 shows its genetic code after some obvious hand-made simplifications, such has merging a tree of PROGNs.

```
SEQ (PROGN(STEP) (DELTAT(1))) (CPI  (SEQ (PROGN(LINEAR)(WEIGHT(-693)
(-1024)(360)(-252)(-300)(-984)(-849)(610))(SBIAS(3497))) (CPO
(PROGN(STEP)(SACT(3458)))  (PROGN(STEP)(DELTAT(39))))) (PAR
(PROGN(LINEAR)(WEIGHT(-693)(-1024)(360)(-252)(-300)(-984)(-706)
(796))(SBIAS(1864))) (PROGN(LINEAR)(WEIGHT(-914)(40)(736)(-622)
(-1024)(-984)(-706)(610))(SBIAS(-2321))))) )
```

Figure 2.6
The genetic code of the Champion leg controller

Neuron e controls the lift, neuron f controls the swing and neuron a is the
input neuron. While the ANN is completely feed-forward, yet it can generate a
short sequence of different leg commands. Because we use neurons with time
constants, different events can happen at different time steps. In Step 1, the
input to the ANN is 0, and the leg is forward down, the input is then changed
to 4096 to initiate the power stroke. In Step 2, we are in the middle of the power
stroke, neuron e receives an even more negative input, this has no effect, since
it was already over negative, the leg just stays on the ground. On the other
hand, neuron f is brought to negative value, so the leg goes backward relative
to the body, and since the leg is on the ground, the body moves forward. In
Step 3, the power stroke is finished, we now initiate the return stroke the input
is set to 0. In Step 4, we are in the middle of the return stroke, neuron a is
0, but neuron c had not yet time to increase its activities, because of the time
constants. Therefore, neuron e is positive, and the leg is up in the middle. When
the return stroke terminates, we are back to Step 1. Neuron c being positive,
forces the neuron e to become negative again, and the leg is back on the ground.
Initially we wanted to terminate the return stroke with the leg up, and to bring
it down on the power stroke, the controller evolved in another way, and we
thought it would be acceptable. We realized later, that it is actually much better
this way, because the robot always has its leg on the ground, except when it
is in the middle of a return stroke. So it does not lose balance often. There is
another unexpected interesting feature of this controller. We put a security on
the robot driver, so that at each time step the leg cannot move more than a small
amount, to avoid warming of the servo motors. The evolutionary algorithm
used this feature. It generates extreme binary leg position. Nevertheless, the
leg moves continuously, because it cannot move more that the predetermined

upper bound. This was totally unexpected.

2.6   The Locomotion Controller

The Challenge

We have previously evolved ANN for a simulated 6-legged robot, see [95]. We had a powerful parallel machine, an IPSC860 with up to 32 processors. We needed 1,000,000 ANNs to find the an ANN solution to the problem. In this study, one ANN takes a few minutes to assess the fitness, because the fitness is manually given, and it takes some time to see how interesting the controller is. One time we even spent an hour trying to figure out whether the robot was turning or going straight, because of the noise that was not clear. The challenge of this study was to help the EA so as to be able to more efficiently search the genetic space and solve the problem with only a few hundreds of evaluations instead of one million.

General Setting

There are some settings which were constant over the successful run 2, and run 4, and we report them here. The way we give the fitness was highly subjective, and changed during the run depending on how we felt the population had converged or not. We realized that the role of the fitness is not only to reward good individuals, but also to control genetic diversity. Since there is a bit of noise when two individuals are compared, the selective pressure can be controlled by the fitness. The rewarding must be done very cautiously; otherwise newly fit individuals will quickly dominate the population. We are quite happy to see a new good performing phenotype, and are inclined to give it a good rank, to be sure that it is kept for a while. However, if we see that same guy reappear again and again, we may kill it to avoid dominance. We followed some general guidelines. The fitness was a sum of three terms varying between 0.01 and 0.03: The first term rewards oscillations, and discourages too slow or too quick oscillations. The second term rewards the number of legs which oscillate, the third term rewards the correct phase between the different leg oscillators, and the correct coupling. We were very afraid to give big fitnesses, and wanted to put fitnesses difference in the range of the noise that exists when a Boltzmann tournament takes place. So our fitness seldom went above 0.1 .

We started with a population of 32 individuals so as to be able to sample building blocks, and reduce it to 16 after 5 generations. At the same time as we reduced the population, we lowered all the mutation rates (set list and tree) to 0.01 except the integer mutation rate which was increased to 0.4, the idea was to assume that the EA had discovered the right architecture, and to concentrate the genetic search on the weights. The weights were mutated almost one time out of two. The selective pressure was also augmented: the number of individual participating in Boltzmann tournament was increased from 3 to 5. Those tournaments are used to delete individuals or to select mates. We no longer wanted genetic diversity, but rather genetic convergence of the architecture, similar to tuning an already working solution. We got the idea to use genetic convergence from the SAGA paradigm of Inman Harvey [97]. It is possible to give a fitness −1, the effect is that the individual is immediately thrown to the garbage, and not counted. We threw away the motionless individuals, and those that did not have the right number of input/output units. As a result, to generate the first 32 individuals in the initial population, we went over one hundred evaluations.

Syntactic Constraints Used in All the Runs

The first part of the syntax remains the same in the different runs. It is represented in figure 2.7.

```
<axiom>::=(LABEL(SEQ
 (SEQ
  (PAR(<command>)(<command>))
  (PROGN
    (WAIT(4))   (CTYPEI(-1)) (RESTRICTI(0)(1)) (STYPEI(0)) (CTYPEI(-1))
    (STYPEI(1)) (CTYPEO(-1))   (STYPEO(0))
    (<evolved>)   )   )
 (PROGN
   (BLOC)
   (TESTIO8)
   (SHARI (JMP12)   (SHARI (JMP12)   (SHARI (JMP12)    (SHARI (JMP12)
        (PROGN (SWITCH) (SHARI (JMP12) (PROGN (SWITCH) (SHARI (JMP12)
        (PROGN (SWITCH) (SHARI (JMP12) (JMP12)
         (1)))   (1)))   (1)))   (1))   (1))   (1))   (1)) )))
```

Figure 2.7
Syntactic constraint specifying the general structure

It just specifies some fixed cellular code that is always to be part of any individual. This codes a general structure which is developed in figure 2.8.

We now detail the execution of the code. First it sets the type of the links to the output pointer cell to 0 and develops an ANN with two input units

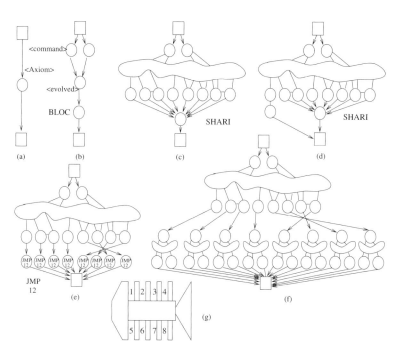

Figure 2.8
What the Syntactic constraint specifying the general structure do: The initial situation is (a), with the two pointer cells represented by a square, and the ancestor cell by a circle. (b) The general structure is specified after the three first divisions, two input units will execute a genetic tree generated by the non-terminal <command>, which is not used anyway. The central cell will develop the core of the controller, the bottom cell waits for the core to develop, then in un-blocs, check that it has exactly 8 neighbor, (it is the case here, but it could not, and then makes 7 SHARI division in (d) and (e), The last four divisions are interleaved with SWITCH operator, so as to set the leg numbers as is indicated in (g). Finally the 8 child cells make a JMP 12, where 12 is just the number of the tree where the cellular code that encodes a leg controller has been stored.

typed 0 and 1. It then generates a cell which will execute the beginning of the evolved code, (<evolved>), and another cell blocked by the BLOC instruction. The input cells are not used. The blocked cell waits that all its neighbors are neurons, then it unblocks and executes the TESTIO instruction which has the effect to check the number of inputs, here it test whether it is equal to 8, and set a flag accordingly. This flag will be used in the fitness evaluation, to throw away those ANNs which does not have exactly 8 outputs units. The unblocked cell then goes on to execute the cellular code that develop the previously evolved leg controller at the right place. For this it used an ad-hoc division called 'SHARI' and also the 'SWITCH' operator which is used to assign number to the output units that match a logical numbering of the legs. This order is specified in figure 2.8 (g).

2.7   Log of the Experimental Runs

We only performed five runs, and we are proud of it. That is a proof that the method works well, it doesn't need weeks of parameter tuning. That's useful because one run is about two days of work. So we report the five runs, even if only one of them was really successful, and the others were merely used to debug our syntactic constraints.

Analysis of Run 0 and Run 1

The first two runs were done with only seven legs, because a plastic gear on the eighth leg had burned, the robot had stubbornly tried to run into an obstacle for 30 seconds. As a result, ANNs were evolved that could made the robot walk with only seven legs. Run 0 brought an approximate solution to the problem. But after hours of breeding we input accidentally a fitness of 23, which had the effect to stop the EA, the success predicate being that the fitness is greater than 1. Run 1 also gave a not so bad quadripod, as far as we can remember, but we realized there was a bug in the way we used the link types which were not used at all. Instead of selecting a link and then setting the type we were first setting and then selecting, which amounts to a null operation. We had simply exchanged the two alleles. When we found out the bug, we were really surprised that we got a solution without types, but we think that's an interesting feature of EAs – even if your program is buggy, the EA will often find workarounds.

Syntactic Constraints Used in the Second Run

The syntactic constraints used for the second run are reported in figure 2.9.
    The core of the controller is developed by the cell executing the non-terminal <evolved>. This cell makes clones, and then generates a sub-ANN. The non-terminal <clone> is rewritten exactly 3 times, and generates exactly 3 clones, therefore an ANN with an 8-fold symmetries will be generated. The non-terminal <nn> is rewritten between 1 and 6 times, and generates a sub-ANN having between one and seven units. Because of the preceding 3 clones, this sub-ANN will be duplicated 8 times, however, one of those 8 sub-ANNs can potentially more than one leg.

The clone division and the normal cell division are specified in a similar way. The general type of the division is to be chosen between FULL, PAR, SEQ, CPI and CPO. Right after dividing, the two cells execute a different sequence of cutting operators generated with the <op> non-terminal. It is possible to adjust the probability of cutting link by first specifying how often we want to cut, and then how much links of a given type we want to cut, using the non-terminal <restrict>. We tune this probability so as to obtain ANNs not too densely connected. The second child sets the type of the newly created link between the two child cells, if there are some, using the non-terminal <settype>. When a cell stops to divide, it sets all its neuron attributes, the cellular code is generated by the non-terminal <unit>. First we reverse some links or/and add a recurrent link. We choose a particular *amount of recurrence* by setting the probability with which recurrent links are created. <unit> then generates a time constant, some weights, a threshold, an initial activity, and finally the sigmoid type. The PI unit makes the product of its input. We use the PI unit with a small probability, because it is highly non-linear, and we do not want to introduce too much non-linearity.

Analysis of the Second Run

The *wavewalk* gait is when the robot moves one leg at a time, the *quadripod* gait is when the robot moves the legs four by four. For the second genetic run, we implemented a mechanism to store nice individuals, and be able to print them and film them afterwards. We now describe a selection of the different champions that were found during the second genetic run. They are shown in figure 2.10.

At generation 0, the ANNs are a bit messy, densely connected. About 75 percent of the ANNs do not have the correct number of outputs, that is 8 outputs, and they are directly eliminated. For this reason, the generation 0 takes quite more time than the other generations. Later individuals have the right number of outputs most of the time. Among those that have the correct number of outputs, most of the ANN do not even make the robot move, also a lot of them make random movements. This happens when a threshold unit is connected directly to the servos and its input is near 0. In this case its output oscillates between 0 and 4096 due to the 1 percent of random noise that is added to the net input. Some ANNs produce a short sequence on one leg before the motionless state. They get a fitness like 0.001. One of them produced an oscillation on four legs. During the next two generations, we concentrated on evolving oscillations on as many legs as possible, giving fitnesses between

0.01 and 0.02, depending on how many legs were oscillating, and how good the period and duration of the return stroke and power stroke were. At generation 3, we started to have individuals with a little bit of coordination between the legs. We watched an embryo of wavewalk which very soon vanished because the leg went out of synchrony. The coupling was too weak. The ANN is represented in figure 2.10 in the second picture, you can see that it is very sparsely connected. The next ANN at generation 4 generated an embryo of quadripod. Four legs moved forward, then four other legs, then the 8 legs moved backward. At generation 6 we got an ANN made of four completely separated sub-ANNs each one was controlling two legs, due to a different initial setting of the activities, the difference of phase was correct at the beginning, and we obtained perfect quadripod, but after 2 minutes, the movement decreased in amplitude, four legs come to a complete stop, and then the four other legs. Generation 7 gave an almost good quadripod, the phase between the two pairs of four legs was not yet correct. The ANN is probably a mutation of the one at generation 3, because the architecture is very similar. Generation 8 gave a slow but safe quadripod walk. The coupling between the four sub-ANNs is strong enough to keep the delay in the phase of the oscillators. Only the frequency needs to be improved, because that's really too slow. Generation 10 produced a correct and fast quadripod, but not the fastest possible. Generation 11 produced one which walked a little bit faster, due to an adjustment of the phase between the two pairs of four legs. The frequency did not improve. Furthermore there was no coupling between the legs. Generation 12 did not improve and we show it because it has a funny feature. The input neuron was not used in all our experiments, it was to control the speed of the robot, but we could not yet go that far. However its activity was set to 2000, and what happened at generation 12 was that an ANN was produced that used this neuron to differentiate the phase between the two pairs of sub-ANNs that were controlling the two pairs of four legs.

Except at generation 0 where we always have a great variety of architectures, you can see that the general organization of the ANN remains similar throughout the whole run. It has 8 sub-ANNs, four of them control 8 legs, one for two contiguous legs, and can potentially ensure that two contiguous legs on one side are out of phase. The four other ANN are in-between, sometimes they are not used at all, as is the case in the champion of generation 11 and 12. The 8 sub-ANNs taken separately have some recurrent links. However, if each sub-ANN is modeled as one neuron, the architecture becomes feed-forward. The sub-ANNs that control the rear legs send information to all the other sub-ANNs. They are the two master oscillators which impose the rhythm. The other sub-ANNs, although they could supposedly run independently, have their phase locked by the master oscillators. We realized that in this run, it was not possible to mutate the general architecture without destroying the whole genetic code, because that would imply replacing a division by another. We think it explains the fact that the general architecture did not change. So we decided to change the syntactic constraints in the next run so as to make the mutation of the general architecture possible, and more thoroughly explore the space of general architectures.

Analysis of the Third Run

The third run lasted only 5 hours, because of a typing mistake in the first generation. We typed a high fitness on the keyboard, for a bad individual who kept reproducing all the time during the next three generation. Being unable to locate it and kill it, we had to kill the whole population, a bit like the story of the mad cow disease which recently happened in England.

Syntactic Constraints Used in the Fourth Run

Our motivation to do another run was to enable mutation of the general structure. We also realized that there were still bugs in the syntactic constraints and we fixed them. The new syntactic constraints are shown in figure 2.11.

To enable mutation of the general structure, instead of implementing <clone> as a recursive non-terminal, we put three occurrences of it, and use it in a non-recursive way. In this way, it is possible to mutate any of them, without having to regenerate the others. Second, we used only the FULL division for the general structure, and forced the EA to entirely determine type by type, which links are inherited and which are not. This can be mutated independently, and may result in making *soft mutation* possible, that can modify a small part of the division. In contrast, if we mutate a division from CPI to PAR, for example, the entire division has to be re-generated from scratch. (We remind the reader that now the division is also genetically determined using link types and cutting links selectively after the division.) The goal of using only FULL was also to augment the probability of coupling between two sub-ANNs. Using only FULL, augments the density of connections, so we augmented the probability of cutting links to keep the density at the same level. Also we made a distinction between cutting links that were created during the development, and cutting the link to the output unit which is now done at the end of the development, by the non-terminal <output>. We felt it was better to encode individually for each neuron whether it was an input or an output unit. These two modifications resulted in producing ANNs whose number of inputs were always a multiple of 8, and each of the sub-ANNs were now forced to control one and exactly one leg, unlike the preceding run. The last modification we did was to ensure that all the newly created links got a type. When a cell divides, the first child cell waits 14 extra time steps before dividing again. This makes sure that the second child cell has time to set the types of the newly created links. Then each time a link is reversed or a recurrent link is added, we also make sure that the type is set, which we had forgotten in the previous constraints.

Analysis of the Fourth Run

A selection of the champions of this run is reported in figure 2.12.

We deleted systematically ANNs that do not have the right number of inputs, or produced no movement at all, as in the second run. We represent at generation 0 a solution that produced oscillation on one leg. At generation one, we had an individual that has a correct oscillation on all the legs. That solution has a quite simple 16 neuron controller made of 8 oscillator neurons with a recurrent connection, and 8 neurons that implement a weak coupling. The oscillators lose synchronization. In generation 1, we had an ANN that produced oscillation, and coupling between the two sides but not within one side. This means that the two front legs for example, or the two right legs are synchronous, but not the left front leg with the left rear leg. Generation 2 produced a fun individual which moved the two front legs two times quicker than the other 6 legs. You can see in figure 2.12 fourth picture, that the ANN that controls the two front legs is much more sparsely connected than the one which controls the other 6 legs. Generation 2 produced another champion: a slow but correct quadripod gait. The genotype is probably a mutation of the second individual at generation 1, because the architectures are very similar. There is one sub-ANN for each leg, as is specified by the syntactic constraints, the sub-ANNs within one side are coupled, but the two sides are independent, as is clearly shown in the picture. Generation 3 produced a funny gait, with four pairs of two coupled oscillators. Inside each pair, one oscillator has double frequency of the other, due to the coupling. The figure clearly shows the structure of the ANN. Generation 5 produced a quadripod gait, not too slow, but there still lacks some coupling between the ANNs controlling the legs of one side. There are diagonal connections between the four groups, which implement coupling between the two sides, but there are no connections from top to bottom. At generation 6 we had a nice ANN with all the connection needed for coupling, but the frequency on the right side was slightly greater than on the left side, as a result the robot was constantly turning right. We would have thought that a higher frequency results in turning in the opposite direction, but the reverse is true at least for those particular frequencies which were almost similar. We got a number of individuals which were always turning right. In generation 7, we finally got success, a perfect quadripod, smooth and fast. We had the robot run for 20 minutes to check the phase lock.

2.8   Comparison of the Interactively Evolved Solution With the Hand-Coded Solution

Performance

We now want to compare this solution with the hand-coded solution. The hand-coded program is a wavewalk that has been done with a loop and a C program, by Koichi Ide, an engineer in Applied AI systems. In wavewalk, only one leg at a time is up. The evolved solution naturally produced a quadripod gait, where four legs are on the ground and four legs in the air. First we just look at the speed. The champion evolved robot moves at 7.5 cm/seconds. Whereas in all the previous runs we could not do better than 15 cm/seconds. The period of leg update is 50 ms. The period of leg update in Koichi's controller was set to 64 ms, (4 cycles), and the speed was 5cm/seconds. If the period of the leg was 50 ms, we assume that the robot would do 6.4 cm per seconds, so our solution walks faster with the same rhythm on the leg impulses.

We used some constraints on the leg movement. The legs had been restricted to move between -96 and +96 to avoid clutch, and they could not move by more than 40 to prevent the motor from warming up. There are no such constraints in Koichi's controller. It can be said that in Koichi's controller, the beta angle which controls whether the leg is backward or forward, sometimes makes an increase of 96 in a single time step, so the genetic controller is more smooth.

Analysis of the Solution

The genetic code of our best solution found in run 4 is shown in figures 2.13 and 2.14, and steps of its development are shown in figure 2.15.

The genetic code is huge compared to the genetic code needed for one leg, that is shown in figure 2.6. This is because we need a lot of elementary cutting instruction, for each cell division, and also we go systematically through all the types to set the weights. By watching the ANN carefully, we found that it was only using LINEAR sigmoids, those are sigmoids which merely compute the identity. Puzzled by this fact we looked into the matter and remembered that when the net input is greater than 1,000,000 (resp. lower than -1,000,000) it is clipped to 1,000,000 (reps. -1,000,000). This is used to avoid a computation artifact that could arise if the integer became too high. What the ANN does is that it exploits this fact by using big weights, and the identity function like a clipped linear sigmoid. Pure identity would always produce either a divergence to plus infinity, or a vanishing of the movement.

2.9   Conclusion

In this work we succeeded in evolving an ANN for controlling an 8-legged robot. Experiments were done without a simulator, and the fitness was determined interactively by hand. We believe that generating an ANN for locomotion controller is not a trivial task, because it needs at least 16 hidden units, unlike most applications that can be found in the literature. To be able to solve this problem in only 200 evaluations, four features were used.

- Cell cloning and link typing.
- Interactive syntactic constraints.
- Interactive problem decomposition.
- Interactive fitness.

   Cell cloning generates highly symmetric ANNs. Link typing makes it possible to encode different types of cell division, and to genetically optimize the cell division itself. Syntactic constraints specify that there is exactly a three fold symmetry and exploits the fact that 8 legs are used. The problem would have been a little more difficult if only 6 legs were used. The hand given fitness allow us to reward behavior that would have been quite difficult to detect automatically.

   Interactive operation of the Evolutionary Algorithm (EA) appears faster and easier than hand-programing the robot. It takes a few trial and errors if we are to generate the ANNs by hand. It is quite easy to say that the development must begin with three clone division, it is more difficult to say how exactly the division must be done. What is hand specified in our work is only the fact that there is a symmetry, not the precise architecture. The EA alone is able to decompose the problem of locomotion into the subproblem of generating an oscillator, and then makes 8 copies of the oscillator, and combines them with additional links so as to provide the adequate coupling. Other researchers have tried to evolve ANNs for legged-locomotion, but they all give more information than we do. In the work of Beer and Gallagher [92] the precise Beer architecture is given. This 6-legged architecture described by Beer in [91] has the shape of the number 8, in which all the sub-ANNs controlling adjacent legs are connected, and the controller of the legs that are symmetric between the two sides are also connected.

In the work of Lewis, Fagg and Solidum [100] not only is the general architecture given but also the precise wiring of all the neurons. This work is the first historic work where the fitness was given interactively by hand, and they also used a decomposition into sub-problem by hand. But the way it is done leaves the EA with only the task of finding four real values. They first generate a leg oscillator using 2 neurons, they only have to find 4 weights to obtain a correct rotation. Then they build the Beer architecture by connecting 6 copies of this 2 neurons oscillator, with some precise links, and weight sharing between similar links. As a result, they once more have only four weights to genetically optimize.

We did not try to generate an ANN by hand, that could produce an efficient quadripod gait. I estimate the time needed to produce one to a few hours, one day for somebody who is not trained to think in terms of recurrent ANNs. We have not proved that the EA is a more efficient technique than direct hand programming, since it took two days. But, first, it is more fun to breed a robot during two days, than to try to understand the dynamics going on inside a recurrent ANN of a few dozens of neurons. Second, I could have asked my girlfriend to do the breeding, which would have reduced the *scientific time* down to less than what is needed to program the robot. Third, if we had 10 robots to give the fitnesses then the time would have been reduced to two hours. This is a direction which we think is most interesting. The natural parallelism when using different robots is quite easily extensible. If you want to add a processor, you just need a bigger room to put your robot inside.

May be the most unexpected thing out of this work, is that the breeding is worth its pain. We are not sure that an automatic fitness evaluation that would have just measured the distance walked by the robot would had been success-ful, even in one week of simulation. There are some precise facts that support this view. First, right at the initial generation, we often got an individual which was just randomly moving its legs, but still managed to get forward quite a bit, using this trick. This is because the random signal has to go through the leg controller and the leg is up when it goes forward and down when it goes backward. Using automatic fitness calculation, this individual would have dominated all the population right at generation 1, and all potentially interesting building blocks would have been lost. With interactive fitness we just systematically eradicate this noisy and useless individual. When we say noisy, it really produces much more noise than all the others, because it moves all the time by the maximum allowable distance. So after a while, we push the kill button as soon as we hear the noise. Second, there are some very nice features which do not result at all in making the robot go forward. We are pretty happy if we see at generation 1, an individual which periodically moves a leg in the air, because that means that somewhere there is an oscillatory sub-structure that we would like to see spreading. Typically, we spend the first generations tracking oscillatory behavior, and tuning the frequency, we then reward individuals who get the signal on all the eight legs, and lastly, we evolve coupling between the legs, with the right phase delay. This is a pretty simple strategy to implement when breeding online, but that would be difficult to program.

In short, we developed in this work a new paradigm for using Evolutionary Computation in an interactive way. Syntactic constraints provide a prior probability (machine learning terminology) on the distribution of ANNs. Modular decomposition allows us to replace one big problem by two simpler problems, and interactive fitness evaluation can steer the EA towards the solution.

Our future direction will be to evolve a locomotion controller with three command neurons: one for forward/backward, one for right/left and one for the walking speed. In order to do that, we need to enhance our method so as to be able to optimize different fitnesses with different populations, and then build one behavior out of two separately evolved behaviors. In the case of turning, or speed controlling, things can be stated more precisely. We think that turning as well as varying speed is only a matter of being able to govern the frequency of the oscillators. Typically we would like to separately evolve an oscillator whose frequency can be tuned using an input neuron, and then recombining it with the locomotion controller evolved in this paper. How to successfully operate this recombination is still an open subject of research.

Acknowledgments

This paper reports on work partially done by Dominique Quatravaux in fulfill-
ment of the master's thesis requirements under supervision of Michel Cosnard
and Frédéric Gruau, on Frédéric Gruau's project at CWI in Amsterdam.

Since Dominique declined to be coauthor, it is proper to carefully delin-
eate his contributions. He developed the gnu C compiler for the robot processor, and the protocol to handle the serial line, that is, to control the robot
from the host computer. The programs can be downloaded from URL page
http://www.cwi.nl/ gruau/gruau/gruau.html, together with user information,
bugs and tips.

Dominique performed about half of the experiments (the leg controller,
run0 and run1 of the locomotion controller) and developed the approach to
first evolve a leg controller with a well defined interface. He can be reached
at (quatrava@clipper.ens.fr). To represent Dominique's involvement we added
the name of his workstations as co-author.

Phil Husband acted as a remote adviser, and we thank him for letting
us use their OCT1 robot. Paul Vitanyi and the Algorithmics and Complexity
(AA1) Group at CWI hosted the whole research, providing a modern computer
environment and tools. We are grateful to Paul for his constructive and positive
comments. F. Gruau was supported by a postdoctoral TMR grant from the
European community. within the evolutionary robotics group at the COGS
department in Sussex University. We also acknowledge help from the pole
Rhone Alpes de Science Cognitive who supplied money to buy a prometheus
Robot in the frame of a joint project with prof. Demongeot. We preferred to use
the OCT1 Robot because it turned out we had the choice and the OCT1 Robot
was 10 time more expensive, more reliable and faster. We did however use
replacement part from the prometeus robot, namely the power supply. Applied
AI system did a good job in sending us replacement part for the OCT1 robot,
together with advice. We thank Ann Griffith and Koichi Ide.

References

[91]R. Beer. *Intelligence as Adaptive Behavior: An Experiment in Computational
Neuroethology.* Academic Press, San Diego, CA, 1990.

[92]R. D. Beer and J. C. Gallagher. Evolving dynamical neural networks for adaptive behavior.
Adaptive Behavior, 1(1), 1992.

[93]D. Cliff, I. Harvey, and P. Husbands. Explorations in evolutionary robotics. *Adaptive
Behavior*, 2:73–110, 1993.

[94]F. Gruau. *Neural Network Synthesis Using Cellular Encoding and the Genetic Algorithm.* PhD thesis, PhD Thesis, Ecole Normale Supérieure de Lyon, 1994. anonymous ftp: lip.ens-lyon.fr (140.77.1.11) directory pub/Rapports/PhD file PhD94-01-E.ps.Z (english) PhD94-01-F.ps.Z (french).

[95]F. Gruau. Automatic definition of modular neural networks. *Adaptive Behavior,* 3(2):151–183, 1995.

[96]F. Gruau. Artificial cellular development in optimization and compilation. In Sanchez and Tomassini, editors, *Towards Evolvable Hardware.* Springer-Verlag, Berlin, 1996.

[97]I. Harvey. Species adaptation genetic algorithm: A basis for a continuing saga. Cogs csrp 221, The Evolutionary Robotics Laboratory, Sussex, 1995.

[98]J. Kodjabachian and J. Meyer. Development, learning, and evolution in animats. In *Proceedings of PerAc'94,* 1994.

[99]J. Koza. *Genetic Programming.* MIT Press, Cambridge, MA, 1992.

[100]M. Lewis, A. Fagg, and A. Sodium. Genetic programming approach to the construction of a neural network for control of a walking robot. In *Proceedings of the IEEE International Conference on Robotics and Automation,* 1992.

```
<clone> [3..3]; <nn> [1..6]; <evolved>::=<clone>
<coef2>::=(SWEIGHTO: list[16..16] of (integer[0..+512]))
<clone>::=(PROGN(FULL(<opi>)(<opo>))(<clone>)|(PROGN(PAR(<opi>)(<opo>))
   (<clone>))|(PROGN(SEQ(<opi>)(<opo>))(<clone>)))|(PROGN(CPI(<opi>)
   (<opo>))(<clone>)))|(PROGN(CPO(<opi>)(<opo>))(<clone>)))|(<nn>)
<nn>::=(FULL(PROGN(<opi>)(<nn>))(PROGN(<opo>)(<nn>)))
   |(PAR(PROGN(<opi>)(<nn>))(PROGN(<opo>)(<nn>))))|(SEQ(PROGN(<opi>)
   (<nn>))(PROGN(<opo>)(<nn>))))|(CPI(PROGN(<opi>)(<nn>))(PROGN(<opo>)
   (<nn>))))|(CPO(PROGN(<opi>)(<nn>))(PROGN(<opo>)(<nn>))))|(<unit>)
<opo>::=(PROGN(<op>)(<settype>)(WAIT(integer[2..4])))
<opi>::=(PROGN(<op>)(WAIT (integer[0..2])))
<op>::=(PROGN(PROGN:set[0..7] of
               (PROGN(CTYPEI (0))(<cuti>)) (PROGN(CTYPEI (1))(<cuti>))
               (PROGN(CTYPEI (2))(<cuti>)) (PROGN(CTYPEI (3))(<cuti>))
               (PROGN(CTYPEI (4))(<cuti>)) (PROGN(CTYPEI (5))(<cuti>))
               (PROGN(CTYPEI (6))(<cuti>)) (PROGN(CTYPEI (7))(<cuti>)))
          ( PROGN: set[0..7] of
               (PROGN(CTYPEO (0))(<cuto>)) (PROGN(CTYPEO (1))(<cuto>))
               (PROGN(CTYPEO (2))(<cuto>)) (PROGN(CTYPEO (3))(<cuto>))
               (PROGN(CTYPEO (4))(<cuto>)) (PROGN(CTYPEO (5))(<cuto>))
               (PROGN(CTYPEO (6))(<cuto>)) (PROGN(CTYPEO (7))(<cuto>))))
<cuti>::=(PROGN(<restricti>)(RMI))<cuto>::=(PROGN(<restricto>)(RMO))
<unit>::=(PROGN(PROGN:set[0..2] of
      (WAIT)(WAIT)(<cyc>)(PROGN: list[0..7] of (<reverse>)))
      (PROGN(DELTAT(integer[1..40])))(<weight>)(SBIAS
      (integer[-4096..+4096]))(SACT(integer[-4096..+4096])))(<type>))
<reverse>::=(PROGN(CTYPEI(integer[1..7]))(<restricti>)(REVERSEI))
<command>::=(PROGN (WAIT(200))(DELTAT(1))(SBIAS(0))
      (PROGN(CTYPEO(0))(<coef2>))(PROGN(CTYPEO (1))(<coef2>))(LINEAR))
<weight>::=(PROGN(PROGN(CTYPEI(2))(<coef>))(PROGN(CTYPEI(3))(<coef>))
      (PROGN(CTYPEI(4))(<coef>))(PROGN(CTYPEI(5))(<coef>))
      (PROGN(CTYPEI(6))(<coef>))(PROGN(CTYPEI(7))(<coef>)))
<coef>::=(SWEIGHT: list[7..7] of (integer[-4096..+4096]))
      (SWEIGHT: list[7..7] of (integer[-256..+256]))
<restricti>::=(RESTRICTI(integer[0..2])(integer[1..10]))
<restricto>::=(RESTRICTO(integer[0..2])(integer[1..10]))
<type>::=(LINEAR)|(LINEAR)|(LINEAR)|(LINEAR)|(LINEAR)|(STEP)|(STEP)
      |(STEP)|(STEP)|(STEP)(PROGN(DELTAT(1))(PI))
<cyc>::=(PROGN(RESETNEW)(CYC)(<settype>))
<settype>::=(PROGN(CNEWI) (PROGN : set[1..1] of
      (STYPEI(2))(STYPEI(3))(STYPEI(4))(STYPEI(5))(STYPEI(6))(STYPEI(7))))
```

Figure 2.9
Syntactic constraints for the second run

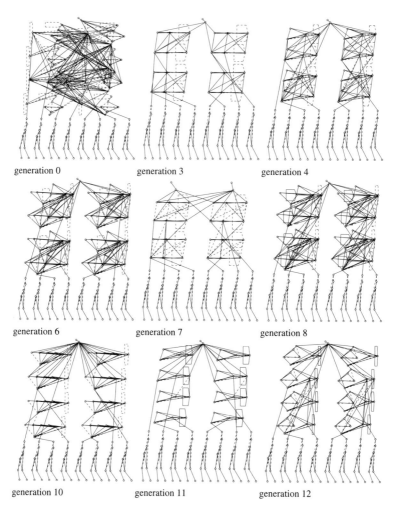

generation 0   generation 3   generation 4

generation 6   generation 7   generation 8

generation 10   generation 11   generation 12

Figure 2.10
Champions of the second run

```
<evolved>::=(PROGN(<clone>)(<clone>)(<clone>)(<nn>))
<clone>::=(FULL(<opi>)(<opo>))
<opo>::=(PROGN(<op>)(<settype>)(WAIT (integer[0..4])))
<opi>::=(PROGN(<op>)(WAIT(integer[14..18])))
<op>::=(PROGN(PROGN:set[0..4] of
                 (PROGN: list[1..2] of (PROGN(CTYPEI (2))(<cuti>)))
                 (PROGN: list[1..2] of (PROGN(CTYPEI (3))(<cuti>)))
                 (PROGN: list[1..2] of (PROGN(CTYPEI (4))(<cuti>)))
                 (PROGN: list[1..2] of (PROGN(CTYPEI (5))(<cuti>))))
           (PROGN: set[0..4] of
                 (PROGN: list[1..2] of (PROGN(CTYPEO (2))(<cuto>)))
                 (PROGN: list[1..2] of (PROGN(CTYPEO (3))(<cuto>)))
                 (PROGN: list[1..2] of (PROGN(CTYPEO (4))(<cuto>)))
                 (PROGN: list[1..2] of (PROGN(CTYPEO (5))(<cuto>)))))
<unit>::=(PROGN (PROGN : set[0..2]  of
          (WAIT)(WAIT)(<cyc>)(PROGN: list[0..7] of (<reverse>)))
          (PROGN(DELTAT (integer[1..40]))(<weight>)
          (SBIAS(integer[-4096..+4096]))(SACT(integer[-4096..+4096])))
          (<input1>)(<input2>)(<output>)(<type>)(END))
<restricti>::=(RESTRICTI(integer[0..2])(integer[1..32]))(WAIT)
<restricto>::=(RESTRICTO(integer[0..2])(integer[1..32]))(WAIT)
<type>::=(LINEAR)(LINEAR)(LINEAR) (LINEAR) (LINEAR)
             (STEP)(STEP)(STEP)(STEP)(STEP)(PROGN(DELTAT(1))(PI))
<cyc>::=(PROGN(RESETNEW)(CYC)(<settype>))
<settype>::=(PROGN(PROGN : set[1..1] of
                 (PROGN (CNEWI)(STYPEI(2))(CNEWO)(STYPEO(2)))
                 (PROGN (CNEWI)(STYPEI(3))(CNEWO)(STYPEO(3)))
                 (PROGN (CNEWI)(STYPEI(4))(CNEWO)(STYPEO(4)))
                 (PROGN (CNEWI)(STYPEI(5))(CNEWO)(STYPEO(5)))))
<input1>::=(PROGN : set[1..1] of (WAIT)(PROGN(CTYPEI(0))(RMI))
                    (PROGN  (CTYPEI(0))(RMI)))
<input2>::=(PROGN : set[1..1] of (WAIT)(PROGN(CTYPEI(1))(RMI))
                    (PROGN(CTYPEI(1))(RMI)))
<output>::=(PROGN : set[1..1] of (WAIT)(PROGN(CTYPEO(0))(RMO))
                    (PROGN (CTYPEO(0))(RMO)))
```

Figure 2.11
Syntactic constraints used during the fourth run, we report only the non-terminal that are
rewritten in a different way, compared to the previous run.

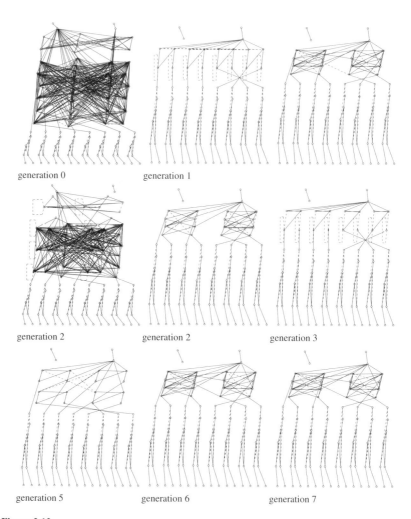

generation 0   generation 1

generation 2   generation 2   generation 3

generation 5   generation 6   generation 7

Figure 2.12
Champions of the fourth run

```
LABEL(SEQ(SEQ(PAR(PROGN(WAIT(200))(DELTAT(1))(SBIAS(0))(PROGN
(CTYPEO(0))(SWEIGHTO(318)(319)(128)(148)(485)(228)(154)(49)(333)
(7)(357)(327)(314)(444)(171)(448)))(PROGN(CTYPEO(1))(SWEIGHTO(268)
(185)(424)(113)(54)(357)(316)(110)(259)(102)(90)(43)(299)(367)(477)
(78)))(LINEAR))(PROGN(WAIT(200))(DELTAT(1))(SBIAS(0))(PROGN(CTYPEO(0))
(SWEIGHTO(453)(461)(82)(56)(283)(111)(385)(43)(409)(312)(391)(210)
(491)(347)(171)(238)))(PROGN(CTYPEO(1))(SWEIGHTO(67)(403)(483)(458)
(104)(219)(505)(323)(234)(94)(291)(330)(154)(198)(355)(324)))(LINEAR)))
(PROGN(WAIT(4))(CTYPEI(-1))(RESTRICTI(0)(1))(STYPEI(0))(CTYPEI(-1))
(STYPEI(1))(CTYPEO(-1))(STYPEO(0))(FULL(PROGN(PROGN(PROGN(PROGN(PROGN
(CTYPEI(2))(PROGN(RESTRICTI(2)(18))(RMI)))(PROGN(CTYPEI(2))(PROGN(WAIT)
(RMI))))(PROGN(PROGN(CTYPEI(4))(PROGN(WAIT)(RMI)))))(PROGN(PROGN(PROGN
(CTYPEO(3))(PROGN(WAIT)(RMO)))(PROGN(CTYPEO(3))(PROGN(RESTRICTO(0)(17))
(RMO))))(PROGN(PROGN(CTYPEO(5))(PROGN(WAIT)(RMO))))))(WAIT(18)))(PROGN
(PROGN(PROGN(PROGN(PROGN(CTYPEI(3))(PROGN(WAIT)(RMI))))(PROGN(PROGN
(CTYPEI(5))(PROGN(WAIT)(RMI)))(PROGN(CTYPEI(5))(PROGN(WAIT)(RMI)))))
(PROGN))(PROGN(PROGN(PROGN(CNEWI)(STYPEI(2))(CNEWO)(STYPEO(2)))))
(WAIT(2))))(FULL(PROGN(PROGN(PROGN(PROGN(PROGN(CTYPEI(5))(PROGN
(RESTRICTI(2)(16))(RMI)))(PROGN(CTYPEI(5))(PROGN(WAIT)(RMI)))))(PROGN))
(WAIT(14)))(PROGN(PROGN(PROGN(PROGN(PROGN(CTYPEI(2))(PROGN(RESTRICTI(1)
(3))(RMI)))(PROGN(CTYPEI(2))(PROGN(WAIT)(RMI))))(PROGN(PROGN(CTYPEI(3))
(PROGN(RESTRICTI(1)(31))(RMI)))(PROGN(CTYPEI(3))(PROGN(WAIT)(RMI))))
(PROGN(PROGN(CTYPEI(4))(PROGN(RESTRICTI(2)(12))(RMI)))(PROGN(CTYPEI(4))
(PROGN(WAIT)(RMI))))(PROGN(PROGN(CTYPEI(5))(PROGN(WAIT)(RMI)))))(PROGN
(PROGN(PROGN(CTYPEO(2))(PROGN(WAIT)(RMO))))(PROGN(PROGN(CTYPEO(3))
(PROGN(WAIT)(RMO)))(PROGN(CTYPEO(3))(PROGN(WAIT)(RMO))))(PROGN(PROGN
(CTYPEO(4))(PROGN(WAIT)(RMO)))(PROGN(CTYPEO(4))(PROGN(RESTRICTO(0)(9))
(RMO))))(PROGN(PROGN(CTYPEO(5))(PROGN(RESTRICTO(0)(15))(RMO)))(PROGN
(CTYPEO(5))(PROGN(RESTRICTO(1)(21))(RMO))))))(PROGN(PROGN(PROGN(CNEWI)
(STYPEI(2))(CNEWO)(STYPEO(2)))))(WAIT(0))))(FULL(PROGN(PROGN(PROGN
(PROGN(PROGN(CTYPEI(5))(PROGN(WAIT)(RMI)))(PROGN(CTYPEI(5))(PROGN(WAIT)
(RMI)))))(PROGN))(WAIT(16)))(PROGN(PROGN(PROGN(PROGN(PROGN(CTYPEI(2))
(PROGN(WAIT)(RMI))))(PROGN(PROGN(CTYPEI(3))(PROGN(WAIT)(RMI)))(PROGN
(CTYPEI(3))(PROGN(RESTRICTI(2)(6))(RMI))))(PROGN(PROGN(CTYPEI(5))
(PROGN(RESTRICTI(0)(2))(RMI)))(PROGN(CTYPEI(5))(PROGN(RESTRICTI(2)(7))
(RMI)))))(PROGN(PROGN(PROGN(CTYPEO(2))(PROGN(RESTRICTO(1)(2))(RMO))))
(PROGN(PROGN(CTYPEO(3))(PROGN(RESTRICTO(2)(9))(RMO))))(PROGN(PROGN
(CTYPEO(5))(PROGN(RESTRICTO(0)(12))(RMO)))(PROGN(CTYPEO(5))(PROGN(WAIT)
(RMO))))))(PROGN(PROGN(PROGN(CNEWI)(STYPEI(4))(CNEWO)(STYPEO(4)))))
(WAIT(2))))(CPO(PROGN(PROGN(PROGN(PROGN)(PROGN(PROGN(PROGN(CTYPEO(2))
(PROGN(WAIT)(RMO))))(PROGN(PROGN(CTYPEO(3))(PROGN(WAIT)(RMO))))(PROGN
(PROGN(CTYPEO(4))(PROGN(WAIT)(RMO)))(PROGN(CTYPEO(4))(PROGN(RESTRICTO
(0)(6))(RMO))))(PROGN(PROGN(CTYPEO(5))(PROGN(WAIT)(RMO))))))(WAIT(18)))
(PROGN(PROGN(PROGN(PROGN(CNEWI)(STYPEI(4))(CNEWO)(STYPEO(4)))))(PROGN
(PROGN(WAIT))(PROGN(DELTAT(4))(PROGN(PROGN(CTYPEI(2))(SWEIGHT(254)(212)
(170)(-63)(-181)(158)(122)))(PROGN(CTYPEI(3))(SWEIGHT(242)(73)(103)(56)
(9)(226)(48)))(PROGN(CTYPEI(4))(SWEIGHT(4003)(1411)(-3628)(3953)(1248)
```

Figure 2.13
The genetic code of the Champion (continued in figure 2.14)

```
(-1062)(1202))))(PROGN(CTYPEI(5))(SWEIGHT(-2642)(-1926)(2968)(-4094)
(-217)(-577)(-2340))))(SBIAS(1896))(SACT(989)))(PROGN(PROGN(CTYPEI(0))
(RMI)))(PROGN(WAIT))(PROGN(PROGN(CTYPEO(0))(RMO)))(LINEAR)(END))))
(PROGN(PROGN(PROGN(PROGN(PROGN(PROGN(CTYPEI(2))(PROGN(WAIT)(RMI))))
(PROGN(PROGN(CTYPEI(3))(PROGN(RESTRICTI(2)(24))(RMI))))(PROGN(PROGN
(CTYPEI(4))(PROGN(WAIT)(RMI)))(PROGN(CTYPEI(4))(PROGN(WAIT)(RMI)))))
(PROGN(PROGN(PROGN(CTYPEO(2))(PROGN(RESTRICTO(1)(24))(RMO))))(PROGN
(PROGN(CTYPEO(4))(PROGN(RESTRICTO(2)(20))(RMO))))(PROGN(PROGN(CTYPEO
(5))(PROGN(WAIT)(RMO)))(PROGN(CTYPEO(5))(PROGN(RESTRICTO(2)(9))(RMO))))
))(PROGN(PROGN(PROGN(CNEWI)(STYPEI(5))(CNEWO)(STYPEO(5)))))(WAIT(3)))
(PROGN(PROGN(PROGN(PROGN(CNEWI)(STYPEI(3))(CNEWO)(STYPEO(3)))))(PROGN
(PROGN)(PROGN(DELTAT(27))(PROGN(PROGN(CTYPEI(2))(SWEIGHT(-3469)(-1379)
(-3329)(-2945)(296)(-1376)(-4096)))(PROGN(CTYPEI(3))(SWEIGHT(196)(3165)
(-1501)(-3442)(2994)(-2912)(1369)))(PROGN(CTYPEI(4))(SWEIGHT(2875)(-575)
(3329)(-770)(-402)(-793)(3496)))(PROGN(CTYPEI(5))(SWEIGHT(-118)(-179)
(-25)(-220)(110)(-240)(170))))(SBIAS(-1697))(SACT(-1746)))(PROGN(WAIT))
(PROGN(WAIT))(PROGN(WAIT))(LINEAR)(END)))))))(PROGN(BLOC)(TESTIO8)
(SHARI(JMP12)(SHARI(JMP12)(SHARI(JMP12)(SHARI(JMP12)(PROGN(SWITCH)
(SHARI(JMP12)(PROGN(SWITCH)(SHARI(JMP12)(PROGN(SWITCH)(SHARI(JMP12)
(JMP12)(1)))(1)))(1)))(1))(1))  (1))(1))))
```

Figure 2.14
The genetic code of the Champion (continued from figure 2.13)

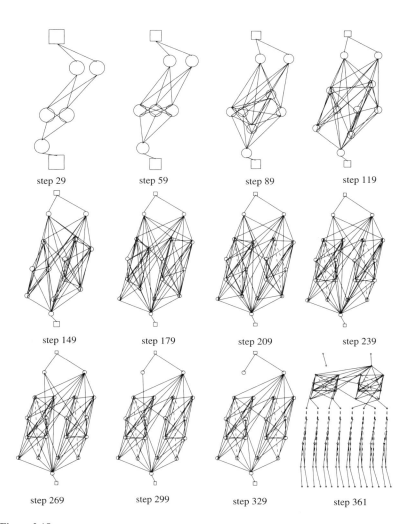

Figure 2.15
Steps of the development of the Champion

3 The Emergence of Communication Through Synthetic Evolution

Bruce J. MacLennan

We describe four series of experiments to study the emergence of *inherently meaningful communication* by synthetic evolution in a population of artificial agents, which are controlled either by finite state machines or by neural networks. We found that the agents can evolve the ability to use single symbols and, to a limited extent, pairs of symbols exhibiting rudimentary syntax. We show that the communication system evolved by the population can be studied in its own right as an evolving emergent phenomenon, and that the emergent communication systems exhibit some of the richness of natural communication.

3.1 Introduction

This article describes a series of experiments to study the emergence of *inherently meaningful communication* by synthetic evolution in a population of artificial agents. By "inherently meaningful" we mean that the communication is meaningful and relevant to the agents themselves, independent and regardless of any meanings we (as observers) may attribute to the communications. (We discuss elsewhere [107, 113] the relevance to the study of intrinsic intensionality of these experimental techniques, which we call *synthetic ethology.*) Briefly, we may say that communication is inherently meaningful if it has some actual or potential relevance to the agents.

However, Burghardt [101] has defined communication as "the phenomenon of one organism producing a signal that, when responded to by another organism, confers some advantage (or the statistical probability of it) to the signaler or his group." Therefore communication acquires its primary, natural meaning through the selective advantage it has conferred on the communicators through their evolution. (Hence, ecologically valid investigations of communication must take place in the agents' natural environment or something close to it.) Thus we may conclude that meaningful communication must be investigated in an evolutionary context, and that if inherently meaningful communication is to emerge in artificial systems, it will do so in a context of *synthetic evolution.*

3.2 Experimental Design

Synthetic World

If we are to design a synthetic world in which genuine communication can be expected to emerge, then we must begin by asking what sort of world will make this likely. For communication to emerge, it must have some selective advantage, such as allowing the agents to coordinate their behavior more effectively.

One way to accomplish this is to give a reproductive advantage to agents that coordinate their behavior, for example, when the behavior of one agent A is appropriate to a *situation* known only to the second agent B. We can think of this *situation* either as being some aspect of B's internal state (so it is not observable by A), or as being some external situation perceivable by B but out of A's range of perception. Of course, these analogies are ultimately irrelevant; all that matters are the formal structures of perceivability and selection. Since our goal has been to design an experiment that is as simple as possible while still exhibiting the phenomenon of interest (communication), these conditions of coordination have been established in a simple way.

These conditions are created by giving each agent a *local environment*, the state of which is perceivable by that agent but by no other. Of course the state can be simple or complex, but in these experiments we have kept it very simple. Furthermore, although one could use any sort of process to determine the states of the local environments, we set them randomly, which makes it as difficult as possible for an agent's local-environment state to be predicted by the other agents.

Our goal is to select for coordinated behavior among the agents and our hope is that communication will emerge as a way of accomplishing this. Therefore we select for an action that corresponds to the local environment of another agent. That is, if the local environment of agent B is in state λ, and a different agent A acts in a way appropriate to λ, then we say that A and B have cooperated and we give them some reproductive advantage. In accord with our goal of keeping the experiment as simple as possible, we have interpreted "acting in a way appropriate to λ" to be a simple match with λ. That is, A has succeeded in cooperating with B when it manages (by whatever means) in matching the state of B's local environment.

There are many ways in which such cooperation could be made to affect reproductive advantage; we have taken the simple approach of awarding a point of abstract credit to each agent that cooperates every time it cooperates. Agents are more likely to reproduce if they have accrued more credit and they are more likely to die if they have accrued less. Cooperation need not be limited to pairs of agents, and so in general if several agents $A_1, \ldots, A_n$ match B's local environment state, then all $n+1$ agents will be awarded credit (n points for the emitter B, 1 point for each of the actors $A_1, \ldots, A_n$. Other variations include imposing credit penalties for unsuccessful attempts to cooperate (i.e. mistaken attempts to match the other's local environment state).

Clearly, communication will never emerge if it is physically impossible in the simulated world. In particular there must be some potential medium of communication and the agents must have the physical capability to alter and sense the state of that medium. (We say "must" because in these experiments the mechanisms of synthetic evolution are incapable of evolving new sensory or effector organs, so we must take these as given. We do not, however, give them any specific function, such as communication.)

Therefore, in these experiments we provide the synthetic world with a *global environment* whose state can be sensed and altered by all the agents. By "sensed" we mean that an agent's behavior may depend on the state of the global environment, and by "altered" we mean that an agent's behavior can modify the state of the global environment. As with the local environments, the state of the global environment may be simple or complex in structure, but in the experiments described below it has been kept as simple as possible. Because communication takes place in time, for example by a signal that varies through time, we must allow temporal variations of the global environment's state; that is, the agents can cause it to change through time and can sense those variations through time.

As a consequence of the foregoing, we can see that the agents must have a behavioral control mechanism with the following faculties:

1. ability to respond to the state of its local environment,
2. ability to respond to the state of the global environment,
3. ability to alter the state of the global environment,
4. internal memory or other mechanism for responding to and influencing the time-course of the global state,
5. ability to attempt cooperative activity with other agents.

There are many mechanisms that can satisfy these requirements, including recurrent neural networks, finite state machines, traditional programs, and rule-based systems such as classifier systems.

One of our goals has been to study the evolution of language, and one of the characteristics of language is that it is a cultural phenomenon transmitted through learning. Therefore, in some of our experiments we allow our agents to learn, which means that there is some means for automatic adaptation of their behavioral control mechanisms. Reinforcement, unsupervised and supervised learning are all possible mechanisms for behavioral adaptation.

Synthetic Evolution

As remarked in section 3.1, ecological validity requires that inherently meaningful communication be investigated in its "natural" environment, that is, in the environment in which it has evolved. This implies that the emergence of communication must occur in the context of synthetic evolution, which allows the behavioral mechanisms of the agents to evolve in accord with the selective pressures of the synthetic world. Our basic approach is straight-forward.

Each agent has a genetic string that encodes its genotype. When an agent is created this string is used to create the agent's phenotype, which represents its behavioral mechanism. In some cases the agent's phenotype can change by means of learning or other forms of adaptation.

Recall that agents are awarded credit for successful cooperation; this credit is used to influence the probability of an agent reproducing or dying. In our experiments reproduction is sexual. Two agents are chosen as parents, with reproductive preference given to agents that have accrued more credit. Their genetic strings are combined by a simplified model of biological crossover with a low probability of random mutation; the result becomes the genetic string of the offspring.

Agents may also die, which means that their phenotypes are removed from the population; agents with less credit are more likely to die than those with more credit. In the experiments to be described we have kept the population size constant with a one-for-one replacement rule: an agent must die for each that is born.

Data Collection

We collect various kinds of data to track the emergence of communication and to study its evolving structure. Since we select for cooperation and cooperation is (by design) difficult in the absence of communication, an important variable is the amount of cooperation in the population. Therefore, we measure the average number of cooperations in a given interval of time (i.e., the average credit accrued in that interval); this quantifies the *degree of coordination* in the agents' behavior.

We are especially interested in the emergence of communication as a collective behavior of the population, that is, we want to study the emergent communication as manifested by the population as a whole and evolving through time. To understand this we can, for example, measure correlations between the apparent signals and external (local environment) states and between them and the internal (memory) states of the agents. In this sense we (as observers) can discover the meanings created by the agents for their (inherently meaningful) signals.

There are several statistics that may be computed. For example, if the global environment is being used sometimes as a medium for communicating the local-environment state, then there should be a correlation between local- and global-environment states when successful cooperations take place. In the absence of communication there should be no systematic relation between global- and local-environment states. One way to quantify this is to count the fraction of times each pair occurs simultaneously with a cooperation. The resulting probability matrix has maximum entropy (reflecting its lack of order), when the signals have no systematic meaning, and the entropy decreases as the signal use becomes more regular. This is one way in which we can quantify the emergence of a communication system. Another statistic of deviation from randomness is the coefficient of variation, which is the standard deviation in units of the mean ($V = \sigma/\mu$).

We may also gather relevant statistics of the population of agents that supports the communication system. For example, to better understand the structure of the populations we may compute statistics on the weight matrices of neural nets or on the transition tables of finite state machines.

Experimental Controls

One of the advantages of studying communication through synthetic evolution is the degree of experimental control that it permits. I will mention a few examples.

Certainly, when compared with the study of communication in nature, one of the advantages is that we can have complete control of the genetic structure of the population. For example, we can run two simulations under different conditions with genetically identical populations, or we can seed the population with selected genotypes for particular experimental purposes. In addition, since learning can be enabled or disabled, we can compare situations in which the agents are able to learn or not, or in which they have different adaptive mechanisms or parameters. Further, if some interesting phenomenon appears in a simulation, we can rerun it and make interventions for the sake of the investigation.

One form of control that we have found especially useful is the external suppression of the possibility of communication: by frequent randomization of the state of the global environment (effectively raising its noise level) we can prevent it from being used for communication and thereby prevent communication from emerging. This permits comparison of population behavior under conditions in which communication can and cannot evolve.

Finally, one of the advantages of our approach is that the behavioral mechanism is completely available for analysis. At any point during the simulation we may subject any individual agent or the entire population to analysis, thus relating the internal behavioral mechanisms to the structure and evolution of the emergent communication system.

3.3   Series 1: One-symbol Communication by FSMs

Setup

The first series of experiments investigated the simplest form of single-symbol communication. The local-environment state λ was drawn from a small discrete set Λ of size $L = |\Lambda|$. In most of these experiments $\Lambda = \{0, \ldots, L-1\}$, where $L = 8$. Likewise, the global environment state γ was drawn from a discrete set Γ of the same size, $G = |\Gamma| = L$. In practice, $\Gamma = \{0, \ldots, 7\}$.

The behavioral control mechanism was a finite state machine (FSM) with one internal state (and hence no memory). We chose finite state machines because they are a simple behavioral model that has the potential of both generating and recognizing sequential signals (although that potential was not exploited in the first series of experiments). Thus, each machine's transition table had GL entries for each possible combination of global- and local-environment states.

The finite state machine can respond in only two ways: to *emit* (or *signal*) by altering the global-environment state or to *act* by attempting to match another machine's local-environment state. (Recall that a machine's local environment is not under its control.) In effect, each table entry represents one of two kinds of rules. An *emission rule* has the form:

$$(\gamma, \lambda) \Longrightarrow \text{emit}(\gamma'),$$

where (γ, λ) is the current global/local state and $\text{emit}(\gamma')$ makes γ' the new (altered) global state. Similarly, an *action rule* has the form:

$$(\gamma, \lambda) \Longrightarrow \text{act}(\lambda'),$$

where $\text{act}(\lambda')$ attempts to match λ' to the local environment of another machine. Thus a machine has $G + L$ possible responses, encoded as an integer in the range $0, \ldots, G + L - 1$.

Observe that a machine's response always depends on both the global state and its local state. This means that its response to a given signal is context-dependent, for it is potentially different in each local situation in which it may find itself. Therefore, it will not automatically respond to a signal in the same way in all situations, although it may evolve to do so; therefore the machines face a difficult evolutionary challenge (more on this in section 3.6).

The genotype of a machine is simply represented by a string of GL genes, each with $G + L$ alleles. In these experiments there were 64 genes with 16 alleles. Two-point crossover was used, which means that two numbers η, θ were chosen randomly from $1, \ldots, GL$. The genetic strings were treated like rings; that is, between η and θ the offspring's genes were copied from one parent, and between θ and η from the other. With low probability (0.01) a single randomly selected gene was mutated to a random allele. Population size was kept constant by having the offspring replace a low-scoring agent.

It is necessary to mention a modification to the rules for cooperation: we judge a cooperation to have taken place only if an agent's action matches the local-environment state of *the last emitter*. The reason is that with only eight possible local-environment states and modest population sizes (e.g. 100), it would be almost certain that any action would match the local environment of *some* other agent. Therefore, cooperation would be easy by "guessing" and there would be little selective pressure toward the emergence of communication. Even with this more restrictive cooperation rule there is a $1/8$ chance of guessing correctly without communication. (Further consequences of this co-operation restriction are discussed under "Partial Cooperation" in section 3.3.)

The process of synthetic evolution is organized into three nested cycles. The outermost are the *breeding cycles*, in each of which one agent is chosen to die and two agents are chosen to breed (producing a single offspring). Each of the B breeding cycles comprises $E = 10$ *environmental cycles*, at the beginning of each of which all the local environments are set randomly. (Thus the states of the local environments cannot be predicted.) Each environmental cycle comprises $A = 5$ *action cycles*, during each of which all the agents have an opportunity to respond to the global- and local-environment states. In these experiments the agents are serviced cyclically (a decision discussed in section 3.7).

The probability of being selected as a parent was proportional to accrued credit (number of cooperations) in a breeding cycle, while the probability of dying was inversely related in a simple way to accrued credit (the exact formulas given elsewhere [106, 107]).

We investigated a very simple single-case learning rule for these FSMs. When a machine attempts unsuccessfully to cooperate, its transition table is altered to give what would have been the correct response in these circumstances. That is, if under conditions (γ, λ) the machine responded $\operatorname{act}(\lambda')$, but the local environment state of the last emitter was $\lambda'' \neq \lambda'$, then the (γ, λ) entry of the transition table is altered to be $\operatorname{act}(\lambda'')$.

We ran our simulations under three different conditions: (1) communication suppressed, (2) communication permitted with learning disabled, and (3) communication permitted with learning enabled. By "communication suppressed" we mean that a random signal was written into the global environment after each agent responded, thus preventing the possibility of communication through the global environment. By "communication permitted" we mean that the global environment was not randomized in this way; however, we do nothing directly to facilitate or encourage its use for communication. By this control we can measure the selective advantage of the emerging communication system.

By "learning enabled" or "disabled" we mean that the previously described learning rule is or is not allowed to operate. In the former case the phenotype can diverge from that determined by the genotype, in the latter it cannot. There are of course many other sorts of controls that can be used with these experiments, but even these few generate interesting phenomena.

In these experiments, the population size was $P = 100$. The simulations were usually run for $B = 5000$ breeding cycles, although some simulations were run for much longer.

Results

We ran a series of more than 100 simulations of this kind; in most cases we ran genetically identical random starting populations under all three conditions. As is to be expected from simulations of this kind, there is considerable variation from run to run, but all the results are qualitatively the same as those we will describe. The experiments are robust and have been replicated in other laboratories [116].

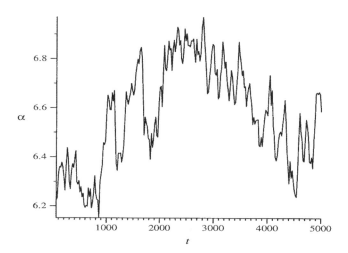

Figure 3.1
Degree of Coordination α: Communication Suppressed

When communication is suppressed, the degree of coordination (average level of cooperation) stays near to 6.25, the calculated level when the agents are "guessing" [106]; figure 3.1 shows how the average number of cooperations per breeding cycle α varies over time (measured in breeding cycles). Although we would expect the degree of coordination to stay near the chance level, a linear regression analysis shows a slight upward trend, 3.67×10^{-5} cooperations/breeding cycle/breeding cycle. This is a stable phenomenon, which will be discussed in section 3.3.

Figure 3.2 shows the evolution of the degree of coordination α, as measured by average cooperations per breeding cycle, when communication is not

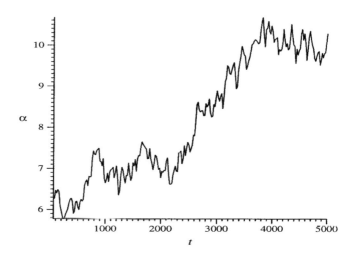

Figure 3.2
Degree of Coordination α: Communication Permitted with Learning Disabled

suppressed. It is apparent to the eye that coordination is increasing much faster than when communication was suppressed, a fact confirmed by linear regression, for the degree of coordination is increasing at a rate of 9.72×10^{-4} cooperations/breeding cycle/breeding cycle, which is 26 times faster than it was when communication was suppressed. After 5000 breeding cycles the average number of cooperations per cycle has grown to 10.28, which is 65% above the level of 6.25 achievable without communication.

In figure 3.3 we see the result when communication is not suppressed and the agents are able to learn from their mistakes. First, it is apparent that communication starts at a much higher level than under the two previous condition. This is because after making a mistake an agent has four more opportunities in an environmental cycle to respond correctly before the local environments are re-randomized. Further, the degree of coordination is increasing much more rapidly than without learning: 3.71×10^{-3} cooperations/breeding cycle/breeding cycle, which 3.82 times the rate without learning and 100 times the rate when communication was suppressed. After 5000 breeding cycles, the degree of coordination has reached 59.84 cooperations/cycle, which is 857% above the level achievable without communication.

The preceding results show us *that* communication has emerged and that

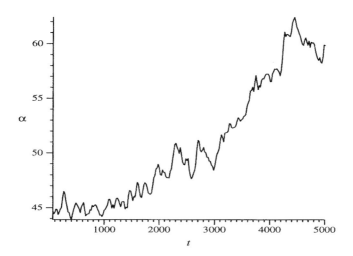

Figure 3.3
Degree of Coordination α: Communication Permitted with Learning Enabled

it has significant selective advantage, but it does not tell us much about the structure of the emerging communication system. As suggested in section 3.2, we can keep track of the co-occurrence of local- and global-environment states that occur together in successful cooperations. That is, whenever a cooperation takes place we increment a count corresponding to the state of the global environment and the state of the local environment of the last emitter. We cannot be sure from such a co-occurrence that the global-environment state *means* the local-environment state, but nonrandom associations between the two will point in that direction.

Since in these experiments we are most interested in the later stages of the evolution, we calculate the co-occurrence tables over the last 50 breeding cycles of the simulation.

Table 3.1 shows the co-occurrence table that resulted when communication was suppressed.[1] Although some structure is apparent, overall the local and global states are weakly correlated. The entropy is $H = 4.95$ bits, which is

---

1 Crumpton [102, App. A] discovered a small error in the calculation of the co-occurrence matrix in the communication-suppressed case, which made it appear less structured than it is. Table 3.1 reflects the corrected calculation; the corresponding tables in prior publications [106, 107, 114] are incorrect. Noble and Cliff [116, table 2] also noted the discrepancy.

Table 3.1
Co-occurrence Matrix: Communication Suppressed

sym.	situation							
	0	1	2	3	4	5	6	7
0	94	130	133	34	166	0	150	682
1	16	105	279	228	261	307	0	118
2	0	199	229	12	0	0	161	274
3	95	19	93	283	669	89	0	201
4	1	97	212	200	112	0	0	0
5	28	135	84	8	600	215	0	351
6	0	0	0	118	59	70	0	690
7	0	33	41	0	371	0	0	0

Table 3.2
Co-occurrence Matrix: Communication Permitted with Learning Disabled

sym.	situation							
	0	1	2	3	4	5	6	7
0	0	0	2825	0	500	20	0	0
1	206	0	0	505	999	231	2	0
2	1	0	0	277	39	4935	1	2394
3	385	1	1	94	0	0	1483	1
4	0	292	0	0	19	555	0	0
5	0	0	1291	0	0	144	0	0
6	494	279	0	403	0	1133	2222	0
7	140	2659	0	202	962	0	0	0

lower (more ordered) than the calculated maximum entropy $H_{\max} = 6$ bits
(derivations given elsewhere [106]). The coefficient of variation is $V = 1.27$.
These numbers will be more meaningful when we compare them to the other
two conditions.

Now consider the co-occurrence matrix that results when communication
is not suppressed (table 3.2). The table is visibly more organized than when
communication was suppressed. This is confirmed by the coefficient of variation $V = 2.13$, which is larger than in the suppressed case, $V = 1.27$,
reflecting a less-random use of signals. For comparison, $V_{\min} = 0$ for a
uniform co-occurrence matrix and $V_{\text{ideal}} = \sqrt{7} \approx 2.65$ for an "ideal matrix" [107], which has a one-to-one correspondence between local- and global-
environment states. The entropy $H = 3.87$ bits, which is closer to the entropy
$H_{\text{ideal}} = 3$ bits of an ideal co-occurrence matrix than it was when communi-

cation was suppressed ($H = 4.95$ bits). Figure 3.4, which shows the change of entropy over time, demonstrates the emergence of an ordered communication system in the population.

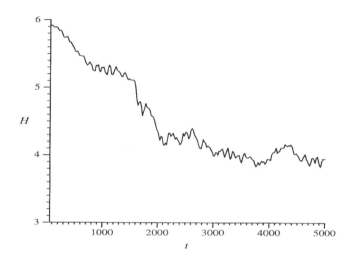

Figure 3.4
Entropy: Communication Permitted with Learning Disabled

Table 3.3 shows the co-occurrence matrix that resulted when communication was not suppressed and the agents were able to learn.

The coefficient of variation is $V = 2.39$, which is a little larger than in the non-learning case; the entropy is $H = 3.91$ bits, which is a little larger than in the non-learning case. This is fairly typical: the entropy with learning may be a little larger or smaller than without it.

Table 3.2 shows some of the richness typical of natural communication. For example symbol $\gamma = 7$ is most often associated with situation $\lambda = 1$ and vice versa, although it sometimes denotes situation 4, and situation 1 is occasionally represented by symbols 4 and 6. There are also cases of synonymy, for example situation 6 may be represented by symbols 3 or 6. Further, we find ambiguity, for example, symbol 4 may represent situations 1 or 5 (or occasionally 4). Such synonymy and ambiguity could result from individual agents using synonymous or ambiguous symbols, from the existence of competing dialects in the population, or from a combination of the two, but

Table 3.3
Co-occurrence Matrix: Communication Permitted with Learning Enabled

sym.	situation							
	0	1	2	3	4	5	6	7
0	3908	29172	1287	12281	2719	1132	93	3836
1	191	634	107	1039	0	0	2078	0
2	4675	1306	0	37960	85	410	7306	26611
3	0	410	0	0	0	126	1306	304
4	0	0	353	62	575	1268	420	519
5	36	0	46	469	0	0	0	26
6	1075	156	0	0	0	951	0	1086
7	0	73	54	0	2764	135	461	102

Table 3.4
Summary of Order Measures

Measurement	Random	Communication/Learning			Ideal
		N/N	Y/N	Y/Y	
Coefficient of Variation, V	0	1.27	2.13	2.39	2.65
Entropy, H (bits)	6	4.95	3.87	3.91	3

experiments by Noble and Cliff (discussed in section 3.7) point to the first possibility.

Finally there is asymmetry in symbol use. For example, situation 7 is virtually always denoted by symbol 2, which is however ambiguous, and more commonly denotes situation 5. Similarly, symbol 5 almost always denotes situation 2, which is however mostly denoted by symbol 0.

The values of the entropy and coefficient of variation in each of the three conditions, along with their extreme values, are collected in table 3.4. Overall it is apparent that not suppressing communication allows the emergence of an organized communication system, regardless of whether the agents are capable of learning.

Partial Cooperation

We must pause to consider a phenomenon we call *partial cooperation* (inaccurately termed "pseudo-cooperation" in some earlier reports) [107, 114]. Recall (section 3.3, p. 71) that we have placed a restriction on cooperation — an actor must match the local state of the last emitter — since otherwise chance cooperations will be much too easy. However, this restriction creates a loophole in the scoring algorithm, which the population may evolve to exploit. Specifically, the agents may coadapt to emit and act in only a subset ($\Lambda' \subset \Lambda$) of the local-environment states. This strategy raises the chances of a correct guess to $1/|\Lambda'|$ from $1/|\Lambda|$. The evolution of the population to exploit the loophole explains the slow increase in the degree of coordination when communication is suppressed (figure 3.1); it also explains why in long simulations the agents communicate about a decreasing subset of the situations. It is *genuine cooperation*, but occurs without the benefit of communication by restricting the opportunities for potential cooperation. In spite of these difficulties, we kept the cooperation restriction, since it facilitated the emergence of communication in shorter simulations. (See section 3.7 for Noble and Cliff's investigation of this phenomenon.)

3.4   Series 2: Two-symbol Communication by FSMs

Setup

A second series of experiments was intended to investigate the possibility of finite-state machines evolving the ability to generate and recognize sequential signals (sequences of global-environment states used for communication). We accomplished this by creating an artificial world in which the number of local-environment states is greater than the number of global-environment states, so a single symbol (global-environment state) cannot uniquely specify a situation (local-environment state). That is, since $G < L$ there is no map from Γ onto Λ, although there are maps from Γ^* onto Λ.

We decided to begin with local environments that could be expressed by two symbols; that is, there are maps from Γ^2 onto Λ, so $G^2 \geq L$. In this case we chose $G = 4$ and $L = 8$, so two symbols are more than enough to express the local states.

Obviously, if the agents are to be able to recognize or generate sequential signals, they must have some memory by means of which to control their sequential behavior. Therefore, in this series of experiments the agents were finite state machines (FSMs) with $S = 4$ possible internal memory states. That is, we gave them the minimum memory necessary to remember a global-environment state ($S = G$). Let Σ be the internal state space, so $S = |\Sigma|$; in practice $\Sigma = \{0, \ldots, S - 1\}$.

These machines are defined in effect by a set of behavioral rules of the form

$$(\sigma, \gamma, \lambda) \implies (\sigma', R)$$

for all possible $\sigma \in \Sigma, \gamma \in \Gamma, \lambda \in \Lambda$. In practice, the rules are represented by a transition table of SGL entries, indexed by $(\sigma, \gamma, \lambda)$. Each table entry contains the pair (σ', R), where $\sigma' \in \Sigma$ is the new internal state and R is a response, either emit(γ') or act(λ'), as before. Thus, a table entry must encode $S(G+L)$ possibilities. In practice we represent this as a pair of numbers, one in the range $0, \ldots, S - 1$, the other in the range $0, \ldots, G + L - 1$. Similarly, the genotype is represented by a string of SGL genes, each chosen from $S(G + L)$ alleles. In these experiments there were 128 genes with 48 alleles.

Except for the difference in genetic structure, the mechanism of synthetic evolution was essentially the same as in the first series of experiments (section 3.3). However, we did try several variations of the selection strategy, such as imposing a penalty for failed attempts to cooperate and making the probability of selection proportional to the square of the number of cooperations per breeding cycle. The nested breeding, environmental and action cycles were also similar, except that the simulations were generally run longer: 10^4 to 2×10^5 breeding cycles. Learning was implemented by a similar single-case algorithm: if the rule $(\sigma, \gamma, \lambda) \implies [\sigma', \text{act}(\lambda')]$ was applied but the correct action was λ'', then the rule is changed to $(\sigma, \gamma, \lambda) \implies [\sigma', \text{act}(\lambda'')]$. For experimental purposes, as before, communication can be suppressed by randomizing the global environment state, and learning can be enabled or disabled. Further, the population size was $P = 100$ and the mutation rate was 0.01, as in the first series.

Results

Table 3.5 shows the co-occurrence matrix resulting from a typical simulation, which ran for 10^4 breeding cycles (communication unsuppressed, learning disabled). When a successful cooperation takes place, we increment the table entry corresponding to the local-environment state (column) and to the *last two* global-environment states (row). There is obvious structure in the matrix. For example, the table falls into 4×4 submatrices of similar degrees of coordination, which means that successful cooperations tend to be more sensitive to the most recent of the two symbols, rather than to the first of the two. For example, local-environment state 5 is usually expressed by signals of the form $X1$ (that is 01, 11, 21, or 31). This suggests that the machines are not making full use of their memory capacity. Nevertheless, the agents sometimes make full use

Table 3.5
Co-occurrence Matrix: Communication Permitted with Learning Disabled

sym.	0	1	2	situation 3	4	5	6	7
0/0	31	22	42	0	144	0	0	0
1/0	26	15	62	0	175	0	0	0
2/0	119	23	44	0	47	0	0	0
3/0	8	9	18	0	31	0	0	0
0/1	0	54	106	2	74	59	516	0
1/1	0	33	174	3	423	227	1979	0
2/1	0	23	65	17	139	74	125	0
3/1	0	1	24	0	48	96	51	0
0/2	50	4	4	366	7	0	8	42
1/2	35	9	0	32	1	0	6	44
2/2	52	76	0	112	7	0	13	135
3/2	52	6	1	215	2	0	2	78
0/3	0	2	13	17	0	3	0	0
1/3	0	66	19	6	0	4	0	0
2/3	0	33	61	27	0	2	0	0
3/3	0	39	38	8	0	0	0	0

of the expressive power of two symbols. For example, 00, 10 and 30 usually mean local state 4, but 20 usually means local state 0, so here the machines are using the first symbol to modify the meaning of the second. Furthermore, order is significant, since 02 usually denotes local state 3 and only occasionally 0.

Nevertheless, in this series of experiments we never observed the agents evolving to make full use of their communicative potential. We can see this in figure 3.5, which shows the decrease of entropy H as communication evolves; it begins at $H_{max} = 7$, reflecting total disorder, and decreases to about $H = 4.5$, which is still substantially more disordered than the $H_{ideal} = 3$ of a "perfect" two-symbol communication system. The entropy appears to have stopped decreasing after about 5000 breeding cycles, so we can see that longer simulations are not likely to help (nor did they, in our experiments).

It appears that two-symbol communication cannot fully self-organize, at least under the conditions investigated in these experiments. We can understand why by considering the task that the agents must evolve the ability to solve. Recall that in each action cycle, all of the machines are allowed to respond as determined by the global environment γ, their local environment λ and their internal state σ. The machines are serviced cyclically, which means that once a machine emits a symbol, it will have to wait while all the other machines are serviced before it has an opportunity to emit a second symbol.

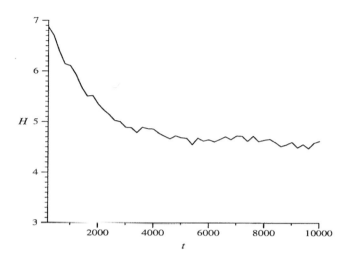

Figure 3.5
Entropy of Two-symbol Communication (Learning Disabled)

Consider what must take place for a machine A to signal its local environment λ^* to another machine B by means of the symbol sequence $\gamma_1\gamma_2$. First, whatever the internal state σ of machine A and whatever the state γ of the global environment, machine A must have a rule $(\sigma, \gamma, \lambda^*) \Longrightarrow [\sigma_1, \mathrm{emit}(\gamma_1)]$. Second, supposing that no machine between A and B has altered the global environment, whatever the internal state σ' of machine B and whatever the state λ' of its local environment, machine B must have a rule $(\sigma', \gamma_1, \lambda') \Longrightarrow [\sigma'', R]$. If R is $\mathrm{act}(\lambda')$, then (a) it is attempting to cooperate prematurely, and will succeed only if $\lambda' = \lambda^*$ by chance. On the other hand, if R is $\mathrm{emit}(\gamma')$, then (b) it will change (unless perchance $\gamma' = \gamma_1$) the global environment, destroying the chances of any other machines responding to A (or of B doing so on later action cycles). Third, machine A must have a rule $(\sigma_1, \gamma'', \lambda^*) \Longrightarrow [\sigma_2, \mathrm{emit}(\gamma_2)]$, where γ'' is the global state resulting from the last machine to emit before the second servicing of A (as conditioned by its own internal and local states and by the global state). Fourth, again supposing that no machine between A and B has altered the global state, machine B must have a rule $(\sigma'', \gamma_2, \lambda') \Longrightarrow [\sigma''', \mathrm{act}(\lambda^*)]$. The emergence of this degree of coordination may be too much to expect, and it is perhaps surprising that we observed as much use of two-symbol signals as we did.

3.5   Series 3: Paired Symbol Emission by FSMs

Setup

The difficulty of evolving two-symbol communication led my student Joseph Crumpton to consider a modification of the experimental design [102]. Because of the likelihood of two-symbol signals being disrupted by intervening emissions, he decided to give each agent *two* chances to respond in each action cycle. Notice that Crumpton's machines do *not* simply emit a pair of symbols emit$(\gamma_1 \gamma_2)$; rather it is still necessary that the machines use their internal state to control the generation or recognition of sequential signals. In an action cycle each machine is allowed to cycle twice before proceeding to the next machine. The global-environment state comprises two symbols, which we may call the first and second components of the global state. On the first of a machine's cycles it is senses the first component and can change the first component by emission; on the second cycle it senses the second component and can change the second component by emission. On both cycles, the machine's response is, as before, dependent on its internal and local-environment states. Furthermore, in addition to emitting or attempting to cooperate, Crumpton's machines are allowed to do nothing, so that they are not forced to emit or attempt to cooperate while waiting for a second symbol. As in the second series of our experiments (section 3.4), Crumpton used $S = 4, G = 4, L = 8, P = 100$, but ran the simulation for 6×10^4 breeding cycles. The selection, breeding and learning processes are also the same as in the earlier experiments.

Results

In a typical simulation run, Crumpton found that the number of cooperations per breeding cycle increased to 65 in the first 10^4 breeding cycles; it remained between 65 and 70 for the remaining 5×10^4 breeding cycles of the simulation, although there was a slight elevation in the average level after $t = 3 \times 10^4$ cycles. This is significantly higher than the 23 cooperations/breeding cycle obtained in the earlier experiments (analysis of variance $p < 0.01$). Similarly, the entropy decreased to about 5.1 bits in the first 10^4 breeding cycles; after a slight elevation between $t = 2 \times 10^4$ and $t = 3 \times 10^4$, the entropy stabilized at $H = 5$ bits for the remaining 3×10^4 cycles. This was *not* significantly different from the entropy achieved in the second series of experiments (section 3.4).

For each local-environment state, Crumpton considered the symbol pair most commonly used in successful cooperations; such a pair might be said to express that state (perhaps ambiguously), and so we'll refer to it as an *expressive pair*. For example, in a typical run he found five expressive pairs $(11, 22, 32, 33, 34)$, which means that the eight environment states could not be expressed unambiguously. The average he measured (4.3) was not significantly different from that found in the earlier experiments (4.0).

Crumpton was especially interested in non-repeating symbol use, that is, signals of the form XY, which require the use of memory in their generation and recognition, as opposed to signals of the form XX, which do not. For example, of the five expressive pairs $(11, 22, 32, 33, 34)$, two are non-repeating $(32, 34)$. In his experiments Crumpton found an average of 1.4 non-repeating pairs, which is significantly higher ($p < 0.01$) than the 0.3 of the earlier series of experiments (section 3.4), thus showing that the machines were making better use of the representational resources of the medium.

Crumpton used his experimental design to investigate several other properties of communication in his synthetic world. For example, he found significant differences in entropy and degree of coordination for population sizes $P = 50, 100, 200, 400$ and 800. (The $P = 800$ case was exceptional in many respects, which Crumpton attributes to the population being too big for communication to have stabilized in the 6×10^4 breeding cycles of his experiments.) In general, larger populations achieved a higher degree of coordination, but $P = 100$ led to the most use of expressive and non-repeating pairs. Degree of coordination was found to be significantly negatively correlated with entropy, as would be expected.

Crumpton also investigated differing amounts of memory for the agents ($S = 2, 3, 4, 5, 6$). With regard to degree of coordination and entropy, smaller numbers of internal states were better, but this was found to be deceptive, since with $S = 2$ or 3 the eight situations were being represented by an average of three expressive pairs, whereas with $S = 4$ they were represented by an average of four expressive pairs. That is, in the former cases the agents were achieving higher degrees of coordination by cooperating in a smaller subset of the situations (as was discussed in section 3.3, p. 78).

Crumpton ran a series of experiments in which there were two "species" of agents: the usual ones, and a breed of memoryless "competitors" who received credit for blocking cooperation by matching the last emitter's local environment.[2] It was hoped that the competitors would push the communicators to use

---

2 That is, if a competitor was able to match the last emitter's local environment, it prevented the signaller and any communicating responders from getting credit, and it received credit for every such blocked communication.

pairs of symbols. The result, however, was a significantly lower ($p < 0.01$) degree of coordination (48) and significantly less ($p < 0.03$) use of non-repeating symbols (0.4). He observed that the competitors either dominated the population or had very little effect.

Crumpton investigated a number of other variations (including variations in learning rule and placement of offspring in the population), that did not lead to significant differences in degree of coordination, entropy, or the use of expressive and non-repeating pairs of symbols.

3.6   Series 4: One-symbol Communication by Neural Networks

Motivation

There are at least two limitations to the FSM behavioral control mechanisms used in the preceding experiments. First, one of the important problems in the evolution of language is the emergence of discrete signal types from a continuum of states [107, 108, 109, 110, 111]. (Steels has addressed this problem directly as part of his investigation of symbol grounding [117, 118].)

Second, since FSMs have in effect a separate rule (i.e. transition table entry) for each possible combination of internal, global and local state, they have no inherent capacity to generalize. For example (and ignoring internal state for now), to consistently signal γ for situation λ, the machine must have in effect the rule $(*, \lambda) \implies \text{emit}(\gamma)$, where "$*$" means "don't care" (i.e. any possible global state). However, conventional FSMs do not permit rules of this form (although alternative rule-based models, such as classifier systems, do). Therefore, the FSM must acquire (through evolution or learning) a rule $(\gamma', \lambda) \implies \text{emit}(\gamma)$ for every possible global-environment state γ'. The situation is even worse when the machines have internal state too. This problem is aggravated by the fact that the size of the table, and hence of the genetic strings, increases with the product of the sizes of the state spaces, so there is no economy for the machines in discovering general rules.

We originally made the decision to use FSMs because they include no *a priori* model of general rules, but this same characteristic means that the population has a much more difficult evolutionary problem to solve. Hence, it seemed appropriate to investigate behavioral control mechanisms more capable of representing and learning general rules.

Setup

My students Rick Stroud and Noel Jerke [115, sec. 2] conducted an exploratory investigation patterned after our first series (section 3.3), but using neural networks instead of FSMs, and continuous rather than discrete local and global state spaces, specifically, $\Gamma = [0, 1] = \Lambda$. Each neural net had two inputs for sensing the states of its local environment and the global environment, and two (continuous-valued) outputs representing the emission/action choice (in $[-1, 1]$) and the emission/action value (in $[0, 1]$). In addition the nets had a single hidden layer comprising six neurons.

The emission/action choice was indicated by the sign of the first output. In the emission case the second output becomes the new state of the global environment. In the action case the second output is compared to the local environment of the last emitter; credit is awarded if they differ by less than $1/8$ (in emulation of the $L = 8$ discrete states of the earlier experiments).

The overall cycle of synthetic evolution was the same as in the first series of experiments (section 3.3). The genetic string represented the connections between the neurons ($+1, -1, 0$; i.e. excitatory, inhibitory, absent) but not their relative strengths, which were adjusted by back-propagation. Generally five to ten cycles of back-propagation were used to train the networks. The emit/act output was trained to ± 1, depending on its sign on its first response (i.e., its native response was strengthened). Further, when the response was an action, the other output was trained to match the last emitter's local-environment state. Simulations were run for 10^4 breeding cycles. The continuous local and global state spaces were each divided into ten bins for compiling a 10×10 co-occurrence matrix.

Results

Stroud and Jerke observed that communication did not emerge when equal credit was awarded to the emitter and actor for successful cooperations (as was done in the FSM experiments), but that it did emerge when the actor was awarded three units and the emitter one. Without this adjustment, they speculated, there was an increase in the tendency of the agents to emit, and therefore an increased probability of emissions interfering with each other; the better coordinated populations seemed to have a small number of emitters and a large number of actors. With increasing coordination, the corresponding co-occurrence matrices displayed an obvious increase of structure, but Stroud and Jerke did not quantify it by entropy or other measures. Although Stroud and Jerke did observe an increase in the cooperation of the agents, it seems to have resulted in part from the "partial cooperation" of the agents exploiting the loophole in the scoring rule (section 3.3), rather than from full-fledged cooperation, for the co-occurrence matrices show cooperations to be taking place in a decreasing subset of the local state space.

3.7   Related Work

Noble and Cliff [116] have replicated our first series of experiments (section 3.3) and extended them in a number of ways. Overall their results agreed with ours, but their experiments exhibited several discrepancies. First, they measured lower entropy in the communication-suppressed condition, as did Crumpton [102] when the program was corrected (footnote 1, page 75). Second, they observed a lower degree of coordination than we did when learning was enabled; this has not been explained. Next, they compared the sequential (cyclic) servicing of the agents that we used with servicing them in a different random order each time, and they found that the results were unaffected except when learning was enabled, in which case coordination increased more quickly with random updating (and in fact agreed with the values we measured). Further, they investigated whether synonymy and ambiguity in the emergent communication system reflects the existence of multiple dialects in the population or ambiguous symbol usage by individual agents (recall section 3.3, p. 77). The latter interpretation was supported, since over time the population tends toward genetic homogeneity. Third, they investigated extreme situations in which there were a small number of possible states ($L \leq G \leq 4$). They found that the agents were able to achieve comparatively high coordination by exploiting the loophole in the scoring rule (section 3.3).

3.8   Conclusions

It will be worthwhile to summarize our results: (1) We have demonstrated consistently that inherently meaningful communication can emerge through synthetic evolution in populations of simple artificial agents. (2) This has been demonstrated for agents controlled by both finite state machines and neural networks. (3) The agents can evolve the ability to use single symbols and, to a limited extent, pairs of symbols exhibiting rudimentary syntax. (4) The communication system evolved by the population can be studied in its own right as an evolving emergent phenomenon. (5) The emergent communication systems exhibit some of the richness of natural communication, including ambiguous, synonymous, asymmetric and context-dependent symbol use.

We will mention a few opportunities for future work. In nature, communication media are inherently continuous, but some functions of communication are facilitated by the use of discrete symbols. This implies that the emergence of discrete symbols from continuous phenomena is an important problem that must be solved by the evolution of language [107, 108, 109, 110, 111, 114]. As mentioned above, Steels has initiated a promising investigation of this problem [117, 118]. In addition to explaining the emergence of words, such research may illuminate the gradual emergence of the rules and hierarchical structure characteristic of human language [108, 111]

We have already remarked on the limitations of the FSM behavioral model (section 3.6), but the simple neural nets employed by Stroud and Jerke are not much better. Animals, on the other hand, independent of any communicative abilities they may have, are able to interpret perceptually complex phenomena and to generate complex, flexible, hierarchically structured motor behaviors. It seems likely that the underlying neural mechanisms of these behaviors may be recruited and adapted for communication, including language. Therefore, we may speculate that our artificial agents may need to be similarly endowed with perceptual-motor abilities before they will evolve complex, structured communication systems. (For this reason, our recent research has been directed toward mechanisms for perception and motor control [112].)

The experiments we have described involve local environments that are extremely simple in structure: a small discrete set (e.g. $\{0, \ldots, 7\}$) or a simple continuum (e.g. $[0, 1]$); the communication systems that have evolved to describe them are correspondingly simple. Although some of the structure (syntax) of communication systems may be emergent phenomena independent of their semantics and pragmatics [103, 104, 105], we expect the complexity of communication to reflect the complexity of the agents that use it and the complexity of their world. That is, structure in the pragmatic interactions of agents induces structure in the semantics that must be expressed, which induces structure in the syntax to express it. This suggests that we will have to construct more structured synthetic worlds in order to study the emergence of more structured communications systems, including language.

References

[101]G. M. Burghardt. Defining 'communication'. In J. W. Johnston Jr., D. G. Moulton, and A. Turk, editors, *Communication by Chemical Signals*, pages 5–18. Appleton-Century-Crofts, New York, 1970.

[102]J. J. Crumpton. Evolution of two symbol signals by simulated organisms. Master's thesis, University of Tennessee, Knoxville, December 1994.

[103]S. Kirby. Language evolution without natural selection: From vocabulary to syntax in a population of learners. Technical Report EOPL-98-1, University of Edinburgh, Department of Linguistics, 1998. Available from http://www.ling.ed.ac.uk/~simon.

[104]S. Kirby. Learning, bottlenecks and the evolution of recursive syntax. In E. J. Briscoe, editor, *Linguistic Evolution through Language Acquisition: Formal and Computational Models*. Cambridge University Press, Cambridge, 2000. Also available from http://www.ling.ed.ac.uk/~simon.

[105]S. Kirby. Syntax without natural selection: How compositionality emerges from vocabulary in a population of learners. In C. Knight, M. Studdert-Kennedy, and J. Hurford, editors, *The Evolutionary Emergence of Language: Social Function and the Origins of Linguistic Forms*. Cambridge University Press, Cambridge, 2000. Also available from http://www.ling.ed.ac.uk/~simon.

[106]B. J. MacLennan. Evolution of communication in a population of simple machines. Technical Report CS-90-99, University of Tennessee, Knoxville, Department of Computer Science, January 1990. Available from http://www.cs.utk.edu/~mclennan.

[107]B. J. MacLennan. Synthetic ethology: An approach to the study of communication. In C. G. Langton, C. Taylor, J. D. Farmer, and S. Rasmussen, editors, *Artificial Life II: The Second Workshop on the Synthesis and Simulation of Living Systems*, pages 631–658. Addison-Wesley, Redwood City, CA, 1992. Santa Fe Institute Studies in the Sciences of Complexity, proceedings Vol. X. Report available from http://www.cs.utk.edu/~mclennan.

[108]B. J. MacLennan. Characteristics of connectionist knowledge representation. *Information Sciences*, 70:119–143, 1993. Also available from http://www.cs.utk.edu/~mclennan.

[109]B. J. MacLennan. Continuous symbol systems: The logic of connectionism. In D. S. Levine and M. Aparicio IV, editors, *Neural Networks for Knowledge Representation and Inference*, pages 83–120. Lawrence Erlbaum, Hillsdale, NJ, 1994. Also available from http://www.cs.utk.edu/~mclennan.

[110]B. J. MacLennan. Image and symbol: Continuous computation and the emergence of the discrete. In V. Honavar and L. Uhr, editors, *Artificial Intelligence and Neural Networks: Steps Toward Principled Integration*, pages 207–24. Academic Press, New York, 1994. Also available from http://www.cs.utk.edu/~mclennan.

[111]B. J. MacLennan. Continuous formal systems: A unifying model in language and cognition. In *Proceedings of the IEEE Workshop on Architectures for Semiotic Modeling and Situation Analysis in Large Complex Systems*, pages 161–172, Monterey, CA, August 1995. Also available from http://www.cs.utk.edu/~mclennan.

[112]B. J. MacLennan. Field computation in motor control. In P. G. Morasso and V. Sanguineti, editors, *Self-Organization, Computational Maps and Motor Control*, pages 37–73. Elsevier, 1997. Also available from http://www.cs.utk.edu/~mclennan.

[113]B. J. MacLennan. Synthetic ethology: A new tool for investigating animal cognition. In C. Allen, M. Bekoff, and G. Burghardt, editors, *The Cognitive Animal: Empirical and Theoretical Perspectives on Animal Cognition*. MIT Press, forthcoming.

[114]B. J. MacLennan and G. M. Burghardt. Synthetic ethology and the evolution of cooperative communication. *Adaptive Behavior*, 2(2):161–187, Fall 1993. Also available from http://www.cs.utk.edu/~mclennan.

[115]B. J. MacLennan, N. Jerke, R. Stroud, and M. D. VanHeyningen. Neural network models of

cognitive processes: 1990 progress report. Technical Report CS-90-125, University of Tennessee, Knoxville, Department of Computer Science, December 1990.

[116]J. Noble and D. Cliff. On simulating the evolution of communication. In P. Maes, M. Mataric, J.-A. Meyer, J. Pollack, and S. W. Wilson, editors, *From Animals to Animats 4: Proceedings of the Fourth International Conference on Simulation of Adaptive Behavior*, Cambridge, 1996. MIT Press.

[117]L. Steels. Constructing and sharing perceptual distinctions. In M. van Someran and G. Widmer, editors, *Proceedings of the European Conference on Machine Learning*, Berlin, 1997. Springer-Verlag.

[118]L. Steels. The synthetic modeling of language origins. *Evolution of Communication*, 1(1):1–34, 1997.

4 Optimization of Classifiers Using Genetic Algorithms

J. J. Merelo, A. Prieto, and F. Morán

Classification is one of the main tasks neural networks perform. A classifier is issued a vector belonging to an unknown class, and returns a class. One of the techniques used for classification is *vector quantization* (VQ), in which the classification task is entrusted to a set of labeled vectors called *codebook*. This codebook, in order to be optimal, must meet two conditions:

1. accuracy in classification, and
2. being a good representation of the training sample, i.e., minimal *distortion*.

Another characteristic should be added: optimal size of the codebook, so that it fills the minimum amount of memory and is fast, or else takes the minimal surface in a hardware implementation.

Kohonen's LVQ is a codebook design method, which, given a set of labeled vectors with an initial value, returns a codebook that meets the two first conditions said above. But it has two problems: the size of the codebook, the vector labels and the initial vector values must be set in advance; and besides, it only finds the optimal value closer to the initial values of the codebook vectors.

These problems are addressed using a genetic algorithm. Codebooks are represented in a chromosome, decoded and trained using LVQ in a training set, and then evaluated on a test set. In order to optimize size, variable length chromosomes are used to represent the initial values of the codebook vectors and its labels; chromosomes vary its length in units of full vectors, using genetic operator that alter the size of the chromosome.

All optimality conditions must be taken into account, so that a single fitness value is substituted by a vector fitness, i.e., all three quantities: accuracy, distortion and size are considered separately in order to select or reject a chromosome. The genetic algorithms guarantees that the search for an optimal codebook does not get stuck in a local minimum.

The resulting algorithm, called G-LVQ (for *genetic* LVQ), is evaluated by applying it to different synthetic (cluster classification, Hart's problem) and real world (sonar classification, benchmark problems) problems. The effect of different genetic operators, like uniform crossover and n-point crossover and different rates of application of the genetic operators is also evaluated.

Obtained codebooks are smaller and more accurate than those obtained with LVQ, and contain less weights than MLP trained with backpropagation with a similar accuracy. Besides, G-LVQ has fewer free parameters to tune than the mentioned algorithms.

4.1   Introduction

Many scientific and engineering fields need to capture data from the environment, and automatically classify it as belonging to one class or another. For instance, quality control would need to classify widgets as "good" or "bad"; a field biologist would need to classify a bug as belonging to species "foo" or "bar", or as being "male" or "female"; and finally, a fingerprint or retina recognition machine would have to classify people as "friend" or "foe". A whole field, generically called *pattern recognition* [125], has arisen from this need.

To classify is to assign a set of features a label from a finite set; a classifier, then, is a function f that maps from a feature space F to a label space L [138],

$$f : F \to L$$
$$f(X) \mapsto Y \tag{4.1}$$

The elements in F (usually called *features*) can be real numbers, integers or even Boolean values (true, false). Labels are usually discrete values, but in some cases, a continuous variation of classification values will be needed (for instance, in the case of grading object qualities).

Many scientific fields are concerned with selecting the right classifier for a task and training it to optimum performance: neural networks, multivariate analysis and pattern recognition [125], to name a few. The main problem is, then, for a certain task represented by a set of *training pairs* $(\vec{x}_i, y_i)$, to choose a classifier algorithm that optimally classifies vectors $\vec{x}_i'$ not previously seen, i.e., to *predict* the label or class of an unknown vector. Sometimes, the classifier will not only have to be optimal with respect to classification accuracy, but also from the point of view of extracting information from the classified items; this means that the classifier will have to *represent* optimally the training sample, and, ideally all possible vectors in the space from which the training sample has been extracted.

In some cases, a first step before classification is to group or *cluster* training samples in different bins; in this way, features that make vectors fall in the same bin stand out. This process is usually called *clustering* or *feature extraction* [125].

Some other practical considerations must be taken into account when designing a classifier. In general, classifier size is important because it means a faster classification of an unknown sample: usually classification is $O(S)$, where S is some characteristic classifier size; less memory usage (which becomes important in embedded controller implementations), and a smaller surface in a custom integrated circuit.

Many different algorithms, with different capabilities and different initial assumptions, have been proposed and are used in scientific and engineering applications. Some of them are purely statistical, like linear regression; some others come from the field of Artificial Intelligence (fuzzy classifiers, tree classifiers like C4.5), and yet others from neural networks: Kohonen's Learning Vector Quantization [131] (LVQ), multilayer perceptrons (MLP) and Radial Basis Functions (RBF).

The quality of a classifier is, thus, usually represented by three quantities: accuracy, distortion and classifier size. The problem of designing a classifier that optimizes these three characteristics is a multiobjective global optimization problem, which implies to search in a vast space of possible classifier configurations for the correct one. Usual classifier training algorithms are local optimization procedures, that find the best configuration in the surroundings of the initial one.

In this paper, we will try to present a general procedure for optimizing classifiers, based in a two-level GA operating on variable size chromosomes, that uses as fitness several of the classifier characteristics. We will first present the state of the art in evolutionary classifier design in section 4.2, then the methodology for genetic classifier design will be presented in section 4.3, to be followed by different implementations of the method to design unsupervised classifiers in section 4.4 and supervised classifiers in section 4.5.

4.2 State of the Art

Despite the vast amount of literature already produced on global optimization of neural networks and other classifiers using genetic algorithms, parameter tuning by hand seems to be yet the state of the art, for instance in backpropagation [142] (BP), and for Kohonen's Self-Organizing Map [135].

Statisticians estimating parameters for classifiers (the statistical equivalent of neural network training), face a similar problem. Some global optimization procedures have been tested: simulated annealing and stochastic approximation, but little mention is made to GAs, except for optimizing k-nearest neighbor [127, 128], an unsupervised clustering algorithm. For this kind of problem, MCMC and bootstrap algorithms are used to obtain the number of clusters, but this is rather costly in terms of computation time.

The usual approach is to optimize one of the three values mentioned above, classification accuracy for supervised learning, or distortion for unsupervised learning, while leaving size fixed. Several size values are usually tested, and the best is chosen.

Some other methods for optimizing LVQ have been based on incremental approaches (for a review, see [121]), which are still local error-gradient descent search algorithms on the space of networks or dictionaries with different size; or on genetic algorithms [134], but in this case they have got a maximum implicit size.

An incremental methodology proposed by Perez and Vidal [136], seems to offer the best results for this kind of methodology. This method adds or takes codevectors after presentation of the whole training sample, eliminating those that have not been near any vector in the training sample, and adding as new codevector a vector from the training sample that has been incorrectly classified, and, besides, is the most distant from all codevectors belonging to its same class. This approach has the advantage of not relying on threshold parameters, but it still has the problem of being a local search procedure, that optimizes size step by step; and besides, it relies on heuristics for the initial weights.

A method for global optimization of LVQ was proposed in [133]. This method is simplified, taking out unnecessary features, and extended here to other kinds of classifier training algorithms besides LVQ, testing it on real world problems taken from machine learning databases.

4.3 Method

The method proposed here for global optimization of classifiers is based on several pillars, which sometimes lean on each other: hybridization of local and global search operators, variable length chromosome genetic algorithm and vectorial fitness.

Hybrid Local/Global Search

Genetic algorithms, as global optimization procedures, are not too efficient for designing good classifiers, since their search method using global sampling takes usually too long to find a solution. This approach, pioneered by Ackley and Littman [119, 120], and Belew [122, 123], has been widely recognized in the GA/NN literature [145, 124]. On the other hand, local gradient descent algorithm are quite fast in finding the local optimum for the initial conditions and parameters they have been given.

The ideal combination is, then, to make the GA search the space of initial combinations and parameters, and then leave the local search procedure to find the optimum. Unsuccessful results have been reported for such a combination of GA and backpropagation by Kitano [130], citing that GA + standard BP is worse than QuickProp, a fast backpropagation algorithm; but this conclusion has been dismissed by Yao [145], terming it "unfair", claiming that QuickProp should have been compared with GA+QuickProp.

The efficiency of this hybrid approach will be proven later on, by testing different approaches to vector quantization.

Variable Length Chromosome Genetic Algorithm

The process of global optimization of classifiers requires to search on the space of different size classifiers, and the comparison among them. This could imply, for example, the simultaneous evaluation between codebooks with different number of levels, multilayer perceptrons with different number of neurons in the hidden layer or different number of hidden layers.

This means that the GA must have variable-size chromosomes and the corresponding genetic operators to implement them. Chromosomes are structured in genes, each one of them coding for a basic building block. In order to always have meaningful classifiers coding, these building blocks are the minimal unit of length change; for instance, a full codevector in a codebook, or a hidden layer neuron with all connections to input and output layers; genetic operators will add a full gene, or kill a gene, eliminating it from the chromosome.

On the other hand, classifiers have usually an internal structure, that allows each building block to be evaluated separately from the others. For instance, in a rule-based classifier, some rules will never fire; or will lead to incorrect classification; in a codebook, some vectors will never *win*, or be the closest to any vector in the training sample. Thus, structures within the classifier can be evaluated, assigned a fitness, and allowed to compete; only the best will survive and/or reproduce, while the worst will be eliminated from the chromosome.

In practice, this means that each generation, the genes within some chromosomes will be evaluated and reproduced or eliminated according to fitness. Length altering operators can be applied in this way.

However, how this process will improve overall performance is not clear. Since size is taken into account in fitness evaluation, classifiers with useless parts will be worse than others that use all their components; and if adding a new structure to a classifier improves performance, it will be preferred in fitness evaluation. These two strategies (directed length alteration, used in a previous version of this work [133], and non-directed length alteration) will be tested against each other. In any case, these "directed" operators can be used to fix classifiers resulting at the end of the combined GA/classifier algorithm training.

Vectorial Fitness

As it has been said above, classifiers will be optimized for three different values, which have differing importance. Instead of normalizing and combining them in a single formula, or giving them different weights, they are evaluated in turn. Accuracy, or number of training/test vectors correctly classified, is usually first, size usually second and distortion last. Distortion minimization must be balanced with size minimization to avoid overfitting; a minimal distortion is not always desirable, since it spells doom for generalization.

Some types of vectorial fitness have already been described in the literature, mainly for multiobjective optimization [141, 140, 143]. In the case of Shaw and coauthors, vectorial fitness is also used to account for constraints (lateness of orders, for instance) in scheduling problems, and uses Pareto optimization to select the best candidates, which are then presented to a human operator. This approach is somewhat different to the one presented in this paper, since here the fitness values are ordered; some values are preferred over others.

Genetic Design of Classifiers

Since GAs have already proved their worth in finding good solutions in a vast search space, they have been chosen to evolve good classifiers. The genetic algorithm used in this work, and based in the previous considerations, can be described in the following way:

1. Initialize randomly chromosome population with lengths ranging from half the number of classes to twice the number of classes.

2. For each member of the population:

   (a) Using the values stored in the chromosome as initial values for classifier parameters, create a classifier and train it using the classifier algorithm, which has been selected in advance. Then evaluate accuracy and distortion in classification using the training set as test set. Set fitness to the triplet (accuracy, size, distortion).

(b)If the "directed" option has been chosen, and with a certain probability, apply "directed" chromosome length changing operators, suppressing or adding new significant structures to the initial values of the classifier.

3. Select the P best chromosomes in the population, comparing their fitness vector, and make them reproduce, with mutation and 2-point crossover (acting over the length of the smallest chromosome of the couple). Apply, if chosen, non-directed duplication and elimination operators.

4. Finish after a predetermined number of generations.

4.4   Unsupervised Codebook Design and Optimization Using GAs

So far, the methodology described above is applicable to many kinds of classifiers, for instance, fuzzy rule classifiers, in which the smallest functional unit is a fuzzy rule; or multilayer perceptrons, with hidden layer neurons with fan-in and fan-out weights as functional units, etc.

However, we have tested it on codebook based classifiers. A codebook C is a set of L *codevectors*. These codevectors are labeled if the codebook is to be used for supervised classification. L is called the *number of levels* of the codebook.

A vector $\vec{x} \in F$ is classified as $\vec{m}_i \in C$, if

$$d(\vec{m}_i, \vec{x}) < min_j d(\vec{m}_j, \vec{x}) \, \forall \vec{m}_j \in C \qquad (4.2)$$

, where d is the Euclidean distance

$$d(\vec{x}, \vec{y}) = \sqrt{\sum_{i=0}^{D} (x_i - y_i)^2} \qquad (4.3)$$

where D is the vector space dimension.

Many algorithms have been proposed for unsupervised and supervised codebook training. Unsupervised classification using codebooks is usually called *vector quantization*, and vectors x belonging to F are said to be *quantized* as $\vec{m}_i$, or simply as i, if the codevectors are known in advance. One of the best known vector quantizer training procedures is *k-means*, also called Linden-Buzo-Gray [132].

An open problem in the statistical community is to find a VQ or clustering algorithm that, besides training the codebook, finds the correct size. Several algorithms have been proposed, including incremental [126], and decremental algorithms. Some of them are versions of another VQ algorithm, Kohonen's Self-Organizing Map [131]. Fritzke's algorithm tends to create too many codevectors, because its main intent is not to create optimal classifiers, but to reproduce accurately the probability density of the training set. Many other algorithms have been proposed in the statistical literature; for a review, see [139].

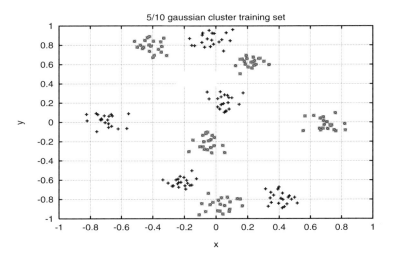

Figure 4.1
Training set for the unsupervised classifier experiment, composed of 5 and 10 Gaussian non-overlapping clusters, with a $\sigma = 0.1$. Stars were used for the 5-cluster training set, stars and crosses form the 10-cluster training set.

What is proposed here is to apply our methodology to the k-means codebook training algorithm, using as fitness distortion and size, in this order. Putting distortion before is obviously dangerous, since the algorithm will tend to minimize distortion increasing size, but has the positive effect that the selection procedure eliminates the bigger of two codebooks with identical distortion. However, this effect has been partially avoided by setting a *threshold*, under which smaller networks with higher distortion will be chosen as better,

Table 4.1
Results of training several algorithms on a 5 and 10 Gaussian non-overlapping cluster classification problem.

Algorithm		Average Distortion	Average length
K-means	5 clusters	16.9	5
	10 clusters	26.16	10
Genetic VQ	5 clusters	6.2	11.08
	10 clusters	14.1	14.05
Genetic K-means	5 clusters	7.2	6.15
	10 clusters	15.14	10.5

if the distortion difference is not over that threshold.

For the genetic algorithm, codevectors were represented with 16 bits per component, and trained initially for 100 generations, with a population of 100 chromosomes and a steady-state selection procedure that keeps 40% of the population each generation.

To prove the superiority of the hybrid approach with respect to VQ using only GA or only k-means, 20 experiments were conducted with each of the two genetic approaches, and 100 with k-means, in a clustering experiment with 5 and 10 Gaussian non-overlapping clusters (both represented in figure 4.1). For k-means algorithm, size was fixed to the number of clusters known in advance, and codebooks were initialized to vectors with component value within the same range than the training set. For genetic k-means and genetic vector quantization, chromosomes were randomly initialized with a length between 10 and 20; these values were the same for genetic VQ and genetic k-means. Training took several seconds for k-means and several minutes for the genetic algorithms in a SGI Indigo R4000.

In this experiment, a "good" performance is defined by a good combination of codebook size and distortion; distortion can only be compared for same size codebooks; since larger codebooks usually have smaller distortions, but worse generalization capability. From this point of view, and as it can be seen in table 4.1, genetic k-means outperforms the other two algorithms.

Comparing genetic VQ with genetic k-means, it can be seen that average size is smaller, and closer to the real values (as shown in the k-means row). Distortion is smaller for genetic VQ, but that is only due to the larger codebook size. Genetic k-means obtains codebooks with lower distortion than k-means for comparable size, and besides, codebooks are close to the real number of clusters. It might be surprising that k-means achieves such bad results, but that is due to the fact that k-means is quite sensitive to initialization: it achieves the optimum sometimes, but in other occasions converges to far from optimum values. That is the reason why genetic k-means outperforms it. No special care was taken to initialize k-means clusters, except that initial codevectors were in the same range as the training set vectors. Probably, better results would be achieved with a better initialization strategy. In any case, the value of genetic k-means is not only on the achievement of good codebooks, but also on finding the number of clusters.

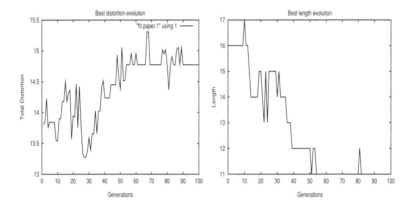

Figure 4.2
Evolution of the distortion and codebook length for the best codebook in each generation, for 100 generations, and for a typical run. Training set was the 10 Gaussian non-overlapping cluster classification problem. As it can be seen, sometimes distortion leaps a bit, if the leap is within the threshold; sometimes, those leaps lead to lower dictionary length.

The evolution of fitness in a typical run of genetic k-means for the 10-cluster unsupervised classification problem has been represented in figure 4.2. The fuzzy definition of "better fitness" is reflected the evolution of distortion. Distortion decreases while length remains constant, but it increases if a code-book with smaller length and the same distortion is found.

4.5 Genetic Optimization of LVQ Algorithm

Following the hybrid spirit of the methodology presented in this paper, we will try to design codebooks, by training them using genetic algorithms and LVQ. This algorithm will be called G-LVQ, for Genetic Learning Vector

Quantization, and has already been described in other papers [133]. However, the algorithm described in that paper relied in some assumptions that will be relaxed on this work:

• One of the usual genetic selection methods, *steady-state* selection, instead of the selection procedure adapted to processor meshes described there. The default action will be to eliminate 40 % of the population, and substitute it by the offspring of the remaining 60 %.

• The worth of the directed application of variable-length operators, as opposed to undirected application will also be evaluated. If directed application of operators is used, ten percent of the evaluated are added new codevectors, and 5 percent have codevectors surgically removed.

• One of the operators used before, `randomAdd`, which added a random unit to the chromosome, has been dropped.

• Two point crossover is used, instead of uniform crossover. Actually, uniform crossover acts as mutation after the initial generations, in which it actually manages to mix building blocks, as has been pointed out by Terry Jones [129]. If directed application of variable length operators is used, half the new population is generated by mutation, and half by crossover; if non-directed application is used, 1/17 undergo crossover, 1/17 mutation, 10/17 are added a new codevector, and 5/17 are decreased by one codevector.

• Only one fitness ordering is used: accuracy, length and distortion. Putting distortion before length leads to big dictionaries with a bad generalization ability.

The codevector representation is shown in figure 4.3, and is the same as used in the previous work. Two bytes are given to each codevector component, and 1 byte to the class. Those two bytes are decoded to the actual floating-point vector representation by scaling them to a range that has been computed from the training set. The class is decoded by extracting the remainder of dividing that byte value by the number of classes. The default population is 100, and the GA is run for 100 generations. Default range of initial codebook levels goes from the number of classes (computed from the training set) divided by two, to twice the number of classes. The GA part has been programmed using the GAGS package, a freeware C++ class library available from the author.

In order to test the two different options for G-LVQ, directed operator application or not, versus other algorithms, several problems have been selected: a difficult synthetic problem, 7 and 10 Gaussian non-overlapping classes clas-

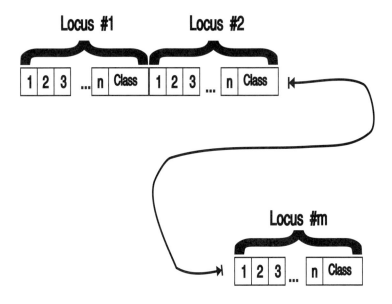

Figure 4.3
Codification of a variable-size neural network in a variable-length genome. The components of a vector are coded together with the vector label; the genome changes size by increments of whole codevectors.

sification as shown in figure 4.4, in which each cluster corresponds to a different class, and a real-world problem: cancer detection problem, taken from the PROBEN1 benchmark [137].

Classification: Synthetic Problems

In order to assess G-LVQ performance, it was tested on a synthetic problem whose main difficulty lies in the number of different classes, be it for G-LVQ, LVQ or BP.

In order to test all algorithms, homebrew programs were written for the SGI architecture, and programs were tested in a wide assortment of SGIs, from a humble Indigo R4000 to a mighty Power Challenge with R8000. The LVQ and LVQ2 [131] algorithms were tested, but LVQ2 did not seem to consistently improve LVQ results, and was thus dropped. Both were programmed using the

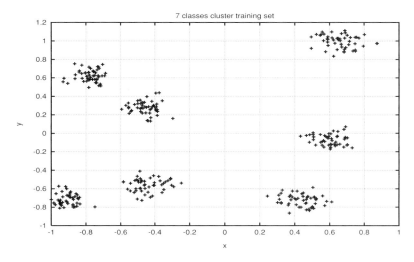

Figure 4.4
Training set for the 7 classes experiment.

latest version of the S-VQ (simple vector quantization) package (available at `ftp://kal-el.ugr.es/pub/s-vq-1.0*`). LVQ codebooks were initialized taking random vectors from the training set. Since LVQ is quite sensitive to initialization, this seemed to be the best option.

A multilayer perceptron with standard backpropagation was used for the backpropagation comparison. Other training algorithms, like RPROP or Quick-Prop were not used since they do not seem to improve accuracy, only training time. Backpropagation, given enough time, will converge, and that was done for the experiments.

The best combination of parameters for LVQ and BP was found by hand tuning parameters (hidden layer size or number of codevectors, number of epochs to train, and so on), until the solution was found. This problem admitted only a solution, 100% training set and test set classification accuracy.

First, the 7 cluster classification problem shown in figure 4.4 was tested. Results are presented in table 4.2. For some reason, this problem was specially difficult for backpropagation, as is shown in the results: the problem required a neural net with a high number of neurons in the hidden layer and many iterations to converge; it can be probably due to the proximity of some clusters. LVQ and backpropagation achieve comparable results, but LVQ is one order of magnitude faster. G-LVQ with standard parameter setting (100 generations of

Table 4.2
Results of training several algorithms on 7-classes classification problem. Times were taken on a SGI Indigo R4000, which is slightly slower than a Pentium 100. G-LVQ parameters were as follow: (1) used standard parameters, (2) increased population and number of generations to 200, and (3) used non-directed application of variable-length operators.

Algorithm	Iterations	Number of weights	Approx. training time
MLP+BP	35000	9 neurons = 9(2+7) = 81	2 minutes
LVQ	20000	17 codevectors = 119	5 seconds
G-LVQ (1)	1000 * 26 generations	8 codevectors = 16	10 minutes
G-LVQ (2)	1000 * 27 generations	7 codevectors = 14	10 minutes
G-LVQ (3)	1000 * 40 generations	8 codevectors = 16	10 minutes

100 individuals, adding rate at 0.1, killing rate at 0.05, 40% of individuals kept each generation), manages to find a codebook with 8 levels; if the population is increased, the right codebook size is found in more or less the same number of generations. Non-directed operator application does not seem to work well in this case; since it is usually only one vector the right one to suppress, it has a chance of one in 8 to succeed; that is why it has to make do with an slightly worse result, even increasing the population.

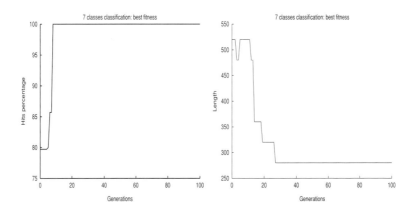

Figure 4.5
Evolution of the classification accuracy and codebook length for the best codebook in each generation, for 100 generations, in the 7-classes classification problem. Left hand side graph represents the evolution of the hit rate, i.e., the number of vectors correctly classified; and left hand side the length in bits of the best codebook (each codevector takes 40 bits). Sometimes, length increases as a results of an increase in hit rate; at the end, 100% accuracy in classification and the correct length is achieved.

The evolution of two of the three fitness parameters is represented in figure 4.5. Initially, the space of codebooks with a high number of levels is explored; when a codebook with 100% accuracy is found, size is optimized; in the last generations; distortion is also optimized.

In this problem, the need to keep genetic diversity high already arises. Since the search space explored is quite high, diversity allows exploitation to work better than exploitation, sifting through the present codebooks to get the best. In this paper, genetic diversity is achieved mainly through two "natural" mechanisms: decreasing the number of individuals eliminated each generation, and increasing population.

Classifying more than 7 different classes is even more difficult: longer training times are needed, and also bigger population and elite rates. Although nets with 100% accuracy were always obtained after a few generations, GA parameters had to be finetuned to obtain networks with the correct number of codevectors.

Classification: Real World Problems

A set of classification problems taken from the benchmark PROBEN1 [137] have been used. They have been already used before, and compared with MLP trained using RPROP, as published in the paper [137]; the same benchmark is used here to show that relaxing some assumptions will still make G-LVQ work; besides, some results have even been improved.

cancer is a breast cancer diagnosis problem with 9 inputs and two possible outputs: sick or healthy. The file cancer contains 699 examples, from which 3 partitions have been made: cancer1, 2 and 3. This data set was originally obtained from Dr. W. H. Wolberg [144]. Results have been compared to a baseline neural classifier, RPROP, which uses a multi-layer perceptron with two hidden layers; the two figures shown in table 4.3 are the number of neurons in the first and second layer; parameters used in RPROP are shown in [137].

In order to test the performance of G-LVQ on this test problem, 3 runs were made for each problem subdivision in a SGI Power Challenge; each one took several minutes. Results shown are average and standard deviation for the best codebook obtained in each of the three runs.

This is a simple problem. Discovered dictionaries have small size, besides, the number of classes is also small. That is the reason why directed or non-directed variable-length operators application does not seem to affect the result much. In any case, results seem to be slightly better for directed application than for non-directed application, and obtained codebook lengths are always

Table 4.3
Results for benchmark problem `cancer1`, `2` and `3`. The "net size" column contains the number of levels in the LVQ codebook, and the size of the two hidden layers in the RPROP case.

	cancer1		cancer2		cancer3	
Algorithm	Error+SD	Net size	Error+SD	Net size	Error+SD	Net size
G-LVQ [133]	3.1 ± 0.5	5	4.6 ± 0.1	3	3.45 ± 0.06	4
G-LVQ directed	2.8 ± 0.3	3.3 ± 0.4	4.6	3	3.4 ± 0.4	3.7 ± 0.9
G-LVQ non directed	2.1 ± 0.5	4.3 ± 0.4	4.4 ± 0.2	3.7 ± 0.9	5.4 ± 0.6	5 ± 1
LVQ 2 levels	3.5 ± 0.8		4.0		4.8 ± 0.3	
LVQ 4 levels	2.8		4.6		4.8 ± 0.3	
RPROP	1.14	4 + 2	5.7	8 + 4	2.3	4 + 4

lower. However, error is higher for G-LVQ, except in the `cancer2` problem, although sizes are always smaller; the published number of weights in the MLPs is higher than the number of weights in the codebooks obtained with G-LVQ. Results are also slightly better, in size and accuracy, than those published before [133].

A comparison was made also with LVQ, by initializing dictionaries with random codevectors, but with ordered labels, and testing dictionaries of size 2 and size 4; usually, codebooks with power-of-two levels are tested. 5 runs, with different random initializations, were made for each problem. Since this is an easy problem, results are difficult to evaluate. Results are usually better for directed operator application, except for the problem subdivision `cancer2`, and lengths obtained are not too different: they are around 3; obviously they cannot be lower than 2, since this is the number of classes. Some of the LVQ runs have not got any standard deviation, since they obtained exactly the same result for the 5 runs.

4.6   Discussion and Future Work

The results published on this paper are steps towards the achievement of an automatic design procedure for classifiers. While with "classical" classifier training methods, the number of levels or any other characteristic classifier size must be set in advance, or several sizes tested, using GAs leads to an exhaustive search in the space of classifiers of different size. Hybridizing GAs with local search algorithms makes search much more efficient.

A lot of work remains to be done in the subject. This future line of work will go in two different directions: application of this methodology to other classifier training algorithms, like backpropagation, radial basis functions and fuzzy rule set , and, at the same time, exploration of several genetic design issues, like the influence of the variable length of the chromosomes in the population size, possible use of variable-size populations, and the need to keep diversity in order to search the space efficiently.

Acknowledgments

We are grateful to C. Ilia Herráiz, who programmed the multilayer perceptron and BP. This work has been supported in part by DGICYT grant number PB-92-0456.

References

[119]D. H. Ackley. *A Connectionist Machine for Genetic Hillclimbing*. Kluwer Academic Publishers, Boston, MA, 1987.

[120]D. H. Ackley and M. L. Littman. Interactions between learning and evolution. In C. G. Langton, C. Taylor, J. D. Farmer, and S. Rasmussen, editors, *Artificial Life II*, pages 487–509. Addison, 1992.

[121]E. Alpaydim. GAL: Networks that grow when they learn and shrink when they forget. Technical Report TR-91-032, International Computer Science Institute, May 1991.

[122]R. K. Belew. When both individuals and populations search: Adding simple learning to the genetic algorithm. In J. D. Schaffer, editor, *Proceedings of the Third International Conference on Genetic Algorithms*, pages 34–41. ICGA89, Morgan Kaufmann, 1989.

[123]R. K. Belew, J. McInerney, and N. N. Schraudolph. Evolving networks: Using genetic algorithms with connectionist learning. CSE Technical Report CS90-174, University of California at San Diego, La Jolla, CA, June 1990.

[124]J. Branke. Evolutionary algorithms for neural network design and training. In *Proceedings of the 1st Nordic Workshop on Genetic Algorithms and its Appplictions*, 1995.

[125]R. O. Duda and P. E. Hart. *Pattern classification and scene analysis*. Wiley and Sons, 1973.

[126]B. Fritzke. Growing cell structures – a self-organizing network for unsupervised and supervised learning. Technical Report TR-93-026, International Computer Science Institute, 1947 Center Street, Suit 600, Berkeley, California 94704, may 1993.

[127]R. Huang. Systems control with the genetic algorithm and the nearest neighbour classification. *CC-AI*, 9(2-3):225–236, 1992.

[128]J. James D. Kelly and L. Davis. Hybridizing the genetic aglorithm and the k nearest neighbors classification algorithms. In R. K. Belew and L. B. Booker, editors, *ICGA91*, San Mateo, CA, 1991. Morgan Kaufmann.

[129]T. Jones and S. Forrest. Fitness distance correlation as a measure of problem difficulty for genetic algorithms. In L. J. Eshelman, editor, *ICGA95*, pages 184–192. Morgan Kaufmann, 1995.

[130]H. Kitano. Designing neural network using genetic algorithm with graph generation system. *Complex Systems*, 4:461–476, 1990.

[131]T. Kohonen. The self-organizing map. *Procs. IEEE*, 78:1464 ff., 1990.

[132]J. Makhoul, S. Roucos, and H. Gish. Vector quantization in speech coding. *Procs. IEEE*, 73(11), Nov 1985.

[133]J. J. Merelo and A. Prieto. G-LVQ, a combination of genetic algorithms and LVQ. In N. D.W.Pearson and R.F.Albrecht, editors, *Artificial Neural Nets and Genetic Algorithms*, pages 92–95. Springer-Verlag, 1995.

[134]E. Monte, D. Hidalgo, J. Mariño, and I. Hernáez. A vector quantization algorithm based on genetic algorithms and LVQ. In *NATO-ASI Bubión*, page 231 ff., 1993.

[135]F. Murtagh and M. H. Pajares. The Kohonen self-organizing map method: An assesment. Technical report, European Space Agency/ UPC, 1993.

[136]J.-C. Perez and E. Vidal. Constructive design of LVQ and DSM classifiers. In J. Mira, J. Cabestany, and A. Prieto, editors, *New Trends in Neural Computation, Lecture Notes in Computer Science No. 686*, pages 335–339. Springer, 1993.

[137]L. Pretchelt. PROBEN1, a set of neural network benchmark problems and benchmarking rules. Technical Report 21/94, Univ. Karlsruhe, Germany, 1994.

[138]B. D. Ripley. Neural networks and related methods for classification. *J. R. Statist. Soc. B*, 56(3):409–456, 1994.

[139]W. Sarle. The number of clusters. published in comp.ai.neural-nets, Adapted Mar 16, 1996, from the SAS/STAT User's Guide (1990) and Sarle and Kuo (1993). Copyright 1996 by SAS Institute Inc, Cary, NC, USA, 1996.

[140]J. D. Schaffer. *Some experiments in machine learning using vector evaluated genetic algorithms*. PhD thesis, Dept. of Electrical Engineering, Vanderbilt Univ, 1985.

[141]J. D. Schaffer and J. J. Grefenstette. Multi-objective learning via genetic algorithms. In *Procs. of the 9th international Conference on Artificial Intelligence*, pages 593–595, 1985.

[142]W. Schiffman, M. Joost, and R. Werner. Optimization of the backpropagation algorithm for training multilayer perceptrons. Technical report, University of Koblenz, Institute of Physics, 1994.

[143]K. J. Shaw and P. J. Fleming. Initial study of multi-objective genetic algorithms for scheduling the production of chilled ready meals. In *Second International Mendel Conference on Genetic Algorithms*. Tech. Univ. of Brno, 1996.

[144]W. H. Wolberg and O. Mangasarian. Multisurface method of pattern separation for medical diagnosis applied to breast cytology. *Proceedings of the National Academy of Sciences, U.S.A.*, 87:9193–9196, December 1990.

[145]X. Yao. A review of evolutionary artificial neural networks. Technical report, CSIRO, 1992.

5 Evolving Neuro-Controllers and Sensors for Artificial Agents

Karthik Balakrishnan and Vasant Honavar

5.1 Introduction

Evolutionary algorithms, loosely inspired by biological evolutionary processes, have gained considerable popularity as tools for searching vast, complex, deceptive, and multimodal search spaces using little domain-specific knowledge [159, 157, 170]. In addition to their application in a variety of optimization problems, evolutionary algorithms have also been used to design control programs (e.g., artificial neural networks, finite-state automata, LISP programs, etc.) for a wide variety of robot tasks [156, 174, 158, 175, 179, 154, 167, 178, 162, 153, 163, 169, 172, 151, 164]. In such cases, evolutionary search operates in the space of robot control programs, with each member of the population representing a robot *behavior*. By evaluating these behaviors on the target robot task and performing fitness-based selection/reproduction, evolution discovers robot behaviors (control programs) that lead to effective execution of the robot's task. Some researchers have also used artificial evolution to design robot sensors and their placements [175, 178, 148], tune sensor characteristics [167, 146], and even evolve robot body plans [165, 164]. Widespread interest in the use of artificial evolution in the design of robots and software agents has given birth to a field that is increasingly being referred to as *evolutionary robotics*.

But why does one need an evolutionary approach for synthesizing robot behaviors? Robot behaviors often involve complex tradeoffs between multiple competing alternatives that are difficult to characterize *a priori*. And even in cases where they are identifiable, it is often hard to specify *a priori*, how to cope with these competing alternatives. For example, suppose a robot has the task of clearing a room by pushing boxes to the walls. Let us also assume that the robot has limited sensing ranges that prevent it from observing the contents of the entire room and it does not have any means to remember the positions of boxes it has observed in the past. Suppose this robot currently observes two boxes. Which one should it approach and push? Or should it ignore both boxes and continue its exploration to find another box to push? This decision is critical as it directly affects the subsequent behaviors of the robot. We may use heuristics such as *approach the closer of the two boxes*, but can we be sure that such a decision made at the local level will indeed lead to any kind of globally optimal behavior? Faced with such competing alternatives and the *lack of* rich supervisory signals, many learning techniques become inapplicable. We have mentioned earlier that evolutionary search works well in feedback-impoverished environments, requiring little prior domain knowledge or information about the structure of the solution. With these benefits, evolutionary approaches are aptly suited for searching the space of complex robot behaviors and designs.

In this chapter, we present a short report on our experiments in the evolutionary synthesis of robotic neuro-controllers. We demonstrate the emergence of intricate, aptly tailored, high fitness solutions on a heavily constrained box-pushing robot task. We also demonstrate the power of evolution in designing robot sensory systems, and its ability to carve out robust designs that operate effectively in noisy environments. We present two broad sets of results. First we present a detailed analysis of solutions discovered by the evolutionary approach. In each of these cases, our analysis of the structures of highly successful box-pushing robots reveals *critical insights* into the behaviors required to successfully overcome the constraints and limitations imposed by the box-pushing task environment. That evolution automatically discovers these intricate workarounds, with little help or human intervention, is testimony to its powerful, population-based search capabilities.

Second, we demonstrate the inherent complexity of the box-pushing task, by showing the difficulty faced by other, simpler, search techniques. Indeed, we argue that the constraints and limitations imposed by this seemingly simple task, result in a complex solution space that cannot be easily traversed using *simple, blind* search algorithms. The thesis, then, is that even a simple robotic task such as this requires a search algorithm with *powerful heuristics*. The results in this chapter can thus be construed as an empirical demonstration of the ability of EAs to execute parallel, population-based search with little domain-specific knowledge, a combination that gives them immense potential as *global search heuristics* [173].

This chapter is organized as follows. Section 5.2 introduces the box-pushing robot task, along with its associated constraints. It also compares this task to other tasks commonly used in the evolutionary robotics community and argues that the constraints make the box-pushing task considerably more interesting and challenging. Details of the simulation setup are presented in section 5.3 and results of different experiments and analysis are presented in section 5.4. The generality of evolved box-pushing behaviors, and the futility of designing effective behaviors through other search techniques, is discussed in Section 5.5. Section 5.6 presents results in the evolutionary design of robot

sensory systems, while Section 5.7 highlights the role of evolution in synthesizing robust behaviors in noisy environments. Research related to our work,
is summarized in section 5.8 and the chapter concludes with a summary in
section 5.9.

5.2 The Box-Pushing Task

Teller proposed an interesting task for studying the evolution of control behaviors in artificial agents and robots [177]. The task environment consisted of a
square room of dimension $N \times N$ cells, which was littered with M boxes, as
shown in Figure 5.1. The room had impenetrable, delimiting walls.

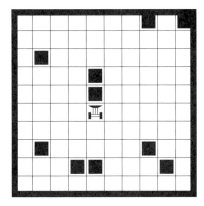

Figure 5.1
The box-pushing environment.

The robot (or agent) had the task of clearing the room by pushing the boxes
to the enclosing walls. The robot had eight sensors capable of detecting boxes,
walls, and empty spaces. These sensors were placed to sense one cell in each of
the eight directions around the robot's current position. Thus, the robots were
sensorily handicapped, with the robot being *blind* beyond one cell in each
direction. The sensors were also assumed to be fixed to the robot and hence
turn with the robot.

Based on its sensory inputs and memory, the robot could choose to perform
one of three actions: forward move, left turn through 90 degrees, or right
turn through 90 degrees. The robot was thus incapable of moving diagonally

through its environment and could only move in directions parallel to the walls. The robot was assumed to turn *in place*, i.e., it remained in the same cell after executing a turn although it was now facing a different direction. Forward moves, on the other hand, took the robot from one cell to the next, in the direction in which it was currently facing. Turn actions executed by the robot were always considered successful, although forward moves could fail under two circumstances. First, if there was a wall in front of the robot, it could not move into the wall (or push boxes through them). Second, the robot could not push more than one box at the same time. For instance in Figure 5.1, if the robot wanted to move forward, the move would fail because there are two boxes in front of the robot and it is only capable of pushing at most one. The first constraint was something we would expect, however, the second constraint was critical to the performance of the robot since it prevented the robot from collecting multiple boxes and pushing them to the walls together. The robots were thus forced to move boxes to the walls one at a time.

What made the robot task even harder was the inability of the robot to *detect* such failed movements. For instance, if the robot happened to be against a wall and attempted to move forward, the move would fail. However, owing to its inability to detect such failures, the robot would consider the move successful. For obvious reasons this had undesirable repercussions on the behaviors of the robot.

These constraints, namely: limited sensor ranges, restricted movements, limited box-pushing ability, and the inability to detect failed actions make the task very hard, and the design of an appropriate robot controller immensely challenging.

Genetic Evolution of Robot Control Programs

Teller used a Genetic Programming framework to evolve robot behavior programs for the box-pushing task. His important contribution was the addition of *state* information to standard Genetic Programming. In particular, his evolved agents had access to 20 *indexed memory elements* which they could use to remember past information. The evolved programs could make use of 10 predefined functions for reading sensory and memory data, performing mathematical operations on them, comparing numerical quantities, branching, and writing to indexed memory elements.

Teller used environments of size 6 × 6 cells with six boxes randomly placed in the inner 4 × 4 grid. Each agent was introduced in a random cell in the arena (facing a random direction), and allowed a maximum of

80 simulation time steps within which to move the boxes to the walls. In each time step, the agent sensors sensed the corresponding cell to which they were tuned, returning a value of 0, 1, or 2 corresponding to an empty cell, a box, or a wall respectively. Using these sensory inputs and its state (index memory) information, the agent behavior program determined an appropriate action to perform and the agent was made to execute the action. At the end of the simulation period, each box against a wall was awarded one point while boxes pushed into corners earned an extra point. Thus, the maximum fitness attainable in this environment was 10 (all six boxes along walls with four of them in corners). Each agent was introduced into 40 such random environments and its average performance over them was declared its fitness. For further details regarding this experiment, the reader is referred to [177].

Teller performed a number of evolutionary experiments with different kinds of agents. He found that without access to indexed memory the evolved programs performed rather poorly, causing the box-pushing agent to obtain an average fitness of less than 0.5 points per test. Teller also evolved *mental* agents that had the ability to access and use indexed memory. These mental agents averaged 4.25 fitness points per test, with the best agent program evolved achieving a fitness of 4.4.

By switching off specific memory elements Teller was able to identify that *memory* was critical for successful box-pushing behaviors. However, he was unable to *analyze* the evolved robot control programs to determine *how* the robots used their memories to achieve their fitnesses. He was thus unable to *characterize agent behaviors* in the box-pushing environment. As we will demonstrate shortly, we have evolved neuro-controllers for successful box-pushing behaviors. In addition, through a critical analysis of the evolved neuro-controller structures we have also gained significant insights into what constitutes successful behaviors in the box-pushing environment.

What Makes the Box-Pushing Task Interesting and Challenging

Most of the robot tasks used in *evolutionary robotics* studies have been simple variants of basic navigation behaviors like obstacle avoidance [156, 174], goal approaching [158], wall following [175, 179], light or target following [154], feeding [167, 178], homing, maze or trail learning [162, 153], simple exploration [163, 169], etc. In contrast, the box-pushing task described above has a number of salient properties that make it significantly more interesting and challenging.

Firstly, the box-pushing task is *dynamic*, in the sense that the robot can *alter* its own environment and hence effect its *fitness landscape*. For instance, suppose the robot is introduced in an environment containing six boxes, where no two boxes are together. Given this state of the environment, the maximum fitness attainable by the robot is 10 (all six boxes against the walls, with four of them in corners). Now suppose the robot moves in such a way that four boxes are somehow collected together in the middle of the arena in the form of a closed square. Since the robot cannot push more than one box at a time, it cannot push any of these boxes to the wall. The maximum attainable fitness has now dropped to 4 (two remaining boxes, both in corners). Thus, the behavior of the robot dynamically alters its fitness landscape. It is much harder to find good control functions (or behaviors) in such dynamic environments, which makes the box-pushing task more challenging than behaviors like obstacle avoidance, wall following, etc., where the environments are static.

Secondly, the robots of Teller have limited sensory and pushing abilities (probably overly limited). In any case, this scenario is more realistic (given the state of contemporary robotics technology) than the assumptions made in a number of other evolutionary robotics tasks. For instance, a number of approaches assume that the robots have infinite sensor range (bounded only by the limits of the environment) [172, 178]. Since all biological and artificial sensors are physically constrained to operate within specific limits (range, resource usage, processing time, etc.), such assumptions are quite unrealistic and will lead to problems if the designs are ever to be implemented on actual robots. In contrast, the sensorily and operationally-constrained robots of Teller offer more realistic conditions to work with.

Finally, the box-pushing task *subsumes* a number of other behaviors mentioned above. For instance, to function well in their environment Teller's robots have to move and explore their environment, approach and push boxes, identify and avoid walls, etc. These primitive behaviors must be interleaved and mixed together in appropriate ways for the robot to excel in pushing many boxes to the walls. Interleaving these primitive behaviors involves multiple tradeoffs. For instance, the robot should be capable of *exploring* different regions of its environment to find boxes to push. In this process, it must identify and avoid bumping into walls. Once it finds boxes, it must decide whether to push them to walls (at the risk of deviating from its exploratory behavior), or continue with its exploratory behavior and find other boxes to move. This is reminiscent of the *exploration versus exploitation* dilemma of search algorithms, i.e., should it exploit what is has found (push box) or should it explore more (find other boxes). Assuming that the robot somehow performs this tradeoff and decides to push a box, it also has to decide when to stop pushing the box and continue its exploration. This is rather difficult in the current setup since the limited sensory range of the robot prevents it from detecting walls ahead of the box which it happens to be pushing. As the robots are also incapable of detecting failed actions, the robot really has no way of knowing when the box it is pushing comes against a wall.

As may be surmised, the behaviors required by robots in the box-pushing task must be well-balanced combinations of the primary behaviors of exploration, approach, and avoidance, modulated in appropriate ways by the constraints associated with the task. For these reasons it is extremely difficult, if not impossible, to *manually* design controllers for these box-pushing robots. In contrast, it is rather easy to manually develop controllers to approach and avoid obstacles, follow walls, or navigate in open spaces.

These aspects set the box-pushing task apart from most of the others used by researchers in the evolutionary robotics community. The challenges inherent in this task offer a multitude of opportunities for the evolution of robots with interesting behaviors, and for these reasons, we use the box-pushing robot task in our research.

5.3   Simulation Details

We have performed a number of experiments in the evolution of neuro-controllers for the box-pushing robot task. In this section we present details of our simulation setup.

Neural Network Structure and Output Coding Strategies

The neuro-controllers in our simulations used up to eight input units, each deriving input from one robot sensor. The robot sensors (and hence the input units) provided a value of 0, 1, or -1 to the neuro-controller, in response to an empty cell, box, or wall respectively. While some experiments did not permit the use of hidden units, others allowed up to 10 hidden units to be used. These hidden units, when used, computed *bipolar threshold* functions, i.e., they produced an output of +1 when the net input activation was greater than zero and a -1 otherwise.

The networks used a *time-bounded* activity propagation mechanism, as detailed in [146]. Here, inputs were supplied to the network and the units in the network computed their activations in a near-synchronous fashion. The activations of the output units at the end of this step were then interpreted as the network response to the inputs. As will become clear later, *recurrent* neuro-controllers could contain arbitrary connections between units, including direct connections between input and output units, recurrent connections between units, etc., although recurrent connections between output and input units were not permitted. *Feed-forward* networks could have arbitrary connections between units so long as they were not recurrent connections.

The number of output units in the neuro-controller (along with their activation functions), were dictated by the *output coding strategy* used, i.e., the mechanism used to translate the neuro-controller outputs into robot actions. For instance, the *Left-Forward-Right* (LFR) output coding strategy requires the use of three output units, one corresponding to the left-turn action, one for forward moves, and one for right-turns. In the LFR scheme, the output units compute their input activations and then engage in a *winner-take-all* computation. This simply means that the unit with the largest activation is declared the winner and it produces an output of +1 while the remaining two units produce outputs of -1. The robot then performs the action associated with the unit that is the winner. This output coding strategy is shown in Table 5.1.

Table 5.1
Left-Forward-Right output coding strategy.

Unit L	Unit F	Unit R	Robot Action
+1	-1	-1	Turn Left
-1	+1	-1	Move Forward
-1	-1	+1	Turn Right

We have also experimented with other output coding schemes. These will be explained in section 5.5.

Multi-Level Variable Length Genetic Representation

The genetic representation used in our experiments was carefully designed to possess a number of properties listed in Section 1.7 (although this is not necessarily the most optimal genetic representation). As shown in Figure 5.2, our representation explicitly encodes the connectivity (or topology) of the neuro-controller. Each *gene* in the representation corresponds to the input connectivity of a hidden or output unit. This gene (or input connectivity) itself corresponds to a number of *connections* between units. For instance, the gene corresponding to hidden unit 0 in Figure 5.2 contains three connections, while the gene corresponding to output unit F contains six connections (the LFR output coding strategy being used in this case). Each connection is specified as a 3-tuple represented by: (LayerID, UnitNo, Weight). Here LayerID is I, H, O, or B corresponding to input, hidden, or output layers, with B denoting the bias (threshold) of the unit. UnitNo identifies the specific unit in LayerID which serves as the *source* of that connection and Weight, an integer in [-100, +100], denotes the strength of the connection.

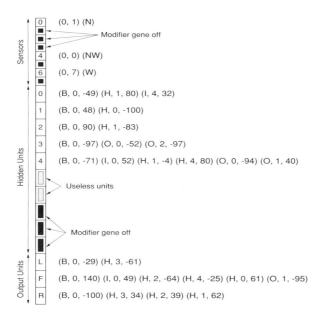

Figure 5.2
Genetic representation uses multi-level modifier genes and variable length chromosomes.

For instance, hidden unit 0 has a bias value of -49, a *recurrent* connection from hidden unit 1 of strength 80, and a connection from input unit 4 with a weight of 32. In our experiments, we have restricted the number of connections to any single unit (also called the *fan-in* of the unit) to a maximum of 10.

In addition to the input connectivities of the neuro-controller units, the genetic representation also supports the evolution of robot sensors. Each such sensor gene encodes the *position* of the corresponding robot sensor. Note that this representation implicitly allows the evolution of not only the placement of the robot sensor but also the tuning of its range. For instance, if a sensor is placed to sense a cell two units away, its range is automatically tuned to two units.

Figure 5.2 shows the genetic encoding of three sensors. While sensor numbered 0 is placed to sense the cell immediately ahead of the robot, sensor 4 observes the cell forward and to the left, and sensor 6 senses the cell to the left of the robot. For convenience, we will label sensors based on the cells they observe when the robot *faces north*. Thus, a sensor that observes the cell immediately ahead of the robot is labeled *N*, while the sensor observing the cell to the left of the north-facing robot is labeled *W*. It should be noted that even though the genetic representation in Figure 5.2 has a W sensor, it is effectively useless as none of the neuro-controller units derive input from it.

Our genetic representation also assumes the existence of *second-level* or *modifier genes* which control the *expression* of entire sequences of other genes [155]. In our representation, these modifier genes control the expression of hidden units and robot sensors. For instance, in Figure 5.2 only the modifier genes corresponding to sensors 0, 4, and 6 are ON. The rest of the genes are OFF, as shown by the black squares in the corresponding gene positions. Thus, the robot using this neuro-controller has access to only three sensors. Similarly, although 10 hidden units are allowed, the representation suggests that only seven of them are expressed. Further, only five of these seven hidden units are actively used, with the other two (shown in grey), not being connected to either the inputs or the outputs (and hence being useless). The neuro-controller (phenotype) that corresponds to this genetic representation, is shown in Figure 5.15.

As can be observed, modifier genes allow evolution to easily manipulate the size of the evolved neuro-controller or the number of sensors at the robot's disposal, thereby entertaining the possibility of discovering *minimal* (or opti-mal) designs.

Properties of this Genetic Representation

The genetic representation we have chosen to use in our experiments has a number of properties described in Section 1.7. It easily supports the evolution of both feed-forward and recurrent neuro-controllers and hence can be used equally well in temporal and non-temporal domains. However, each weight in our network is restricted to be an integer in [-100, 100]. It would appear that networks with *arbitrary* weights between units cannot evolve in our system.

However, as our representation allows *multiple connections* between units, arbitrarily large weights between units can be easily realized via appropriate combinations of multiple connections. This endows our representation with the important property of *completeness*.

The same genotype in our representation can be decoded into a feed-forward or a recurrent network by simply changing the decoding mechanism to disable or enable the expression of recurrent connections. Similarly, the expression of hidden units, recurrent links, etc., can also be controlled during decoding by altering the expression of modifier genes. Thus, multiple phenotypes *can* result from the same genotype, which leads to the property of *phenotypic multiplicity*. Also, since the order of the connections in a given gene (input connectivity of a hidden or output unit) does not matter, the exact same neuro-controller can be encoded using multiple genotypes. Thus, our representation exhibits *genotypic multiplicity*, with *different* genotypes decoding to the same phenotype.

We have also mentioned that in our genetic representation a given unit (target) can have multiple connections from another unit (source). This allows multiple links between two units. This feature corresponds to *genotypic redundancy* as well as *phenotypic redundancy*. Genotypic redundancy allows the system to maintain backup copies of good genes, which is of considerable value if the genetic operators are disruptive and/or the decoding process is error prone (e.g., it does not read entire gene sequences, etc.). Phenotypic redundancy is a useful feature in scenarios where phenotypic components fail. For instance, if our robots operate in hazardous environments that cause neuro-controller links and units to fail, phenotypic redundancy can compensate for such effects through robust and fault-tolerant designs that make use of multiple identical units and links.

Since our representation supports genotypic multiplicity (multiple genotypes decode to the same phenotype), we can easily bias our evolutionary system to preferentially choose *compact representations*. As described in Section 1.7, notions of *topological* as well as *functional compactness* can be incorporated in our system by appropriately defining *cost-functions* to characterize compactness. One such approach is presented in [146].

As can be seen, the genetic representation used in our experiments possesses a number of interesting properties that make it suitable for the evolution of neuro-controllers for the box-pushing robot task.

Miscellaneous Details

Our simulations used populations of size 500 and the evolutionary runs lasted 100 generations. We used *binary tournament selection* to choose parents for mating in each step [157]. Our experiments made use of two genetic operators: crossover and mutation. We used *uniform crossover* with the probability of crossover set at 0.5. In uniform crossover each gene in the offspring has a uniform chance of coming from either of its parents [176]. This requires a random coin-toss at each of the gene positions to determine the parent the offspring inherits that particular gene from.

In our implementation, crossover respected gene boundaries, i.e., off-springs inherited entire genes *intact* from their parents (subject to muta-tion). Since genes in our representation encoded input connectivities of neuro-controller units or positions of sensors, crossover had the effect of producing offspring with a mix of units and sensors available in the parents. Mutation, on the other hand, operated within genes. Each neuro-controller unit and robot sensor was mutated with probability 0.1. Further, once a unit (or sensor) was chosen for mutation, either the modifier gene bit was flipped with probabil-ity 0.1 or the gene (input connectivity or sensor position) was mutated. For neuro-controller units, mutation involved a random modification of either the LayerID, UnitNo, or the Weight of one randomly chosen connection. For sen-sors, this gene mutation resulted in a random change of the sensor position.

As with the experiments of Teller, each individual in the population (a neuro-controller for a robot) was evaluated in 40 random box-pushing envi-ronments and its average performance was used as a measure of fitness for se-lection. In each experiment, we performed 50 evolutionary runs, each starting with a different random seed. This was done to ensure statistical significance of the results obtained. Further, in order to directly compare the fitnesses of the different neuro-controllers, we computed *standardized* fitnesses for each of them. This was done by evaluating the performance of the neuro-controller over a fixed set of 1000 box-pushing environments. Unless otherwise men-tioned, the fitnesses reported in the following experiments refer to the stan-dardized fitnesses.

5.4   Evolving Neuro-Controllers for Box-Pushing Behaviors

In this section we present results of experiments in the evolutionary synthesis of neural network controllers for the box-pushing robot task described earlier.

Evolution of Improved Behaviors

Figure 5.3 shows the improvement in box-pushing performance in the course of one evolutionary run. This experiment involved the evolution of recurrent networks with no hidden units and three output units (the LFR output coding strategy was used). Note that the plot appears smooth because we have shown the best, average, and worst fitness in the population every ten generations rather than at every generation.

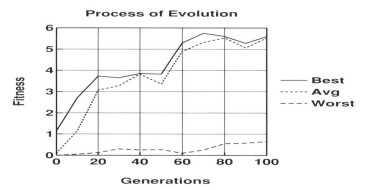

Figure 5.3
From initial populations consisting of highly unfit robot controllers, evolution produces better, fitter controllers.

It can be easily observed that the networks in the initial population (Generation 0) are highly unfit, i.e., they lead to poor box-pushing performance. This is to be expected given that initial populations are *randomly* created. Most robots endowed with these networks either keep spinning in the same position or attempt to move into walls. As a result, the best network in the initial population has a fitness of 1.2 and the population, an average fitness of 0.15.

From this modest beginning, the fitnesses can be seen to improve over generations, with the best network in generation 100 having a fitness (non-standardized) of 5.6 and the population an average fitness of 5.5. Notice that the fitness of the worst member of the population remains consistently low (< 1) over the generations. This is due to the disruptive effects of the genetic operators which modify parts of the network crucial to the survival of the robot.

The networks of generation 100 demonstrate effective navigation behaviors, particularly when compared to the primitive capabilities of their ancestors. The robots in generation 100 address the box-pushing task well – they move about in their environment, avoid walls, and importantly, approach and push boxes. Thus, evolution discovers neuro-controller designs that give rise to effective box-pushing behaviors.

Evolving Feed-forward and Recurrent Networks

In our experiments, we evolved both feed-forward and recurrent neuro-controllers. As explained earlier, we conducted 50 complete evolutionary runs to present results of statistical significance. Figure 5.4 shows a comparison of the fitnesses of feed-forward and recurrent networks evolved without any hidden units. In this figure, AFF refers to the fitness of the best feed-forward network produced in each of the 50 evolutionary runs, averaged over the runs, while BFF denotes the fitness of the best feed-forward network discovered by evolution in the 50 runs. ARR and BRR denote similar fitness measures but for recurrent networks. These fitness values are *standardized*, i.e., they denote the fitness of the robot over a fixed set of 1000 box-pushing environments and hence are directly comparable.

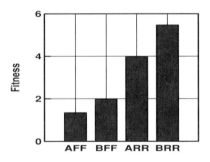

Figure 5.4
Performance of feed-forward and recurrent neuro-controllers. Recurrent networks possess limited-depth memory, and hence do well on the task while feed-forward networks perform rather poorly.

From Figure 5.4 one can observe that the fitness of the best feed-forward networks, averaged over the 50 evolutionary runs and denoted by AFF, was approximately 1.65, while the best feed-forward network discovered by evolution (denoted by BFF) had a fitness of 2.0. On the other hand, the average of the fitnesses of the best recurrent networks evolved (ARR) was approximately

4.0, with the best recurrent network (BRR) having a fitness of 5.46. Some of these recurrent neuro-controllers thus have considerably higher fitnesses than the control programs evolved by [177].

One can also observe that the recurrent networks are over twice as effective as feed-forward ones. This is largely due to the differences in the abilities of feed-forward and recurrent networks. While feed-forward networks are constrained to make action choices based *solely* on current sensory inputs, recurrent networks can additionally exploit their *memory* of the actions undertaken by the robot in the recent past.

This ability to make use of information from the past (albeit recent past) is critical because the networks used in our experiments are *deterministic*, i.e., they always produce the same action in response to a given input. In such cases, if the sensory inputs available at a given place trigger a robot action but the robot action fails, then the robot remains at the same location indefinitely. This is because the sensory inputs remain the same at subsequent time steps (since the robot does not move) and the deterministic controller produces the same action, which keeps failing. This leads to a *permanently* stuck robot. This might happen, for instance, if the robot wanted to push a box and the box happened to be against a wall or another box. This would lead to failed actions and a permanently stuck robot. *All* the feed-forward networks in this experiment suffered from this affliction.

When faced with a similar situation, an appropriately designed recurrent network can exploit its knowledge of the action taken by the robot in the previous step to determine the action to perform. For instance, as we will explain in the following section, a recurrent network could make the robot turn if had moved forward in the previous step, thereby preventing it from getting permanently stuck.

Effective Box-Pushing Behaviors

We have shown earlier that the fitness of the neuro-controllers is rather low in the initial populations but then improves considerably as evolution progresses. We also showed that recurrent networks have much higher fitnesses than their feed-forward counterparts. Why are the robots in the initial populations less fit and why is it that recurrent networks outperform feed-forward ones? What behavior must the robot possess to do well in this box-pushing environment?

Since one of the constraints of the box-pushing task is the inability of the robot to detect failed moves, the robots often get into situations where they remain stuck till the end of simulation. For instance the robot might keep spinning in the same place, try to move into a wall, attempt to push two or more boxes simultaneously, etc. What, then, would be the most effective strategy under such circumstances? Obviously, the key is to avoid getting stuck. Since repeated actions of the same kind (e.g., turning in place or continually moving forward and eventually into the wall), lead the robot to stuck states, they must somehow be avoided. One way of doing this would be for the robot to remember its previous action and choose to perform an action that is different from it. For instance, if the robot moved forward in the previous time step, it should be inclined to turn now.

A careful analysis of the structure of the recurrent networks produced in our evolutionary experiments indicates that over generations these networks develop structures that permit them to do just that. These networks evolve a *strong negative self-loop* at the output unit that codes for forward moves (unit F), as shown in Figure 5.5 (unit F has a recurrent link with weight -81).

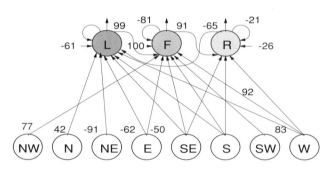

Figure 5.5
The best recurrent (RR) neuro-controller (without any hidden units) that was discovered by evolution. A strong negative self-loop at the forward move (F) unit makes the robot *alternate* move and turn actions.

Such structures force the robot to *interleave* or *alternate* forward moves with turns. Thus, if the current action of the network is to move forward the output of the *F* unit is a 1. The strong negative self-loop at the *F* unit automatically *biases* the robot towards a turn action at the next time step. Of course, strong sensory inputs can override this automatic bias, still, it provides an effective safeguard mechanism against getting into states in which it might be stuck forever. Feed-forward networks cannot exploit this feature since self-loops of this sort qualify as recurrent links. Consequently, these networks perform poorly in comparison.

This observation is further reiterated by Figure 5.6, which shows a typical plot of the actions performed by the robot in the course of one simulation run.

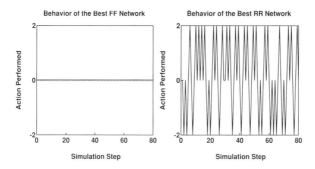

Figure 5.6
Actions performed by the robots using the best feed-forward (FF) and recurrent (RR) neuro-controllers discovered by evolution. Here, 0, 2, and -2 represent forward moves, right turns, and left turns respectively. The robot behavior on the right was produced by the recurrent neuro-controller shown in Figure 5.5.

The ordinate axis in these figures codes for the action performed by the robot, with 0 representing forward moves and 2 and -2 denoting right and left turns respectively. The figure on the left shows the behavior of the robot with the best feed-forward network evolved. The relatively poor fitness of the robot is a direct consequence of its inability to change actions, in this particular case, its inability to determine when the box it was pushing actually came against a wall. As a result, the robot continues (at least tries to) move ahead with the box little realizing that it is in fact against the wall. It remains stuck in this state till the end of simulation, obtaining a fitness of merely 1.

The figure on the right shows the behavior of the robot with the best recurrent network found (shown in Figure 5.5). This network frequently switches actions, interleaving motions of moving forward and turning. It does not choose one box and push it all the way to the side, rather, it pushes many different boxes by steps. This behavior reduces its chances of getting stuck indefinitely, thereby contributing to its higher fitness. This neuro-controller obtains a fitness of 6 in the same environment.

A few other observations can be made about the neuro-controller shown in Figure 5.5. Notice that the bias (or thresholds) of the L and R units are negative values while that of the F unit is a large positive value. Thus, in the absence of any sensory input this robot moves forward first. We have already pointed out the strong negative self-loop at the F unit that biases the robot to interleave moves and turns. In addition to this feature, this neuro-controller also has other mechanisms that produce a move-turn behavior. Consider the large weight (99) between units L and F. This attempts to equalize the number of moves and left turns. For instance, if the robot did not turn left, the output of the L unit is a -1. This lowers the chances of the robot choosing to move forward at the next time step. Conversely, if the robot turned left, the output of the L unit is a +1. This, in conjunction with the large weight between the L and F units, biases the robot to move forward at the next time step. A similar role is played by the link between F and R units, which has a weight of 91. These different features together endow the robot with a characteristic move-turn behavior.

Let us now consider the effect of the right sensor (E). If it detects a box (sensor value of 1), it provides negative input values to L and F units, thereby biasing the robot to chose R as the winner. The robot thus turns towards the box. Equivalently, when the E sensor detects a wall to the right of the robot (sensor value of -1), the L and F units receive positive activations. In this case the robot either turns left, away from the wall, or moves forward along the wall. In a similar fashion, the left sensor (W) allows the robot to turns towards boxes and avoid walls. Such features prevent the robot from wasting valuable time bumping into walls.

Perhaps the most interesting feature of the evolved network is its response to a box immediately ahead (N sensor detects a +1). Since the objective of the task is to push boxes to the walls, one might expect the robot to respond to such a sensory input with a forward move. However, a closer inspection of the network suggests that such a box has little or no effect on the action choices made by the robot. Although this is a little counter-intuitive, it makes sense when we realize that any commitment on the part of the neuro-controller to sense and push boxes immediately ahead of the robot has the potential to lead to a permanently stuck robot, as explained earlier. Further, since the task constraints do not require the robot to sense a box in order to push it (if the robot moves forward and there is a box in front of it, the box is automatically pushed unless, of course, the box is against a wall or another box), there is no need to really sense and respond to boxes immediately ahead. This is precisely what is achieved by the neuro-controller shown in Figure 5.5. It does not respond directly to boxes appearing in front of the robot. Instead, it uses its left and right sensors to turn towards boxes, and relies on its move-turn behavior to automatically push boxes.

We have carefully analyzed the different neuro-controllers evolved in the various simulation runs. In each case we have found that the best network *functionally* resembles that shown in Figure 5.5. Analysis of this kind has helped us identify not only the kinds of behaviors that lead to high-fitness box-pushing behaviors, but also the roles played by the different network components in realizing such behaviors.

Using a simple experiment we can further demonstrate that recurrent links in these evolved networks play a crucial role in the box-pushing performance of the robots. We take the best recurrent network produced in each of the 50 evolutionary runs, and determine its standardized fitness *with* and *without* the recurrent links, as shown in Figure 5.7.

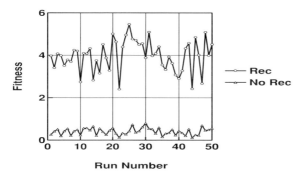

Figure 5.7
The importance of recurrent links can be demonstrated by comparing the fitnesses of the best robots with and without their recurrent links. Removal of the recurrent links can be seen to drastically reduce robot fitness.

Since these fitnesses are standardized (the robots are evaluated on the same set of box-pushing environments), any change in fitness is a direct result of the change in the neuro-controller (e.g., presence or absence of recurrent links) and is devoid of other random or environmental influences. It can be observed that the fitness of the neuro-controller drops significantly when the recurrent links are removed. For instance, run 25 produced a network with fitness 5.46 (shown in Figure 5.5). Without its recurrent links the fitness of this network drops to a mere 0.42. Recurrent links are thus critical to the effective box-pushing performance of these neuro-controllers.

Using Hidden Units in Box-Pushing Behaviors

Although evolution discovers recurrent and feed-forward neuro-controllers that endow robots with the ability to move, approach and push boxes, and avoid walls, the recurrent networks manage higher fitnesses than their feed-forward counterparts by evolving an intuitively appealing strategy that involves the use of recurrent links to remember past actions. However, even with recurrence, the robot's memory is only *one* time-step long, i.e., the robot remembers the action performed in the previous time step and nothing more. It is natural to wonder if a robot with a longer memory will perform better, since in that case, its decision can be expected to benefit from its history of past input activations and output actions. This motivates us to explore networks with hidden units, since in our model of neural computation, a network with two hidden layers can remember network activations two time steps earlier.

In order to study the effect of hidden units in the evolution of box-pushing behaviors, we allowed evolution to choose up to 10 hidden units. As explained in Section 5.3, the genetic representation used in our simulations allowed arbitrary connections to be formed between units. However, the *fan-in* or the input connectivity of any unit was restricted to a maximum of 10, as explained earlier. In feed-forward networks, connections between input-output, input-hidden, and hidden-output units were permitted. However, the connectivity between hidden layer units were constrained in such a manner as to allow lower numbered units to connect to higher numbered ones but not vice versa. Recurrent networks, on the other hand, could have connections between arbitrary pairs of units. In both kinds of networks, connections *into* input units were not allowed.

As can be observed from Figure 5.8, hidden units improve the performance of both kinds of networks. While the improvement is only marginal for recurrent networks, feed-forward networks benefit tremendously from the addition of hidden units. In fact, the average and best fitnesses of feed-forward networks almost double (a 100% improvement). Note that the best feed-forward network (BFF) evolved with hidden units has a fitness of almost 4.0, which is nearly equal to the average fitness of the best recurrent networks (ARR) without hidden units. It is clear that the hidden units somehow help the robots with feed-forward neuro-controllers, avoid or escape from situations where they used to get stuck earlier.

Just as we did with recurrent links earlier, we can perform a simple experiment to demonstrate the importance of hidden units. We simply take the

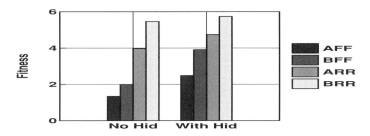

Figure 5.8
Robot fitnesses when hidden units are allowed in the neuro-controllers. Hidden units can be seen to significantly enhance the fitnesses of feed-forward networks.

best neuro-controller produced in each of the evolutionary runs and compute its fitness with and without its hidden units. Figure 5.9 shows the result of this experiment for the feed-forward neuro-controllers. It can be observed that in every case the fitness decreases alarmingly when the hidden units are disabled. Feed-forward networks thus appear to rely heavily on the hidden units.

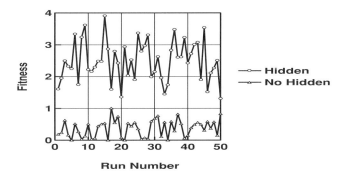

Figure 5.9
Performance of the best feed-forward neuro-controllers from each of the evolutionary runs, with and without hidden units.

A similar experiment performed on the evolved recurrent neuro-controllers suggests that these networks too use hidden units when they are available. However, though disabling hidden units results in a marked decrease in the fitness of these networks, they are not as badly impacted as feed-forward ones. These results suggest that recurrent networks perform well on the box-pushing task by making use of recurrence or hidden units, depending on what is available. When hidden units are not available, evolution relies on recurrence. However, when hidden units are available, the tendency of evolution is to exploit them to attain higher fitnesses.

Figure 5.10 shows the behavior of the best feed-forward network evolved with hidden units, on *one* box-pushing environment. Unlike feed-forward networks evolved earlier (Figure 5.6), this neuro-controller can be observed to switch effectively between forward moves and turns. In particular, one can easily notice that this robot either moves forward or turns right. It should also be noted that unlike the recurrent networks shown earlier, this robot does not necessarily *alternate* actions. For instance, between simulation steps 6 and 9, the robot moves forward on *four* consecutive time steps before turning right. It displays this behavior many times during the course of its box-pushing exercise, as can be confirmed from Figure 5.10. This ability to turn after moving forward on consecutive time steps, allows the robot to escape from states where it might be stuck indefinitely, thereby attining higher fitnesses. Feed-forward neuro-controllers evolved in other simulation runs possess similar behaviors.

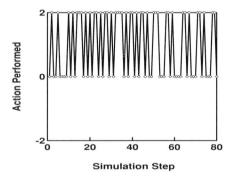

Figure 5.10
Behavior of the best feed-forward network with hidden units, that was discovered by evolution. Here 0, 2, and -2 represent forward moves, right turns, and left turns respectively.

Figure 5.11 shows the best feed-forward network (with hidden units), that was discovered by evolution. It may be noted that though the evolved neuro-controller has 7 hidden units, only three of them are in *active* use. From the thresholds of the three output units and the three hidden units, one can infer that in the absence of other sensory inputs the robot is biased towards forward moves. This is because the activation at the output unit corresponding to forward moves, F, is given by 127 (62+14+51), which is significantly greater than the activations at the other two output units. It can also be noticed that a box detected by the N sensor biases the robot towards a forward move by suppressing left and right turns (through weights of -32 and -62 respectively), while a box detected by the SE sensor biases the robot towards a right turn by increasing the activation of the R unit (through a weight of 91).

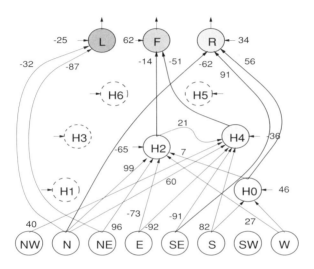

Figure 5.11
The best feed-forward network with hidden units, discovered by evolution. Although this network has seven hidden units, it effectively uses only three.

   The hidden units H0, H2, and H4 play a critical role in preventing the robot from pushing a box too long. This is achieved as follows. Suppose the units in the network are at their default activations dictated by their thresholds. Hence, H0=+1, H2=-1, H4=-1, L=-25, F=127 (62+14+51), and R=90 (34+56). Since the output unit F has the highest activation, the robot moves forward. Suppose the robot now finds a box immediately ahead and there are no other boxes or walls within its sensory range. This box is detected by the sensor N, which provides an input of +1 at the next step. It can be easily verified that this causes the following activations in the network units: H0=+1, H2=+1, H4=+1, L=-57, F=127, and R=28. Hence the robot moves forward again, possibly pushing the box (if it is not against another box or wall).

At the next time step, assuming the robot does not sense any additional boxes or walls, the changed activations of H2 and H4 cause the output activations to become: L=-57, F=-3 (62-14-51), and R=28 (34-62+56). Now the unit R is declared the winner and the robot turns right.

Thus, hidden units enable the feed-forward neuro-controllers to remember previous sensory *inputs* (although they still cannot remember past actions owing to the unavailability of recurrent links). With such hidden units the networks can choose wise actions by taking past observations into account. For instance, in the above example, the hidden units H2 and H4 record the fact that the robot has sensed a box ahead (N=1), by changing their activations from -1 to +1. The robot is then offered one chance to push the detected box, after which it is made to turn. Once the robot turns away from the box, the activations of these two hidden units return to -1.

When we analyzed the feed-forward neuro-controller designs discovered by evolution, we found a similar *switching* mechanism in place in each. The evolved networks used the hidden units to implement a *trigger* mechanism to prevent them from getting stuck pushing boxes. The evolved trigger mechanisms varied from pushing the box once and then turning, to pushing the box by up to 5 steps and then turning. It is evident that without the benefit of such trigger mechanisms, the feed-forward neuro-controllers would result in poor box-pushing performance.

5.5 Discussion

These different experiments in the evolution of neuro-controllers for box-pushing robots have not only helped us conclude that *memory* of past actions and activations is critical, but also show precisely how the evolved networks use this memory (either through recurrent links or hidden units) to produce effective box-pushing behaviors. It must be pointed out that though Teller recognized that memory might be important in the box-pushing task, he was unable to analyze the programs to decipher agent behaviors or explain how memory was used by his evolved agents [177].

Our experiments have revealed that robots with recurrent networks attain high fitnesses by interleaving actions of moving forward and turning. We also showed that such behaviors arise through the use of hidden units, which remember and exploit past input activations. However, are such behaviors truly characteristic of the constraints of the box-pushing task, or merely artifacts

Table 5.2
Braitenberg (BR) and Action-Direction (AD) output coding strategies.

Unit L	Unit R	Braitenberg Strategy	Action-Direction Strategy
-1	-1	Move Forward	Turn Right
-1	+1	Turn Left	Turn Left
+1	-1	Turn Right	Move Forward
+1	+1	Move Forward	Move Forward

of the neuro-controller structure (e.g., the LFR output coding mechanism). Further, is an evolutionary approach really necessary to design good box-pushing behaviors? We discuss these questions in the following sections.

Generality of Box-Pushing Behaviors

One way to absolve the output coding strategy from the primary role in the evolved behaviors is to evolve robots with *different* output coding mechanisms, analyze the resulting behaviors, and show that the behaviors are qualitatively similar. In order to do this, we repeated the evolutionary experiments described above, with two other output interpretations.

In the Braitenberg strategy [150], the neuro-controller uses two output units computing bipolar-threshold functions. The two output units are considered to be directly connected to the two wheels of the robot (assuming the robot has one wheel on either side). In this scheme, if an output unit produces a +1, the corresponding wheel turns in the forward direction and vice-versa. Appropriate combinations of the two wheels then lead to forward and backward moves, and to left and right turns.

The second strategy, called *Action-Direction* (AD), makes use of two output units that compute bipolar-threshold functions. The output of the first unit is interpreted as the *action* to be performed (+1 to move forward and -1 to turn) while the second unit indicates the direction of *turn* (+1 to turn left and -1 to turn right). These schemes are illustrated in Table 5.2.

As shown in Figure 5.12, there is little difference between the robot fitnesses using the three schemes. A careful analysis of the structures evolved using Braitenberg and Action-Direction output coding strategies confirms our earlier observation that high fitnesses on the box-pushing task are realized by interleaving or alternating forward moves and turns. The networks using the Braitenberg strategy evolve *large recurrent links* at the two output units. While one link is *positive*, the other is *negative*. Thus, the output of one unit is biased towards remaining constant, while the output of the other unit is biased to change at every time step. In the Braitenberg strategy this leads to alternating moves and turns.

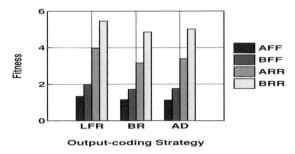

Figure 5.12
Performance of the robots with different output coding strategies.

The neuro-controllers using the Action-Direction strategy consistently evolve a large *negative* recurrent link at the output unit coding for action. This mechanism makes the robot alternate between moves and turns at each time step. A number of results with the Action-Direction output coding strategy are presented in [147, 148, 149].

It thus appears that the behavior of interleaving moves and turns is characteristic of the task environment and is consistently discovered by evolution irrespective of the output coding mechanism used.

These results lead us to believe that evolution automatically comes up with ways to effectively counter the constraints and limitations of the task environment. Given the box-pushing task and its associated constraints, evolution uses the neuro-controller structures at its disposal to sculpt behaviors that involve alternating moves and turns.

Baseline Experiments: Random Walk and Random Search

When we presented the box-pushing task, we argued that it was a challenging environment that made the design of appropriate behaviors rather hard. One might be tempted to ask for some quantitative measure of the *difficulty* of achieving good fitnesses on this task. Although we cannot provide a generic measure, we can show that the box-pushing task cannot be effectively addressed by simple behaviors like a *random walk*. We can easily demonstrate this by conducting simulations where the robots randomly choose an action to perform at each step.

We have also alluded to the fact that evolution is capable of effectively searching vast, multimodal, and complex search spaces, using little domain-specific knowledge. But can we show that the space of neuro-controllers for this box-pushing task is indeed vast and complex? Can we show that other algorithms for searching this neuro-controller space will indeed falter? Although we cannot really *prove* that other search algorithms will fail to effectively search the neuro-controller space, we can show that *simple* search algorithms like exhaustive or random search, will be inefficient.

First, let us consider the size of the search space. Assuming that the neuro-controllers do not have any hidden units, the search procedure must determine appropriate connectivities for the three output units (assuming an LFR output coding scheme). Since there are eight input units, three output units, and a threshold for each unit, the search algorithm must determine $(8+3+1 = 12)$ parameters for each of the output units. Now, since the weights are restricted to be integers in the range [-100, +100], there are 201 possible values for each weight. Thus, the *total size* of the neuro-controller space, i.e., the space of possible values for the weights of the three output units, is $(201)^{36}$, which is a truly large quantity. Remember that this figure is for a neural network without any hidden units. Adding hidden units leads to an exponential increase in the size of the search space. This vast space plays havoc with simple search algorithms. While an exhaustive search of this space is *infeasible* and *impractical*, random search is confronted with a *needle-in-a-haystack* situation. Thus, simple search algorithms like exhaustive and random search are unsuitable for searching the space of neuro-controllers for the box-pushing task.

Figure 5.13 compares the fitnesses of neuro-controllers produced by evolution with two *baseline* experiments. The first involves the average fitness of a random walking robot (RW) and the second is a random search of the space of neuro-controllers. As can be seen, random walk results in extremely poor performance in this environment, with the average random walk (over 10,000 such environments), producing a fitness of a mere 1.0 point and the best random walk producing a fitness of approximately 1.6.

Figure 5.13 also shows the best and average fitnesses of 10,000 randomly created neuro-controllers. As can be observed, this random search yields a best fitness of 4.2 and an average fitness less than 1.0. In contrast, the evolutionary approach produces individuals of fitness over 4.5 within 20 generations (i.e.,

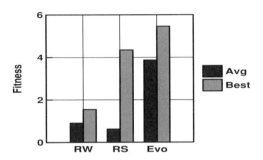

Figure 5.13
Baseline experiments to compare random walk, random search, and evolutionary search.

total evaluation of $500 \times 20 = 10,000$ neuro-controllers). Thus, with the same effort (measured in terms of the number of neuro-controllers evaluated), evolutionary search finds better neuro-controllers than random search.

Further, when continued to 100 generations, the evolutionary approach produces neuro-controllers with a best fitness of 5.46 with *all* the neuro-controllers produced (and evaluated) yielding an average fitness of approximately 3.9. Thus, searching the neuro-controller space using population-based evolutionary algorithms has a higher likelihood of discovering highly fit designs (on an average).

One of the factors that make the box-pushing task hard is that the boxes in the room are randomly placed for each trial. Also, the robot does not start from a single fixed position in the room, rather, it starts from randomly chosen places. This makes the task particularly hard because the robot has to develop behaviors that work well across all the random environments. What would happen if the robot always found the boxes in the same locations every time? In addition, if the robot were to be introduced into the room at the same place in every trial, would evolution produce robot behaviors of higher fitnesses? It should be noted that with the box positions fixed and the robot starting at the same location every time, the box-pushing task acquires the same flavor as that of *trail-following* or *maze-running* tasks.

Figure 5.14 shows the results of such a modified experiment. TR1 refers to the *trail-like* box-pushing task (with box and robot start positions fixed across trials). In this case the robots used feed-forward neuro-controllers without any hidden units. As can be seen, the best feed-forward neuro-controller attains a fitness of 4.0 on this task, which is twice the fitness of the best feed-forward neuro-controller evolved for the regular box-pushing task (Section 5.4). When hidden units are permitted, evolution discovers feed-forward networks with an average fitness of 8.2 and a peak fitness of 9.0, as shown by TR2 in Figure 5.14. Contrast this with the average and peak fitnesses of 2.6 and 3.9 achieved by feed-forward neuro-controllers on the regular box-pushing task. TR3 shows the fitnesses of recurrent networks *without* any hidden units. While the average fitness of these networks is 8.2, the best recurrent network produced by evolution has a fitness of 10, which is the maximum fitness attainable in this box-pushing environment. Thus, evolution discovers neuro-controllers with optimal behavior in the modified, trail-like environment.

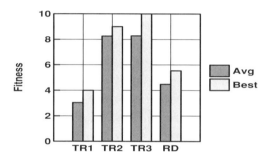

Figure 5.14
Comparison of trail-like behaviors (TR1, TR2, and TR3), with regular box-pushing behaviors (RD).

Contrast these results with the best fitnesses observed in the regular box-pushing environment (where the box positions and the robot start locations are randomly chosen). The label RD in Figure 5.14 shows the average and peak fitnesses of the recurrent networks discovered by evolution. It can be observed that the peak fitness of 5.46 is much lesser than the maximum attainable fitness of 10.

Thus, by relaxing some constraints, the regular box-pushing task can be transformed into a trail-following one. Given the fact that evolution appears perfectly capable of discovering designs (and behaviors) of maximum fitness in trail-following environments, its failure to do so in the regular box-pushing environment may be construed as an indication of the inherent difficulty of the box-pushing task.

These results show that it is rather difficult to determine good box-pushing behaviors in general. They also demonstrate the ability of artificial evolution to efficiently and effectively search the space of neuro-controller designs.

5.6 Sensor Evolution

Although our experiments in the evolutionary synthesis of neuro-controllers for box-pushing behaviors were quite successful, the question remains whether the box-pushing task really requires the eight sensors that Teller had stipulated or could it be equally well-addressed using fewer sensors. This question is motivated by the fact that real sensors on real robots have acquisitional and operational costs associated with them, and one would want to use the minimum number necessary for the task. This consideration forces us to recognize a tradeoff between performance on the task and the incidental cost of providing and operating extra sensors. For instance, we might be willing to tolerate a certain amount of *decrease* in box-pushing performance provided the designs offer significant savings in sensor costs, and vice-versa. But the question then is "How can we determine the *best* number, placement, and kind of sensors required for a given task?" Or alternatively, "How can we decide which sensors to use from the set of sensors at the disposal of a robot?"

The wide variety of sensory systems represented in nature is suggestive of the power of evolution in determining good designs over many dimensions including — sensors of different *types* (e.g., vision, tactile, olfactory, etc.), *characteristics* (e.g., range, sampling frequency, response function, etc.), *numbers* (e.g., two eyes, one nose, etc.), *placement* (e.g., front, rear, top, etc.), and modes of *sensory information integration* (e.g., through the use of appropriate neural circuits for reactive behaviors, cognitive behaviors, etc.). Given the role evolution seems to have played in developing organisms with varied behaviors realized through the *combined* or *co-evolved* design of sensory and neural information processing systems, it only seems natural to presume that the field of robotics, or any enterprise that aims to produce autonomous agents of a certain behavioral repertoire, would benefit from similar co-evolutionary design considerations.

Since evolutionary techniques are already being used quite successfully in the design of neuro-controllers for robots, we would like to explore the use of evolution in the design of sensory systems as well [148]. By evolving the sensory system of these robots along with the neuro-controllers, we expect evolution to not only determine efficient sensory system designs but also develop effective behaviors tailored to these sensory characteristics.

Results in Sensor Evolution

In the following experiments, we allow evolution to determine the number, placement, and range of the robot sensors. As explained in Section 5.3, the genetic representation used in our work contains a gene for each allowable robot sensor. Each gene encodes the placement and range of the corresponding sensor. In addition, the second-level or modifier genes used in our representation allow mutation to turn off (or discard) sensors. Given these features, the designs that evolve may be expected to have sensors that are of *adaptive value* to the box-pushing robots and that allow the robot to sense in *critical* directions around themselves.

As in our earlier experiments, we used populations of size 500 and the evolutionary runs lasted 100 generations. In order to make statistically meaningful interpretations, we performed 50 evolutionary runs, each starting with a different random seed. Further, based on our earlier results, we only evolved recurrent neuro-controllers with up to 10 hidden units. Since the sensors in Teller's experiments could only sense cells immediately around the robot, we set the maximum range of our sensors to 1 cell.

Our results indicate that the average fitness of the best neuro-controllers discovered in the 50 evolutionary runs is 4.63, while the best neuro-controller has a fitness of 6.32. Further, this neuro-controller only employs *three* sensors, as shown in Figure 5.15. Not only does this robot use 62.5% fewer sensors than the number allowed ($\frac{8-3}{8}$) but also its fitness is 16% more ($\frac{6.32-5.46}{5.46}$) than the best neuro-controller with 8 sensors (Section 5.4). Although the neuro-controller in Figure 5.15 has three sensors and seven hidden units, it effectively uses only two sensors and five hidden units. It should also be noted that this robot uses its sensors to sense cells in the front, in particular, the cell immediately ahead (labeled N) and the cell diagonally to the left in front (labeled NW). Thus, there are no sensors that provide input from behind the robot.

It can be observed that owing to its strong positive bias (90), the hidden unit H2 always produces an output of 1. This changes the bias on units F and R to 76 and -61 respectively. Given these biases, it is clear that the robot is inclined to move forward in the absence of any sensory inputs. Further, the strong negative loop at the F unit (-95) makes the robot interleave moves

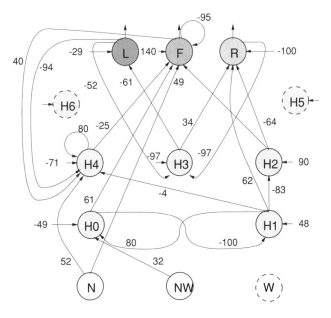

Figure 5.15
Best network with sensor evolution.

and turns. However, the hidden units lead to more complex dynamics. For instance, suppose the robot moved forward (F=1, L=R=-1) and encountered a wall immediately ahead. This causes the N and NW sensors to produce a -1 at the next time step, which leads to values of +1 and -1 at the hidden units H3 and H0 respectively. Now, the action performed by the robot depends on its past history, in particular on the activation of unit H1. If H1 happens to be in state +1, the output activation becomes: L = -29-61 = -90, F= 76-95-49 = -68, and R = -61+34+62=35, which makes the robot turn right. However, if H1 happens to be in state -1, the activation of the R unit becomes -61+34-62=-89, which makes the robot move forward. Although this causes the robot to bump into the wall, it can be easily verified that at the next time step H1 produces an output of +1 (since the output of H0 becomes a -1), making the robot turn right.

Our empirical results indicate that, on an average, the robots evolved in this study employ only 4.58 sensors out of the maximum possible 8. Further, the best designs found in *each* of the 50 evolutionary runs make use of fewer than 8 sensors, thereby suggesting that 8 sensors are possibly superfluous for this box-pushing task. As shown in the design in Figure 5.15, even two appropriately positioned sensors appear to be sufficient for successful box-pushing behaviors to emerge.

What is most noteworthy is that the sensors are automatically discarded *without* the imposition of any explicit penalty. For instance, we do not penalize robots that make use of their 8 sensors; nor do we favor robots that use fewer than 8 sensors. The only evolutionary pressure appears to be the effect of sensory information on robot behavior. We strongly suspect that having more numbers of sensors leads to *sensory inundation* and *conflict*, making the robot perform actions that are eventually *self-defeating*. Such conflicts possibly take the robot away from optimal behaviors. Our results indicate that this discarding of superfluous sensors also leads to an *increase* in robot fitness.

Given that eight sensors are not necessary for box-pushing behaviors, can we identify the sensor placements that indeed contribute to the robot fitness? Are certain sensor placements absolutely critical to robot performance? We can answer these questions by analyzing data from our 50 evolutionary runs and observing the distribution of sensors used by successful agents, as shown in Figure 5.16. As can be seen, 48.3% (almost half) of the sensors used by the evolved robots are placed so as to sense cells ahead of the robot (N, NE, and NW). Further, almost 75% of the sensors are used by the evolved robots to observe cells on the front (N, NE, and NW) and sides (E and W). Few sensors, if any, are tuned to the three cells behind the robots (S, SE, and SW).

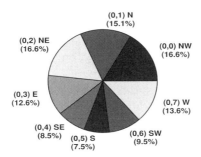

Figure 5.16
Distribution of sensors in the best robots produced in each of the evolutionary runs.

Thus, sensor evolution leads to effective designs that in *all* cases employ fewer than the maximum permissible 8 sensors. Further, the placement of sensors is largely biased towards the region ahead and to the sides of the robot, which makes intuitive sense since the robot cannot directly respond to sensors behind it. For instance, if the S sensor detects a box, the robot has to turn *twice* before it can get into a situation where it can push the box. Not surprisingly, evolution automatically veers away from such sensory system designs. Similar observations using two other output coding strategies are presented in [148], which also discusses the effect of increasing the range of the sensors.

It should be stressed that these designs are evolved without any explicit penalties or costs on the use of sensors. As we mentioned earlier, the only evolutionary pressure against the use of sensors appears to be the possibility of too much sensory information leading to conflicting behavioral choices. One might expect the designs to become more optimal if the sensors had real costs associated with them. We have explored one such approach wherein the robot has limited battery power and sensors require energy to operate. This leads to very interesting and minimalist designs [146].

At the concept level, the design of robot sensory systems is reminiscent of the *feature selection problem* in machine learning applications where a problem is associated with a number of features and the reasoning system, owing to a variety of performance related constraints, has to choose to use a subset of them in arriving at a solution. For instance, in our case, the robot is allowed to use many sensors, but the evolutionary design system chooses to use just a few that somehow translate into performance gains on the box-pushing task. Such evolutionary approaches are thus attractive options for the feature selection problem, as has also been demonstrated by [180].

5.7   Sensor Noise and Evolution of Fault-Tolerant Designs

Noise plays a very important role in robotics research largely because of the noise inherent in real-world environments and robot components. For example, visual sensory readings corresponding to the same object may be quite different at different times owing to a number of environmental effects like lighting, reflection, interference, occlusion, etc., or due to defects and malfunctions of the sensory apparatus. Similarly, robot actions are often sizable deviants of their intended ones, with factors like friction, improper tire-inflation, battery power, motor manufacturing defects, gradients, etc., causing marked changes from the expected trajectories of mobile robots. If robots are to be built to operate in such real-world environments, they must possess mechanisms for dealing reliably with such noises.

In our work, we are concerned with manifestations of noise in the system components. In particular, we would like to study the effects of noise caused by *faulty sensors*. These failures and malfunctions may be a result of factors intrinsic to the sensors (e.g., manufacturing defects, etc.), or they may be caused by environmental features like excessive concentration of radiation, corrosive substances, moisture, etc. Whatever might be the cause, we expect the robots to function reliably in the presence of such noise.

In general, sensor noise can be modeled in a number of ways. For instance, sensors could either *fail* and thereby not sense at all, or they might return sensory inputs corrupted by noise. This noise in sensing may be random white noise, or characterized by some probability distribution based on the properties of the operating domain. In addition, sensors may either fail completely, i.e., for the entire duration of simulation, or may simply be unoperational for a few time-steps of the trial. In our work, we assume that each sensor has a certain *a priori* probability of being faulty, where a fault is modeled by the sensor returning a value of 0 instead of what it currently senses. This is tantamount to saying that each sensor (with a pre-specified probability) confuses boxes and walls with empty spaces. The goal, then, is to design robot behaviors that are robust to the noise caused by such faulty sensors.

Our simulations were performed with a 10% probability of each sensor being faulty. Thus, at each time-step, each sensor *independently* determines (with probability 0.1), whether to provide a 0 or the sensed value to the neuro-controller. In these experiments, the robots could use up to 10 hidden units in their neuro-controllers and up to 8 different sensors. Evolution was allowed to co-design the neuro-controller and the sensory system of the box-pushing robot with the experimental details same as in the studies in Section 5.6.

When the sensors were assumed to be noisy, we found that evolution discovered robot designs that used 4.46 sensors on average. Of these, 24.7% of the sensors were placed to sense the cell immediately ahead of the robot (labeled N), as shown in Figure 5.17. When compared to the sensor evolution results without any sensor noise (Figure 5.16), it is apparent that a significantly larger fraction of sensors are now used to sense the cell immediately ahead of the robot.

Since 4.46 sensors were used (on an average) by the evolved robot designs, each evolved design has *at least* one sensor (actually 1.1 = 24.7% of 4.46) placed to sense the cell immediately ahead of the robot (labeled N). We also found that 28% of the evolved robots have *two or more* N sensors, while 8%

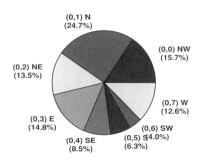

Figure 5.17
Distribution of sensors in robots evolved with sensor noise.

of the robots use three N sensors. Since the sensors are faulty, one may infer that evolution discovers robust designs that involve *duplication* of the faulty resource, namely sensors, in the critical sensing position in front of the robot. Thus, even if one sensor fails, the other functions with high probability, thereby allowing the robot to sense the cell in front of it. We have shown similar results with a different output coding strategy in [149].

In our experiments the average fitness of the evolved designs (over 50 evolutionary runs), was found to be 4.53 while the best evolved network had a fitness of 5.64. Further, the best evolved network made use of two N sensors, two NE sensors, and one E sensor.

Probably the most important observation in these experiments was the fact that though sensory noise hinders box-pushing performance, evolution discovers designs that are tailored to *use* this noise. For instance, one may suppose that the box-pushing performance of robots evolved in the presence of sensory noise will improve when the sensory noise is removed. However, empirical evidence suggests otherwise. Figure 5.18 shows the *difference* between the fitnesses of the best neuro-controller from each of the 50 evolutionary runs, evaluated on a set of random environments with and without sensory noise. A positive value for this difference represents a *decrease* in fitness with the removal of sensory noise, while a negative value represents an *increase* in fitness.

It can be easily observed that in many cases the removal of sensory noise leads to a marked decrease in robot fitness. On the other hand, though some designs show an increase in performance when sensory noise is removed, this improvement is not appreciable in most cases. A closer inspection of the evolved neuro-controllers reveals that evolution often discovers designs

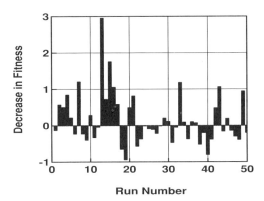

Figure 5.18
Decrease in fitness with the removal of sensory noise.

that *exploit* or benefit from the sensor faults. For example, most such designs utilize sensor faults to break away from their fixed-cycle paths, rather than recurrent links in their neuro-controllers. In many cases, we also found that the neuro-controllers had contradictory behaviors programmed within. For instance, one design made use of two N sensors placed to observe the cell immediately ahead of the robot. However, the two sensors biased the robot towards different behaviors. While one N sensor made the robot move forward towards a box, the other had an opposite effect. It biased the robot towards turning away from a box. Although seemingly contradictory in their effects, the two sensors worked well in tandem. When both sensors functioned correctly, the first sensor dominated the second one and the robot responded to boxes by moving towards them. However, in situations when the first sensor failed and the second was active, the robot responded to boxes by turning away from them. Careful thought reveals that unlike the use of recurrent links (which force the robot into alternating moves and turns), this design allows the robot to push a box multiple steps forward and to stop pushing the box when the first sensor fails momentarily. It is no surprise then that the removal of sensor noise causes a decrease in the fitness of these designs.

5.8   Related Work

As we mentioned earlier, evolutionary robotics is a rich and blossoming field. Here we present a sample of related work that compares and compounds the approach we have followed in this chapter.

Floreano and Mondada (1994) were perhaps the first to evolve a neural network controller for the Khepera robot [171]. They chose to evolve navigation and obstacle avoidance behaviors, using recurrent neuro-controllers with a fixed architecture containing 8 input and two output units. The output units computed sigmoid activation functions, and directly controlled the two stepper-motors associated with the robot wheels. Importantly, all their evaluations were performed on the robot, i.e., each member of each population was evaluated on the Khepera.

Miglino et al. (1994) evolved neuro-controllers for a *wandering* robot that effectively performed a variation of navigation and wall-avoidance tasks. The neuro-controllers contained two input units, two hidden units, one memory unit, and two output units. The units computed a threshold activation function. The binary output produced by the network was interpreted into four robot actions: forward/backward move, or left/right turn through 45 degrees. The researchers evolved effective exploration behaviors, analyzed them, and implemented the evolved behaviors on a Lego robot. However, they found considerable differences between robot behaviors in simulation and reality. They also found that by evolving designs for simulated robots that had *noisy* actions, the simulated and actual behaviors matched rather well.

In other related work, Miglino et al. (1995) evolved neural networks for obstacle avoidance behaviors. They used simple feed-forward neuro-controllers with 8 input units and two output units. Their simulations used a model of the Khepera robot, which has 8 infrared sensors and two stepper-motor driven wheels. Instead of performing their evolutionary experiments directly on the Khepera, they built a *simulation environment* by placing the Khepera at various positions and orientations in the real environment and recording its sensory inputs. They also built a *motor model* by executing specific motion commands on the Khepera and observing its displacements. This simulation model was then used to evolve robot behaviors in simulation.

Lund and Parisi (1995) attempted to study the effect of environmental changes in the behavioral inclinations of evolving agent populations for a foraging task. Agent behaviors were realized using a fixed neural network architecture containing 5 input, 9 hidden, and 2 output units. While two input units provided the distance and angle of the *nearest* food element, the other three units signaled the *type* (A, B, or C) of this food element. The two neuro-controller outputs were interpreted as a turn angle and forward move step size for the robot. Thus the robot could directly approach specific food elements.

By *co-evolving* the fitness function, the researchers discovered that the robots develop preferences for specific food types.

Walker (1995) studied a variation of a foraging task where the robots had to locate and approach *radiative* energy sources. These robots used extremely simple feed-forward networks with two input units and two output units. Each input unit provided the robot with a *measure* of the *energy field* (field strength of each energy source, normalized by its distance from the corresponding robot sensor). The two output units directly controlled the speed of the corresponding wheel of the robot. The researchers evolved behaviors for approaching energy sources, avoiding walls, etc.

It may be noted that most of these approaches involve relatively simple robot tasks (exploration, approach, avoidance, etc.). As we have argued earlier, such behaviors are often easy to program manually. In contrast, the constraints and limitations of the box-pushing task make it hard to manually develop effective behaviors. Secondly, some of these approaches assume that the robot sensors have unlimited ranges [166, 178]. This design choice is unrealistic for large environments. The box-pushing task, on the other hand, makes use of sensorily-constrained robots. Importantly, all of these approaches evolve neuro-controllers of fixed size. In contrast, our approach uses modifier-genes to evolve neuro-controllers of different sizes, providing evolution with the opportunity to automatically discover minimal designs.

While most of the work in evolutionary robotics concerns the design of controllers, some researchers have also considered the role of evolution in the design of agent sensory systems. Menczer and Belew [167] studied the evolution of sensors for food-seeking agents in a controlled environment that they termed *latent energy environments* or LEEs. Their environments contained food elements of different types (e.g., A, B, and C) and combinations of these elements led to exothermic or endothermic reactions. Instead of simple foraging (find food and eat), the agents thus had to learn to distinguish between food types and recognize useful combinations (exothermic reactions that produce energy). In their work on sensor evolution, the number and placement of sensors was fixed and evolution effectively determined the type of sensor (e.g., A, B, or C). In contrast, our work in this chapter deals with the number, placement, and range of sensors rather than their types.

Reynolds [175] also explored the use of evolution in the design of sensory systems for a corridor following robot task. The sensors in his work were assumed to be *noisy* range sensors and he evolved programs for robust corridor navigation behaviors. Sensory system design consisted of determining the number and placement of the range sensors. Thus, our work is rather similar to the approach adopted by Reynolds, albeit on a different (and arguably harder) problem. Also, we consider the effects of noise caused by sensor *faults* rather than noisy range estimation.

Walker [178] studied a variation of a foraging task where the robots had to locate and approach *radiative* energy sources. Using two sensors and a simple neural network, he evolved effective foraging strategies. His work on sensor evolution dealt with the design of sensor placements and he found that co-evolving the sensor placements and the robot controller leads to marked improvements in robot performance. In contrast, we have used the evolutionary approach to also determine the number of sensors required for the robot task.

Although a number of researchers have used noise in their simulation studies, most have been to develop designs that are robust when transferred on to real robots [169], [168], and [161]. In such cases the researchers have found that robot controllers, evolved in simulation environments that contain noise (usually random white noise), perform much better when tested on real robots when compared to the designs evolved without noise. This is in contrast to the sensor noise studied in our experiments.

There has also been some work in the evolution of noisy neuro-controllers for robots [152] and [160]. In this particular model, each neuro-controller unit was considered noisy, with its output being modulated by an additive random white Gaussian noise. The researchers found that this led to robust behaviors. In contrast, the work reported in this chapter assumes reliable neuro-controller units and deals with noise caused by faulty sensors.

5.9   Summary

In this chapter we have explored an evolutionary approach to the design of neuro-controllers and sensory systems for a box-pushing robot. Evolution is perfectly suited for this design challenge since the constraints associated with the box-pushing task make it particularly hard to develop good box-pushing behaviors via simple techniques like random-walking or a random search over the space of behaviors. In addition, even understanding the constraints of the task offers little insight into the kinds of sensory and neural structures that would lead to effective box-pushing behaviors.

We showed that against these odds evolution discovers neuro-controller designs that endow the robots with effective box-pushing strategies. Through a detailed analysis of the evolved designs we were also able to show how the robots address the constraints of the box-pushing task. For instance, we were able to conclude that robots with recurrent neuro-controllers interleave moves and turns, thereby avoiding situations that may lead them to a permanently stuck state. Although feed-forward networks do not have recurrent links, we showed that evolution discovers designs that employ hidden units to produce qualitatively similar behaviors.

In addition to the design of the neuro-controller, we also evolved the number, placement, and range of the robot sensors, in addition to designing the neuro-controller. This approach produced a number of interesting results. We found that the box-pushing task did not require eight sensors and each of our evolutionary runs produced robot designs that made use of fewer than eight sensors. It should be pointed out that there was *no explicit pressure* towards using fewer sensors and the optimization of the numbers of sensors was an *emergent property* of this system. We believe that having fewer sensors leads to lesser sensory conflicts and hence is favored by evolution. In this regard, the sensory design problem is simply the *feature selection problem* in a different guise. This study also confirmed our intuition that sensors located to sense cells ahead and to the sides of the robot play a more significant role in their performance than sensors located behind the robot.

We also considered the design of robust robot behaviors in the presence of sensor noise. Since noise is omnipresent in the real-world, this consideration makes the box-pushing task a little more realistic. We introduced noise in the form of sensor faults. We found that evolution discovered designs that were well adapted to effectively handle the noise. For instance, evolution produced robots that employed two (sometimes even three) sensors to sense the cell immediately ahead of the robot. In effect, evolution discovered robust designs by *duplicating* the *faulty resource* (namely the sensors) in critical directions around the robot.

We also found that when noise was present in the system, evolution often discovered designs that were tailored to exploit them. When such designs were later tested in environments without noise, their performance *decreased*. A closer inspection of such designs revealed novel ways in which sensor faults were being exploited. For instance, we found that multiple sensors placed to sense the same cell, often made the robot react in opposite ways. While one made the robot approach boxes, the other biased the robot to turn away from them. This combination, modulated by sensor faults, led to interesting behaviors wherein the robots pushed boxes through multiple steps and then turned away from them. Little wonder then, that the fitness decreased when noise was removed.

Although the box-pushing task has provided an interesting computational context for exploring the evolution of robot behaviors and sensory systems, there is an important dimension that we did not consider in this chapter. We have assumed that the robots have an inexhaustible source of energy that allows them to survive through their entire simulation time. This is in contrast to most real-world situations where the robots must be designed keeping such energy considerations in mind. For instance, real-world sensors require energy to operate. In such a scenario, unnecessary or irrelevant sensors must be discarded (or switched off) by the robot. Similarly, useless units must be discarded from the neuro-controllers. A number of robot designs presented in this chapter include examples of such excesses where sensors and units are retained by the robot, but are never used in any fruitful computation. We need mechanisms to circumvent such design faults. We have developed one such approach that imposes energy penalties on the robot components and uses evolution to discover energy-efficient designs [146]. Other mechanisms need to be explored.

Acknowledgments

We would like to thank David Levine, Brian Walenz, and other members of the PGAPack development team, for use of their parallel genetic algorithm library in the experiments reported in this paper. We also thank the Scalable Computing Laboratory in Ames Laboratory for use of their distributed computing cluster. We gratefully acknowledge the support provided by the Department of Computer Science at Iowa State University where much of this research was completed. This research was partially supported by grants from the National Science Foundation (NSF IRI-9409580) and the John Deere Foundation to Vasant Honavar, and an IBM Fellowship to Karthik Balakrishnan. We are also grateful for support provided by Obongo Inc. and Allstate Research and Planning Center.

References

[146] K. Balakrishnan. *Biologically Inspired Computational Structures and Processes for Autonomous Agents and Robots*. PhD thesis, Department of Computer Science, Iowa State University, Ames, IA, 1998.

[147]K. Balakrishnan and V. Honavar. Analysis of neurocontrollers designed by simulated evolution. In *Proceedings of IEEE International Conference on Neural Networks ICNN'96*, 1996.

[148]K. Balakrishnan and V. Honavar. On sensor evolution in robotics. In *Proceedings of Genetic Programming Conference – GP-96*, 1996.

[149]K. Balakrishnan and V. Honavar. Some experiments in the evolutionary synthesis of robotic neurocontrollers. In *Proceedings of the World Congress on Neural Networks*, pages 1035–1040, 1996.

[150]V. Braitenberg. *Vehicles: Experiments in Synthetic Psychology*. MIT Press, Cambridge, MA, 1984.

[151]F. Cecconi, F. Menczer, and R. Belew. Maturation and evolution of imitative learning in artificial organisms. *Adaptive Behavior*, 4(1):179–198, 1995.

[152]D. Cliff, P. Husbands, and I. Harvey. Analysis of evolved sensory-motor controllers. In *Second European Conference on Artificial Life*, 1993.

[153]R. Collins and D. Jefferson. Antfarm: Towards simulated evolution. In *Proceedings of the Second International Conference on Artificial Life*, pages 579–601, 1991.

[154]M. Colombetti and M. Dorigo. Learning to control an autonomous robot by distributed genetic algorithms. In *From Animals to Animats 2: Proceedings of the Second International Conference on Simulation of Adaptive Behavior*, 1992.

[155]D. Dasgupta and D. McGregor. Designing application-specific neural networks using the structured genetic algorithm. In *Proceedings of the International Conference on Combinations of Genetic Algorithms and Neural Networks*, pages 87–96, 1992.

[156]D. Floreano and F. Mondada. Automatic creation of an autonomous agent: Genetic evolution of a neural-network driven robot. In *from Animals to Animats 3: Proceedings of the Third International Conference on Simulation of Adaptive Behavior*, pages 421–430, 1994.

[157]D. Goldberg. *Genetic Algorithms in Search, Optimization, and Machine Learning*. Addison Wesley, Reading, MA, 1989.

[158]I. Harvey, P. Husbands, and D. Cliff. Seeing the light: Artificial evolution, real vision. In *From Animals to Animats 3: Proceedings of the Third International Conference on Simulation of Adaptive Behavior*, 1994.

[159]J. Holland. *Adaptation in Natural and Artificial Systems*. The University of Michigan Press, Ann Arbor, 1975.

[160]P. Husbands, I. Harvey, and D. Cliff. Analysing recurrent dynamical networks evolved for robot control. In *Proceedings of the 3rd IEE International Conference on Artificial Neural Networks*, 1993.

[161]N. Jakobi, P. Husbands, and I. Harvey. Noise and the reality gap: The use of simulation in evolutionary robotics. In *Proceedings of the Third European Conference on Artificial Life*, 1995.

[162]J. Koza. Genetic evolution and co-evolution of computer programs. In *Proceedings of the Second International Conference on Artificial Life*, pages 603–629, 1991.

[163]M. Lewis, A. Fagg, and A. Sodium. Genetic programming approach to the construction of a neural network for control of a walking robot. In *Proceedings of the IEEE International Conference on Robotics and Automation*, 1992.

[164]H. Lund, J. Hallam, and W.-P. Lee. Evolving robot morphology. In *Proceedings of IEEE Fourth International Conference on Evolutionary Computation*, 1997.

[165]H. Lund, J. Hallam, and W.-P. Lee. Evolving robot morphology. In *IEEE 4th International Conference on Evolutionary Computation*, 1997.

[166]H. Lund and D. Parisi. Preadaptations in populations of neural networks evolving in a changing environment. *Artificial Life*, 2(2):179–198, 1995.

[167]F. Menczer and R. Belew. Evolving sensors in environments of controlled complexity. In *Proceedings of the Fourth International Conference on Artificial Life*, 1994.

[168]O. Miglino, H. Lund, and S. Nolfi. Evolving mobile robots in simulated and real environments. *Artificial Life*, 2(4):417–434, 1995.

[169]O. Miglino, K. Nafasi, and C. Taylor. Selection for wandering behavior in a small robot. *Artificial Life*, 2(1):101–116, 1994.

[170]M. Mitchell. *An Introduction to Genetic Algorithms*. MIT Press, Cambridge, MA, 1996.

[171]F. Mondada, E. Franzi, and P. Ienne. Mobile robot miniaturization: A tool for investigation in control algorithms. In *Proceedings of the Third International Symposium on Experimental Robotics*, 1993.

[172]S. Nolfi, J. Elman, and D. Parisi. Learning and evolution in neural networks. *Adaptive Behavior*, 3(1):5–28, 1994.

[173]C. Peck and A. Dhawan. Genetic algorithms as global random search methods: An alternative perspective. *Evolutionary Computation*, 3(1), 1995.

[174]C. Reynolds. Evolution of corridor following behavior in a noisy world. In *From Animals to Animats 3: Proceedings of the Third International Conference on Simulation of Adaptive Behavior*, 1994.

[175]C. Reynolds. Evolution of obstacle avoidance behavior: Using noise to promote robust solutions. In K. Kinnear, editor, *Advances in Genetic Programming*. MIT Press, Cambridge, MA, 1994.

[176]G. Syswerda. Uniform crossover in genetic algorithms. In *Proceedings of the Third International Conference on Genetic Algorithms*, pages 2–9, 1989.

[177]A. Teller. The evolution of mental models. In K. Kinnear, editor, *Advances in Genetic Programming*, pages 199–219. MIT Press, Cambridge, MA, 1994.

[178]J. Walker. Evolution of simple virtual robots using genetic algorithms. Master's thesis, Department of Mechanical Engineering, Iowa State University, Ames, IA, 1995.

[179]B. Yamauchi and R. Beer. Integrating reactive, sequential, and learning behavior using dynamical neural networks. In *From Animals to Animats 3: Proceedings of the Third International Conference on Simulation of Adaptive Behavior*, pages 382–391, 1994.

[180]J. Yang and V. Honavar. Feature subset selection using a genetic algorithm. In Motoda and Liu, editors, *Feature Extraction, Construction and Selection - A Data Mining Perspective*. Kluwer Academic, Boston, MA, 1998.

6 Combined Biological Metaphors

Egbert J. W. Boers and Ida G. Sprinkhuizen-Kuyper

As computer hardware becomes more powerful, increasingly large artificial neural networks will become feasible. There will be no limit to the size of the networks, in principle, and it will become increasingly difficult to design them and understand their internal operation. That is why it is very important to find design methods that are scalable to large network sizes. In this chapter we describe our explorations into a new scalable method for the construction of good neural network architecture for a given task. Reverse-engineering the only example available, the evolution of our own brains, we have combined several ideas from evolution, embryology, neurology, and theoretical psychology.

The method we describe in this chapter allows the coding of large modular artificial neural network architectures while restricting the search space of the genetic algorithm that is used for the optimization. This done by using a scalable, recipe-like coding (as opposed to a blueprint-like coding).

Currently, it is still very time-consuming to train artificial neural networks, which has to be done many times in our method to establish their evolutionary fitness. Therefore, we are working on all kinds of improvements to accelerate the process. In this chapter we will describe some new techniques that can make architectural improvements to a given artificial neural network during their fitness evaluation. These techniques can speed-up and improve the evolutionary search for good network architectures, an effect that has become known as the 'Baldwin effect'.

6.1 Introduction

When designing artificial neural networks, the question often arises of how to choose the (initial) network architecture: how many layers, how many nodes per layer, which nodes are connected, and so on (i.e., the underlying graph topology). More general, a network *architecture* specifies the number of nodes and the way they are connected (it does not describe the actual strengths of the connections' weights).

The choice of a specific architecture determines to a large extent which functions can be implemented by the neural network. It also has a strong influence on the ability of the training algorithm to learn the desired function. This ability of course also depends on the task itself. Given the same training samples and learning algorithm, a different initial network architecture will in general show a different behavior of the network. For example: a network that has to approximate training data as close as possible will need a different network architecture than a network that has to generalize as much as possible. Choosing the right initial architecture is currently one of the major problems encountered when applying neural networks to complex tasks. In section6.2 we will give some examples of the importance of choosing a proper network architecture for a given task. Considering the small size of the given examples and the fact that it is already difficult to design a suitable network architecture to solve them, it should be obvious that it is almost impossible to design network architectures for large problems by hand. That is why several authors (e.g., [193, 194, 195, 206, 208, 209, 210, 211]) have designed learning methods that automatically generate an architecture as part of the learning algorithm. For small problems, these methods give good results, but for large problems they have their limitations. We will describe these later in this chapter.

Very little theoretical knowledge exists about how to find a suitable network architecture for a given task. Missing this knowledge makes it almost impossible to find the best network architecture by hand or by using some analytic method. Even for the simplest networks, a complete analysis of their functioning is very difficult (e.g., [219]).

Evolving Neural Network Architectures

Evolutionary computation is one of the few optimization methods that can operate even if no analytic knowledge about the problem is available. Therefore, it is a technique that can be used to search automatically for suitable network architectures. In evolutionary computation a population of candidate solutions, or individuals, is maintained and optimized using selection and reproduction. When optimizing neural network architectures, each individual contains a description of a network architecture. The goal is to find the optimal architecture for a given task. This also needs a description of how to measure the final quality of a network, after training it on the training data. The performance of the trained network is then transformed into a *fitness* measure which is used by the evolutionary algorithm to determine the selection probabilities of this individual. Section 6.3 will give an overview of the different ways to optimize artificial neural networks using evolutionary computation. The bottleneck of these procedures is, of course, the long training time that is needed to evaluate each network architecture. An important topic of this chapter is the presentation of several ways to improve the performance of this evolutionary process.

Scalability Through Modularization

A key concept in artificial neural network research is modularity. Fully connected artificial neural networks usually perform worse than networks that are not fully connected but have a modular architecture specific for the task at hand. Typically, if a problem can be divided in several subtasks, assigning a subnetwork to each subtask makes it a lot easier for the learning algorithm to come up with a solution. Besides the fact that designing modular network architectures specific for a task will result in better performances, modularization also allows for a more scalable coding scheme. When large networks are to be designed using evolutionary computation, a scalable coding scheme has to be found to code the candidate networks into the chromosomes of the individuals. Scalable means that the size of the coding that is needed to specify a network does not grow too much when the size of the network increases. It is very important to keep the size of the needed coding as small as possible to minimize the search space of the evolutionary algorithm. The necessity to design large artificial neural networks has caused several researchers to start looking for coding schemes that use graph grammars that are scalable and can easily generate modular networks (for an overview see [215]). The idea behind these coding schemes is to code a recipe instead of a blueprint. A recipe does not have to code the architecture of a neural network in every detail, but only codes a growth process that describes how to construct it. The grammar we developed will be described in 6.4 together with a possible coding. Both our grammar and our coding are strongly inspired by biology.

Combining Local Search with Evolution

Section 6.5 of this chapter will elaborate on how to use local search techniques, like gradient descent techniques, in order to *direct* the evolutionary process. It has been shown (e.g., [181, 182, 200, 221]) that a combination of 'local' and 'global' search strategies can improve the final quality of the result of an evolutionary search process. Moreover, a combination with local search techniques can increase the speed of convergence of an evolutionary algorithm. In principle there are two different ways of utilizing the result of a local search process:

1. Use the local search process only to calculate the fitness of the members (changing the fitness landscape only). This method is comparable to Darwinian evolution [189]. When the speed of convergence and/or the final quality of the

solution increase as a result of adding local search, we speak of the 'Baldwin effect'.

2. Code the solution found by the local search process into the inheritable characters of the population members (changing the evolutionary process). This kind of evolution is called 'Lamarckism' after Lamarck [205].

In 6.5 we will first discuss the differences between Darwinian evolution with the Baldwin effect and Lamarckian evolution from a general perspective. After that, we will discuss the possibilities of using these ideas when optimizing neural network architectures in 6.6. Most importantly, we will show that it is possible to use a local search algorithm as part of an evolutionary process that optimizes neural network architectures. This may result in the Baldwin effect. We will also explain why Lamarckian evolution can not be implemented when using a graph grammar coding.

6.2   Artificial Neural Network Architectures

Many tasks cannot be trained easily by a learning algorithm using conventional fully connected layered neural networks (e.g., [185, 218]). Some of the possible causes for this are (see e.g., [199]):

• The artificial neural network is too small and cannot implement the correct input output behavior. It should be obvious that it then also will not be able to learn it. Note that the other way around is not always the case: *implementability* does not imply *learnability*.

• Only the training set is learned correctly, input samples that are not seen during training are mapped in a wrong way. The network is then said to have a poor *generalization*.

• Sometimes a network's generalization is good after a short training period, but decreases after prolonged training when it will try to fit the training date even better. The network then becomes *overtrained* (see e.g., [199]). This effect can happen if the network has too many degrees of freedom.

• Two or more subtasks that have to be solved compete for resources within the network. Learning can be almost impossible in this case. This problem is called *interference*.

• A network should be flexible enough to keep learning new data, but it also should be stable enough not to forget data it has previously learned. This is still very difficult for most learning algorithms, and it is referred to as the *stability-plasticity dilemma*.

• The *training speed* of the network is very slow. This can be the result of an unfortunate starting-point in the weight space of the network, but also the result of a bad architecture.

These problem causes can usually be solved by using the right learning paradigm and by using a network architecture that is specifically tuned for the problem at hand. As stated earlier, by network architecture we mean the graph topology of the nodes and connections of the artificial neural network. Given a learning paradigm and a task to be trained, the performance of the artificial neural network depends to a large extent on its architecture. We will restrict ourselves in this chapter to the effect of the network architecture. To give an impression of the importance of the network architecture for the network's performance, we will look at two examples:

1. *Interference.* The problem of interference (or crosstalk) occurs when one *neural pathway* has to learn two or more unrelated problems (e.g., [203, 216]). When a network is very small it is possible that it can only implement one of the problems. But even if a network is large enough to implement all tasks at the same time, it may still not be able to learn the task. It is possible that the different problems are in each others way: if a training sample of one of the problems is presented to the network this can erase knowledge learned for the other problem, and vice versa. An example of such an interference between several classifications is the recognition of both position and shape of an input pattern. Rueckl et al. [216] conducted a number of simulations in which they trained a two layer backpropagation network with 25 input nodes, 18 hidden nodes and 18 output nodes to process simultaneously the *form* and the *place* of the input pattern (see figure 6.1).
They used nine 3×3 binary input patterns at nine different positions on a 5×5 input grid, so there were 81 different combinations of shape and position. The network had to code both form and place of a presented stimulus in the output layer. It appeared that the network learned faster and made less mistakes when the tasks were processed in separated parts of the network, while the total number of hidden nodes stayed the same. Of importance was the number of hidden nodes allocated to each of the subnetworks. When both networks had 9 hidden nodes the combined performance was even worse than that of the single network with 18 hidden nodes. Optimal performance was obtained when

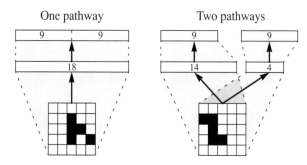

Figure 6.1
Two networks for the "What-Where problem" [216]. The separation of the two tasks into different pathways improves the performance. In this notation, each arrow corresponds with a complete connection between two modules; the number inside the module gives the number of nodes.

4 hidden nodes were dedicated to the *place* network and 14 to the apparently more complex task of the *shape* network. The task of determining the place of the stimulus is linearly separable and can be learned without hidden units. However, the number of weights needed when there is no hidden layer is larger than when a small hidden layer is used. The experiment they did showed that processing the two tasks in one unsplit hidden layer caused interference. In a follow-up paper Jacobs et al. [203] distinguished two types of crosstalk:

Spatial crosstalk occurs when the output units of a network provide conflicting error information to a hidden unit.

Temporal crosstalk occurs when units receive inconsistent training information at different times.

2. *Training speed.* The third and smallest example of the importance of the architecture of a neural network is the XOR problem (e.g., [217]), in which a neural network has to learn to calculate the logical exclusive-or function. If the network has a simple layered architecture, two input units, two hidden units and one output unit (see figure 6.2a), it takes on average 1650 epochs to train it. If two additional connections are made (see figure 6.2b), connecting the input directly to the output, only 30 epochs are needed to achieve the same residual error [185].

In some cases it is very important to have these direct connections between input and output layers, and more in general connections between layers and modules in a free fashion, because these seem to remove flat spaces in the error surface. We proved that a network like figure 6.2b, but with only one hidden

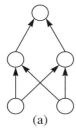 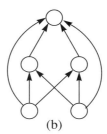

(a)   (b)

Figure 6.2
Two networks able to learn the XOR function. Despite two extra connections, network (b) learns much faster than network (a).

node, does not have any local minima on its error surface at all [219]. However, the training time of this network is longer.

Architecture Optimization During Training

As shown with some small examples in the previous subsection, the architecture of the artificial neural network can strongly influence its learning behavior. It is therefore very important, when designing an artificial neural network application, to find an architecture that is particularly suited for the problem you want to solve. For small problems, or problems for which the solution is already known using different techniques, it is possible to design the network architecture by hand. However, when dealing with a complex problem with no analytic solution the process of finding the right architecture by hand becomes almost impossible. When dealing with large artificial neural networks, it is no longer possible to handle the huge complexity. There are two basic approaches to automate the design process of artificial neural network architectures. The first approach is to start with an initial architecture, and start training the network while adding or deleting nodes as part of the training process. The other approach, which will be discussed in the next section, is to use evolutionary computation to find the right architecture. Here we will give a short overview of the architecture search strategies as part of the training process.

To find the 'correct' network architecture one can incorporate on-line architectural change in the learning algorithm. Most of the existing methods for on-line architecture adaptation can be classified into two categories:

constructive algorithms which add complexity to the network starting from a very simple architecture until the network is able to learn the task. When the remaining error is sufficiently low, this process is halted (e.g., [193, 194, 208,

209]).

destructive algorithms which start with large architectures and remove complexity, usually to improve generalization, by decreasing the number of free variables of the network. Nodes or edges are removed until the network is no longer able to perform its task. Then the last removal is undone (e.g., [206, 210, 211]).

The two described classes of algorithms can perform very well on small problems. But they are not capable to find network architectures for difficult tasks that need specific modular architectures in order to be able to learn those tasks. For both classes of algorithms we will explain why.

Before one can start with a destructive algorithm one needs to find an initial architecture to start the training process. When the training process has started, the learned information from the training samples will be distributed over all the weights, depending on their random initialization. This means that possible clues to decompose the problem will no longer be available for the learning algorithm. Though it will be possible to increase generalization by reducing the complexity of the network, a specific (optimal) modular network architecture will generally not be found.

All existing constructive algorithms produce architectures that, with respect to their topologies, are problem independent because they add nodes in a predefined way. Only the size of the produced architecture varies depending on the problem. Clearly, this also does not create specific modular network architectures.

Since the architecture of a network greatly affects its performance, the inability to find optimal network architectures is a serious problem. Using these on-line search techniques alone will not be enough to solve difficult problems. As will be described in 6.5, these kind of techniques can help an evolutionary algorithm to improve it's search process for modular architectures.

6.3 Evolutionary Computation and Neural Network Architectures

There are several aspects of neural networks that can be optimized using evolutionary computation. One can for example optimize the learning parameters of a learning algorithm. One can also optimize the weights themselves, using the evolutionary algorithm as training method. But, as stated earlier, this chapter focuses on the optimization of architecture alone. To be able to optimize neural network architectures, one needs a coding scheme by which the candidate solutions can be coded in the members of the population of an evolutionary algorithm.

Coding Schemes for Neural Networks

Analogous to a historic debate in embryology [190], we can discern two different kinds of coding schemes. The first is like a *blueprint* and has an exact description of the architecture of the network. The second is like a *recipe*—it only describes the mechanism which is used to construct the architecture.

Blueprint representations In blueprint representations a one-to-one relationship exists between the parts of an artificial neural network architecture and their genetic representation in the chromosomes of the evolutionary algorithm (e.g.,[192, 198]). The simplest blueprint codings are the ones that store the adjacency matrix of the underlying graph of the network architecture into the chromosomes of the evolutionary algorithm.

Recipe representations In this approach it is not a complete network that is coded into a chromosome, but a description of the *growth process* of a network architecture. This description usually is in the form of some kind of graph grammar describing the states of a network [185, 196, 197, 204].

The philosophy behind these recipe representations using (graph) rewriting systems is the *scalability* of the coding, which can not be achieved when using blueprint methods. When using blueprint codings, problems needing large neural network architectures will need very large chromosomes. The resulting search space is very large and will make it very difficult for the evolutionary algorithm to find the right architectures.

Our G2L-system formalism [185, 186, 187] is a graph grammar based on the parallel string rewriting mechanism of L-systems [207]. When using this formalism in a genetic algorithm, each member of the population contains a set of production rules from which the architecture of a feedforward network grows. Section 6.4 will describe the G2L-system in detail.

Gruau proposed a similar approach using *cellular encoding* [196, 197]. In his method the tree representation of genetic programming is used to store grammar trees that contain instructions which describe the architecture as well as the (discrete) weights of the network. The consequence of coding the weights is that all weights conform to the same layout when recursion is used.

6.4   G2L-Systems Coding Neural Networks

Having motivated the need for a scalable mechanism to code large modular neural networks, we will describe in this section a grammar that can do just that and which, moreover, due to its string notation, can easily be coded into chromosomes consisting of bit strings.

Origin and Motivation

The development of plants and animals is governed by the genetic information contained in each cell of the organism. Each cell contains the same genetic information (the *genotype*), which determines the way in which each cell behaves and, as a result of that, the final form and functioning of the organism (the *phenotype*). This genetic information is not a blueprint of that final form but can be seen as a *recipe* [190], that is followed not by the organism as a whole but by each cell individually. The shape and behavior of a cell depend on those genes that are expressed in its interior. Which genes actually are expressed depends on the context of the cell. Already at the very beginning of an organism's life, subtle inter-cellular interaction takes place, changing the set of genes that are expressed in each cell. This process of *cell differentiation* is responsible for the formation of all different organs.

In order to model this kind of development in plants the biologist Lindenmayer developed a mathematical construct called 'L-systems' [207]. With an L-system, a string of symbols can be rewritten into another string by using so-called 'rewriting rules'. A special property of L-systems, compared with other string rewriting formalisms, is that all rules are applied in parallel. Whether a specific rewriting rule can be applied or not depends on which rules have been applied in the past as well as on the neighboring symbols of the symbol to be rewritten. Thanks to these properties, this formalism can implement some of the basic growth mechanisms of plants. We will give some examples of basic L-systems later in this chapter.

In our research [185, 186, 187] we tried to find a way to implement a growth model that could generate artificial neural networks instead of plant-like structures. To optimize the architecture of a neural network for a specific task, we could then use a genetic algorithm to optimize the *rules* of the growth model instead of the network architecture itself. What we needed was a context sensitive graph rewriting system that could generate *modular* graphs. After trying several alternatives [185] we focused on L-systems because they make use of context and because they have already been used to generate biological structures. The changes to the L-system mechanism which were needed to construct a graph grammar will be described.

Principles of L-Systems

The L-system formalism is a parallel string rewriting mechanism. An L-system grammar, which defines a *language* in formal language theory, consists of an alphabet, a starting string and a set of rewriting rules. The starting string, also known as the *axiom*, is rewritten by applying the rewriting rules: each rule describes how a certain symbol should be rewritten into a string of symbols. Whereas in most other grammars rewriting rules are applied sequentially, within an L-system all rewriting rules are applied in parallel in order to generate the next string of the rewriting process.

The L-system grammar G of a language L is defined as: $G = \{\Sigma, \Pi, \alpha\}$ where Σ is the finite set of symbols or alphabet of the language, Π is the finite set of rewriting rules (or production rules), and $\alpha \in \Sigma^*$ is the starting string (axiom) of L. $\Pi = \{\pi | \pi : \Sigma \to \Sigma^*\}$ is the set of rewriting rules. Each rewriting rule defines a unique rewriting of a symbol of Σ, the left side of the rewriting rule, into a string $s \in \Sigma^*$, the right side of the rewriting rule. All symbols in Σ that do not appear as the left side of a rewriting rule are, by default, rewritten into themselves. For clarity, these default rewriting rules are usually not included in Π.

For example, if we take the L-system $G = \{\Sigma, \Pi, \alpha\}$ with

$$
\begin{aligned}
\Sigma &= \{A, B, C\} \\
\Pi &= \{A \to BA, B \to CB, C \to AC\}, \text{ and} \\
\alpha &= ABC,
\end{aligned}
$$

we get the following language:

$$L = \{ABC, BACBAC, CBBAACCBBAAC, \ldots\}.$$

The example shows that all rewriting rules are applied in parallel in consecutive *rewriting steps*. After each rewriting step, all symbols of the original string which *matched* the left side of a rewriting rule have been rewritten into their successor, as defined by the right side of this rewriting rule. The language L is the set of all strings that are generated by applying the rewriting rules; each rewriting step generates the next string of the language until no more rules apply.

Extensions of L-Systems

The simple L-systems described in the previous paragraph can be extended with *context sensitivity*, which is used to generate conditional rewriting rules.

For example, the rewriting rule $A < B \rightarrow C$ expresses that B may only be rewritten if it is preceded by an A. In general, context sensitive rewriting rules will have this form: $L < P > R \rightarrow S$ with $P \in \Sigma$ and $L, R, S \in \Sigma^*$. P, the predecessor, and S, the successor, are what we earlier called the left and right side of a rewriting rule. L and R, the left and right context respectively, determine whether or not a rewriting rule will be applied to a symbol P in the string. Only those symbols P that have L on their left and R on their right side will be rewritten. One or both contexts may be empty, in which case only the context that is present in the rewriting rule will be checked.

For example, suppose our current string in the rewriting process of an L-system is: $ABBACAADBAABBAC$, and we have the following set of rewriting rules:

$$
\begin{aligned}
CA < A &\rightarrow EG, \\
A < A > B &\rightarrow BE, \\
B &\rightarrow RT,
\end{aligned}
$$

then the string that results after one rewriting step is:

$$ARTRTACAEGDRTABERTRTAC.$$

L-systems without context are called 0L-systems. L-systems with one-sided or two-sided context are called 1L-systems or 2L-systems respectively. It is allowed to have empty contexts, which implies that:

0L-systems $\subset$ 1L-systems $\subset$ 2L-systems.

If two rewriting rules apply for a certain symbol, one with and one without context, the one with context is used. In general, the rewriting rule that is more specific will be used. It is however possible to have conflicting rules.

Interpretation of Strings

When we attach a specific meaning (based on a LOGO-style turtle, [220]) to the symbols in a string, we are able to visualize the strings resulting from the rewriting steps.

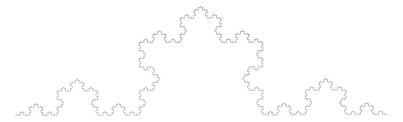

Figure 6.3
The Koch graph (after 5 rewriting steps). If the number of rewriting steps goes to infinity, so does the length of the curve.

The usual interpretation of the symbols used is the following one (see e.g., [214]):

Symbol	Interpretation
F	draw a line in the current direction
$+$	rotate $\varphi°$ to the left
$-$	rotate $\varphi°$ to the right

For example, the well-known Koch graph which is shown in figure 6.3, can be described by the following L-system:

$$G \;=\; \{\{F,+,-\},\{F \to F+F--F+F\},F\},$$
$$\varphi \;=\; 60°.$$

Other symbols that are frequently mentioned in literature are:

Symbol	Interpretation
f	move in the current direction but do *not* draw a line
[	push the current position and direction on the stack, and continue
]	pop a position and direction from the stack and continue from here

The usage of brackets for push and pop operations while interpreting the string was introduced by Lindenmayer [207] in order to achieve more realistic representations of plants and trees. Hogeweg and Hesper [201] have generated many examples of what can be modeled with G2L-systems. One of their examples, extended with *stochastic rewriting* [213], is given in figure 6.4.

Introducing brackets in 2L-systems has some effect on the determination of the left and right contexts of the rewriting rules. The left context consists of the path before the predecessor, and the right context consists of a subtree

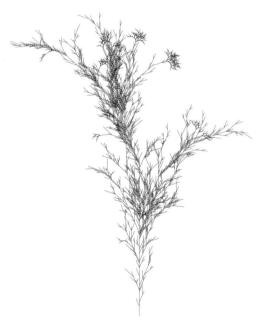

Figure 6.4
Drawing of a stochastic 2L-system.

behind the predecessor. To detect this, the tree representation of the string must
be examined at each rewriting step.

For example (from [214]), a rewriting rule with the following left-side:

$$BC < S > G[H]M,$$

can be applied to the symbol S in the string

$$ABC[DE][SG[HI[JK]L]MNO].$$

Figure 6.5 gives a graphical interpretation of this match.

For an extensive look at the possibilities of this kind of interpretation of
the strings resulting from an L-system and for some more extensions to it, see
for example [201, 213, 214].

A Graph Interpretation: GL-Systems

For an L-system to generate the graph topologies that are needed for the coding
of neural network architectures, a suitable interpretation has been constructed

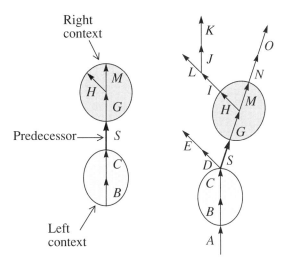

Figure 6.5
Matching in bracketed 2L-systems.

earlier [185, 186]. Here, a generalized interpretation is given, allowing the construction of cyclic graphs, which also allows for recurrent networks [187].

Instead of the graphical interpretation of a string resulting from the rewriting steps, a direct transformation into a graph is possible using $\Sigma_g = \mathbb{Z} \cup \{[,]\} \cup \Sigma$ with $\mathbb{Z}$ the set of integer numbers where each $j \in \mathbb{Z}$ is read as one symbol, called a *connector*. The symbols [and] are used to denote subgraphs (see below). Each $n \in \Sigma$ in the string represents a node in the corresponding graph. The numbers j, directly behind a symbol from Σ or], connect the node or subgraph with a directed edge to the jth node or subgraph to the left or right in the string, depending on the sign of j.

For example, the string $A1\,2B2C0\,1D - 3$ represents the graphs drawn in figure 6.6.

The symbols in the nodes are not labels of the graph, but are used as matching symbols for the GL-system.

THEOREM 6.1:   All possible finite unlabeled directed graphs can be represented and generated with a finite GL-system.

Proof   Label all nodes of an arbitrary graph F with $A_i, i = 1 \dots n$, with n the number of nodes in F. For each edge (A_i, A_j) insert the connector calculated

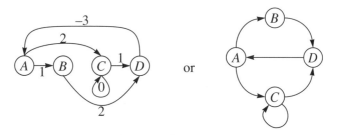

Figure 6.6
The graph of example 6 drawn in two different layouts. The left drawing shows the node names
as represented in the string as well as the connectors.

by $j - i$ directly after A_i in the string $A_1 \ldots A_n$. The resulting string, S, can
now be used directly to construct the GL-system G that generates the graph,
simply by taking the string S as axiom. ■

The special symbols [and] are used to group nodes into subgraphs (or
modules), which can be recursively repeated. Each subgraph is assigned a
level, which is calculated by counting the number of surrounding bracket pairs.
In calculating the jth node or subgraph when making the connections, each
subgraph is seen as a unity, and can be regarded as one node on the same level
as the subgraph. The connectors directly to the right of a closing bracket will
connect all *output nodes* of the subgraph. All connections made *to* a subgraph
are connected with all its *input nodes*. There are two possible definitions of in-
and output nodes:

• The first possibility defines the output nodes of a subgraph as those nodes
that have no outgoing edges to other nodes of the same subgraph. The input
nodes of a subgraph are those nodes that do not have incoming edges from
within the same subgraph. GL-systems with this interpretation will be referred
to as *strictly modular*. This definition is particularly suited for generating
layered networks, and is therefore the one we used.

• The second possibility takes into account the order of the symbols in the
string representing the graph. Besides having the input and output nodes as
defined in the previous definition, also those nodes that have no edges to nodes
in the same subgraph that are denoted to the right in the string are output
nodes and those nodes that do not have edges from nodes of the same subgraph
that are denoted to the left in the string are input nodes. GL-systems with this
interpretation will be referred to as *not strictly modular*.

As a consequence, specific edges to nodes within a subgraph can not be made from outside of the subgraph, while edges from a node in a subgraph to nodes or other subgraphs outside its own subgraph are possible, after counting across the subgraph boundary, the level at which the nodes are counted is decreased by one. This idea of limiting the possible connections from and to a subgraph corresponds to a sense of information hiding and improves the capability of the GL-system to generate modular graphs, which is important for our purposes.

A nice example of defining a recursive graph is the following not strictly modular GL-system:

$$G = \{\{A, B, [,], 1, -2\}, \{A \to [BB]1[AB]1B - 2\}, A\}.$$

After three rewriting steps the graph will look as shown in figure 6.7.

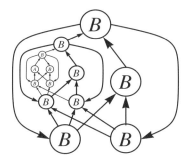

Figure 6.7
An example of a recursive GL-system.

The string corresponding to the figure is:

$$[BB]1\,[[BB]1\,[[BB]1[AB]1B - 2B]\,1B - 2B]\,1B - 2.$$

Context in G2L-Systems

The left context of a node (or subgraph) is defined as the set of all symbols and subgraphs in the string that have edges to the node (or subgraph) in the graph interpretation of the string. The right context is defined in the same way, looking at the edges going away from the node (or subgraph). When, if present in the rewriting rule, both context parts of the rule are a subset of the left and right context in the graph, the rule is said to match and can be applied.

The definition of *context* in G2L-systems is not the same as in normal L-systems. Usually the context of a symbol that is being rewritten is directly on the left and right side of that symbol. In bracketed 2L-systems, context can be seen by looking at the path towards, and a subtree directly after the predecessor. This limits the part of the string that has to be interpreted in order to match context.

In G2L-systems, however, context can only be determined after the complete string has been interpreted. Also, not only single symbols may be rewritten, but complete substrings can be replaced by others. Here, a left to right order for matching the rewriting rules is followed, and a preference for more specific rewriting rules when more rules are possible. The specificity of a rewriting rule is determined simply by counting the number of symbols in the left side of the rule. G2L-systems that have no conflicts, which means that no ambiguity exists about which rule has to be applied, will be called *conflict-free*.

For example, examine the following strictly modular G2L-system: $G = \{\Sigma_g, \Pi, \alpha\}$ with

$$
\begin{aligned}
\Sigma &= \{A, B, C, D\}, \\
\Pi &= \{A \to B1B1B, \\
&\quad\; B > B \to [CD], \\
&\quad\; B \to C, \\
&\quad\; C < D \to C, \\
&\quad\; D > D \to C2\}, \\
\alpha &= A.
\end{aligned}
$$

The successive steps in the rewriting process are shown in figure 6.8.

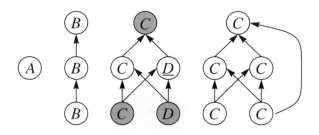

Figure 6.8
The graphs corresponding to successive rewriting steps of a G2L-system.

After the last step no more rules apply:

$$A$$
$$\Downarrow$$
$$B1B1B$$
$$\Downarrow$$
$$[CD]\,1\,[C\underline{D}]\,1C$$
$$\Downarrow$$
$$[CC2]\,1\,[CC]\,1C$$

To show the workings of left and right context, these are drawn in figure 6.8 for the underlined symbol $\underline{D}$ after the second rewriting step. The left context of $\underline{D}$ is the set $\{C, D, [C, D]\}$ and the right context is $\{C\}$. Note that the other D does not have a C in its left context.

The Genetic Code of G2L-Systems

To code the production rules of G2L-systems in binary strings we turned to nature for inspiration. The 'production rules' of nature are proteins. Proteins are large molecules made of a large number of amino acids which are connected in a long folded chain. There are 20 different amino acids. The shape of a protein, which determines its chemical function, results from the specific order in which the amino acids are added during its creation. This sequence of amino acids is coded in DNA by triplets of four possible bases. Three of the 64 possible triplets are used as start and stop markers, telling where a description of a protein starts and ends. The remaining 61 triplets (redundantly) code for the 20 amino acids.

The genetic coding of the G2L-systems we use mimics this coding scheme. We use six bits (triplets of two bits) to code for a symbol of a production rule. Reading a bit string (or chromosome), six bits at a time, the symbols can be looked up in a look-up table[1]. As extra symbol, comparable to the start and stop markers of DNA, we use an asterisk. The process of constructing a production rule starts at the first encountered asterisk. The symbols that follow until the next asterisk, or marker, will be interpreted as the left context of a rule. After that, the predecessor, right context, and successor are read, each time separated by a marker. This process will start at each encountered marker in the chromosome. Figure 6.9 shows how an example bit string is converted

---

1 As the optimal coding is unknown, Wiemer [222] has applied a genetic algorithm to optimize this lookup-table.

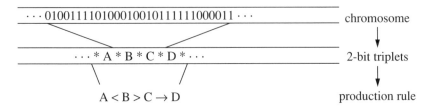

Figure 6.9
The process of decoding a chromosome into a production rule. A complete production rule from it's starting asterisk to it's end will be called a gene.

to a production rule.

Overlapping Genes

One of the striking results from the study of genetics is that it is possible to find genes for different proteins that overlap in the DNA. There are even examples of codings that are completely contained within the coding of another protein. This, of course, is possible because it is possible to start reading DNA starting at every possible starting position. If transcription starts one position further, a complete new set of triplets can be read and decoded. This can also be done with the coding scheme used here. The chromosome can be read starting at each bit, giving six different readouts of one string. Moreover, it is also possible to read the string in the opposite direction. This means that, when reading the chromosome as were it a cycle, the chromosome is read *twelve* times. The nice thing about this way of coding is that genetic operators like inversion, where a substring is cut from the string and pasted back in reverse order, keep genes that are included inside the bit string intact.

Repairing Mechanisms

When starting from random bit strings, it is very unlikely that there are many correct production rules resulting from the decoding of the bit string. Moreover, having correctly formulated production rules still does not mean that the G2L-system can produce a useful network. For a start, given the axiom of the G2L-system, there has to be a production rule that is applicable.

This is why we have incorporated several repairing mechanisms in the decoding process. Not only do we try to fix each production rule, removing spurious brackets and jumps, but also we remove parts of the resulting network that are not used, or have no function.

G2L-Systems in Practice

In our experience with the G2L-system, we have often been surprised with the kind of architectures that were found. In most of the cases these architectures outperformed the architectures constructed manually, with respect to the chosen properties to optimize [185, 186]. However, due to the long evaluation time needed for determining the fitness of an architecture, the problems we tried were relatively simple. To show the full potential of the G2L-system, it will be necessary to work with problems that really need a large architecture.

To show the strength of optimizing large graph topologies with genetic algorithms that use the G2L-system formalism we needed a faster method to determine the fitness of a graph. Using a neural network training algorithm is too time consuming. Instead, we used some simple fitness criteria that looked at properties of the graph like the average number of nodes and connections per module and the total number of modules. Our method found optimal solutions for all cases we tried. To optimize this process, Wiemer [222] applied a genetic algorithm to optimize the parameters of our genetic algorithm and the genetic lookup-table, and was able to find settings that resulted in faster (up to a factor 4) and more consistent convergence.

6.5   Lamarckian Evolution and the Baldwin Effect

In the previous sections we have given an overview of the evolutionary algorithms and on-line adaptation algorithms able to find an artificial neural network architecture that is able to learn a specific task. In this section we will describe how the evolutionary process can be improved by using the on-line architecture adaptation algorithms as part of the fitness evaluation.

Adding local search techniques to evolution can increase the speed of evolution. When members are allowed to optimize themselves as part of their fitness evaluation, the *ability* to optimize becomes the most important character for selective pressure.

Combining Local Search and Evolution

The most important properties of evolutionary computation and local search algorithms are that, respectively, evolutionary computation optimizes globally while local search is good at finding local optima.

We distinguish three different ways to combine evolutionary computation and local search algorithms into one joint optimization strategy that improves

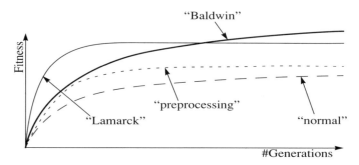

Figure 6.10
General behavior of the three different combinations for hard problems (see e.g., [212].

the results of either of the methods separately:

1. Preprocessing
2. Lamarckian evolution
3. Darwinian evolution with Baldwin effect

The first technique is already proposed by Holland [202] to improve the result found by a genetic algorithm in numerical optimization problems. He used the genetic algorithm to find an approximate solution, which is then further optimized with a local search algorithm. So this technique uses the genetic algorithm as "preprocessor" for a local search algorithm.

Preprocessing will give good results when the evolutionary algorithm indeed gives a reasonable approximation of a global optimum with a high probability. When the complexity of the fitness landscape is large, the other techniques, and especially the Baldwin effect, is expected to give better results. Of course, no matter what kind of algorithm is used to find an approximated solution for a problem, it is always a good idea to see if a simple local optimization algorithm can improve the result found. So in general we can expect that an evolutionary algorithm used as preprocessor for a local optimization algorithm will give slightly better results than a pure evolutionary algorithm (see figure 6.10).

In the second and third possible combination, the evolutionary algorithm and the local search are more closely intertwined: each candidate solution is improved by a local search technique, *before* its fitness is determined. We speak about Lamarckian evolution when the chromosomes of the candidate solutions are replaced by the coded results of the local optimization before

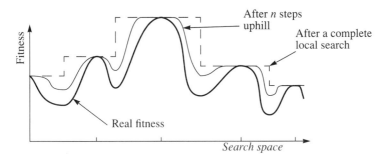

Figure 6.11
Effect of local search on the fitness landscape. Adapted from Whitley et al. [221]. Attractors in search space for the local-search algorithm are indicated at the horizontal axis.

reproduction. The third combination uses local optimization only as part of the fitness evaluation. The contents of the chromosomes is not changed as a result of the local search.

Both combinations that use local search as part of their fitness evaluation function, consider a neighborhood of the point in search space that is represented in the chromosome of the evaluated member. The fitness of that member is the fitness of the best solution in its neighborhood instead of an isolated point in search space. The size and shape of this neighborhood depends on the kind of local search algorithm.

The effect (see figure 6.11) of this local search is that, seen from the perspective of the evolutionary algorithm, the search space becomes simpler. Local minima can even disappear entirely. The proverbial needle in a haystack has learned to speak: it is much easier to find the needle if you can hear it call 'Here I am!', when you are in its neighborhood.

An evolutionary algorithm based on Lamarckian evolution will use the codings of the improved candidate solutions to generate the next generation. So, especially when the fitness landscape of the problem is not too complex, it can be expected that the evolutionary algorithm will very quickly converge to a good solution. Lamarckism, however, will decrease the genetic variation within the population, since the improved solution replaces the original solution before reproduction. The local maxima in the fitness landscape will work as attractors for the local search algorithm (see figure 6.11), so when the local search algorithm is run until no further progression is possible, almost all of the genetic variation will be lost.

The actual effect of local search in Lamarckian evolution will depend on the depth (number of steps) of the local search algorithm. If the local search algorithm is used to improve the solution coded in a member only a little bit, it is expected that Lamarckian evolution will in general result in a faster convergence to a better solution, compared with 'normal' Darwinian evolution (see figure 6.10). If, on the other hand, the local search algorithm will search for the best reachable solution for each candidate solution, there is a high probability that the evolutionary algorithm converges too early to a suboptimal solution, especially for complex search spaces, since the algorithm will be confronted with too less variation in its population.

The only difference in implementation between Darwinian evolution with local search as part of the fitness evaluation and Lamarckian evolution, is that when trying to create the Baldwin effect one does not do the coding step from the locally optimized individual back into it's chromosomes before reproduction. In most cases when the fitness landscape is not too complex, Lamarckian evolution will outperform the Baldwin effect because it makes better use of the information acquired by the local search. If however the fitness landscape is complex, making use of the Baldwin effect can in the long run find better solutions, because it does not reduce the genetic variation. In other words: Lamarckian evolution moves the population itself directed by the local search algorithm, while the Baldwin effect is caused by only changing the selection mechanism of the Darwinian evolution.

Whitley et al. [221], for example, found that incorporating Lamarckism in a genetic search often resulted in an extremely fast form of evolutionary search. However, they also found that functions exist where both the simple genetic algorithm without learning and the Lamarckian strategy used, converge to local optima while the simple genetic algorithm exploiting the Baldwin effect converges to a global optimum. Also in our own experience, Baldwin scores better in terms of how often it finds the global optimum.

6.6   Evolving Network Architectures Directed by Local Search

Evolutionary computation is currently the only available approach that is able to find well suited modular network architectures for a given task. The current bottleneck of this approach is the long training time needed for each network evaluation, but specialized neural hardware may be able to solve this problem in the future (e.g., [191]).

The G2L-system formalism can code large network architectures efficiently [222], but it is very difficult for an evolutionary algorithm to fine-tune the final solution. Fine-tuning is problematic for most evolutionary algorithms, but even more so if a complex coding scheme is being used. Because of this, we started looking for other ways to speedup the evolution of neural network architectures [183].

In this section we will describe how the ideas of Lamarck and Baldwin, as explained in the previous section can be used to improve the performance of the evolutionary search for optimal neural network architectures. Gruau and Whitley also experimented with the effect of learning on the evolution of neural networks [197], but their approach restricted the local search to the optimization of weights that were partially coded in their cellular coding. By leaving some of the weights unspecified in their coding, training those weights using a learning algorithm instead, they found a speed-up of evolutionary convergence compared with the case where all the weights were coded. However, they reported no significant advantage of Baldwin over Lamarck: most of their results showed a slightly better performance when using Lamarckian evolution.

What is needed for speeding up the evolution of modular artificial neural network architectures using Lamarckian evolution or Darwinian evolution with the Baldwin effect, is a local search strategy that locally optimizes the architecture of an already existing modular network. Earlier, we already described several search strategies that are able to change the architecture of neural networks. These methods, however, are not able to operate on a given modular architecture. In [184] we introduced a constructive method that is able to operate on *modular*^{2} architectures. We restricted ourselves to the addition of nodes to existing modules. Here we will shortly present two more general algorithms that also allow the generation of new modules. These constructive algorithms determine *where* to perform the adaptation, and so will provide the means for implementing the Baldwin effect or Lamarckian evolution when evolving neural network architectures.

Adding Nodes to Existing Modules

We will first describe a method that looks at the absolute weight changes in the network during training to determine which module should receive a new

---

2 Since we restricted ourselves to feedforward networks trained by backpropagation [217] or quickprop [193], a module should here be interpreted as a 'layer' of neurons embedded in and part of a modular network.

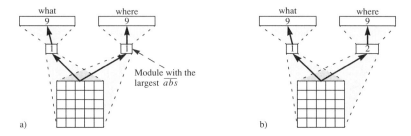

Figure 6.12
The network before and after adding the first node to the 'where subnetwork' for the what-where
problem.

node. After each presentation of a training sample we calculate

$$\text{abs}_{ij}(t) = |\Delta w_{ij}(t)| + m \cdot \text{abs}_{ij}(t - 1),$$

with $0 < m < 1$ and t the time-step, for each weight in the network. After
a number of training cycles we calculate for each hidden module the average
abs_{ij} over all its in- and outgoing weights. Then the module that has the largest
average receives a new node, see figure 6.12.

This process can be repeated for a number of times, after which the fitness
of the final network is determined.

We also did experiments with several variations of the criteria described
above to calculate the position of the new node to be added, for example
looking just at incoming or outgoing weights or looking at changes in the sign
of the weights. These variations rarely led to differences in the path through
'architecture space' that was followed by the algorithm. This indicates the
robustness of the concept.

An important issue is the initialization of the new weights to and from
the added node, and the possible ways to change the existing weights. Ideas
taken from cascaded-correlation [193] were implemented, which increased the
learning speed compared with random initializations [188].

To give an impression of the results of this relatively simple algorithm we
show one experiment we did with the What-Where problem described in 6.2.

Figure 6.13 gives the average sum-squared error of 10 repetitions of training 300 cycles using backpropagation with momentum for several sizes of the
two hidden modules. Table 6.1 gives the consecutive module sizes of our algorithm for the two subnetworks (we started with two hidden modules with one
node each, see figure 6.12a).

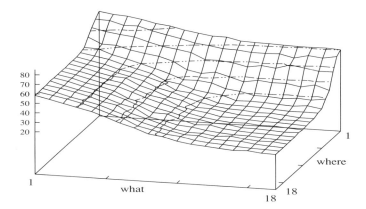

Figure 6.13
The remaining error plotted as function of the sizes of the two hidden modules.

Table 6.1
Results of the what/where experiment.

Step	0	1	2	3	4	5	6	7	...	19
What	1	1	1	1	1	2	2	3	...	15
Where	1	2	3	4	5	5	6	6	...	6

It is easy to see that our algorithm follows the optimal path, and learns the task, which demonstrates that it is correctly determining the module where the next node should be added. More experiments are described in [188].

Adding Modules

To extend the local search techniques for architecture optimization of neural networks we investigated the effects of adding a module at the output side or at the input side of a module selected with criteria as described above. A module added at the output side of a module receives input from the selected module and gives output to all the output modules of the selected module, see figure 6.14.

A module at the input side can be connected similarly. After adding a number of modules, we can add some nodes in the same way as described above. The number of modules and nodes added are parameters determining the depth of the local search.

Figure 6.14
Adding a new module at the output-side of module A.

From experiments with problems like XOR, TC, mapping problem, or the
Spiral problem, we learned that for some problems and starting architectures
it is better to add modules at the output side, while for other problems it is
better to add modules at the input side. More experiments are needed to find
a criterion to decide at what side a module is to be added. Currently we are
doing experiments with a simpler method that adds a new module (or extra
node) parallel to the weight that has the largest summed absolute partial weight
change. We will report on this method in future publications.

Exploiting the Baldwin Effect

The local search algorithms described above can now be used to improve
the architectures specified by our G2L-system formalism. We expect to see a
significant speed-up of our genetic algorithm as a result of the Baldwin effect.
With the algorithms presented in this chapter, it is now possible to optimize
modular artificial neural network architectures, exploiting the Baldwin effect
not just by learning weights, but by adapting the modular structure itself. As
said before, Lamarckian evolution is not possible with the described local
optimization method in combination with a recipe coding like the G2L-system.
The reason for this is that there is no sensible way to change the set of
production rules in such a way that the changes made by the local optimization
method become part of the grammar.

6.7   Conclusion

The L-system based graph grammar described in this paper allows for a very
compact coding of modular neural network architectures. Although it is shown
that all possible graphs can be generated with a G2L-system, iterative and recursive application of a set of rewriting rules usually leads to modular networks. G2L-systems make it possible to search for very large modular neural
network architectures using a genetic algorithm, without needing extremely

large chromosomes.

To speed-up the slow process of evolutionary architecture optimization, caused by the long time needed for each network evaluation, we presented in this chapter several algorithms to adapt the network architecture as part of the training process. We expect a large speed-up as a result of the Baldwin effect, when they are implemented in our method. These algorithms can of course also be used by themselves, when, for example, a normal training algorithm is trapped in a local minimum and adding some nodes in the right place will do the trick.

It is made clear that when recipe-like coding methods are being used, Lamarckian evolution is not possible. Using local search in a Darwinian evolutionary algorithm has the effect of changing the fitness landscape which can result in the Baldwin effect.

The main theme of this chapter was to demonstrate how we can reverse-engineer biological systems into an integrated framework for the synthesis of artificial neural networks. The combination of biologically inspired representations and optimization strategies, at all levels of complexity (the genetic algorithm, reading chromosomes in multiple ways, fixing defect rewriting rules, the graph rewriting mechanism, pruning the resulting networks, training weights, and adding nodes and modules), results in a powerful system providing a solution to the difficult problem of artificial neural network architecture design.

Acknowledgments

We would like to thank some of our students for implementing many of the ideas presented in this chapter: Boekman, Borst, Pit, and Wiemer [183, 188, 212, 222].

References

[181]D. H. Ackley and M. L. Littman. A case for Lamarckian evolution. In C. G. Langton, editor, *Artificial Life III*, pages 3–10. Addison-Wesley, Reading, MA, 1994.

[182]R. K. Belew. When both individuals and populations search: Adding simple learning to the genetic algorithm. In J. D. Schaffer, editor, *Proceedings of the Third International Conference on Genetic Algorithms*, pages 34–41. Kaufmann, San Mateo, CA, 1989.

[183]D. M. E. Boekman. Structure optimization of modular neural networks. Master's thesis, Department of Computer Science, Leiden University, The Netherlands, 1995.

[184]E. J. W. Boers, M. V. Borst, and I. G. Sprinkhuizen-Kuyper. Evolving artificial neural networks using the 'Baldwin effect'. In *Artificial Neural Nets and Genetic Algorithms, Proceedings of the International Conference in Alès, France*, 1995.

[185]E. J. W. Boers and H. Kuiper. Biological metaphors and the design of modular artificial neural networks. Master's thesis, Department of Computer Science, Leiden University, The Netherlands, 1992.

[186]E. J. W. Boers, H. Kuiper, B. L. M. Happel, and I. G. Sprinkhuizen-Kuyper. Designing modular artificial neural networks. In H. A. Wijshoff, editor, *Computing Science in The Netherlands: Proceedings (CSN'93)*, pages 87–96. Stichting Mathematisch Centrum, Amsterdam, 1993.

[187]E. J. W. Boers and I. G. Sprinkhuizen-Kuyper. Using L-systems as graph grammars: G2L-systems. Technical Report 95-30, Department of Computer Science, Leiden University, The Netherlands, 1995.

[188]M. V. Borst. Local structure optimization in evolutionary generated neural network architectures. Master's thesis, Department of Computer Science, Leiden University, The Netherlands, 1995.

[189]C. Darwin. *On the Origin of Species*. J. Murray, London, 1859.

[190]R. Dawkins. *The Blind Watchmaker*. Longman, 1986. Reprinted with appendix (1991). Penguin, London.

[191]H. de Garis. CAM-BRAIN, the evolutionary engineering of a billion neuron artificial brain by 2001 which grows/evolves at electronic speeds inside a cellular automata machine (CAM). In D. W. Pearson, N. C. Steele, and R. F. Albrecht, editors, *Artificial Neural Nets and Genetic Algorithms, Proceedings of the International Conference in Alès, France*, pages 84–87. Springer-Verlag, Wien, 1995.

[192]N. Dodd. Optimization of network structure using genetic algorithms. In B. Widrow and B. Angeniol, editors, *Proceedings of the International Neural Network Conference, INNC-90-Paris*, pages 693–696. Kluwer, Dordrecht, 1990.

[193]S. E. Fahlman and C. Lebiere. The Cascaded-correlation learning architecture. *Advances in Neural Information Processing Systems*, 2:524–532, 1990.

[194]M. Fréan. The upstart algorithm: a method for constructing and training feedforward neural networks. *Neural Computation*, 2:198–209, 1990.

[195]B. Fritzke. Growing cell structures—a self-organizing network for unsupervised and supervised learning. Technical Report 93-026, ICSI, 1993.

[196]F. Gruau. *Neural Network Synthesis Using Cellular Encoding and the Genetic Algorithm*. PhD thesis, l'Ecole Normale Supérieure de Lyon, 1994.

[197]F. Gruau and D. Whitley. Adding learning to the cellular development of neural networks: Evolution and the Baldwin effect. *Evolutionary Computation*, 1:213–233, 1993.

[198]S. A. Harp, T. A. Samad, and A. Guha. Towards the genetic synthesis of neural networks. In J. D. Schaffer, editor, *Proceedings of the Third International Conference on Genetic Algorithms (ICGA)*, pages 360–369. Kaufmann, San Mateo, CA, 1989.

[199]J. A. Hertz, A. Krogh, and R. G. Palmer. *Introduction to the Theory of Neural Computation*. Santa Fe Institute Studies in the Sciences of Complexity. Addison-Wesley, Redwood City, CA, 1991.

[200]G. E. Hinton and S. J. Nowlan. How learning can guide evolution. *Complex Systems*, 1:495–502, 1987.

[201]P. Hogeweg and B. Hesper. A model study on biomorphological description. *Pattern Recognition*, 6:165–179, 1974.

[202]J. H. Holland. *Adaptation in Natural and Artificial Systems*. University of Michigan Press, Ann Harbor, 1975.

[203]R. A. Jacobs, M. I. Jordan, and A. G. Barto. Task decomposition through competition in a modular connectionist architecture: the What and Where vision tasks. *Cognitive Science*, 15:219–250, 1991.

[204]H. Kitano. Designing neural network using genetic algorithm with graph generation

system. *Complex Systems*, 4:461–476, 1990.

[205]J.-B. P. A. Lamarck. *Philosophie Zoologique: ou Exposition des Considérations Relatives à l'Histoire Naturelle des Animaux*. Paris, 1809.

[206]Y. le Cun, J. S. Denker, and S. A. Solla. Optimal brain damage. In D. Touretzky, editor, *Advances in Neural Information Processing Systems, 2*, pages 598–605. Morgan Kaufmann, 1990.

[207]A. Lindenmayer. Mathematical models for cellular interaction in development, parts I and II. *Journal of Theoretical Biology*, 18:280–315, 1968.

[208]M. Marchand, M. Golea, and P. Ruján. A convergence theorem for sequential learning in two-layer perceptrons. *Europhysics Letters*, 11:487–492, 1990.

[209]M. Mezard and J.-P. Nadal. Learning in feedforward layered networks: the tiling algorithm. *Journal of Physics A*, 22:2191–2204, 1989.

[210]M. Mozer and P. Smolensky. Skeletonization: a technique for trimming the fat from a network via relevance assessment. In *Advances in Neural Information Processing Systems 1*, pages 107–115. Morgan Kaufmann, 1989.

[211]C. W. Omlin and C. L. Giles. Pruning recurrent neural networks for improved generalization performance. Revised Technical Report 93-6, Computer Science Department, Rensselaer Polytechnic Institute, Troy, N.Y., 1993.

[212]L. J. Pit. Parallel genetic algorithms. Master's thesis, Department of Computer Science, Leiden University, The Netherlands, 1995.

[213]P. Prusinkiewicz and J. Hanan. *Lindenmayer Systems, Fractals and Plants*. Springer-Verlag, New York, 1989.

[214]P. Prusinkiewicz and A. Lindenmayer. *The Algorithmic Beauty of Plants*. Springer-Verlag, New York, 1990.

[215]S. G. Roberts and M. Turega. Evolving neural network structures: an evaluation of encoding techniques. In D. W. Pearson, N. C. Steele, and R. F. Albrecht, editors, *Artificial Neural Nets and Genetic Algorithms, Proceedings of the International Conference in Alès, France*, pages 96–99. Springer-Verlag, Wien, 1995.

[216]J. G. Rueckl, K. R. Cave, and S. M. Kosslyn. Why are 'What' and 'Where' processed by separate cortical visual systems? A computational investigation. *Journal of Cognitive Neuroscience*, 1:171–186, 1989.

[217]D. E. Rumelhart, G. E. Hinton, and R. J. Williams. Learning internal representations by error propagation. In J. L. McClelland, D. E. Rumelhart, and the PDP research group, editors, *Parallel Distributed Processing, Volume 1: Foundations*, pages 318–362. MIT Press, Cambridge, MA, 1986.

[218]S. A. Solla. Learning and generalization in layered neural networks: the contiguity problem. In L. Personnas and G. Dreyfus, editors, *Neural Networks: from Models to Applications*, pages 168–177. I.D.S.E.T., Paris., 1989.

[219]I. G. Sprinkhuizen-Kuyper and E. J. W. Boers. The error surface of the simplest XOR network has only global minima. *Neural Computation*, 8:1301–1320, 1996.

[220]A. L. Szilard and R. E. Quinton. An interpretation for D0L-systems by computer graphics. *The Science Terrapin*, 4:8–13, 1979.

[221]D. Whitley, V. S. Gordon, and K. Mathias. Lamarckian evolution, the Baldwin effect and function optimization. In Y. Davidor, H.-P. Schwefel, and R. Männer, editors, *Lecture Notes in Computer Science 866*, pages 6–15. Springer-Verlag, 1994.

[222]M. Wiemer. Optimalisatie met een genetisch algoritme van een genetisch algoritme om neurale netwerken te ontwerpen. Master's thesis, Department of Computer Science, Leiden University, The Netherlands, 1995.

7 Evolutionary Neurogenesis Applied to Mobile Robotics

Olivier Michel

This chapter describes an evolutionary process producing dynamical neural networks used as controllers for mobile robots. The main concepts used, namely genetic algorithms, neurogenesis process, artificial neural networks and artificial metabolism, illustrate our conviction that some fundamental principles of nature may help to design processes from which emerge adaptive robot behavior. The artificial neurogenesis model described in this chapter, inspired from developmental and molecular biology, allows the generation of any complex modular neural structure. The evolutionary process is applied to a simulated mobile robot. The resulting neural networks are then embedded on the real mobile robot *Khepera*. We emphasize the role of the artificial metabolism and the role of the environment which appear to be the motors of evolution. Early results demonstrate the efficiency of this methodology and give hints to continue research investigations towards the generation of more complex adaptive neural networks.

7.1   Introduction

Most of artificial life researchers try to obtain synthetic forms of organization inspired from biological principles of life. The interdisciplinarity of this research area induces the integration of biological concepts inside artificial constructions. Although most of the vocabulary and inspiration are borrowed from biology, we do not claim to model biological processes. Our aim is to apply fundamental principles of evolution and self-organization to autonomous agents.

The evolutionary approach applied to autonomous agents is today a rising research area. Various methods might be mentioned which make use of evolutionary processes on different structures. Rodney Brooks proposed a high level language, GEN, which may evolve under genetic control, and which can be compiled into BL (Behavior Language), a lower level language, dedicated to a real mobile robot [226]. He outlines the danger of the lack of realism of simulators but also acknowledges that such tools seem to be necessary for evolutionary processes.

Marco Colombetti and Marco Dorigo make use of classifier systems for the control of mobile robots [228]. Different kinds of classifier systems are used for different kinds of behaviors, the overall system being also supervised by a classifier system. Experiments are presented on a simulator and on a real robot.

Artificial neural networks paradigm is a very powerful AI tool since it allows an infinite number of schemes to be built using a very wide variety of learning rules [239]. For practical applications, engineers have to address both problems of designing a suitable topology and defining an appropriate learning rule in order to obtain accurate artificial neural networks. These tasks, and especially the first one, are not easy and may be inspired by neurobiological observations for the learning rules [238] as well as for the topology [232, 227, 245]. Image processing is a good example where biology gave hints to engineers [233, 248]. But biological data relative to the activities of large groups of neurons are often inextricable and hence difficult to understand. Although the principles of synaptic strengths modifications are better understood [240], most of the functions of biological brains are still unknown. This is mainly due to the big numbers of interconnected units forming complex structures and leading to very complex dynamics.

An alternative to trying to copy biological brains is modeling the biological process of Evolution. Computer investigations addressing artificial evolution are often referred as Evolutionary Computation (EC) or Genetic Algorithms (GA) [234]. The application of evolutionary algorithms to artificial neural networks has been investigated by a number of authors. A distinction must be done between evolutionary techniques used as learning algorithms (i.e. to calculate the synaptic weights of a neural network whose architecture is fixed [242]) and evolutionary techniques used to optimize the topology of a neural network. This chapter will focus on the second point since it represents a promising challenge in the search for adaptive artificial neural networks.

7.2   State of the Art in Artificial Neurogenesis

The artificial morphogenesis of neural networks (neurogenesis) is a process that uses information lying on a chromosome to build up a structure of neurons interconnected via a number of links of different types. A resume of research in developmental neurogenesis can be found in [244]. These recent attempts to automatically generate artificial neural networks, are usually designed to produce behavioral controllers for autonomous agents equipped with sensors and actuators.

Most of these researches make an extensive use of production rules at different levels: On one hand, Boers and Kuiper use Lindenmayer systems [249] for rewriting groups of neurons [224] and Gruau applies a complex encoding scheme using a grammar tree as rewriting rules for neurons [235]. On the other hand, such production rules can be applied to lower level objects, corresponding to chemical elements inside neurons, inducing actions at the neuron level like cell division, cell migration, axon growth, etc. Harvey proposed such a theoretical framework allowing the modeling of polypeptide chains inside the cells [236]. Vaario and Shimohara developed such a system that models attractions and repulsions between cells leading to the formation of structures [256]. Kitano observed the emergence of artificial patterns of axon growth similar to those observed in nature [243]. Dellaert and Beer built a morphogenesis process inspired from Kauffman's genetic regulatory networks [241] in which a steady state of the genetic network fires a morphogenesis action: a cell division [230].

Although they do not use production rules, Nolfi and Parisi developed an interesting dynamical neurogenesis model featuring dendritic growth and allowing the environment to influence the morphogenesis process while the agent is interacting with the environment [255, 254].

De Garis proposed a cellular automaton based morphogenesis involving CAM machines (powerful parallel computers dedicated to cellular automata) [229]. This approach is fascinating since neurogenesis occurs in a huge 2 or 3-dimensional cellular automata space where dendrites and axons grow and where the neural dynamics are modeled, i.e. the neural signals propagate using cellular automata rules. Unfortunately, this model doesn't include yet any cell division process, nor cell migration.

Finally, Floreano and Mondada [231], as well as Harvey, Husband and Cliff [237] have been among the first ones to test evolutionary neural networks on real robots.

The approach presented in this chapter features a dynamical genomic network, involving artificial proteins, which is the heart of a neurogenesis process, allowing cell differentiation, cell division, cell migration, axon growth, axon guidance and target recognition in a two dimensional space. The resulting neural networks are embedded in a simulated mobile robot which has to travel across a maze while avoiding obstacles.

7.3 Application to Mobile Robotics

Most of the evolutionary neural networks research has been applied to autonomous agents [244]. This application area was preferred for three main reasons:

- Other traditional robotics approaches failed in proposing a powerful general framework.
- Simple autonomous agents may involve a relatively simple input to output processing. They are easily expandable and hence may require an increasing structural complexity [225]. This expandability ability makes them very well suited for evolutionary computation.
- The recent emergence of scientific interest in the field of Artificial Life [246] reinforced this research since this way of obtaining artificial neural networks is "biologically plausible" and hence of fundamental interest.

The last point may provide very interesting guidelines for the development of an evolutionary robotics project. Such a framework will give powerful metaphors for the design a self-sufficient, yet powerful, evolutionary system. This research philosophy may help to design a fitness function using something similar to an artificial metabolism to make an evaluation of the individuals.

The evolutionary loop we propose (see figure 7.1) involves successively a genetic algorithm evolving chromosomes, a morphogenesis process allowing to decode a chromosome into a neural network, a dynamical neural network model used for driving a mobile robot and finally an artificial metabolism defining the viability domain of the robots and returning a fitness value to the genetic algorithm. This methodology was applied in order to observe the emergence of mobile robot behaviors. The genetic evolution occurred in simulation and the resulting neural networks were then embedded on the real robot [251].

7.4 Dynamical Neural Network Model

Many reasons led us to use dynamical neural networks. This family of networks includes multi-layer perceptrons as well as recurrent networks. Consequently, it seems to be rather universal. Moreover, the properties of such networks are very interesting for autonomous agents (temporal processing, sequence generation and recognition, models of memory, etc.). It is possible to

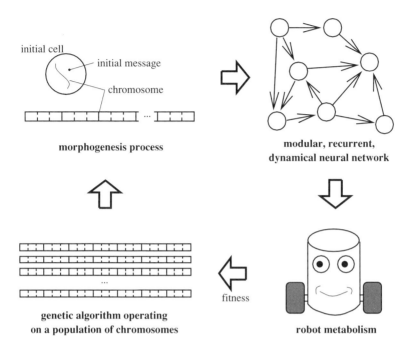

initial cell

initial message

chromosome

morphogenesis process

modular, recurrent, dynamical neural network

genetic algorithm operating on a population of chromosomes

fitness

robot metabolism

Figure 7.1
The evolutionary loop

implement local learning algorithms, cheap in computation time and friendly to parallel computation. Their very complex dynamics make their structural design very difficult. Genetic Algorithms may be suitable for such a task.

All the neurons have the same transfer function (linear thresholds). When the state of a neuron is close to 1, it will be said to be excited. If the state of a neuron is close to 0, it will be said to be inhibited (or at rest). Let $x_i(t)$ be the state of the neuron i at iteration t and ω_{ij}, the weight of the link between neuron j and neuron i. The state of neuron i updates as described here:

$$x_i(t+1) = \begin{cases} 0 & \text{if } \sum_j \omega_{ij} x_j(t) \leq 0 \\ 1 & \text{if } \sum_j \omega_{ij} x_j(t) \geq 1 \\ \sum_j \omega_{ij} x_j(t) & \text{otherwise} \end{cases}$$

Different kinds of links exist. Some links have a fixed given synaptic weight equal to a positive or a negative real number, while other links have a variable

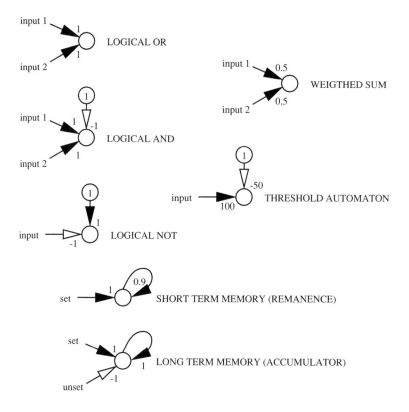

Figure 7.2
Different neural schemes: excitatory links are represented in black and inhibitory links are represented in white

synaptic weight whose value is evolving according to a specific Hebbian learning rule. This system may be easily expandable by adding other learning rules such as different versions of Hebb rule, Anti-Hebb rule, etc. A collection of different fixed weight links has been carefully designed, allowing to build various neural schemes (see figure 7.2) that can be seen as building blocks for larger neural networks.

7.5 Artificial Morphogenesis

The artificial morphogenesis process allows to build dynamical neural networks using a chromosome organized in a linear structure. It takes inspiration

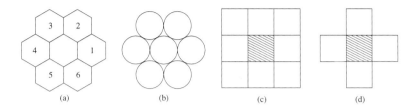

Figure 7.3
Two dimensional space discretizations: hexagonal neighboring (a) is the better approximation of circles neighboring (b) while square grids allows either the 8-neighbors model (c) or the 4-neighbors model (d).

from the biological explanation of protein synthesis regulation [252]. This recurrent process allows an easy generation of modular neural networks (where the same sub-structures may exist at different places in the same overall network). Moreover, due to a strong epistasis, it features some properties of dynamical systems that permit to generate complexity at the edge between chaos and order [241].

Morphogenesis Space

SPACE STRUCTURE

The morphogenesis process runs in a two dimensional space discretized using a hexagonal grid. The choice of hexagons relies on the interesting neighboring property of such grids: Like the circle, the hexagon has exactly 6 neighbors. Moreover, it eludes the typical problem of choosing between the 4-neighbors model and the 8-neighbors model induced by a square grid (see figure 7.3).

Chemicals diffusion, cell migrations and axon growth were implemented within this hexagonal grid. A hexagon usually contains various chemicals (artificial proteins concentrations) ; it may also contain one cell (a single cell per hexagon). An initial rectangular size of $38 \times 28 = 1064$ hexagons was chosen since it represents a big enough space for containing enough artificial neurons necessary for most autonomous agents applications. For systems using a high input data flow like image processing systems, this size should be increased according to the size of the input flow. The hexagon space was configured as a torus (i.e. the upper side communicates with the lower side and the left hand side communicates with the right hand side) to avoid border effects.

CHEMICAL DIFFUSION

A model of diffusion was designed to allow various chemicals (artificial proteins) to diffuse through this space. Each hexagon contains several concentrations of different artificial proteins. These concentrations diffuse to the neighboring hexagons according to equations using the preservation of the quantity of proteins associated with a diffusion coefficient:

$$C_{ik}(t+1) = \frac{K_{diff}}{6} \times \sum_{j=1}^{6}[C_{ik}(t) - C_{N_{ij}k}(t)]$$

$C_{ik}(t)$ represents the concentration of protein k in hexagon i at time t. K_{diff} is the diffusion parameter, it must be lower than 0.5 to avoid oscillation effects due to a too coarse discretization (we set it to 0.3 in our experiments). Finally, $N_{ij}, j \in \{1, 2, 3, 4, 5, 6\}$ represents the jth neighboring hexagon of hexagon i (see figure 7.3, a).

NEURAL CELLS

Each neural cell occupies a unique hexagon, while a hexagon contains at the most one cell. Each cell is associated with a non unique identifier (i.e. a numerical value) corresponding to a cell type. Consequently, two different cells may have the same identifier, which means that they are not differentiated (the one relatively to the other), and hence, they will behave roughly the same way. The cell identifier is used to produce systematically inside the cell's body a protein whose identifier is equal to this cell identifier. A cell moves according to chemicals gradients: if the concentration of a protein matches the cell type, the cell moves towards the neighboring hexagon that contains the highest (or the lowest) concentration of such a protein. This attractive (or repulsive) cell behavior depends upon the cell type and the protein type:

• Attractive cells are attracted by activator proteins.

• Attractive cells are repulsed by repressor proteins.

• Repulsive cells are repulsed by activator proteins.

• Repulsive cells are attracted by repressor proteins.

If a cell is already situated on a local maximum (or minimum) of a matching protein concentration, it will not move. Cell division and axon growth will be detailed after describing the chromosome structure and the genomic network.

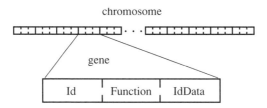

Figure 7.4
Genotype structure: variable length chromosomes contain genes made up of three parts

Table 7.1
Gene functions

Value	Name	Description
000	F_INT_A	protein synthesis: create an internal activator protein
001	F_EXT_A	protein synthesis: create an external activator protein
010	F_CELL_A	cell split: create an attractive cell
011	F_LINK_A	axon growth: create an attractive axon
100	F_INT_R	protein synthesis: create an internal repressor protein
101	F_EXT_R	protein synthesis: create an external repressor protein
110	F_CELL_R	cell split: create a repulsive cell
111	F_LINK_R	axon growth: create a repulsive axon

Chromosome Structure

A chromosome is divided into a variable number of genes. As depicted on figure 7.4, each gene contains an identifier part, Id which is an integer value ranging from 0 to $n - 1$, a function part, Function, made up of 3 bits (see table 7.1) and a data part, IdData which is also an integer value ranging from 0 to $n - 1$. The value of n, representing the number of proteins available in the system and depending on the size of the chromosome, will be explained in the genetic algorithm section.

Genomic Network

PROTEIN SYNTHESIS REGULATION IN BIOLOGY

There are many ways to regulate protein synthesis, here we focused on two interesting points. Of course, we assumed many simplifications in order to be clearer, but the key ideas remain: If a particular protein called repressor is present, it can sit on the start codon of a specified gene on the chromosome, so that RNA polymerase cannot read it, and thus the corresponding proteins cannot be synthesized. This system can be recurrent when a synthesized protein can be a repressor for another gene. The other mechanism can be seen as the positive version of the first one. A molecule called activator is necessary to initiate the process of transcription of the DNA into mRNA at a specific locus, and thus to initiate the proteins synthesis process. Recurrence remains possible when a synthesized protein causes the synthesis of other ones.

Such a system is not closed since a protein may also initiate various cell behaviors (possibly cell division, cell migration, axon growth for neural cells, etc.). This process can be seen as a kind of production system, where proteins (repressors and activators) are conditions to the production of other proteins. If each protein is represented as a vertex of a graph, the genes will be represented as connections between proteins. This is called the genomic network (see figure 7.5).

ARTIFICIAL GENOMIC NETWORK

Before the morphogenesis process runs, the chemical contents of all the hexagons are cleaned and a number of initial cells (possibly one single cell) are laid in some hexagons of the morphogenesis space. These cells are of a given type (defined by their identifier). Consequently, they start to produce the corresponding proteins inside their own cell body. These proteins initiate the complex process occurring in the genomic network: They activate some genes that will produce other proteins and so on.

A gene can influence another through the production of a protein. Let assume that a gene is active. If the Function of this gene leads to the synthesis of an activator (resp. repressor) protein, the gene will use its IdData value to build up such protein. The synthesized protein will be defined by its type: activator (resp. repressor) and its identifier equal to the value of the IdData of the gene. Such a protein will then be able to influence other genes if its identifier matches (i.e. is equal to) Id values of other genes.

Functions leading to the production of activator (resp. repressor) proteins include F_INT_A (resp. F_INT_R) which produces proteins that remain inside the cell body while F_EXT_A (resp. F_EXT_R) produces activator (resp. repressor) proteins that diffuse through the cell body. Proteins remaining inside the cell body cannot move outside of it while diffusion proteins enter the hexagon where the cell lies and diffuse to its neighboring hexagons according to the diffusion model, and so on. When a diffusion protein meets a cell, it enter its body, thus brings a chemical messages to this cell. This extends the notion of genomic network outside the cell body, allowing cells to communicate with each other.

The following equation models the gene activation process where A_k is the activity of gene k, P_k representing the set of proteins matching with A_k, C_i being the concentration of protein i and $T_i \in \{-1, 1\}$ representing whether the protein i is a repressor (-1) or an activator (1). A_k will be said to be active if its value is strictly positive and inhibited otherwise.

$$A_k(t) = \begin{cases} 0 & \text{if } \sum_{i \in P_k}(C_i \times T_i) \leq 0 \\ 1 & \text{if } \sum_{i \in P_k}(C_i \times T_i) \geq 1 \\ \sum_{i \in P_k}(C_i \times T_i) & \text{otherwise} \end{cases}$$

Morphogenesis Actions

CELL DIVISION

A gene may initiate a cell division process if its `Function` is `F_CELL_A` (resp. `F_CELL_R`). This will produce a new attractive (resp. repulsive) cell whose identifier is equal to the gene's `IdData` parameter. A copy of the chromosome of the mother cell is given to the child cell, so that all the cells have the same genotype (just like in Nature). The two cells initially occupy the same hexagon, so they will have to move away from each other during next iteration or else, the new cell will be destroyed (since two cells cannot occupy the same hexagon).

AXON GROWTH

Artificial cells may have several axons connecting them to several other cells and thus allowing different types of synapses to be created. An axon is generated by a gene whose `Function` is `F_LINK_A` (resp. `F_LINK_R`). The axon identifier is set to the `IdData` value of the gene. The newly created attractive (resp. repulsive) axon will growth towards the direction of the positive (resp. negative) chemical gradient corresponding to its identifier using the same principle as cell moving mechanism. Once an axon arrives on a hexagon with a null chemical gradient, it dies, unless the hexagon contains a cell and in this case, it connects to the cell. The resulting synaptic type is corresponding to the axon identifier. It may be a fixed weight synapse (positive or negative) or a synapse associated with a learning law (various forms of Hebbian learning, Anti-Hebbian learning, etc.)

genomic network   chromosome

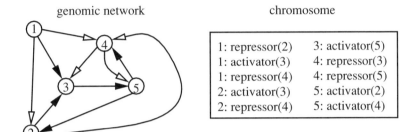

1: repressor(2)	3: activator(5)
1: activator(3)	4: repressor(3)
1: repressor(4)	4: repressor(5)
2: activator(3)	5: activator(2)
2: repressor(4)	5: activator(4)

Figure 7.5
The genomic network represented as a graph and as a set of chromosome genes

7.6 Genetic Algorithm

A genetic algorithm was designed to operate on a population of variable length chromosomes. New operators were defined to allow gene addition, gene deletion, crossover between individuals of different sizes, etc.

At the beginning, an initial population of 100 individuals is randomly generated. Each chromosome is initially made of 16 genes. The maximum values of the fields `Id` and `IdData`, n, corresponding to the maximum number of different proteins is computed using Kauffman's NK model of dynamical Boolean networks [241].

Let N be the number of elements (genes) of the genomic network. If each gene depends on K other genes (on average), the corresponding genomic network will have N links and $N \div K$ vertices (see figure 7.5). Hence, the maximum number of proteins equals $n = N \div K$. It has been shown by Kauffman that the value of K determines the dynamics of the genomic network: on one hand, if $K = N$, the behavior of the network is chaotic, that is very sensitive to initial conditions and to perturbations. On the other hand, if $K = 1$, the network is said to be a *set of independent chain* with very simple dynamics. The most fascinating case corresponds to $K = 2$ where interesting behaviors appear: the network becomes resistant to most of the perturbations and a sort of order seems to emerge through complex structures. Such networks feature dynamics at the edge of chaos, which may lead to interesting results since complex structures in life exists at the edge of chaos [247].

We choose to set $K = 2$ in our genomic network, in order to have a chance to observe such interesting dynamics. Consequently, the initial number of proteins available in the system is given by $n = N \div K = 8$ for the initial chromosome. However, since the size of the chromosome may change during the evolutionary process, this value is updated dynamically during evolution. Consequently, the system will create new proteins when the size of the chromosomes increase.

Metabolism Based Fitness Value

In some of our experiments, the fitness value used by genetic algorithms to perform selection was modeled using the concept of artificial metabolism: At the beginning, each robot receives an initial amount of energy points. The definition of the interactions between the robot and its environment will rule the variation of energy points of the robot. For example, in the case of a mobile robot, one could choose to define the loss of one energy point at regular period of time to penalize slowness or idleness ; the loss of one energy point at each move would penalize useless moves and finally the gain of several energy points would reward satisfactory behaviors. An example of satisfactory behavior could be something like *wall following*, *moving while avoiding obstacles*, *target pursuit*, or *object seeking*.

Each robot is set in the environment with its initial amount of energy points during a given time t. At the end, the remaining energy points will be used to assign a fitness value to the robot. This value will be used by the genetic algorithm to select the best individuals.

7.7 Experimental Setup

Khepera Simulator

Experiments were driven on *Khepera Simulator* [250], a mobile robot simulator allowing to transfer easily the controllers to the real robot *Khepera* [253]. We added specific functions to *Khepera Simulator* including a dynamical neural network simulator connected to the sensors and effectors of the simulated robot, a morphogenesis process used to generate neural networks from chromosomes and a genetic algorithm evolving a population of chromosomes. This simulator is tool for the design of controllers that can be directly embedded on the real robot. Even if the simulator is not perfect, i.e. if some divergence between the simulated robot and the real one are observed, it remains possible to continue the evolutionary process on the real robot for a few generations in order to fine tune parameters of the neural network. Our first series of experi-

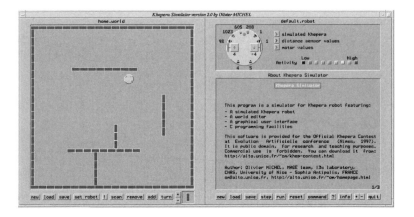

Figure 7.6
Snapshot of *Khepera Simulator* graphical user interface. *Khepera Simulator* is now a freeware
mobile robot simulator running on Unix operating systems with X11 library. It is available from
the World Wide Web at $\texttt{http}://\texttt{wwwi3s.unice.fr}/\sim\texttt{om/khep}-\texttt{sim.html}$

ments did not necessitate such an operation, which demonstrates the reliability
of the simulator concerning the behaviors we evolved.

DESCRIPTION OF THE ROBOT

Like the real robot *Khepera*, the simulated mobile robot includes 8 infrared
sensors (small rectangles) allowing it to detect the proximity of objects in
front of it, behind it, and to the right and the left sides of it. Each sensors
return a value ranging between 0 and 1023. 0 means that no object is perceived
while 1023 means that an object is very close to the sensor (almost touching
the sensor). Intermediate values may give an approximate idea of the distance
between the sensor and the object. Sensors are connected to the inputs of the
neural network according to the following description: The state of the first
input neuron I_0 is always 1 to ensure at least one active input in the neural
network (necessary for some neural schemes), the states I_x of the other input
neurons are computed according to the values of the sensors S_{x+1}, $x \in [0; 7]$.

$$\begin{cases} I_0 = 1 \\ I_x = S_{x+1} \div 1023 \quad \text{with } x \in [0; 7] \end{cases}$$

Each of the right and left motors are driven by two output neurons. Each motor
can take a speed value ranging between -10 and $+10$. Each neuron can take

Figure 7.7
Khepera (5 cm diameter) and its simulated counterpart

a state value ranging between 0 and 1. The speed value of a motor is given by the state value of the first neuron minus the state value of the second one, the resulting value being multiplied by 10. This choice makes that, on one hand, when both neurons are inhibited, no motor action occurs (no excitation induces no move), and on the other hand, when the "move-forward" motor neuron and the "move-backwards" motor neuron are simultaneous active, the actual move results of the competition between these two neurons. The direction of the speed is given by the winning neuron, and the amplitude of the speed corresponds to the amplitude of the success of a neuron against the other. Let Vl (resp. Vr) be the velocity of left motor (resp. right motor) and let O_x, $x \in [0; 3]$ be the states of the output neurons of the network, the velocity of the motors is given by the following equations:

$$\left\{ \begin{array}{rcl} V_g & = & (O_0 - O_2) \times 10 \\ V_d & = & (O_1 - O_3) \times 10 \end{array} \right.$$

Description of the Environment

Bricks (rectangular objects) laid by the user in the environment allow the design of mazes of differing complexities (see figure 7.8). It is also possible to add smaller objects such as corks. Light sources are also available. The simulated robot can perceive them through its infra-red sensors. The real dimensions of this simulated environment (comparing to an actual Khepera) are $1\,m \times 1\,m$.

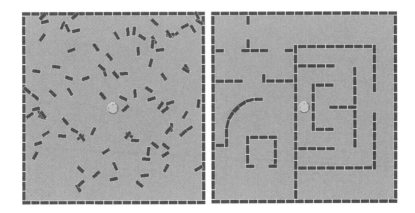

Figure 7.8
Two examples of simulated environments: chaos.world on the left hand side and lab.world on the right hand side

7.8   First Series of Experiments

This early series of experiments used a very simplified neurogenesis model. The space of neurogenesis was not a two dimensional space with chemical diffusion through an hexagonal grid, but a single dimensional space implemented as a chained list of cells which are able to communicate with their ancestor and successor in the list and with other cells through axonal connections. However, the principles of the genomic network dynamics and some fundamental neurogenesis proteins (for cell division, axon growth and target recognition) are included in this simple model.

Preliminary Experiments: Artificial Metabolism

This subsection describes the very first experiments driven on a primitive version of *Khepera Simulator* (the robot has only three front sensors and a single back sensor). There are no obstacles on the path of the robot, but blocks of "food" are scattered randomly over the simulated environment. The robot perceives them through its sensors. These experiments involve a metabolism based fitness function, making the robot eat up as many blocks of food as possible.

METABOLISM BASED FITNESS FUNCTION

The metabolism of the robot was designed in order to observe the emergence of food seeking behavior. It corresponds to a kind of internal energy implemented as a real variable. Each robot has initially the same amount of energy. The energy of a robot is increased each time it eats up a block of food (i.e. goes towards a block of food, making it disappear). Each motor of a robot consumes an amount of energy proportional to its speed. And finally, even if a robot remains motionless, it consumes a small amount of energy, thus forcing it to look for food in order to survive. If the energy runs down to 0, the robot "'dies": its evaluation stops and its corresponding chromosome is removed from the population. Crossing-over and mutations occur on the surviving robots and give birth of a new generation of robots. The initial size of the population, which is set to 100, oscillate around this value along the evolutionary process. Indeed, the environment dynamically regulates this value. On one hand, when the population size is low, the environment becomes more friendly (i.e. more food blocks are generated) and hence the robots live longer and reproduce better. On the other hand, when the population size is too high above 100, the environment becomes more hostile (i.e. less food block than usual), thus leading to a decrease of the population size.

RESULTS

The evolutionary process needed 200 generations to discover neural networks having the right number of inputs and outputs, corresponding to *Khepera* sensors and actuators. The next 50 generations show the emergence of various behaviors in the population (see figure 7.9). At the very beginning, most of the robots don't move at all. But this inefficient behavior rapidly disappears. Some fixed trajectories appear to be efficient at the beginning (circle, line), but finally, a new behavior is discovered around epoch 210, that makes the robots attracted by food blocks. Since this is the best behavior it slowly becomes the most dominating in the population.

Fitness Function

The fitness function used in further investigations is not metabolism based, as described earlier. It optimizes a criterion (a distance). Anyway, the robot has an artificial metabolism which is not used for the calculation of the fitness function, but which allow to optimize the time of evaluation for a robot (a good robot could "live" longer that a bad one). Like in our previous work, our future

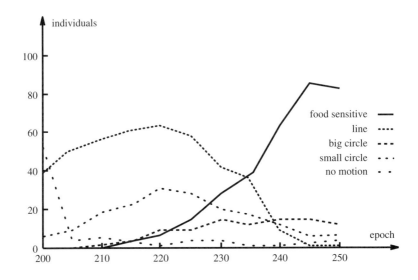

Figure 7.9
Preliminary experiments: Evolution of the behavior of the robots

research will make use of a metabolism based fitness function.

A robot staying motionless avoids obstacles perfectly. A robot that turns around on itself indefinitely, will probably avoid obstacles as well. Finally, a robot that goes forward, and then backwards and then forward again, etc., will certainly avoid surrounding obstacles. All these solutions have been discovered by our genetic algorithm and have led us to define a fitness function that forces the robot to make big moves in order to observe more elaborate behaviors than those observed earlier.

Consequently, we chose to reward (gain of energy points) the robots that get as far as possible from their initial position. The reward is proportional to the difference between the new position of the robot and the last position the more away from the initial position. A punishment (loss of energy points) is inflicted to the robot as soon as it hits an obstacle. It consists in a reduction to zero of its energy points. This punishment will allow evolution to design robots that avoid the obstacles they face. Moreover, a regular slow diminution of the energy points disadvantages motionless or idle robots. As soon as the energy of a robot reaches 0, the robot is stopped and assigned a fitness value equal to the d_max distance it reached. Here is the principle of the corresponding algorithm:

```
d_max  = 0;
energy = 100;
while(energy > 0)
{
   RunRobot();        /* compute d and HitObstacle */
   energy = energy - 1;
   if (d > d_max)
   {
      energy = energy + (d - d_max);
      if (energy > ceiling) energy = ceiling;
      d_max = d;
   }
   if (HitObstacle) energy = 0;
}
fitness = d_max;
```

d is the distance between the robot and its initial position, d_max is the maximal value of d, *energy* is the amount of energy points of the robot (artificial metabolism), *ceiling* is the maximal amount of energy points the robot can reach, $HitObstacle$ is a Boolean variable saying whether the robot hits an obstacle or not, and finally $fitness$ is the fitness value returned.

The environment being closed, the robot could not go away indefinitely (d_max is bounded), even if it doesn't hit any obstacle, it will gradually loose all its energy points, so the evaluation will be over.

Simulation Results

We tested the evolutionary process in two different environments depicted on figure 7.8: lab.world and chaos.world. In each environment, the evolutionary process was stopped after 1000 generations. Various results are observed in each environment.

In lab.world, which is a maze with rectilinear walls and right angles, evolution generated robots that follow the walls on their right. This behavior drives them significantly far away from their initial position. The figure 7.11 (a) illustrates the convergence of the fitness function while the figure 7.10 (a) shows the best neural network resulting from evolution.

In chaos.world, where the obstacles are randomly laid in the environment, the evolution generate robots that move forward and strongly turn to the left as soon as they detect an obstacle, then they start again moving forward

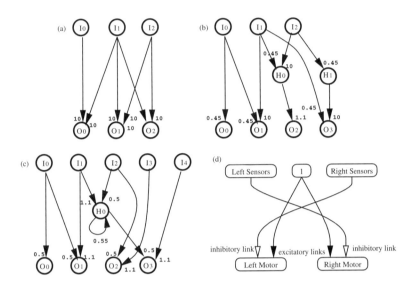

Figure 7.10
Resulting neural networks (a, b, c), looking like Braitenberg simplest vehicles (d)

in their new direction (see figures 7.11 (b) and 7.10 (b)). The fitness jump observed around generation 150 shows the random discovery of a neural connection giving to the robot a better behavior. This feature illustrates the ruggedness of the fitness landscape, making it harder for the genetic algorithms.

In both cases, robots are finally able to avoid obstacles most of the time, they are also able to turn back in a dead end. However, robots generated in lab.world are "lost" if set in chaos.world far from any obstacle. Indeed, if they perceive no obstacle, those robots will turn round, with the "hope" of finding a wall to follow. This strategy, which is very efficient in lab.world because the obstacles are always sufficiently close to the robot, appears to be inefficient in chaos.world because it may happen that the robot is far away from any obstacle, and so the robot cannot find any wall to follow using the "turn round" strategy. The "lost" robot will then turn round indefinitely.

A second test performed in chaos.world led to the emergence of robots whose behavior resembles the behavior of those obtained during the first test, but that remain anyway slightly less efficient (not so fast, fitness value not so good, see figure 7.11 (c) et 7.10 (c)). This result is a consequence of the fact that genetic algorithms use random values. So, the evolutionary process seems to be very sensitive to this random aspect of genetic algorithms.

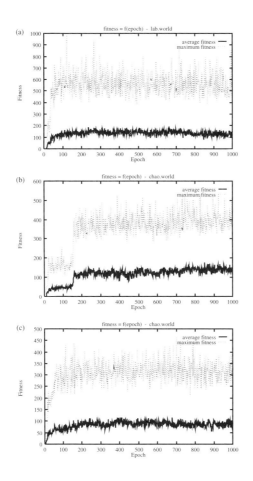

Figure 7.11
Fitness evolution

One could notice that the structures of the resulting neural networks is rather simple and could be compared to the simplest Braitenberg's vehicles [225] (see figure 7.10 (d)). Even if they are perfectly adapted to the given problem, networks (a) and (b) exhibit only pure reactive behaviors and thus are unable to learn. Special attention should be paid to network (c). This neural architecture includes a short term memory unit (or remanence) as depicted on figure 7.2. An interpretation the role of this unit could be that it makes it more easy for the robot to turn properly when facing an obstacle. Indeed, the short term memory unit helps the robot in such a task: when the robot starts turning, it will soon perceive no more obstacle and, if it had no short term memory, it would immediately move forward again, bumping its side to the obstacle. The short term memory unit "remembers", for a short time, that the robot perceived an obstacle and makes it continue turning in order to avoid bumping it on its side. The function of such a memory unit could be seen as a temporary knowledge acquisition. It is a first step towards adaptive behavior and learning.

Transfer to the Real Robot

The neural networks obtained with the simulation were directly transferred to Khepera. The behaviors observed on the real robot seem to be similar to the ones observed on the simulator: wall following for the first robot and forward move with left turn if an obstacle is seen for the second and third robots. These first behaviors are very simple, thus it is difficult for the moment to make a precise evaluation of the reliability of the simulator. The only observable differences between simulated and real behavior are only quantitative. For example, we observed in the wall following behavior that the real robot slightly rubbed the walls while its simulated counterpart didn't touch the wall, although it came very close.

Discussion

In both cases, the evolutionary process discovered solutions that correspond to the given problems. These results outline the important role of the environment which, associated with the definition of fitness function, seems to be one of the motors of the evolutionary process.

Moreover, several runs of the same evolutionary process in the same initial conditions underlined the random aspect of genetic algorithms leading to different solutions. This fact might be explained by the shape of the fitness landscape which is very rugged, so the genetic algorithm gets caught in local optima. Adding ecological niches to our evolutionary model could be an answer to that problem. Evolution would occur independently in different ecological niches and migrations would be rare to allow the really best individuals to settle in neighboring niches and to explore from there various directions of the search space.

The resulting robots developed the ability to turn always to the same side (i.e. to the left in our experiments). This may come from the specific topology of the maze we chose for evolution where turning to the left might be a better strategy than to the right. But it may also come from the fact that it is not necessary for the robot to be able to turn both to the right and to the left. So why make it complicated when a simple solution exists? In the second series of experiments, the ability to turn on both side was a necessary condition to the robot to get a good fitness.

7.9   Second Series of Experiments

In this second series of experiments, the two dimensional model of neurogenesis, involving cell migration and chemical diffusion within a hexagonal grid, was implemented.

Interface to the Artificial Neural Network

To connect artificial neural networks, resulting from the evolutionary process, to the robot, it is necessary to define how to feed the inputs of the neural network using the robot sensors and how to feed the robot motors using the outputs of the neural network. In order to simplify this process, we chose to set on the initial morphogenesis space all the input and output neurons needed inside different hexagons. Three experiments were conducted using three different initial layouts of input and output neurons made of 8 inputs corresponding to the distance sensors available on the robot, 2 inputs corresponding to bumper sensors (added in the simulator but not available on the real robot) and 4 outputs corresponding to the forward and backward speeds of each motor. Since our neural model needs a bias input, this kind of input was also added (see figure 7.12). During the first experiment, the input and output cells were initially set accordingly to the real position of the sensors and motors of Khepera. During the second and the third experiment, several layers were formed where similar neurons were aligned. The third experiment features big spaces between input and output layers.

Robot Behavior

The goal of the experiment is to obtain robots able to travel across a maze forming a kind of cross (see figure 7.13). This shape forces the robot to develop the ability to turn left and right in order to avoid the walls.

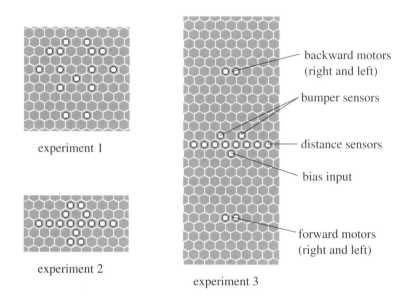

experiment 1

experiment 2

experiment 3

backward motors
(right and left)

bumper sensors

distance sensors

bias input

forward motors
(right and left)

Figure 7.12
Initial positions of input and output neurons

Early Results

Since the distance input neurons are not differentiated (i.e. they have the same numerical identifier), we can expect to observe a similar behavior (connection pattern , migration, etc.) for each of these neurons. The bumper sensors are differentiated, as well as the motor sensors. This should allow the emergence of pre-wired reflexes relying upon these bumper sensors while the neural structures processing the distance information should be trained using for example the available Hebbian links as a learning law and the bumper sensors as reinforcement signals. We successfully built a handmade neural network that learns to associate the distance sensors with the right motor actions according to the reinforcement signals sent by the bumper sensors. Now let see whether the evolutionary process found a similar structure.

After 200 generations of the genetic algorithm, different artificial neural networks were obtained that exhibited various performances in the maze. The best ones were obtained during experiment 1: the best neural network of the population was able to drive the robot across the maze without touching any wall, as long as we could observe it. The neural network was a single layer

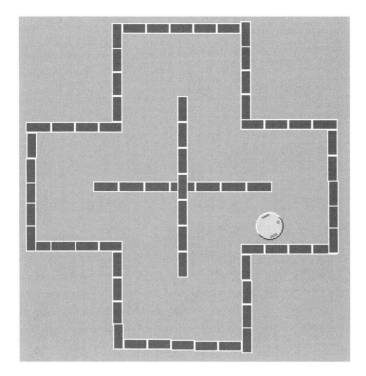

Figure 7.13
Cross-like maze

feed-forward network connecting the distance sensors inputs to three of the four motor outputs with an appropriate set of fixed weight (see figure 7.14). The values 0.5 and 51 of the synaptic weights were chosen by the evolutionary process within a set of weight values given a priori. We were a bit disappointed since we didn't expect that the evolutionary process succeed in establishing different connections starting from the non-differentiated distance input neurons. Different connection schemes were achieved by using the fact that the non-differentiated input cells were initially at different geographical locations on the hexagonal grid and hence received different chemical messages from their neighborhood, leading to different dynamics inside the cell bodies.

To try to minimize the difference of behavior between non-differentiated cells, the input cells were aligned in a layer as described in figure 7.12, experiment 2. The resulting neural networks were very complex made of lots of hidden neurons and lots of connections especially between inputs and hidden

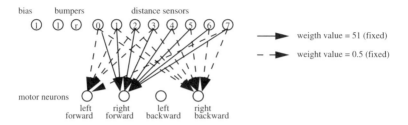

Figure 7.14
Resulting best neural network during experiment 1

neurons. The non-differentiated cells had a roughly similar behavior while slight differences in the connection patterns made the overall scheme perform almost as good as in the first experiment: the corresponding robots were able to travel in the cross maze even if they sometimes hit a wall.

Finally, we decided to set the output neurons far away from the input neurons so that their chemical influence on the input neurons would be rather similar for all input neurons. The results were similar to those obtained in experiment 2, except that the resulting networks were not so complex.

7.10   Conclusions

This attempt to design a powerful artificial neurogenesis system inspired from biology and applied to mobile robotics leads to interesting early results. The evolutionary process turned out to be able to find optimal architectures for simple navigation tasks involving food seeking or obstacle avoidance. In the first series of experiments, the evolutionary process discovered reactive neural networks and a primitive adaptive neural network involving a short term memory unit. The goal of the second series of experiments was to obtain adaptive networks implementing adaptive connections (using Hebb law). The efficient results, achieved with rather simple reactive artificial neural networks, should be compared with our expectations of getting more complex structures involving learning. On one hand, the complex structures we imagined, associated with complex learning behavior, need that the robot learns by trial and error and hence hits some walls to learn to avoid them. On the other hand, simple structures discovered by the evolutionary process don't need to make such errors since their adapted behavior is innate. This demonstrates the ability of the morphogenesis process to be able to connect in a different way non-differentiated cells if necessary and the ability of the overall evolutionary process to find out simple yet optimal solutions.

Primitive animals, like most of the insects, are often capable of walking as soon as they are born, without any learning, just like the robots discovered by the evolutionary process. Human beings and other mammals usually need a learning stage before they are able to walk. This may be explained by the fact that such evolved species developed elaborated learning abilities exempting them from developing and preserving complex hardwired behaviors in their genotype. Moreover, for complex tasks (like walking with two legs), adaptive behaviors are far more efficient than hardwired behaviors.

Further investigations will involve problems in which learning is a mandatory issue for the robot in order to be selected by the evolutionary process. Such a methodology could give birth to a new generation of adaptive autonomous robots able to learn in unknown environments.

References

[223]J. Anderson and E. Rosenfeld, editors. *Neurocomputing: Foundations of Research*. MIT Press, Cambridge, 1988.

[224]E. Boers and H. Kuiper. Biological metaphors and the design of modular artificial neural networks. Master's thesis, Departments of Computer Science and Experimental Psychology at Leiden University, The Netherlands, 1992.

[225]V. Braitenberg. *Vehicles: Experiments in Synthetic Psychology*. MIT Press, Cambridge, 1984.

[226]R. Brooks. Artificial life and real robots. In F. Varela and P. Bourgine, editors, *Towards a Practice of Autonomous Systems, Proceedings of the First International Conference on Artificial Life, Paris*. MIT Press, 1992.

[227]Y. Burnod. *An adaptative neural network: the cerebral cortex*. Masson, 1989.

[228]M. Colombetti and M. Dorigo. Learning to control an autonomous robot by distributed genetic algorithms. In J.-A. Meyer, H. Roitblat, and W. Wilson, editors, *From animals to animats 2: Proceedings of the Second International Conference on Simulation of Adaptive Behavior*. MIT Press, Bradford Books, 1992.

[229]H. De Garis. Cam-brain: The evolutionary engineering of a billion neuron artificial brain by 2001 which grows/evolves at electronic speeds inside a cellular automata machine (cam). In D. W. Pearson, N. C. Steele, and R. F. Albrecht, editors, *Proceedings of the International Conference on Artificial Neural Networks and Genetic Algorithms (ICANNGA'95)*. Springer-Verlag Wien New York, 1995.

[230]F. Dellaert and R. Beer. Toward an evolvable model of development for autonomous agents synthesis. In R. Brooks and P. Maes, editors, *Proceedings of the Fourth International Workshop on Artificial Life*, Cambridge, MA, 1994. The MIT Press / Bradford Books.

[231]D. Floreano and F. Mondada. Automatic creation of an autonomous agent: Genetic evolution of a neural-network driven robot. In D. Cliff, P. Husband, J.-A. Meyer, and W. Wilson, editors, *From animals to animats 3: Proceedings of the Third International Conference on Simulation of Adaptive Behavior*. MIT Press, 1994.

[232]N. Franceschini and F. Mura. Visual control of altitude and speed in a flying agent. In

D. Cliff, P. Husband, J.-A. Meyer, and W. Wilson, editors, *From animals to animats 3: Proceedings of the Third International Conference on Simulation of Adaptive Behavior*, pages 91–99. MIT Press, 1994.

[233]K. Fukushima. Neocognitron : A self-organizing neural network model for a mechanism of pattern recognition unaffected by shift in position. *Biological Cybernetics*, 36:193–202, 1980.

[234]D. Goldberg. *Genetic Algorithms in Search, Optimisation and Machine Learning*. Addison Wesley, Massachussets, 1989.

[235]F. Gruau and D. Whitley. Adding learning to the cellular development of neural networks: Evolution and the baldwin effect. *Evolutionary Computation*, 1(3):213–234, 1993.

[236]I. Harvey. *The Artificial Evolution of Adaptive Behavior*. PhD thesis, University of Sussex, 1993.

[237]I. Harvey, P. Husbands, and D. Cliff. Seeing the light: Artificial evolution, real vision. In D. Cliff, P. Husband, J.-A. Meyer, and W. Wilson, editors, *From animals to animats 3: Proceedings of the Third International Conference on Simulation of Adaptive Behavior*. MIT Press, 1994.

[238]D. Hebb. *The Organization of Behavior*. Wiley, New York, 1949. Partially reprinted in [223].

[239]J. Hertz, A. Krogh, and R. Palmer. *Introduction to the Theory of Neural Computation*. Addison-Wesley, Santa Fe Institute, 1991.

[240]E. Kandel and J. Schwartz. Molecular biology of an elementary form of learning: modulation of transmitter release through cyclic amp-dependent protein kinase. *Science*, 218:433–443, 1982.

[241]S. Kauffman. *The Origins of Order: Self-Organisation and Selection in Evolution*. Oxford University Press, 1993.

[242]H. Kitano. Empirical studies on the speed of convergence of neural network training using genetic algorithms. In *Proceedings AAAI*, pages 789–795, 1990.

[243]H. Kitano. Cell differentiation and neurogenesis in evolutionary large scale chaos. In F. Morán, A. Moreno, J. Merelo, and P. Chacón, editors, *Advances in Artificial Life, Proceedings of the Third European Conference on Artificial Life, Granada*. Springer, June 1995.

[244]J. Kodjabachian and J.-A. Meyer. Development, learning and evolution in animats. In P. Gaussier and J.-D. Nicoud, editors, *Perception To Action Conference Proceedings*. IEEE Computer Society Press, 1994.

[245]T. Kohonen. *Self-Organization and Associative Memory*. Springer-Verlag, 1989. (3rd ed.).

[246]C. Langton, editor. *Artificial Life, proceedings of the First International Conference on Artificial Life*. Addison-Wesley, 1988.

[247]C. Langton. Adaptation to the edge of the chaos. In C. Langton, J. Farmer, S. Rasmussen, and C. Taylor, editors, *Artificial Life II: A Proceedings Volume in the Santa Fe Institute Studies in the Sciences of Complexity*, volume 10, Mass, 1992. Addison-Wesley, Reading.

[248]Y. Le Cun, B. Boser, J. Denker, D. Henderson, R. Howard, W. Hubbard, and L. Jackel. Handwritten digit recognition with a back-propagation network. In D. Touretzky, editor, *Advances in Neural Information Processing Systems II*. Morgan Kaufmann, 1990.

[249]A. Lindenmayer. Mathematical models for cellular interactions in development, I & II. *Journal of Theoretical Biology*, 18:280–315, 1968.

[250]O. Michel. Khepera simulator package version 2.0. Freeware mobile robot simulator downloadable from the World Wide Web at URL: http ://wwwi3s.unice.fr/ ∼ om/khep − sim.html.

[251]O. Michel. An artificial life approach for the synthesis of autonomous agents. In J.-M. Alliot, E. Lutton, E. Ronald, M. Schoenauer, and D. Snyers, editors, *Artificial Evolution*, volume 1063 of *LNCS*, pages 220–231. Springer Verlag, 1996.

[252]O. Michel and J. Biondi. Morphogenesis of neural networks. *Neural Processing Letters*,

2(1), January 1995.

[253]F. Mondada, E. Franzi, and P. Ienne. Mobile robot miniaturisation: A tool for investigation in control algorithms. In *Third International Symposium on Experimental Robotics*, Kyoto, Japan, October 1993.

[254]S. Nolfi, O. Miglino, and D. Parisi. Phenotypic plasticity in evolving neural networks. In P. Gaussier and J.-D. Nicoud, editors, *Perception To Action Conference Proceedings*. IEEE Computer Society Press, 1994.

[255]S. Nolfi and D. Parisi. Evolving artificial neural networks that develop in time. In F. Morán, A. Moreno, J. Merelo, and P. Chacón, editors, *Advances in Artificial Life, Proceedings of the Third European Conference on Artificial Life, Granada*. Springer, June 1995.

[256]J. Vaario and K. Shimohara. On formation of structures. In F. Morán, A. Moreno, J. Merelo, and P. Chacón, editors, *Advances in Artificial Life, Proceedings of the Third European Conference on Artificial Life, Granada*. Springer, June 1995.

8 Development in Neural Networks

Domenico Parisi and Stefano Nolfi

8.1 Development

The changes that occur in an individual organism during the individual's life-time can be studied in a number of different ways. If one uses computer sim-ulations to analyze and explain these changes, one first goal can be to train neural networks in such a way that the networks go through successive stages during training that replicate the change observed in real organisms. One can use the backpropagation procedure for training a single network or the genetic algorithm for training an entire population of different networks. The back-propagation procedure changes the connection weights of the single network in such a way that the network's output progressively approximates the desired output. The genetic algorithm is based on the selective reproduction of the in-dividuals that are best in terms of a fitness criterion and the constant addition of new variants, and after a certain number of successive generations it usually results in networks that perform as desired. If the individual network trained with the backpropagation procedure exhibits changes in behavior during train-ing that are similar to the changes observed in real organisms, or if successive generations of networks trained with the genetic algorithm go through succes-sive stages that correspond to the changes observed in individual organisms, one can be said to have reached a certain measure of success in explaining those changes.

For example, using the backpropagation procedure to teach networks the balance beam task McClelland [273] has been able to show that his networks not only are able to learn the task but they change their behavior during training in ways that correspond to the stages of acquisition of the task in children. Similarly, Schlesinger, Parisi, and Langer [274] have used the genetic algorithm to train a population of networks to reach a visually perceived object using a two-segment arm. Successive generations of networks subdivide the task into sub-portions that are acquired sequentially, the easiest ones first, thus following a principle of "starting small" [269] which may also be followed by real organisms in acquiring their capacities.

In this approach the researcher can use any kind of training procedure that makes it possible to analyze successive stages of acquisition. The changes occur because of the internal organization of the training process itself and one does not investigate whether it is the environment or the genetic material contained in the organisms that causes the changes. But to explain the changes that take place during an individual's lifetime one can also follow a different approach that distinguishes between individual and population training and asks if it is the environment or the genetic material that triggers the observed changes.

In fact, not all changes that occur in organisms are development. If an organism changes exclusively because of environmental causes, the organism cannot be said to develop. To call the changes that take place in an organism developmental changes (or ontogeny) it is necessary that some of the causes that determine the changes are genetic, i.e., that the changes can be traced back at least in part to the information contained in the individual's genome and, therefore, to the evolutionary history of the population of which the individual organism is a member.

Most of the work that has been done on neural networks so far has been concerned with learning, not development. A neural network is exposed to some input and, in supervised learning, to some teaching input coming from outside and, as a consequence of this input and teaching input, the network changes its connection weights. (The network architecture is typically fixed.) Because of the changes in the connection weights the network's behavior changes, that is, the network responds in different ways to the same input presented at successive stages of learning. However, since the network starts its learning with a random set of weights, i.e., with no inherited genetic information, and the changes that occur in the network are exclusively due to external causes - the input and teaching input - these changes cannot be called development.

One might object [270, 271] that the network's architecture, the learning algorithm (e.g., backpropagation), and the specific values that are chosen for the activation and learning parameters constrain learning and could be considered as genetically inherited information. The decisions made by the researcher with respect to these properties of the network can be interpreted as embodying his or her hypotheses about the genetic information constraining how some particular behavior is learned. These hypotheses are verified by observing if the network actually learns and if the course of learning reflects the ontogeny which is observed in real organisms.

Although this approach to development in neural networks can be productive and it can generate important insights [267], it seems to be preferable to apply the term "genetic" to information which is the actual result of an evolutionary process, not to information that is arbitrarily put into the network by the researcher. Furthermore, while the network's architecture, the learning algorithm and the algorithm's parameters are decided by the researcher once and for all at the beginning of learning, the information contained in the genome can be expressed at various stages during the development of the phenotype and can influence development in different ways at different stages of development. Finally, it is not only the case that genetic information influences development but it is also true that development can influence the evolutionary process that results in the inherited genetic information. To capture the reciprocal influence between development and evolution it is necessary to simulate both processes.

We conclude that to talk properly about neural networks that develop it is necessary that the networks are members of evolving populations. Each individual network has an associated genome which is inherited from the network's parents and which is mapped into the phenotypical network. Since the population of networks reproduces selectively and with the constant addition of variability to the genetic pool (the totality of genotypes of the population) due to sexual reproduction and random mutations, the genetic pool is subject to change across successive generations of networks. The genome that a particular network inherits from its parents is the result of this evolutionary process of change. If the inherited genome is among the causes of the changes that occur during the lifetime of the individual, we are entitled to say that the network develops.

Much work has been done in the last ten years or so on evolving populations of neural networks [287]. Some kind of evolutionary algorithm (e.g., Holland's genetic algorithm; cf. [265, 272]) is applied to an initial population of randomly generated genomes. Each genome is mapped into a phenotypical network, the networks have a lifetime of finite duration during which they are tested to determine their goodness at some task, and the networks that are better at the task have more chances to generate offspring. (In some cases the mapping of the genome into the phenotype, especially if it is a complex mapping, is called development. However, if the mapping results in a phenotype which does not change during its life, we do not think the term development is appropriate.) An offspring inherits the genome of its single parent if the population reproduces nonsexually or a recombination of parts of the genome of one parent and parts of the genome of another parent if the population reproduces sexually. Inherited genomes are subject to random mutations. The constant addition of variability by means of sexual recombination and random mutations and the selective reproduction of the best networks tend to cause an increase across generations in the average level of task performance until the level reaches a stable state. In populations with variable population size and limiting resources in their environment, population size first decreases due to the networks' low initial level of ability and then it increases until it reaches a stable state that corresponds to the carrying capacity of the environment.

As we have said, a great amount of work has been done on designing neural networks using evolutionary algorithms and this work has produced many interesting results. However, in most of this work there are no changes during the lifetime of the individual networks. The inherited genotype specifies both the architecture and the connection weights of the phenotypical network and it maps into a network that remains identical in all stages of life. Since nothing happens to the network during its life that modifies either the network's architecture or its connection weights, these evolving networks cannot be said to develop.

In the remaining portions of this Chapter we will review simulations in which neural networks have an inherited genome and are members of evolving populations and, furthermore, the individual networks change during life because of their experience. (For more work in this area, cf. [278]). These changes are the result of an interaction between the genetically inherited information and the experience of the individual network in the particular environment and, therefore, they can be called development.

8.2   Evolution of Initial Conditions

A first step toward developing networks is taken in simulations in which a population of neural networks evolves and at the same time the individual networks learn during their life. In such conditions, evolution can select initial conditions that enable or increase the adaptive effect of learning. Since the inherited genetic information that specifies these initial conditions interacts with the externally provided input and teaching input in determining the learned changes, this can be considered as a form of development.

Evolution and Learning in "Classical" Neural Networks

Imagine an evolving population of networks with a fixed architecture that learn some task during their life using the backpropagation procedure. The networks with the smallest error at the end of learning reproduce by generating offspring that inherit the same initial weights of their parents with some added random mutations. While "classical" learning in neural networks starts from a "blank slate" (the random initial weights), learning in these evolutionary networks starts from an initial state that embodies the results of the evolutionary process that has been going on at the population level in the preceding generations.

We already know that learning in neural networks can be influenced by the network's initial state. Individual networks with different initial connection weights will tend to learn more or less from the same learning experience as a function of the goodness of their initial weights [268]. The evolutionary process based on selective reproduction and genetic mutations can be used to find good initial weights for learning. If the learning performance constitutes the criterion for the selective reproduction of individuals, the individuals of the later generations will learn more or better (i.e., more quickly) than the individuals of the earlier generations because they inherit better initial weights than the individuals of the earlier generations.

Belew, McInerney, & Schraudolph [277] had a population of networks learn a set of simple tasks. The initial population was made up of networks with random genomes encoding the network's connection weights. All the networks were subject to the same training using the backpropagation procedure. The networks with the best learning performance, which was presumably due to their initial weights, reproduced by generating offspring similar to their parents (mutations and sexual recombination were used). After a certain number of generations the initial weights that evolved in the population resulted in organisms that learned better than the organisms of the early generations.

Inherited genomes can encode other initial conditions for learning that are usually arbitrarily decided by the researcher, for example the learning rate or momentum [277], or the network architecture ([263, 264]. In these simulations too, evolution finds values and properties of these initial conditions that result in better learning.

Evolution and Learning in Ecological Neural Networks

In Belew et al.'s simulations there is an interaction between genetic information (the inherited genotype specifying the initial connection weights) and environmentally provided information (the input and the teaching input) in determining the changes that occur in the individual networks. The inherited initial weights influence the changes that occur in the network's connection weights during learning. Therefore, it is legitimate to talk about development in the case of these networks. However, the role of the genetic information is quite limited. The genotype specifies only the initial state for learning. It is true that given the nature of learning in neural networks - learned changes in connection weights depend on both the input/teaching input and the current weights - the effects of the inherited initial weights are cumulative and tend to be preserved at all stages of learning. But it is clear that most of what changes in these networks is due to the environmentally provided information.

A more important role the genetically inherited information can play if learning occurs in ecological neural networks. Belew et al.'s networks are "classical" neural networks. Classical neural networks do not live in an independent physical environment. Their "environment" is the input and teaching input arbitrarily provided by the researcher. Ecological networks [260], on the other hand, have a simulated physical body and they live in a simulated physical environment. It is not the researcher but the independent structure of the environment that decides what input and, possibly, teaching input will be experienced by the network at any given time. (On the importance of embodiment and situatedness, cf. [257, 275].)

The critical difference between classical and ecological neural networks is that while classical networks are passive receivers of input, ecological networks can partly determine their own input. If an ecological network's output units encode motor actions, the network's output can influence the kind of input to which the network is exposed. With its motor actions the network can change either the physical relation of its body to the external environment or the external environment itself. As a consequence, the input experienced by the network can be influenced by the network's own output. For example, a network can turn its body (with its sensory organs) to the right and, as a consequence, the input from the environment will change. Or the network can displace with its "hand" an object present in the environment and, as a consequence, the sensory input from the object will change. Therefore, ecological networks partly self-select their own input from the environment [281].

Imagine a population of ecological networks that both evolve and learn during life. The inherited genotype encodes the initial weights of the networks, as in the preceding simulation. However, the inherited weights can have a more important role in determining what changes occur during the life of these networks. In classical networks, e.g., Belew et al.'s networks, the initial weights can only influence the learned changes in the connection weights. But the environmentally provided information that causes these changes is independent from and uninfluenced by the genetic information. In ecological networks, on the other hand, the genetic information (the initial weights) can have a role in determining not only the learned changes in the connection weights but also the learning experience of the network, that is, the kind of inputs to which the network is exposed during learning. Since ecological networks partly determine their inputs with their motor actions, the inherited initial weights can cause the network to generate motor actions that tend to expose the network to preferred environmental inputs. The network learns on the basis of these self-selected environmental inputs and, therefore, that appears to be another way in which the genetic information can influence what is learned.

In Nolfi, Elman, and Parisi [284] we describe an experiment in which simulated organisms, living in a two-dimensional grid-world, are selected for reproduction on the basis of their ability to find (and eat) the food present in the environment. However, they also have the possibility to learn to predict the consequences of their motor actions, i.e., to predict how the sensory stimuli will change after a planned motor action is physically executed.

The organisms's nervous system is modeled by a feedforward neural network consisting of three layers of units (Figure 8.1). The input layer contains two units which encode sensory information from the environment (direction and distance of the currently nearest food element) and another two units encoding the currently planned action (moving one step forward, turning 90 degrees to the left or right, do nothing). These four units are connected to an intermediate layer of seven units. The seven hidden units are connected to two output units encoding the planned motor action and two units encoding a prediction on what the future position (direction and distance) of the nearest food element will be given its current position and the currently planned action. Networks are trained during life by using the back-propagation procedure. However, it is important to notice that the teaching input for this learning task is directly available in the environment. When the movement is executed it will physically cause some consequences that will determine the next input for the network. These actually produced consequences are the teaching input. The network compares the predicted consequences of its behavior with the actually realized consequences and learns to make better predictions in the future by modifying its connection weights using the backpropagation procedure.

As we have suggested, if the genetic information that influences development in the individual is the (current) result of an independent process of evolutionary change and is not simply hardwired in the network by the researcher, it is possible to study the reciprocal influence of evolution on development and of development on evolution. In fact, population of evolving individuals that learn during their life to predict the consequences of their action show that

Action   Predicted Sensory Input

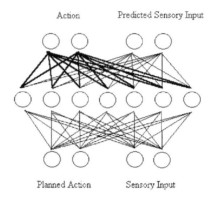

Planned Action   Sensory Input

Figure 8.1
Architecture of a neural network that learns to predict the consequences of its own planned motor
actions. Thin lines indicate learnable weights, thick lines fixed weights.

both evolution affects learning and learning affects evolution. This is true even
if the effects of learning (weight changes) are not genetically inherited and,
unlike Belew et al.'s simulations described above, what is learned (predicting
the consequences of actions) is an independent task with respect to the task in
terms of which individuals are evaluated for their fitness (finding food in the
environment). In particular, it can been shown that: (a) populations that learn
during life to predict the sensory consequences of their actions show a better
evolutionary increase in the average ability to find food in the environment; (b)
after a certain number of generations learning to predict produces an increase
in the ability to find food during life; (c) individuals that have evolved an ability to find food do not directly inherit an ability to predict but they do inherit
a predisposition to learn to predict, this predisposition being demonstrated by
better learning results obtained by the networks of later than of earlier generations [284]. Harvey [266] has claimed that (a) is not due to an interaction
between learning and evolution but to a form of relearning after the weight per-
turbation represented by mutations. However, further analysis of the simulation
data clearly shows that Harvey's hypothesis is wrong and that the obtained results can only be explained by an interaction between learning and evolution
[279].

  Another simulation in which evolution of the initial state and learning interact with each other has been described by Floreano and Mondada [258].
Their genomes encode some general properties for each connection of the phe-

notypic network (i.e., whether it is excitatory or inhibitory, the type of unsupervised (Hebbian) learning rule used, and the learning rate) but not its actual weight. The connection weights are assigned randomly at birth and they are modified during life by learning. By studying a population of physical robots that should move efficiently in a simple environment the authors show how evolution is able to select initial conditions for the neural network controlling the robots' behavior that enable the unsupervised learning mechanism to develop the desired behavior.

Self-Teaching Networks

Since ecological networks partially control their own input, in the simulations described in the preceding section the inherited genetic information (the initial weights) interacts with the structure of the physical environment to determine the inputs that are experienced by a network during learning and, therefore, the changes that occur in the network as a result of learning. However, the genetically inherited initial weights play no role with respect to the other environmental component of learning, the teaching input provided to the network to effect learning using the backpropagation procedure. While the input experienced during learning results from an interaction between genetic and environmental information the teaching input originates in the environment and it remains a purely experiential factor in learning.

The role of genetic information in development can be extended to the teaching input, however. Imagine a network architecture made up of two connected (sub-)networks (Figure 8.2). The two networks share the input layer that encodes the sensory information from the environment but have separate hidden and output layers. In other words, the environmental input is separately elaborated by the two networks. One network, called "student" network, is the usual network that maps sensory input into motor actions. The other network, called "teacher" network, is a special network that maps the sensory input into an output which is used by the "student" network to change its weights according to the backpropagation procedure. In other words, the "teacher" network generates the teaching input on the basis of which the "student" network learns. As in the preceding simulation, the network controlling the behavior of the organism in the environment learns during life but it learns on the basis of a teaching input which is not directly provided by the environment, as in the preceding simulation, but is internally generated by another portion of the organism's nervous system, the "teacher" network, on the basis of the sensory input provided by the environment. (Ackley and Littman [261] have used a similar approach in which one portion of the network generates the reinforcement signal to be used by a second portion to learn using the reinforcement procedure.)

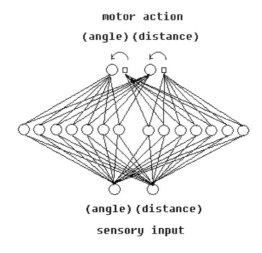

Figure 8.2
Self-teaching architecture. The network is made up two sub-parts, a student network and a teaching network. The two networks share their input units but each has a separate set of hidden and output units.

In these self-teaching networks the genetically inherited information influences not only the sensory input from the environment through the mechanism of self-selection of input, as in the preceding simulation, but also the teaching input on the basis of which the network learns. Therefore, the interaction between genetic and environmental information in determining developmental changes is more complex. Notice that the genetically inherited weights have a double influence on the changes that occur in the "student" network during learning. First, the initial weights of the "student" network are genetically inherited and we know that the initial weights influence learning (cf. earlier sections). In addition, the initial weights of the "student" network, by determining the motor behavior of the individual, partially determine the learning experiences (environmental input) of the network that in turn affect the results of learning (cf. earlier sections). Second, the weights of the "teacher" network are also genetically inherited and they do not change during life. These weights cause the "teacher" network to elaborate the environmental input in order to generate a teaching input for the "student" network. In other words, the genetically inherited weights of the "teacher" network determine what teaching input for the "student" network will be generated by the "teacher" network on the basis of the environmental input, and therefore they also influence learning. In addition, the weights of the "teacher" network, by determining how the weights of the "student" network change, have an influence on how the learning experiences (environmental input) of the network itself will change during life.

It can be shown that evolution in self-teaching networks selects both the initial weights of the "student" network that will be modified by learning and the fixed weights of the "teacher" network [280]. After a certain number of generations the networks that learn during life on the basis of self-generated teaching input exhibit a very efficient behavior (cf. the dotted curve of figure 8.3). However, if we exclude learning and we test the performance of evolved organisms at birth, i.e., prior to learning, their behavior is very inefficient (figure 8.3, thin curve). This shows that the initial weights of the "student" networks do not incorporate a genetically inherited capacity to find food. The organisms need learning to be able to find food in the environment. Learning is based on the teaching input generated by their "teacher" network and, therefore, the genetically inherited weights of their "teacher" network are critical for learning to occur. But the initial weights of the "student" networks are also critical. If we randomize the genetically inherited initial weights of the "student" networks at birth and we let the organisms learn on the basis of such random initial weights and the teaching input generated by their "teacher" network, no learning occurs and the organisms' performance remains very poor throughout their life (Figure 8.3, thick curve).

We conclude that evolution results in the co-evolution of the two distinct sets of genetically inherited weights which determine the way in which environmental information modifies the nervous system of the creatures and, as consequence, their behavior during life.

In other simulations [283] it has been shown that these self-teaching networks can allow an organism to adapt to the particular type of environment in which the organism happens to be born and to develop. Alternate generations of the population are born in two different types of environment that generate different sensory input for the organisms and require different behaviors for optimal adaptation. In evolved organisms the genetically inherited weights of their teaching network generate different kinds of teaching inputs for the stu-

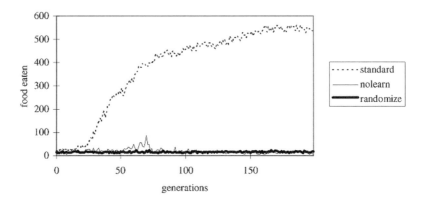

Figure 8.3
Food finding performance across generations. The dotted curve represents the standard
performance with life-learning based on the inherited weights, the thin curve represents the
performance at birth, i.e., prior to learning, the thick curve represents the performance after
learning with randomized initial "student" weights. Each curve represents the average of 10
different simulations.

dent network based on the different environmental inputs. But these different
teaching inputs induce (different) learned changes in behavior that are adapted
to the particular environment in which the individual happens to develop.

8.3   Developmental Genomes

In the preceding Sections we have reviewed various simulations in which neural networks can be said to develop in that they undergo changes during their
life and these changes are the result of an interaction between genetically inherited information and environmental information. However, all the simulations
we have described have a serious limitation as models of development. The genetic information contained in the individual's genome is entirely decoded (or
expressed) in a single event at birth and therefore the genotype-to-phenotype
mapping is not a process that takes place in time throughout the life of the individual or at least during its developmental age. Although the effects of the
initially expressed genetic information continue to be cumulatively felt at all
stages of life (learning), all the information contained in the genome is immediately and completely expressed at birth. In contrast, in real organisms the

information contained in an individual's genome continues to be expressed throughout the individual's lifetime and the genotype-to-phenotype mapping itself is a process that unrolls in time. Real organisms inherit what could be called developmental genomes, that is, genomes that incorporate a temporally distributed program of development with different parts of the program being expressed at successive stages during the life of the individual.

Neural Networks that Develop in Time

Developmental genomes can be simulated in the following way [282]. Imagine a population of randomly generated genomes that encode various parameters controlling the growth process of the branching axon of each of a set of neurons. For each neuron the genome specifies the angle of branching of the neuron's axon and the length of the branching segments. The genotype-to-phenotype mapping consists in each neuron growing its axon according to the parameters specified in the genome. If during the axonal growth process one branch of the growing axon of a neuron makes contact with another neuron (or with another neuron's dendrites), a connection is established between the two neurons. Therefore, the genotype-to-phenotype mapping eventually results in a network architecture (Figure 8.4). Different architectures are constructed on the basis of different genomes and architectures are genetically transmitted with mutations modifying some of the genetic parameters. The evolutionary process progressively selects for architectures that are adapted to the task.

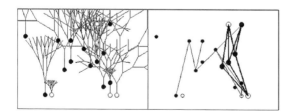

Figure 8.4
Development of a neural network from a randomly generated genetic string. The growing and branching process of axons is shown on the left, the resulting neural network after removal of nonconnecting branches on the right. Isolated or nonfunctional neurons and connections are represented by small circles and thin lines, respectively. Functional neurons and connections are represented as large circles and thick lines.

This model of the genotype-to-phenotype mapping can be realized in two alternative versions. In one version the genotype-to-phenotype mapping is executed all at once at birth so that an individual is born with an already adult nervous system that does not change in any way during life. (The connection weights are also specified in the genome and there is no learning.) In this case not only the genome cannot be called developmental but there is no development at all since there are no changes during the life of the individual. (For other examples of instantaneous genotype-to-phenotype mappings that construct network architectures, cf. [264, 276].

But consider a variant of the genome we have just described. Imagine that among the genetic parameters specifying the axonal growth process of each neuron there is an additional parameter that specifies the age of the individual at which each particular neuron will grow its axon. Different neurons "mature", i.e., grow their axon, at different ages. Some neurons will grow their axon early in life while other neurons will grow their axon at some later stage. Since a neuron can become part of the effective network architecture that maps sensory input into motor actions only if the neuron has already developed its axon and, hopefully, has established a connection with some other neuron, the effective network architecture controlling the behavior of the organism in the environment will change during the life of the organism. Since the growth age parameter of each neuron is inherited along with the other parameters of the neuron and is subject like the other parameters to genetic mutations, the evolutionary process can change the growth age parameters of the various neurons inside a genome and therefore it can modify the process of development of the neural network in individuals of successive generations.

This single change in the content of the genetic information, i.e., the addition of the age parameter, transforms the genome into a developmental genome. In fact, with the addition of the age parameter the genome incorporates a program of development. The genotype-to-phenotype mapping ceases to be an instantaneous process and it becomes a process that unrolls in time. Some portions of the genetic information are expressed in the phenotype at some time during the life of the individual and other portions are expressed at some later time. The phenotype ceases to be a single, "adult", unchanging neural network and it effectively becomes a succession of developmental forms (networks).

An important consequence of using developmental genomes is that evolution can select not only for well adapted "adult" networks but also for well "adapted" courses of development for neural networks [282]. In the version of the model without the growth age parameter, the evolutionary process can only succeed in finding network architectures that allow individuals to exhibit efficient behaviors. What is selected is a single phenotype, i.e., the fixed network architecture the individual already possesses at birth. In the version of the model in which the genome incorporates the growth age parameter for neurons, evolution selects for sequences of developmental changes in network architecture during life rather than just for the final result of this process of development. Since the reproductive chances of the individual are determined at each successive stage during development – when the individual is represented by different developmental phenotypes (network architectures) – the global reproductive chances of the individual will be a complex function of the reproductive chances of each developmental form of the individual. This implies that evolution will select for appropriate sequences of developmental forms that guarantee (a) the best performance of the individual at each stage (minimally guaranteeing the survival of the individual at each stage), and (b) the smooth passage from each stage to the next.

By comparing evolutionary and developmental sequences a number of interesting results are observed. (a) The maturation of adaptive traits, i.e., of traits that increase the reproductive chances of the phenotypes that carry them, but not of neutral or maladaptive ones, tends to be anticipated in development during the course of evolution. (b) Mutations affecting traits that mature later in development are more likely to be retained than mutations with earlier effects and, as a consequence, traits that mature late are more likely to be subject to changes and innovations than traits that mature early in development. (c) Results (a) and (b) only apply to nonneutral traits. As a consequence, neutral characters tend to develop in later stages and, by being strongly affected by mutations that are retained in successive generations, are free to experiment with a huge set of variations and combinations that may eventually result in the discovery of new adaptive traits.

Developmental Genomes with Phenotypic Plasticity

Given our definition of development as changes during the life of an individual that are due to an interaction between genetic and environmental information, the model we have just described can at best be considered as a model of maturation, not of development. The changes that occur in the individual's neural network and, as a consequence, in the individual's behavior in the environment, are exclusively due to the information contained in the inherited developmental genome. There is no role in these changes of the information arriving to the network's input units from the environment.

However, real genomes tend to exhibit phenotypic plasticity. They result in different phenotypes, or in different courses of development of phenotypes, as a function of the particular environment in which the particular individual happens to live and develop. The genome specifies the class of phenotypes that can result from the genotype-to-phenotype mapping (norm of reaction) but it is the environment that selects the particular phenotype that actually develops from the genotype.

To incorporate in the genome a form of phenotypic plasticity the model of developmental genome described in the preceding Section can be modified in the following way. In the preceding model the growth age parameter of each neuron directly specifies the age of the individual at which each particular neuron grows its branching axon. The environment has no role in determining this age. In the modified genome that incorporates phenotypic plasticity the genome only specifies an "activation variability threshold" for each neuron. The activation variability of a neuron is the variability of the activation level of the neuron over a fixed number of successive input/output cycles. The genome specifies for each neuron a threshold for this variability such that only when the threshold is reached the neuron grows its branching axon. However, it is the environment that determines if and when the threshold is reached and, as a consequence, if and when the neuron will grow its axon. In other words, the model incorporates the idea that the sensory information from the environment has a critical role in the maturation of the connectivity of the nervous system and, more specifically, that the maturation process is sensitive to the variability of activation of single neurons [259, 286].

If some particular neuron tends to have always the same level of activation on the basis of the excitations and inihibitions arriving to the neuron, this implies that the neuron is having no great role in deciding with what output the network responds to the various inputs. Hence, it is not important for the neuron to grow its axon so that it can establish connections with other neurons and contribute to determining the network's output. However, if and when the variability of the activation level of the neuron exceeds the genetically specified threshold for that neuron, the neuron will grow its axon and it possibly will establish connections with other neurons further down the input-to-output pathways. Since the activation level of a neuron is ultimately determined by the environmental input, it is clear that any changes in network architecture due to the axonal growth of neurons will depend on the interaction between some genetically specified information, i.e., the "activation variability threshold" of neurons, and the sensory information arriving from the environment, i.e., the information that decides if and when the threshold is exceeded and the neuron can grow its axon.

By using this type of model, plastic individuals able to adapt to different environments can be obtained (cf. [285]. Figure 8.5 and 8.6 show how the same "cloned" genome results in two different phenotypical neural architectures and two different behaviors when the genome develops in two different environments. In this simulation organisms that can develop either "light" sensors or "wall (obstacle)" infrared sensors or both should be able to find a target area that may or may not be illuminated. Figure 8.5 shows how the evolved genome, when placed in an environment in which the target is illuminated, results in a neural network that takes into account the sensory information coming from the light sensors and produces a behavior that approaches the target following the light gradient.

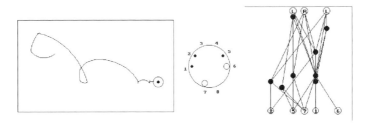

Figure 8.5
An evolved genotype developing in a "light" environment. The picture on the left shows the organism's behavior. The environment and the target area are represented as a rectangular box and as a circle, respectively. The picture shows the organism's trajectory from the starting position to the target area. The central picture represents the sensors that have developed in the organism. Large empty circles represent light detectors and small full circles represent wall (obstacle) detectors. Finally, the picture on the right side represents the organism's entire nervous systems. The bottom layer circles labeled with progressive numbers represent sensory neurons, the upper layer circles labeled with "L" and "R" represent the left and right motor neurons, and the remaining layers represent internal neurons.

Figure 8.6 shows how the same genome, when placed in a dark environment, results in a neural network that does not include connections from the light sensors and that produces a type of exploratory behavior that will in any case allow the individual, although somewhat less efficiently, to reach the non-illuminated target area.

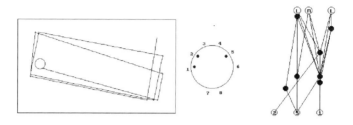

Figure 8.6
The same genotype of Figure 8.5 developing in a "dark" environment.

Learning at Different Genetically Determined "Ages"

A developmental genome can influence the phenotype in a general way by reminding the phenotype of its increasing "age". The phenotype can respond to this temporally varying information provided by the genome by changing its behavior or the way it learns at successive ages.

Imagine a genome specifying a "clock" that tells the organism its age. One can simulate the genetic clock by adding a special input unit to a sensory-motor neural network. The activation state of this "age" unit is zero at birth and is progressively increased during the organism's life. At any given time the organism generates some behavior in response to both the sensory input coming from the environment and the temporally varying activation state of its "age" unit. As a consequence, the organism's behavior can change during its life, i.e., the organism can respond in different ways to the same sensory input in successive epochs of its life. This change is purely genetically determined since the changing activation state of the special "age" unit is assumed to be caused by the genome. However, since these organisms learn during their life they can also change because of their experience with the particular environment. We can then study how the actual changes that occur in the organisms during their life are caused by the interaction between the genetic information provided by the genome (the temporally changing activation state of the "age" unit) and the environmental information the organism is using for learning.

The organisms live in an environment containing prey individuals that tend to run away when an organism approach them. An organism's reproductive chances depend on its ability (and luck) in capturing the prey. A prey individual will move from its current location to another randomly chosen location with some probability that increases with the vicinity of the organism acting as a predator. The predator's behavior is controlled by a neural network with two sensory input units encoding direction and distance of the single nearest prey and an additional "age" input unit whose activation state is zero at birth and is progressively increased by some fixed quantity in each successive epoch of the individual's life. The total lifespan is 20 epochs for all predators. The network's two output units encode a movement of the predator. One unit encodes the angle of turning and the other unit encodes the length of the step forward of the organism.

In addition to responding to the sensory input encoding the position of the nearest prey and to the genetically specified information about their own age with some movement aimed at capturing the moving prey, the organisms learn during their life to predict how the prey's position will change as a function of their planned movements and the current position of the prey. (Prey are allowed to move only after the predator's planned movement has been executed.) To this purpose the network has an additional set of two input units encoding planned movements and two output units encoding predictions about changes in prey position after the physical execution of the planned movements. In other words, the network architecture is identical to that of Figure 8.1 except for the addition of the "age" input unit.

Unlike the network of Figure 8.1 that generates planned movements and predictions in a single step, in the new network each input/output cycle includes two steps. In Step 1 the network generates a planned movement in response to (a) the sensory input encoding the prey's position and (b) its current age as specified in the special "age" input unit. In this step the planned movement input units have zero activation level and the prediction output units are ignored. In Step 2 the planned movement generated in Step 1 is encoded in the planned movement input units and the network generates a prediction about the next sensory input encoding the prey's position resulting from the execution of the planned movement. Then the planned movement is physically executed. This leads to the actual next sensory input. This sensory input is used (a) as the new sensory input for the next cycle, and (b) as teaching input for back-propagation learning. The predicted next sensory input is compared with the actual sensory input and the network's weights are changed based on the dis-

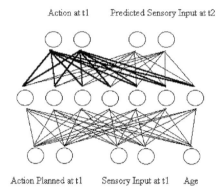

Action at t1   Predicted Sensory Input at t2

Action Planned at t1   Sensory Input at t1   Age

Figure 8.7
Architecture of a network that predicts the consequences of its planned actions with the addition of an "age" input unit.

crepancy between the two in such a way that after a number of cycles (learning trials) the network learns to generate accurate predictions about the sensory consequences of its planned movements.

Notice that the network's behavior, i.e., how the network tries to capture the prey but also how the network predicts the consequences of its movements, changes during the organism's life and these changes are due to both genetic and environmental causes. The genetic causes are the change in the activation value of the "age" input unit in successive epochs of the individual's life and the inherited initial weights that influence learning. The environmental causes are the input and teaching input coming from the environment that determine the changes in the network's connection weights. As we will see, these two causes interact during the individual's life in determining the behavior of the developing individual.

One way of describing the developmental changes that occur in the individual organisms during their life is to count the number of prey captured by a certain individual in the successive epochs of its life. Figure 8.8 and 8.9 show the number of prey captured in each successive epoch of their life by individuals of successive generations in a population of organisms that learn to predict but are not informed by their genes about their current age (Figure 8.8) and in a population of organisms that both learn to predict and are informed by their genes about their current age (Figure 8.9).

In both populations learning to predict has a positive influence on the

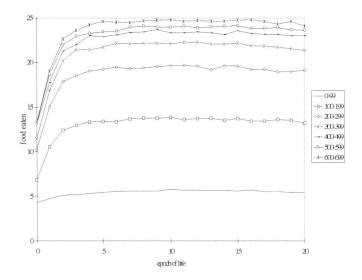

Figure 8.8
Number of prey captured by individuals of successive generations in each of the 20 epochs of their life for a population that learns to predict but does not have a genetically determined "age". Each curve represents the average results of the best individuals of 100 successive generations in 10 replications of the simulation. Performance at epoch 0 is determined by letting an individual live for one epoch with no changes in weights due to learning.

ability to capture the prey during lifetime (cf. Section 2.2). As an individual learns to predict the sensory consequences of its planned movements, the individual's ability to capture the prey improves.

This phenomenon takes a certain number of generations to emerge (almost no increase in number of prey captured in successive epochs of life in the first 100 generations) presumably because evolution takes some time to evolve good initial connection weights for learning. This is observed in both populations. However, after a certain number of generations, the developmentally early improvement in prey capturing behavior is significantly larger in the population with genetic information about age than in the population without age information. The reason it is smaller in the population without age information is that in this population there appears to be a stronger form of genetic assimilation, with information learned during life being progressively transferred into the genes. In both populations there is some genetic assimilation in that indi-

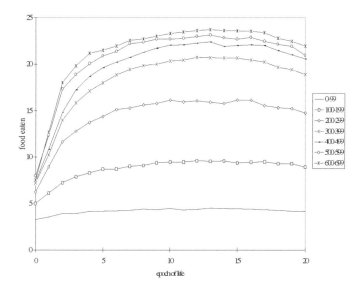

Figure 8.9
Number of prey captured by individuals of successive generations in each of the 20 epochs of
their life for a population that both learns to predict and has a genetically determined "age". Each
curve represents the average results of the best individuals of 100 successive generations in 10
replications of the simulation.

viduals of successive generations tend to be born with an increasing capacity
to capture prey already present at birth. However, the process of genetic assimilation tends to stop sooner in the population with genetic information about
age.

That both genetic and environmental information have a role in determining the developmental changes that are observed in the individuals of the population with genetic information about age can be demonstrated in the following way. We test these individuals in two different experimental conditions in
which the genetic and the learning information are separately manipulated. In
one condition the individuals are deprived of the genetic information about
their age but they still learn to predict during their life. In the other condition
they receive the genetic information about their age but their learning to predict
is discontinued. The results are shown in Figure 8.10 and 8.11.

Depriving an evolved network of either the genetic or the learning information negatively affects its performance. In both cases performance increases

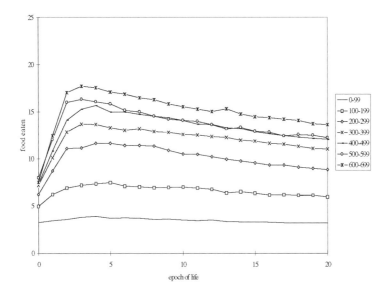

Figure 8.10
Number of prey individuals captured in successive epochs of life by individuals that learn to predict but are deprived of genetic information about age. Each curve represents the average results of the best individuals of 100 successive generations for 10 replications of the simulation.

much less in the first epochs of life and then it starts to decrease. These experimental tests seem to imply that the developmental changes that occur during the lifetime of these individuals, as manifested in the changing number of prey captured in the successive epochs of life, are the result of an interaction between genetic and environmental information. If either of these two types of information is eliminated, the performance during life instead of improving deteriorates.

Notice that in this simulation information about age is provided to the organisms by the genome but is not actually evolved. It is rather hardwired by us in the genome. Elman [269] has done some simulations in which a developmental increase in the memory span of neural networks is also hardwired in the genome. His networks learn to predict the next word in a text given the current word by cumulatively storing information about the preceding words in a set of "context" or memory units and using this stored information together with the current word to predict the next word. Elman has shown that the task can

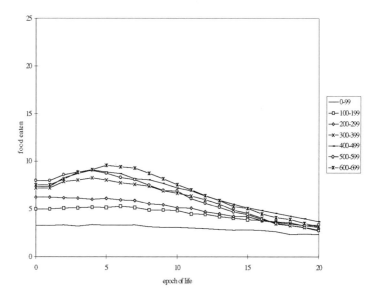

Figure 8.11
Number of prey individuals captured in successive epochs of life by individuals that are informed
about their age by their genes but do not learn to predict during their life. Each curve represents
the average results of the best individuals of 100 successive generations for 10 replications of the
simulation.

be learned if the text contains short (syntactically simple) sentences but not if it
contains both short and longer (more complex) sentences. However, networks
with a memory span that increases during learning can learn to predict the next
word in texts that include both simple and complex sentences. The memory
span of a network with context or memory units is the number of cycles after
which the information stored in the memory units is canceled. Elman shows
that a network will learn the task if its memory span is restricted at the beginning of learning and then it is progressively enlarged at successive stages
during learning.

Elman imagines that the increase in memory span is controlled genetically
much as the increasing age of the organism in the simulation described above.
In both cases the genetic information is hardwired by the researcher rather then
evolved. However, in Elman's networks the genetic information hardwired by
the researcher directly determines the increase in memory span. In the simulation on age the information about age is elaborated by the network's connec-

tion weights which <u>are</u> evolved. Therefore, it is the evolutionary process that decides which use some part of the inherited genetic information (the evolved connection weights) should make of another part of the genetic information which is hardwired by us (information about age).

8.4   Life History

In the simulations described in the preceding sections the changes that occur during the lifetime of an organism are quantitative. The organism is supposed to be able to do a single thing and it can only change because its performance improves or perhaps deteriorate. An individual's reproductive chances are determined using the same criterion in all stages of its life and, as a consequence, the total fitness of the individual is simply the sum of the partial fitnesses of each successive stage in its development.

However, real organisms have a life history, that is, they go through a succession of stages in which they exhibit qualitatively different behaviors and learn different things. Their "performance" is evaluated using different criteria at each stage and their total fitness is a more complex function of the fitnesses at each stage than the simple sum of these fitnesses.

To begin to address the problem of the evolution of life histories, we have done the following simulation [262]. Imagine an organism whose entire lifetime includes two successive stages: a reproductively immature stage followed by a mature stage. The role of genetic information in the development of the organism consists in specifying the time of transition from the first to the second stage.

When an individual reaches reproductive maturity it generates (nonsexually) an offspring each time its energy reaches a certain threshold. The offspring is given half of the energy of its parent. This energy is reduced by a certain amount at each time step (each input/output mapping) and is increased by a certain amount each time the individual succeeds in capturing a food element. If the individual's energy goes to zero, the individual dies. (All individuals die when they reach a certain maximum age.)

The offspring inherit from their (single) parent a genome which encodes (a) a set of connection weights for their neural network (the network architecture is fixed and identical for all individuals), and (b) an "age at maturity gene", i.e., a real number that specifies the age at which the offspring will reach reproductive maturity. Different individuals have different connection weights (and, therefore, behaviors) and they reach reproductive maturity at different ages. Both the connection weights and the value of the age at maturity gene are identical to those of the parent except that random changes (mutations) can slightly modify some of the connection weights and slightly increase or decrease the value of the age at maturity gene.

Before reaching reproductive maturity an individual does nothing and nothing happens to the individual. The individual does not move and it does not increase or decrease its energy. However, if the parent of an immature individual dies the energy of the offspring is decreased by some quantity for each cycle after the parent's death. Hence, immature individuals can die before reaching maturity. If an individual is able to reach the stage of reproductive maturity it begins to use its neural network to look for food to survive and possibly to generate offspring.

In these conditions in which nothing useful happens during immaturity the average value of the age at maturity gene tends to go to zero after a few generations (Figure 8.12). In other words, the stage of reproductive immaturity tends to disappear from the life history of the population. All individuals are born as already mature individuals. This of course results from the fact that individuals that reach reproductive maturity as early as possible tend to have more offspring.

However, imagine that during immaturity something happens that tends to increase the reproductive success of the adult individual. For example, during immaturity an individual learns some ability that will increase the energy value of the food the individual is able to capture as an adult. If the advantage of learning this ability during immaturity (learning is discontinued at maturity) is greater than the cost of having a reproductively immature stage, the average value of the age at maturity gene will reach a steady state and the stage of reproductive immaturity will become a stable feature of the life history of the population.

These simulations are a first step toward the evolution of life histories, that is, of genetically controlled sequences of qualitatively different stages in the development of an individual. Life histories emerge if each stage has its role in the global adaptive pattern of the population and it contributes to the overall fitness of the individual. In the simulations described both the immature and the mature stages contribute each in its own distinct way to determining the reproductive chances of the individual. The age in which the individual reaches maturity is completely under genetic control in these simulations but learning and experience could be easily assigned a role, for example, by making age

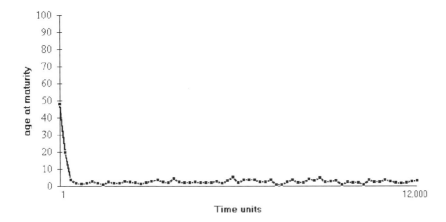

Figure 8.12
Changes in the age in which individuals become reproductively mature in a population in which nothing useful happens during reproductive immaturity. The stage of reproductive immaturity rapidly disappears from the life history of the population. (From [262].

at maturity sensitive to the reaching of a given level of performance in the learning that occurs during immaturity.

8.5 Conclusions

Development is change taking place in an individual organism which is caused by an interaction between the genetically inherited information inside the organism and the information arriving to the organism from the environment in which the organism happens to live. (Biological entities at all levels, e.g., cells, develop, not only organisms. This definition of development applies to all levels.) If the nervous system that controls the organism's behavior is modeled as a neural network, development can be studied as changes in the network that depend on both an explicitly represented inherited "genome" and the environment. The inherited genome is the current result of another process of change, evolution, that takes place not at the level of the individual organism but at the level of the entire population of which the individual organism is a member. Therefore, development in individual neural networks can only be properly studied together with evolution in populations of neural networks. By studying development and evolution together it becomes possible to tackle important research topics such as the reciprocal influence between evolution and development, the similarities and differences between evolutionary and developmental sequences, the evolution of developmental genomes that incorporate temporally distributed programs of development, and the evolutionary emergence of species-specific life histories.

In the last few years some initial attempts have been made to study development in neural networks in an evolutionary perspective. In some simulations the inherited genome specifies the initial state of networks that learn. Learning in neural networks always depends on the initial state: the network architecture, the initial set of weights, the learning parameters, etc. However, it is one thing to decide the initial state more or less arbitrarily, as is done in "classical" connectionist research, and another thing to study how evolution in a population of networks spontaneously converges on some initial state that is appropriate for learning. In other simulations using ecological networks the interaction between genetic and environmental information that causes development is not restricted to the genetic specification of the initial state for learning but it extends to the self-selection by the neural network of its learning experiences. Unlike "classical" networks, ecological networks partly determine with their output their own input. Therefore, the inherited information can influence the network's output which in turn can influence the environmental input on the basis of which the network learns. In still other simulations, networks self-generate their own teaching input for learning by elaborating the environmental input using genetically inherited connection weights. In these simulations the interaction between genetic and environmental information becomes even more complex.

One of the critical aspects of the genetic influence on development is that the genetically inherited information does not only specify the initial state for the changes that occur in the organism during its life but it continues to be phenotypically expressed and to influence these changes throughout the life of the organism. Some simulations have addressed this aspect of the genetic control of development by evolving developmental genomes that contain information portions of which are expressed at successive ages during the life of the individual. While in genomes that are restricted to specifying the initial state of the organism developmental changes are driven by the environment and the genetically inherited information only influences these changes, with developmental genomes the genetically inherited information can drive development and the role of the environment can be restricted to influencing the genetically driven changes. However, even in this case the interaction between genetic and environmental information can be quite complex and intimate as is shown in simulations in which neurons grow their axon and establish connections with other neurons as a function of both a genetically specified threshold for activation variability and the influence of the environment in determining the actual value for this variability.

The continuing influence of the genetic information on development is more globally captured in simulations in which the genome informs the phenotype (in our case, the neural network) about its constantly increasing age. The phenotype can take into account its changing age in the changes that occur in the phenotype as a function of its interactions with the environment (learning). These simulations show that age and learned changes co-evolve. In evolved organisms neither age alone nor learning alone are able to cause useful changes in the phenotype but useful changes can only result from an interaction between the genetically specified age changes and the environmentally caused learned changes.

Evolution is also responsible for the general qualitative changes in the lifetime of an individual organism that constitute the life history of the species. On the basis of the contribution of each stage to the total fitness of the organism evolution specifies what stages constitute the life history, their succession, and the approximate duration of each stage. Some simulations begin to address the evolution of life histories by having evolution select for organisms with a life history divided up into an initial stage of reproductive immaturity and a second mature stage and by identifying the appropriate duration of the immature stage.

Let us conclude this Chapter with some general remarks on the nature of change in neural networks viewed in an ecological and evolutionary perspective.

In section 8.1 we distinguished between development and learning by using the distinction between endogenous and exogenous change. Learning is exogenous change, i.e., change that reflects the external environment in which an individual organism happens to live. Development is endogenous change, i.e., change that is directed by the genetic information contained inside the organism, more specifically, in the DNA present in the nuclei of the organism's cells.

But development is more complex than just genetically directed change. First, the endogenous factors that cause and shape development are not restricted to the individual's DNA. Second, development is a function of the interactions among the various endogenous factors and between endogenous and exogenous factors, rather than just a sum of these factors [267].

There are at least two other important endogenous factors that play a role in development beyond the information contained in the inherited genome. One such factor is already captured in classical connectionist learning given the intrinsic nature of neural networks. The changes that take place in a network's connection weights during learning are not only due to the input and the teaching input arriving to the network from outside but also to the current value of the connection weights. This means that the effects of the external environment in neural network's learning, i.e., the effects of the input and teaching input, are mediated by the constantly changing internal structure of the neural network itself. A neural network does not learn by just absorbing in its internal structure the external environment, but by cumulatively incorporating in its internal structure (connection weights) the results of the interactions between the external environment (input and teaching input) and its internal structure (cf. Piaget's notion of assimilation). In this sense one could say that learning in neural networks has an inherently temporal character since the effect of each learning experience on the network (e.g., a cycle of backpropagation learning) reflects the past and not only the current experience.

The other endogenous factor in development, however, cannot be captured if one uses classical neural networks but it is necessary to use ecological networks. Unlike classical networks, ecological networks live in an independent environment and their input and teaching input comes from this independent environment, and not from the arbitrary decisions of the researcher. The most important consequence of using ecological networks to study development is that ecological networks can influence with their actions the input they receive from the environment. This implies that both learning and development have a constructivist component in ecological neural networks which is lacking in classical networks. By a constructivist component we mean that even the exogenous factors that determine learning and development, that is, the external input and teaching input, are influenced and "constructed" by the organism itself rather than being an uncontrolled purely external source of information. More specifically, at any given developmental stage the external input to which the organism is exposed and which determines its learning is influenced by the behavior of the organism at that stage. Therefore, in ecological networks the external environment is "filtered" by the organism's changing behavior and is "constructed" rather than being passively absorbed by the organism.

Development in neural networks viewed in an ecological and evolutionary perspective, thus, appears to be the result of a constant interaction among the three endogenous factors (the genetic information, the current internal structure of the network, and the behavior of the network that influences the input arriving from the environment) and between these endogenous factors and the exogenous factor represented by the environment.

References

[257]C. A. and T. C. Trading spaces: Computation, representation, and the limits of uniformed learning. *Behavioral and Brain Sciences*, (20):57–90, 1997.

[258]F. D. and M. F. Evolution of plastic neurocontrollers for situated agents. In P. Maes, M. Mataric, J.-A. Meyer, J. Pollack, and S. Wilson, editors, *From Animals to Animats 4, Proceedings of the International Conference on Simulation of Adaptive Behavior*, Cambridge, MA, 1996. MIT Press.

[259]P. D. *Neural activity and the growth of the brain*. Cambridge University Press, Cambridge, 1994.

[260]P. D., C. F., and N. S. Econets: neural networks that learn in an environment. *Network*, (1):149–168, 1990.

[261]A. D.E. and L. M.L. Interactions between learning and evolution. In C. Langton, C. Taylor, J. Farmer, and S. Rasmussen, editors, *Artificial Life II*, Reading, MA, 1991. Addison-Wesley.

[262]C. F. and P. D. Learning during reproduction immaturity in evolving population of neural networks. Technical report, Institute of Psychology, C.N.R., Rome, 1994.

[263]M. G.F., T. P.M., and H. S.U. Designing neural networks using genetic algorithms. In L. Nadel and D. Stain, editors, *Proceedings of the International Conference From Perception to Action*, Los Alamitos, CA, 1989. IEEE Press.

[264]K. H. Designing neural networks using genetic algorithms with graph generation system. *Complex Systems*, (4):461–476, 1990.

[265]J. Holland. *Adaptation in Natural and Artificial Systems*. The University of Michigan Press, Ann Arbor, 1975.

[266]H. I. Relearning and evolution in neural networks. *Adaptive Behavior*, (1):81–84, 1996.

[267]E. J., B. E., K.-S. A., J. M., P. D., and P. K. *Rethinking Innateness. A Connectionist Perspective on Development*. MIT Press, Cambridge, MA, 1996.

[268]K. J.F. and P. J.B. Back propagation is sensitive to initial conditions. *Complex Systems*, (4):296–280, 1990.

[269]E. J.L. Learning and development in neural networks: The importance of starting small. *Cognition*, (48):71–99, 1993.

[270]M. C. J.L. The interaction of nature and nurture in development: a parallel distributed processing perspective. Technical report, Carnegie Mellon University, U.S.A., 1992.

[271]P. K. Development in a connectionist framework: rethinking the nature-nurture debate. Technical report, Newsletter of the Center for Research on Language, UCSD, San Diego, CA, 1996.

[272]M. M. *An Introduction to Genetic Algorithms*. MIT Press, Cambridge, MA, 1996.

[273]M. J. M. Parallel distributed processing: Implications for cognition and development. In R. M. Morris, editor, *Parallel Distributed Processing: Implications for Psychology and Neurobiology*, New York, 1989. Oxford University Press.

[274]S. M., P. D., and L. J. Why starting small help: learning to reach by constraining the movement search space. *Developmental Science*, in press.

[275]P. R. and S. C. *Understanding Intelligence*. MIT Press, Cambridge, MA, 1999.

[276]B. R.K.   Interposing an ontogenetic model between genetic algorithms and neural networks. In J. Cowan, editor, *Advances in Neural Information Processings*, San Matteo, CA, 1993. Morgan Kaufmann.

[277]B. R.K., M. J., and S. N.   Evolving networks: using the genetic algorithm with connectionist learning.   In C. Langton, C. Taylor, J. Farmer, and S. Rasmussen, editors, *Artificial Life II*, Reading, MA, 1991. Addison-Wesley.

[278]B. R.K and M. M.   *Adaptive Individuals in Evolving Populations*.   SFI Studies in the Science of Complexity, Addison-Wesley, Reading, MA, 1996.

[279]N. S.   How learning and evolution interact: The case of a learning task which differs from the evolutionary task. *Adaptive Behavior*, in press.

[280]N. S. and P. D.   Auto-teaching: networks that develop their own teaching input.   In J. Deneubourg, H. Bersini, S. Goss, G. Nicolis, and R. Dagonnier, editors, *Proceedings of the Second European Conference on Artificial Life*, Brussels, 1993. Free University of Brussels.

[281]N. S. and P. D.   Self-selection of input stimuli for improving performance.   In G. A. Bekey, editor, *Neural Networks and Robotics*. Kluwer Academic Publisher, 1993.

[282]N. S. and P. D.   Evolving artificial neural network that develop in time.   In F. Moran, A. Moreno, J. Merelo, and P. Chacon, editors, *Advances in Artificial Life: Proceedings of the Third European Conference on Artificial Life*, Berlin, 1995. Springer Verlag.

[283]N. S. and P. D.   Learining to adapt to changing environments in evolving neural networks. *Adaptive Behavior*, (5):99–105, 1997.

[284]N. S., E. J.L., and P. D.   Learning and evolution in neural networks. *Adaptive Behavior*, (1):5–28, 1994.

[285]N. S., M. O., and P. D.   Phenotypic plasticity in evolving neural networks.   In D. P. Gaussier and J.-D. Nicoud, editors, *Proceedings of the International Conference From Perception to Action*, Los Alamitos, CA, 1994. IEEE Press.

[286]Q. S. and S. T. J.   The neural basis of cognitive development: A constructivist manifesto. *Behavioral and Brain Sciences*, (4):537–555, 1997.

[287]Y. X.   Evolutionary artificial neural networks. *International Journal of Neural Systems*, (4):203–222, 1993.

9 Evolution and Learning in Radial Basis Function Neural Networks – A Hybrid Approach

Brian Carse, Terence C. Fogarty, and John C. W. Sullivan

A hybrid algorithm for determining Radial Basis Function (RBF) neural networks is proposed. The genetic algorithm is applied to the problem of learning optimal network architecture (number of hidden layer nodes, radial basis function centers and widths) in conjunction with gradient based learning for the tuning of connection weights. Each candidate network architecture is trained then evaluated over a test set to determine the network error from which a fitness function is derived. It is observed that such network errors arise from two causes: suboptimal network architecture and incomplete training. Although candidate networks could be trained until their weights converge in order to fully evaluate the network structure this is computationally very expensive. A method is proposed which, in conjunction with a novel crossover operator, varies the amount of training applied to networks during the process of evolution in order to accelerate the overall learning process.

9.1 Radial Basis Function Neural Networks

Radial Basis Function (RBF) neural networks [295, 338] originate from the use of radial basis functions in the solution of the real multivariate interpolation problem [339]. Such networks have been applied successfully in a number of applications including image processing [337], speech recognition [334], time series analysis [295, 330] and adaptive equalization [319]. In its basic form, a radial basis function neural network involves three functionally distinct layers. The input layer is simply a set of sensory units. The second layer is a hidden layer of sufficient dimension which applies a non-linear transformation of the input space to a higher-dimensional hidden-unit space using radial basis functions. The third and final layer performs a linear transformation from the hidden-unit space to the output space. The most general formula for any radial basis function is :

$$h(\mathbf{x}) = \phi((\mathbf{x} - \mathbf{c})^T \mathbf{R}^{-1} (\mathbf{x} - \mathbf{c}))$$

where ϕ is the function used, $\mathbf{c}$ is the centre and $\mathbf{R}$ is the metric. Several types of function are commonly employed (e.g. the linear, $\phi(z) = z$, the cubic $\phi(z) = z^3$, the thin plate spline, $\phi(z) = z^2 \log(z)$, the Gaussian, $\phi(z) = e^{-z}$, the multiquadratic, $\phi(z) = \sqrt{(1 + z)}$, the inverse multiquadratic, $\phi(z) = 1/((1 + z))$ and the Cauchy, $\phi(z) = (1 + z)^{-1}$). When the metric $\mathbf{R}$

is Euclidean, then $\mathbf{R} = r^2\mathbf{I}$ for some scalar radius r and the above equation simplifies to

$$h(\mathbf{x}) = \phi\left(\frac{(\mathbf{x} - \mathbf{c})^T(\mathbf{x} - \mathbf{c})}{r^2}\right)$$

In this contribution Gaussian RBF functions are considered. Figure 9.1 shows such a network with Gaussian RBF functions G_i, inputs x_j and weights W_i. The output Y of this RBF network is evaluated from the input vector x_j as follows :-

$$Y = \sum_{i=1}^{P} W_i G_i(x_1 \ldots x_j, \ldots x_N)$$

where

$$G_i(x_1 \ldots x_j, \ldots x_N) = \prod_{j=1}^{N} \exp\left(-\frac{(x_j - C_{ij})^2}{2R_{ij}^2}\right)$$

where C_{ij} and R_{ij} are centers and radii of Gaussian basis functions.

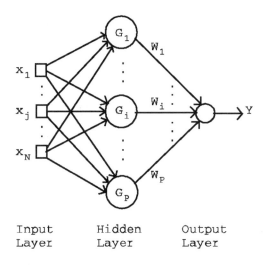

Figure 9.1
RBF Network Architecture

Compared to multi-layer perceptron (MLP) networks, RBF networks differ in a number of respects [313]:

• MLP networks may have more than one hidden layer whereas RBF networks only employ a single hidden layer.

• Nodes in an MLP network typically share a common neural model (usually weighted activations from previous layer nodes are summed and an activation function applied), whereas hidden and output nodes of an RBF network are functionally distinct (hidden layer nodes apply radial basis functions, output layer nodes calculate the linear weighted sum of the resulting activations of the hidden layer).

• MLP networks construct "global" function approximations whereas RBF networks construct "local" function approximations using exponentially decaying localized non-linearities (usually Gaussian functions). As a result, MLP networks can generalize (interpolate) better in regions where no training is available, whereas RBF networks can learn faster and show less sensitivity to the order of presentation of training data. The latter advantages of RBF networks are bought at the expense of a potentially large number of radial basis functions required to span the input space adequately.

Both MLP and RBF networks have been proved to be universal approximators [302, 335] and therefore there exists an RBF network which is functionally equivalent to any MLP network and vice-versa. However, while theoretically extremely important results, these existence proofs offer little insight into how networks may be designed or learned efficiently.

9.2 Evolution of Multi-Layer Perceptron Networks using the Genetic Algorithm

A copious amount of research effort has recently been applied to evolutionary learning of MLP networks in both straight feedforward and recurrent forms. This extensive literature has already been thoroughly reviewed by a number of authors [344, 353, 350, 291] so here we only summarize the primary approaches used and offer a set of representative references of this large body of work. The taxonomies suggested in the different GA/MLP reviews are broadly similar and include the following combinations:

• Evolutionary learning of connection weights for fixed MLP architectures (e.g. [298, 329, 351, 352, 346, 354]), possibly in conjunction with gradient-based learning (e.g. [290, 321, 315]).

• Evolution of MLP architectures (number of nodes and connections between them), again, often with gradient-based learning for weight determination. This includes direct representations, where network topology is directly coded onto the genotype, and also indirect codings of grammar structure which generate architectures by development ("neurogenesis") rather than directly representing the architectures themselves. (e.g. [327, 311, 312, 306, 320, 345, 290, 325, 310]).

- Simultaneous evolution of both network architectures and connection weights (e.g. [316, 304, 326, 292, 293, 343])
- Using an evolutionary approach to preprocessing training data, (e.g. [299, 294]) or to interpret the behaviour of networks (e.g. [308, 307]).
- Evolution of learning rules and parameters (e.g. [290, 311, 312, 332, 331]).

In this contribution, we are primarily concerned with the second of these categories, and in particular, direct representations where the genotype encodes network topology directly. The problem of evolving MLP neural network topologies (nodes and connections) is a difficult one, since the search surface (fitness landscape) possesses the following characteristics [328]:

- The surface is effectively infinitely large (unbounded number of nodes and connections).
- The surface is nondifferentiable since changes in the number of nodes and connections are discrete and can have a discontinuous effect on network performance.
- The surface is complex and noisy since the mapping from architecture to performance is indirect, strongly epistatic, and dependent on initial conditions.
- The surface is deceptive since networks with similar architectures may have dramatically different performances.
- The surface is multimodal since networks with different architectures can have very similar capabilities.

Indeed many of the difficulties experienced in the evolution of MLP architectures have stemmed from one or more of these characteristics. One such difficulty, described by Schaffer et al. [344], and by Radcliffe [340, 341] is the "competing conventions" or "permutations" problem. This problem arises from the fact that a number of distinct genotypes can map to phenotypes (in this context network instantiations) which are functionally equivalent since permuting the hidden nodes in the same layer of a feedforward network does not alter its function. Applying recombination to two successful parents employing different conventions is unlikely to produce successful offspring, thus, as Schaffer et al. [344] point out "rendering crossover essentially impotent as a search operator, at least until the population has converged to a single convention". The same argument is put forward by Angeline et al. [288] who advocate the use of evolutionary programming (EP) which does not employ recombination operators. A further difficulty in evolution of directly coded MLP networks using the GA is the degree of epistasis between elements on the genotype. The distributed way in which learned information is stored in an MLP network, while explaining the excellent generalization properties of such networks, can be difficult for a traditional GA to work on using direct encoding on the genotype. Changing a single weight or adding/deleting a node can have a serious "knock-on" effect regarding the effectiveness of other nodes and weights. This type of strong and non-linear interaction translates to high levels of epistasis between genotype elements. Very high levels of epistasis are known to present difficulties for a traditional GA [305]. Another problem specifically relating to hybrid learning using the GA in conjunction with gradient-based methods is the amount of CPU time spent training and evaluating each candidate network architecture. This is also, of course, a serious problem when applying the approach to RBF networks.

9.3   Evolution of Radial Basis Function Networks Using the Genetic Algorithm – Previous Work

Much less attention has been paid to the artificial evolution of RBF networks, although both direct and indirect encodings have been investigated, along with evolution of learning parameters, and hybrid GA and gradient-based learning combinations. In this section we offer a summary of recent work.

In [348], Whitehead and Choate present an elegant approach which evolves "space filling curves" to determine basis function centers in conjunction with gradient-based learning to learn weights. Rather than encoding individual basis function centers and widths directly on the genotype, this approach applies the GA to binary coded strings representing parameters for an algorithm which generates basis function centres. The learning rate employed in gradient-based learning for evaluation of individual fitness during evolution is encoded on the genotype and is evolved along with the space-filling curve parameters. Mutation involves two operators: a creep operator and a bit-wise operator, in an attempt to avoid the "blocking problem" [309] associated with high cardinality representations. Networks with large numbers of hidden nodes are indirectly penalized by setting the number of passes through the training data during the gradient-based learning phase to be inversely proportional to the number of hidden nodes. The method is applied to learning of a chaotic time-series and RBF networks are evolved that outperform networks determined using the k-means clustering algorithm in conjunction with gradient-based learning, using fewer hidden nodes, although the reported GA/RBF learning approach takes about 35-40 times as much CPU time as the k-means based algorithm.

In [349], the same authors propose a very different way of applying the genetic algorithm to the evolution of RBF networks. Although this work also evolves RBF centers and widths it employs a completely different notion of what the GA population comprises. In this later paper the population of individuals comprises a single evolving network (rather than a population of networks) and each individual represents a single RBF. Selection, recombination and mutation operate at the level of the individual RBF. The potential problem in applying this approach, as Whitehead and Choate point out is that of "co-operation" versus "competition" (reminiscent of similar problems in learning classifier systems): individual RBFs which together produce accurate function mappings over the input space later go on to compete for selection. In order to overcome this problem, they propose a niche sharing method based on the inner product of normalized activation sequences, $\phi(x)$, where the latter is the set of normalized activations of the ith node over the training set x. Two nodes having a large inner product (close to 1) are likely to have very similar basis function centers and widths and are attempting to do nearly the same job; such nodes should compete under action of the GA. However, two nodes with a small inner product (close to 0) then the two nodes are making relatively independent contributions and should not compete (they are cooperative). The method is applied to time series prediction and pattern classification problems using a variety of basis functions (Gaussian, thin plate spline, inverse multi-quadratic) where it is shown to produce much superior solutions than achieved using k-means clustering.

Chen et al. [300] describe a two level learning approach for RBF networks using a regularized orthogonal least squares (ROLS) algorithm at the lower level to learn connection weights. The ROLS learning algorithm employs a regulation parameter λ and basis function width ρ. The GA operates at a higher level by evolving values for λ and ρ to be applied during ROLS learning. Hence the GA is essentially being used to evolve both an architecture related parameter (basis function width) and a learning parameter. Regularization is a technique used to improve the generalization properties of trained networks by minimizing a cost functional $\xi(F) = \xi_s(F) + \lambda_c(F)$, where F is the learned functional mapping, ξ_s is the standard error term (e.g. sum squared error) and ξ_c is the regularizing term. The effect of regularization in learning is to engender smoother input-output function mappings from a finite set of training examples, possibly containing noise. The regularization parameter λ determines the relative contributions of the standard error term and the regularizing term to the cost functional to be minimized during training. In the approach of Chen et al. networks are trained using the ROLS algorithm on a training set for particular values of λ and ρ. The trained networks are then tested on a separate test set and the inverse of the generalization performance is the fitness for that particular (λ, ρ) pair used by the GA. It is shown that even for a simple scalar function, the generalization performance surface as a function of λ and ρ is highly complex and multimodal and therefore the GA may be an appropriate optimization technique. This complex interaction between architectural parameters (basis function widths) and learning rate is an issue we discuss later in this paper. The hybrid approach adopted by Chen et al. is applied to learning of a simple scalar function with added noise; to learning prediction of Mackey-Glass time series; and to learning prediction of sunspot time series. In reported experiments, the GA operating on λ and ρ together gave significantly better results compared with the GA operating on ρ only.

Neruda [333] addresses the matter of functionally equivalent network parameterizations [314] in relation to the evolution of directly encoded RBF networks using the GA. This again raises the issue of the "competing conventions" problem described by Schaffer et al. [344] in relation to evolution of MLP networks. Both relate to the degree of symmetry in direct coded representations in the sense that exchanging two or more nodes in a hidden layer (along with their weights) produces a network with identical input/output characteristics. It is shown that two RBF network parameterizations are functionally equivalent if and only if they are interchange equivalent. Neruda proposes a solution to the problem by selecting a single parameterization for each class, or "convention" (called a "canonical parameterization" and restricting the search space of the GA accordingly. Crossover and mutation operators are defined which ensure that the offspring generated by the GA obey the same "convention" Although no experimental results are presented in Neruda's paper, the arguments presented are compelling and later in section 9.5 we describe an RBF genotype representation and associated genetic operators, independently arrived at and borrowed from studies in evolution of fuzzy controllers, which effectively implement a "canonical parameterization".

9.4   Evolution of Fuzzy Rule Based Systems

The similarity of RBF networks and certain types of fuzzy rule based systems is demonstrated in [317]. This work suggests that an interchange between the two fields is likely to be of benefit. A large amount of research has been carried out to date on artificial evolution of fuzzy rule bases, and much of this work can be carried over to the evolution of RBF networks. A fuzzy rule based system typically comprises a "knowledge base" - a set of fuzzy set membership functions defined over appropriate universes of discourse for input and output variables; and a "rule base" which defines input-output relations (rules) using such a knowledge base. In an, admittedly loose, translation between fuzzy rule based system and RBF network parlance, fuzzy logic membership functions become radial basis functions and fuzzy rules become RBF hidden layer nodes. Therefore published work from the field of evolution of fuzzy systems may be germane to the evolution of RBF networks.

In [318] a GA is used for optimizing fuzzy membership functions using a fixed rule base; this is similar to evolving RBF network function centers and widths for a fixed architecture network. In [347] a GA is used to evolve fuzzy rules which use fixed fuzzy membership functions; translated to RBF networks this is equivalent to evolving connections between RBF network nodes using fixed radial basis functions. Learning of fuzzy rules and membership functions simultaneously is reported in [322, 336, 301, 324, 323].

In [296] a Pittsburgh-style fuzzy classifier system is proposed which is evaluated in [297]. This system employs a variable length genotype directly encoding fuzzy relations and membership functions, and uses a crossover operator based on crosspoints in the input variable space (and therefore the space of possible fuzzy rule membership function centers) instead of position on the genotype string. This operator was devised to preserve building blocks of fuzzy rules whose input membership functions overlap and experiments reported in [297] demonstrate that the new crossover operator significantly outperforms simple one-point and two-point crossover operators in a function identification task and a control task using reinforcement learning. Bearing in mind the demonstrated similarities between RBF networks and fuzzy inference systems, it seems reasonable to extend this GA/Fuzzy approach to the evolution of RBF network architectures, supplementing it with gradient-based learning. This is described in the following section.

9.5 Evolving Radial Basis Function Neural Networks

This section describes the encoding of RBF architectures as genotypes and the genetic operators we propose. In particular, a novel crossover operator is used which recognizes the epistasis between overlapping radial basis functions. The crossover operator is also designed to avoid hidden layer node duplication and the competing conventions problem. The genotype is of variable length (allowing different network sizes) and a simple mechanism is employed to apply selection pressure toward smaller networks.

Genotype Representation

The genotype comprises a variable length concatenated string of composite "genes" where each gene encodes the parameters (basis function centre and widths) of a single hidden layer node. Each composite gene, G_i, which encodes parameters for a hidden layer node is represented by the $2N$-tuple

$$(C_{i1}, R_{i1}, \ldots C_{ij}, R_{ij}, \ldots, C_{iN}, R_{iN})$$

where N is the number of inputs, M is the number of outputs, and (Cij, Rij) are the centre and width of the Gaussian radial basis function of the hidden layer node for the jth input variable. All parameters are encoded as real numbers.

Crossover Operator

The crosssover operator operates as follows. Two vector crosspoints X_{1j} and X_{2j}, where each crosspoint vector contains an element for each input variable (N inputs), are chosen as follows:

$$X_{1j} = MIN_j + (MAX_j - MIN_j).(R_1)$$

$$X_{2j} = X_{1j} + (MAX_j - MIN_j).(R_2)^{\frac{1}{N}}$$

R_1 and R_2 are selected randomly in the range $[0, 1]$ with uniform probability density. $[MIN_j, MAX_j]$ is the allowed range of the jth input variable. After crossover, Child 1 contains those "genes" (i.e. encoded hidden layer nodes) which satisfy:

$$\forall j, ((C_{ij} > X_{1j}) \wedge (C_{ij} < X_{2j})) \vee ((C_{ij} + MAX_j - MIN_j) < X_{2j})$$

together with "genes" from Parent 2 which do not satisfy this condition. Child 2 contains the remaining "genes" from both parents. The crossover operator therefore juxtaposes complete sets of radial basis functions in the input space as opposed to the space of position on the encoded string. Its effect is to exchange hidden layer nodes whose RBF centers are contained in the hypervolume (in the input space) defined by X_{1j} and X_{2j}. Since this crossover is carried out with reference to the space of the input variables rather than distance along the genotype string, two strings which are different but interchange equivalent (i.e. represent different permutations of the same set of hidden layer nodes and therefore belong to different "conventions") are treated as identical for the purposes of crossover.

Mutation

Mutation operators are relatively straightforward. Real number creep is applied to basis function centers and widths, and is intended to perform the role of local search. Hidden layer node creation and deletion operators are employed. The node creation operator introduces a new hidden layer node with random centre and width. The node deletion operator simply deletes a hidden layer node selected at random.

Fitness Evaluation

Fitness evaluation employs network training to modify hidden layer output connection weights using the Least-Mean-Square(LMS) algorithm (see [313] for a full description of the LMS algorithm). The LMS algorithm proceeds as follows. An input $x(n)(n = 1, 2, \ldots)$ of the training set is applied to the network input and the error e(n) is evaluated. This error is the difference between the suggested network output and the correct output. Network weights are adjusted according to the equation:

$$W_i(n + 1) = W_i(n) + \eta e(n) A_i(n)$$

where $A_i(n)$ is the activation of the ith hidden layer node and η is the learning rate parameter. After training, the fitness of the individual is evaluated. In this way, the GA is used to modify the number of hidden layer nodes and their associated radial basis function centers and widths and supervised learning is used to tune connection weights. During the course of evolution, the fitness evaluation of each individual representing an encoded RBF network is a function of the error over the training set.

Clearly with this method, as with other similar methods, a tradeoff has to be made in choosing the number of training epochs before evaluating the prediction accuracy over the target function and therefore fitness. Large amounts of training will more clearly demonstrate the potential of a candidate network architecture but will also take large amounts of CPU time for fitness evaluation. In [289] it is suggested that in evaluating a network in terms of the error it produces over the target function, the total error comes from two sources:

Approximation Error: the distance between the target function and the closest neural network function of a given architecture, and

Estimation Error: the distance between this closest network function and the actual function estimated by the neural network given its actual set of weights.

Approximation error arises from incorrect network architecture (number of nodes, connections, basis function centers and widths in the case of RBF networks); even if such a network was fully trained there is a residual error which can never be reduced due to the incorrect architecture. Estimation error arises from incomplete training. In the specific case of hybrid evolution and learning of RBF networks with which we are concerned here, it might be expected that at early generations approximation error is large and that this reduces as evolution proceeds as better network structures are evolved. It might then be argued that there is little point wasting valuable CPU time on large numbers of training epochs in early generations. Using this premise as a basis, we propose to vary the number of training epochs used in fitness evaluation as evolution proceeds. In early stages of evolution, when encoded network architectures may be highly suboptimal, fewer training cycles are applied. As higher quality network architectures evolve, a larger number of training cycles are applied to more fully evaluate the performance of encoded networks.

9.6   Experimental Results and Discussion

Experiments described in this section address the following issues:

- Evaluation of the proposed representation and genetic operators compared with more "standard" representations and operators when evolution and learning are applied together.

• What are the contributions of estimation error and approximation error to the overall error of evolved neural networks and how do these contributions vary with the number of learning epochs employed and generation number?

• Can the results of measuring the contributions of estimation and approximation error be fruitfully used to speed up the overall learning process by applying a parsimonious choice of number of training epochs in early stages of the evolution process in order to produce better network architectures in less time?

Two sets of experiments are presented. The first involves the learning of RBF architectures for a simple single input, single output function $y = \sin(20x^2)$ in the input range [0,1]. This function is chosen since its input/output mapping varies in complexity over the input range, and therefore genetic learning of RBF network architectures with variable RBF centers and widths might be expected to outperform networks with fixed parameters. It also provides a simple function with which to compare the proposed representation and genetic operators with more "conventional" ones. In addition, and perhaps more importantly, the use of such a simple function allows practical evaluation of approximation and estimation errors (in terms of CPU time) in order to evaluate the contribution of the two types of error to the overall network error. The second set of experiments presented tackles a benchmark problem of chaotic time series prediction (the Mackey-Glass series).

Evaluation of the Representation and Genetic Operators

The method proposed employs a variable length genotype and a new crossover operator designed to work in the space of radial basis function centers. Experiments were performed to compare the performance of the proposed approach with a more "standard" (fixed length) representation and more standard crossover operators. Experiments were performed in learning the sinesquare function using fixed length genotypes representing 8, 10, 12, 15 and 20 hidden layer nodes. In the case of variable length genotypes, networks were allowed to evolve up to these maximum sizes. The GA was run in each case for 50 generations with a population of 50, replacing the weakest 40 individuals at each generation, and using rank-based selection with s = 1.8. In each case, the chromosome mutation rate was 0.2 and the crossover rate 0.8. LMS learning was applied for 40 epochs over a set of 40 equally spaced points in the range [0,1] with the learning rate parameter, η set to 0.3. The evaluation function used to determine fitness was the inverse of the sum squared error over the training set after training. Node creation and node deletion operators were applied to new offspring with probability 0.1 and in the case of fixed length genotype, these operators were applied together.

Figure 9.2 shows the error of the best evolved networks using different networks sizes and different crossover operators. These graphs show the average of 20 runs in each case with a different initial random seed. Clearly evolution of variable length genotypes with the new crossover operator is outperforming that using fixed length genotypes and one- and two-point crossover operators. The difference in performance is particularly marked when smaller networks are evolved (e.g. those containing 8 or 10 hidden layer nodes). This is particularly encouraging if the proposed method is to scale up to produce relatively small but efficient networks using higher dimensional input spaces.

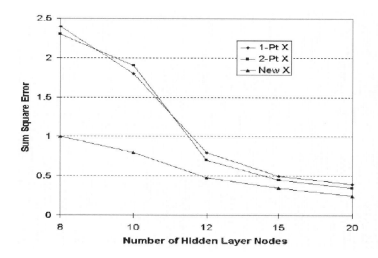

Figure 9.2
Network Error versus Number of Hidden Layer Nodes for Different Crossover Operators

Figure 9.3 illustrates the accuracy of an evolved solution; this functional mapping is achieved with a network containing 7 hidden layer nodes.

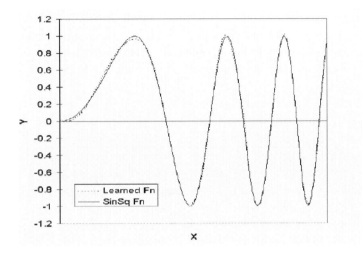

Figure 9.3
An Evolved Solution for the Function $y = \sin(20x^2)$

Varying the Number of Training Epochs

The previous set of experiments employed a fixed number (40) of training epochs. As mentioned earlier, the contribution to network error comes from two sources: approximation error (poor network architecture) and estimation error (incomplete training). Although evolution is attempting to discover good network architectures, the fitness function depends on both network architecture and the degree of training used during evolution. Obviously if networks could be fully trained before evaluation, then a good measure of approximation error could be obtained. However, this is computationally very expensive and we seek to evolve good network architectures with less training employed during evolution.

To investigate this, network architectures were evolved using different numbers of training epochs. Experiments in this section pertain to networks allowed to have up to 15 hidden layer nodes and using the same sinesquare target function as in the previous section. Networks were evolved for 30 generations using the same GA parameters as previously described. The number of training epochs were chosen from $\{5, 10, 20, 40\}$ with respective learning rates from $\{0.7, 0.5, 0.4, 0.2\}$. The results are the average of 5 runs using different initial random seeds.

Figure 9.4 shows the error of evolved networks versus generation number using different numbers of training epochs. Not surprisingly, the larger the number of training epochs employed, the more accurate the evolved networks after a particular number of generations. However, the number of generations is not a good measure of the actual CPU time spent in evolving the individual networks. The innermost loop of the complete hybrid learning method (GA plus LMS learning) is the calculation of weight changes using the LMS algorithm. A more accurate measure of computational effort expended in evolving networks is the product of the number of epochs employed and the number of generations.

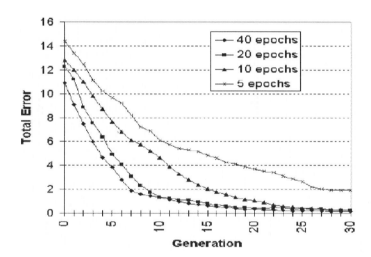

Figure 9.4
Network Error versus Generation for Different Numbers of Training Epochs

Figure 9.5 shows the evolved network errors versus this (Epochs × Generations) product in the early stages of evolution using different numbers of training epochs. The maximum product value of 200 corresponds to 5 generations using 40 learning epochs, 10 generations using 20 epochs, 20 generations using 10 epochs and 40 generations using 5 epochs. Figure 9.5 suggests that faster overall learning, certainly in early stages of evolution, is achieved using smaller numbers of training epochs. This is despite the fact that a smaller number of training epochs implies a less accurate estimation of the approximation

error of networks. It appears that concentrating the computational effort on
the exploration of the space of individual network architectures (the evolutionary component of the hybrid algorithm) rather than on the accurate estimation
of the approximation error (the LMS learning component) is producing faster
overall learning in the early stages.

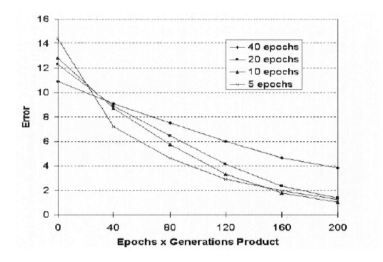

Figure 9.5
Evolved Network Error versus (Epochs × Generations) Product for Different Numbers of Epochs

To further investigate this, the approximation and estimation error of networks evolved with different numbers of training epochs were measured. This
was done as follows: at each generation, the total error, E_T of the elite population member was evaluated over the training set. This population member
was then fully trained until its weights converged and no further performance
improvement could be achieved using LMS learning. This fully trained population member was then evaluated over the training set to give an estimate of
the approximation error, E_A. The estimation error was calculated as $E_T - E_A$.
Figures 9.6,9.7,9.8 and 9.9 show the results of these measurements. In the case
of 40 training epochs, approximation error is the dominant term throughout the
run. This is to be expected since with a large number of training epochs individual networks are better trained and estimation error is small. As the number
of training epochs is decreased, estimation error becomes the dominant term
over much of the course of evolution.

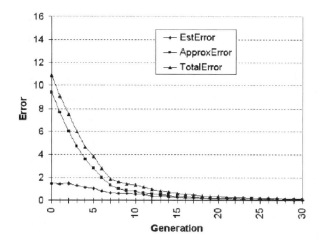

Figure 9.6
Error Contributions versus Generation Number (40 Training Epochs)

These results would indicate that an efficient strategy (in terms of computational effort) is to apply less training in evaluation of networks in early generations, when approximation error is large, and apply more training later on in evolution as good network structures emerge. In pure gradient based learning, such learning rate annealing was suggested in 1951 by Robbins and Munroe [342] and more recently Darken and Moody [303] propose a similar "search then converge" schedule. Here we are proposing a similar approach for hybrid GA/LMS learning. To investigate this using the simple sinesquare function, RBF networks were evolved by varying the number of training epochs employed over the course of evolution. The number of training epochs was linearly increased from 5 to 40 over 30 generations.

When network error versus generation number was inspected for variable training epochs compared with 40 training epochs, the latter method produced good solutions faster. After 30 generations, both methods were evolving networks of similar quality. However, as stated before, comparing methods based only on numbers of generations does not tell us much about the computational effort expended.

Figure 9.10 shows the network error versus (Epochs × Generation) product. This shows that varying the number of epochs evolves better networks af-

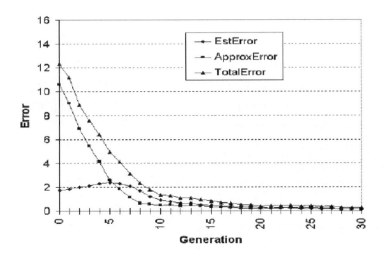

Figure 9.7
Error Contributions versus Generation Number (20 Training Epochs)

ter about 100 training episodes and that networks of similar accuracy to those evolved using 40 training epochs can be evolved in about half the time.

Scaling Up – Mackey-Glass Time Series Prediction

This section extends the proposed approach to a much more challenging problem – that of learning to predict the chaotic time series generated by the Mackey-Glass differential equation:

$$\frac{dx(t)}{dt} = -bx(t) + a.\frac{x(t-T)}{1 + x(t-T)^{10}}$$

Following previous research [330, 348], the time series was generated with parameter values $a = 0.2, b = 0.1$ and $T = 17$. Training data comprised 500 randomly selected points in the time series and test data comprised the 500 points in sequence following the training data. The task for the neural network is to predict the value of the time series at point $x[t + I]$ from the earlier points $x[t], x[t - D], x[t - 2D]$ and $x[t - 3D]$ where $D = 6$ timesteps and $I = 85$ timesteps into the future. Radial basis function neural networks for doing this prediction therefore have 4 inputs and a single output.

For this more challenging problem, the GA was supplemented with a cover

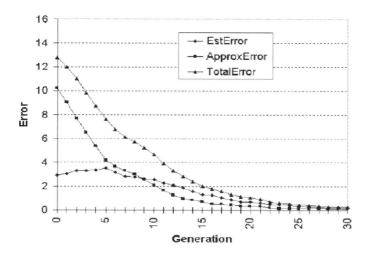

Figure 9.8
Error Contributions versus Generation Number (10 Training Epochs)

operator which generates a new hidden layer node if an input vector is encountered which does not activate any of the encoded basis functions. This new hidden layer node has its basis function centers placed at the position of the input vector, with randomly assigned basis function widths and output weight. After training on the training set is completed, the fitness of an individual is based on the "normalized" network error which is calculated as the root-mean-squared error over the training set divided by the standard deviation of the set of correct outputs. After evolution, the best evolved RBF networks were fully trained on the training set and then finally evaluated on the test set.

Networks were evolved using maximum network sizes (number of hidden layer nodes) of 20, 40, 60, 80 and 100. Evolution was carried out over 200 generations. During evolution, the learning parameters were varied as follows:

$$TrainingEpochs = 5 + GenerationNumber/10$$

$$LearningParameter = 0.6 - 0.002 * GenerationNumber$$

In this way, at early stages of evolution, fewer numbers of training epochs are applied, with more training being applied later in the run as good network structures arise. Figure 9.11 shows the results of using the variable length representation with the new crossover operator versus fixed length representations

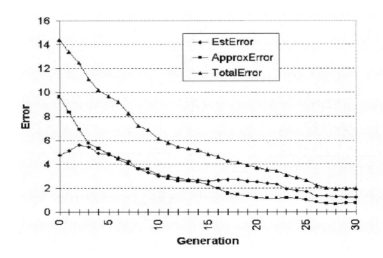

Figure 9.9
Error Contributions versus Generation Number (5 Training Epochs)

using one-point and two-point crossover. Clearly the new crossover operator is providing higher quality solutions for all sizes of network used.

Experiments were carried out using networks of maximum sizes 40, 70 and 110 to allow comparison with results reported by Whitehead and Choate [348] using k-means clustering and using evolved space filling curves. Figure 9.12 shows the comparison.

The proposed method appears to compare well. In looking at the maximum number of weight changes required to obtain this accuracy (weight changes represent the innermost loop of the hybrid learning algorithm), the proposed method employed 220 million weight changes compared with 1 billion weight changes used in [348]. The performance of evolved networks also compare well with the smallest networks described in [330] using non-GA learning for setting basis function centers and widths. In [330] normalized errors are reported which are approximately 0.25 (first nearest neighbor, 500 hidden layer nodes), 0.16 (adaptive units, 500 hidden layer nodes) and 0.27 (k-means clustering, 100 hidden layer nodes). However, we note that the small networks we have evolved (up to 110 hidden layer nodes) are an order of magnitude poorer than some of the largest networks reported in [330] (for example, a 5000 node network is reported which achieves a normalized error of 0.02 using k-means clustering). We have not experimented with evolving such large

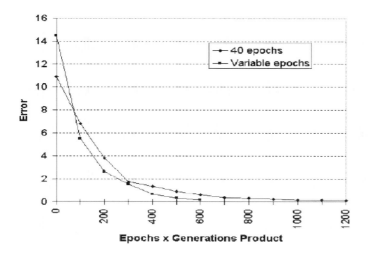

Figure 9.10
Error versus (Training Epochs × Generation) Product using 40 Training Epochs and using a
Variable Number of Epochs

networks using the genetic algorithm but suspect that difficulties might be
encountered due the size of the search space. We are therefore in agreement
with Whitehead and Choate [348] that the main contribution of evolving RBF
networks with a GA, at least for the moment, is to provide high performance
networks with relatively small numbers of nodes.

9.7   Conclusions

A representation and modified genetic operators have been proposed for the
evolution of radial basis function neural networks using the genetic algorithm.
The approach is a hybrid one, using the GA to learn network architecture
(number of hidden layer nodes, basis function centers and widths) and using
gradient-based learning for ascertaining connection weights. It was found that
during early stages in the evolution of such networks, approximation error is
the dominant contributor to overall network error and that CPU resources in
these early stages should be applied to the discovery of new network structures
rather than fully evaluating network structures by extensive training. A method
has been proposed which employs smaller numbers of training epochs early
on in the evolution process with more training later on as good network

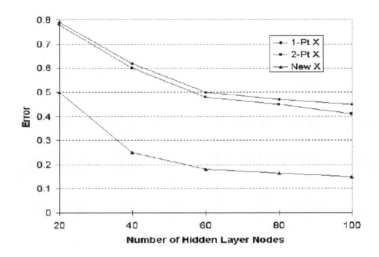

Figure 9.11
Error using Different Crossover Operators on the Mackey-Glass Prediction Problem

structures evolve. Experiments in learning a simple single-input, single-output function, and in learning to predict the Mackey-Glass time series using this method show that evolution combined with a variable gradient-based learning rate can produce relatively small RBF networks with good performance using a relatively small number of training epochs. In the experiments described, this variation in learning rate parameters is set by hand. Further work might investigate ways in which this learning is varied automatically as evolution proceeds.

References

[288] P. Angeline, G. Saunders, and J. Pollack. An evolutionary algorithm that constructs recurrent neural networks. *IEEE Transactions on Neural Networks*, 5(1):54–65, January 1994.

[289] A. Barron. Approximation and estimation bounds for artificial neural networks. In *Proceedings of the 4th Annual Workshop on Computational Learning Theory*, pages 243–249, 1991.

[290] R. Belew, J. McInerey, and N. Schraudolph. Evolving networks: using the genetic algorithm with connectionist learning. Technical Report Technical Report CS 90-174, Computer Science and Engineering Department, UCSD (La Jolla), 1990.

[291] J. Branke. Evolutionary algorithms for neural network design and training. Technical Report Bericht 322, Institut für Angewandte Informatik und Formale Beschreibungsverfahren, University of Karlsruhe, Germany, September 1995.

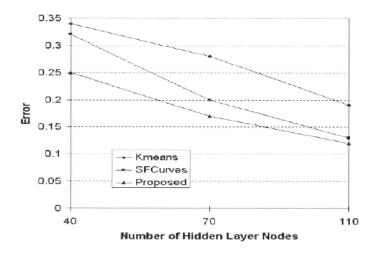

Figure 9.12
Performance Comparison of Different Learning Methods on the Mackey-Glass Prediction Problem

[292]H. Braun and J. Weisbrod. Evolving neural feedforward networks. In *Proceedings of the Conference on Artificial Neural Nets and Genetic Algorithms*, pages 25–32. Springer Verlag, 1993.

[293]H. Braun and P. Zagorski. Enzo-m - a hybrid approach for optimising neural networks by evolution and learning. In Y. Davidor, H.-P. Schwefel, and R. Männer, editors, *Parallel Problem Solving from Nature III*, pages 440–451. Springer Verlag, 1994.

[294]F. Brill, D. Brown, and W. Martin. Fast genetic selection of features for neural network classifiers. *IEEE Transactions on Neural Networks*, 3(2):324–328, 1992.

[295]D. Broomhead and D. Lowe. Multivariable functional interpolation and adaptive networks. *Complex Systems*, 2:321–355, 1988.

[296]B. Carse and T. Fogarty. A fuzzy classifier system using the pittsburgh approach. In Y. Davidor, H. Schwefel, and R. Männer, editors, *PPSN III- Proceedings of the International Conference on Evolutionary Computation*, pages 260–269, Berlin Heidelberg, 1994. Springer-Verlag.

[297]B. Carse, T. Fogarty, and A. Munro. Evolving fuzzy rule based controllers using genetic algorithms. *Fuzzy Sets and Systems*, 80:273–293, 1996.

[298]T. Caudell and C. Dolan. Parametric connectivity: training of constrained networks using genetic algorithms. In *Proceedings of 3rd International Conference on Genetic Algorithms*, pages 370–374, Arlington, 1989.

[299]E. Chang and R. Lippman. Using genetic algorithms to improve pattern classification performance. In R. Lippman, J. Moody, and D. Touretsky, editors, *Advances in Neural Information Processing 3*, pages 797–803. Morgan Kauffman, 1991.

[300]S. Chen, Y. Wu, and K. Alkadhimi. A two-layer learning method for radial basis function networks using combined genetic and regularised OLS algorithms. In *Proceedings of the 1st IEE/IEEE International Conference on Genetic Algorithms in Engineering Systems: Innovations*

and Applications, pages 245–249, 1995.

[301]M. Cooper and J. Vidal. Genetic design of fuzzy controllers: the cart and jointed pole problem. In *Proceedings of the Third IEEE International Conference on Fuzzy Systems*, pages 1332–1337, Piscataway NJ, 1994. IEEE.

[302]G. Cybenko. Approximation by superposition of a sigmoidal function. *Mathematics of Control, Signals and Systems*, 2:303–314, 1989.

[303]C. Darken and J. Moody. Towards faster stochastic gradient search. In J. Moody, S. Hanson, and Lippmann, editors, *Advances in Neural Information Processing Systems 4*, pages 1009–1016. Morgan Kaufmann, San Mateo, CA, 1992.

[304]D. Dasgupta and D. McGregor. Designing application-specific neural networks using the structured genetic algorithm. In *Proceedings of the International Workshop on Combinations of Genetic Algorithms and Neural Networks*, pages 87–96, 1992.

[305]Y. Davidor. Epistatic variance: suitability of a representation to genetic algorithms. *Complex Systems*, 4:369–383, 1990.

[306]N. Dodd. Optimisation of network structure using genetic techniques. In *Proceedings of the International Joint Conference on Neural Networks*, pages 965–970, 1990.

[307]R. Eberhart. The role of genetic algorithms in neural network query-based learning and explanation facilities. In D. Whitley and J. Schaffer, editors, *Combinations of Genetic Algorithms and Neural Networks*. IEEE Computer Press, 1992.

[308]R. Eberhart and R. Dobbins. Designing neural network explanation facilities using genetic algorithms. In *IEEE International Joint Conference on Neural Networks*, pages 1758–1763. IEEE, 1991.

[309]D. Goldberg. Real-coded genetic algorithms, virtual alphabets, and blocking. *Complex Systems*, 5:139–167, 1991.

[310]F. Gruau. Genetic synthesis of modular neural networks. In S. Forrest, editor, *Proceedings of the 5th International Conference on Genetic Algorithms*, pages 318–325, San Mateo CA, 1993.

[311]S. Harp, T. Samad, and A. Guha. Towards the genetic synthesis of neural networks. In *Proceedings of the 3rd International Conference on Genetic Algorithms*, pages 360–369. Morgan Kaufmann, 1989.

[312]S. Harp, T. Samad, and A. Guha. Designing application-specific neural networks using genetic algorithms. In D. Touretski, editor, *Advances in Neural Information Processing II*, pages 447–454. Morgan Kaufmann, 1990.

[313]S. Haykin. *Neural Networks*. Macmillan College Publishing Company, New York, NY, 1994.

[314]R. Hecht-Nielson. On the algebraic structure of feed-forward network weight spaces. In *Advanced Neural Computers*, pages 129–135. Elsevier, 1990.

[315]J. Heistermann. Different learning algorithms for neural networks - a comparative study. In Y. Davidor, H.-P. Schwefel, and R. Männer, editors, *Parallel Solving from Nature, Workshop Proceedings*, pages 368–396. Springer Verlag, 1994.

[316]K. Hintz and J. Spofford. Evolving a neural network. In *Proceedings of the 5th IEEE International Symposium on Intelligent Control*, pages 479–484, 1990.

[317]J. Jang and C. Sun. Functional equivalence between radial basis function networks and fuzzy inference systems. *IEEE Transactions on Neural Networks*, 4(1):156–159, 1993.

[318]C. Karr. Design of an adaptive fuzzy logic controller using a genetic algorithm. In R. Belew and L. Booker, editors, *Proceedings of the Fourth International Conference on Genetic Algorithms*, pages 450–457. Morgan Kaufmann, 1991.

[319]S. Kassam and I. Cha. Radial basis function networks in nonlinear signal processing applications. In *Proceedings of the 27th Annual Asilomar Conference on Signals, Systems and Computers*, Pacific Grove, CA, 1993.

[320]H. Kitano. Designing neural networks using genetic algorithms with graph generation

system. *Complex Systems*, 4:461–476, 1990.

[321]H. Kitano. Empirical studies on the speed of convergence of neural network training using genetic algorithms. In *Proceedings AAAI*, pages 789–795, 1990.

[322]M. Lee and H. Takagi. Integrating design stages of fuzzy systems using genetic algorithms. In *Proceedings of the Second IEEE International Conference on Fuzzy Systems*, pages 612–617, San Francisco, 1993. IEEE.

[323]D. Linkens and H. Nyongesa. Genetic algorithms for fuzzy control: Part 1: Offline system development and application. *IEE Proc. Control Theory Appl*, 142(3):161–176, May 1995.

[324]J. Liska and S. Melsheimer. Complete design of fuzzy logic systems using genetic algorithms. In D. Schaffer, editor, *Proceedings of the Third IEEE International Conference on Fuzzy Systems*, pages 1377–1382, Piscataway NJ, 1994. IEEE.

[325]M. Mandischer. Representation and evolution of neural networks. In *Proceedings of the Conference on Neural Nets and Genetic Algorithms*, pages 643–649. Springer Verlag, 1993.

[326]L. Marti. Genetically generated neural networks II: searching for an optimal representation. In *Proceedings of the International Joint Conference on Neural Networks*, volume 2, pages 221–226, 1992.

[327]G. Miller, P. Todd, and S. Hegde. Designing neural networks using genetic algorithms. In *Proceedings of the 3rd International Conference on Genetic Algorithms*, pages 379–384, Arlington, 1989.

[328]G. Miller, P. Todd, and S. Hegde. Designing neural networks using genetic algorithms. *Complex Systems*, 4:461–476, 1990.

[329]D. Montana and L. Davis. Training feedforward neural networks using genetic algorithms. In *Proceedings of the International Joint Conference on Artificial Intelligence*, pages 762–767, 1989.

[330]J. Moody and C. Darken. Fast learning in networks of locally-tuned processing units. *Neural Computation*, 1:281–294, 1989.

[331]H. Mühlenbein. Limitations of feedforward neural networks - steps towards genetic neural networks. *Parallel Computing*, 14:249–260, 1990.

[332]H. Mühlenbein and J. Kindermann. The dynamics of evolution and learning - towards genetic neural networks. In R. Pfeifer, Z. Schreter, F. Fogelman-Soulie, and L. Steels, editors, *Connectionism in Perspective*, pages 173–197. Elsevier (North-Holland), 1989.

[333]R. Neruda. Functional equivalence and genetic learning of rbf networks. In D. Pearson, N. Steele, and R. Albrecht, editors, *Artificial Neural Nets and Genetic Algorithms*, pages 53–56. Springer-Verlag, 1995.

[334]K. Ng and R. Lippmann. Practical characteristics of neural network and conventional pattern classifiers. In R. Lippmann, J. Moody, and D. Touretzky, editors, *Advances in Neural Information Processing Systems*, volume 3, pages 970–976. Morgan Kaufmann, San Mateo, CA, 1991.

[335]J. Park and I. Sandberg. Universal approximation using radial-basis-function networks. *Neural Computation*, 3:246–257, 1991.

[336]D. Pham and D. Karaboga. Optimum design of fuzzy logic controllers using genetic algorithms. *Journal of Systems Engineering*, 1:114–118, 1991.

[337]T. Poggio and S. Edelman. A network that learns to recognise three-dimensional objects. *Nature*, 343:263–266, 1990.

[338]T. Poggio and F. Girosi. Networks for approximation and learning. *Proceedings of the IEEE*, 78:1481–1497, 1990.

[339]M. Powell. Radial basis functions for multivariable interpolation: a review. In J. Mason and M. Cox, editors, *IMA Conference on Algorithms for the Approximation of Functions and Data*, pages pp143–167. Oxford University Press, 1987.

[340]N. Radcliffe. *Genetic neural networks on MIMD computers*. PhD thesis, University of

Edinburgh, Edinburgh, Scotland, 1990.

[341]N. Radcliffe. Genetic set recombination and its application to neural network topology optimisation. Technical Report EPCC-TR-91-21, University of Edinburgh, Edinburgh, Scotland, 1991.

[342]H. Robbins and S. Munroe. A stochastic approximation method. *Annals of Mathematical Statistics*, 22:400–407, 1951.

[343]S. Saha and J. Christensen. Genetic design of sparse feedforward neural networks. *Information Sciences*, 79:191–200, 1994.

[344]J. Schaffer, D. Whitley, and L. Eschelman. Combinations of genetic algorithms and neural networks: a survey of the state of the art. In *Proceedings of the International Workshop on Combinations of Genetic Algorithms and Neural Networks (COGANN-92)*, pages 1–37. IEEE, 1992.

[345]W. Schiffmann, M. Joost, and R. Werner. Performance evaluation of evolutionary created neural network topologies. In H.-P. Schwefel and R. Männer, editors, *Parallel Problem Solving from Nature*, pages 274–283. Springer Verlag, 1990.

[346]D. Thierens, J. Suykens, J. Vandewalle, and B. D. Moor. Genetic weight optimisation of a feedforward neural network controller. In *Proceedings of the Conference on Artificial Neural Nets and Genetic Algorithms*, pages 658–663. Springer Verlag, 1993.

[347]P. Thrift. Fuzzy logic synthesis with genetic algorithms. In R. Belew and L. Booker, editors, *Proceedings of the Fourth International Conference on Genetic Algorithms*, pages 509–513. Morgan Kaufmann, 1991.

[348]B. Whitehead and T. Choate. Evolving space-filling curves to distribute radial basis functions over an input space. *IEEE Transactions on Neural Networks*, 5(1):15–23, January 1994.

[349]B. A. Whitehead and T. D. Choate. Cooperative - competitive genetic evolution of radial basis function centers and widths for time series prediction. *IEEE Transactions on Neural Networks*, 7(4):869–880, 1996.

[350]D. Whitley. Genetic algorithms and neural networks. In G. Winter, J. Périaux, M. Galan, and P. Cuesta, editors, *Genetic Algorithms in Engineering and Computer Science*, pages 203–216. Wiley, 1995.

[351]D. Whitley and T. Hanson. Optimising neural networks using faster, more accurate genetic search. In *Proceedings of the 3rd International Conference on Genetic Algothms*, pages 391–395, 1989.

[352]D. Whitley, T. Starkweather, and C. Bogart. Genetic algorithms and neural networks: optimising connections and connectivity. *Parallel Computing*, 14:347–361, 1990.

[353]X. Yao. A review of evolutionary artificial neural networks. *International Journal of Intelligent Systems*, 8:539–567, 1993.

[354]B. Yoon, D. Holmes, G. Langholz, and A. Kandel. Efficient genetic algorithms for training feedforward neural networks. *Information Sciences*, 76:67–85, 1994.

10 Co-Evolution and Ontogenetic Change in Competing Robots

Dario Floreano, Stefano Nolfi, and Francesco Mondada

We investigate the dynamics of competitive co-evolution in the framework of two miniature mobile robots, a predator with a vision system and a faster prey with proximity sensors. Both types of robots are controlled by evolutionary neural networks. A variety of efficient chase-escape behaviors emerge in few generations. These results are analyzed in terms of variable fitness landscapes and selection criteria. A new vision of artificial evolution as generation and maintenance of adaptivity is suggested and contrasted with the theory and practice of mainstream evolutionary computation. In a second stage, different types of ontogenetic changes applied to the robot controllers are compared and the results are analyzed in the context of competitive co-evolution. It is shown that predators benefit from forms of directional changes whereas prey attempt to exploit unpredictable behaviors. These results and their effect on co-evolutionary dynamics are then considered in relation to open-ended evolution in unpredictably changing environments.

10.1 Introduction

In a competitive co-evolutionary system the survival probability of a species is affected by the behavior of other species. In the simplest scenario of only two competing species, such as a predator and a prey, or a parasite and a host, the survival probability of an individual is tightly related to the behaviors of the competitors both on the ontogenetic and on the evolutionary time scale. Behavioral changes in one lineage might affect the selection pressure on the other lineage and, if the other lineage responds with counter-adaptive features, one might observe what some biologists call a "a co-evolutionary arms race" [358]. Consider for example the well-studied case of two co-evolving populations of predators and prey [379]: the success of predators imply the failure of prey and viceversa. Evolution of a new behavior in one species represents a new challenge for the other species which is required to evolve new strategies. The continuation of this co-evolutionary process may produce increasingly higher levels of complexity in the behavioral strategies of the two competing species (although this is not guaranteed).

On the ontogenetic time-scale, it has been argued that pursuit-evasion contests might favor the emergence of "protean behaviors", that is behaviors which are adaptively unpredictable [359]. For example, prey could take advantage of unpredictable escape behaviors based on short sequences of stochastic motor actions. On the other hand, predators could take advantage of adaptation abilities that occur on a faster time-scale than generations.

The purpose of this research is to investigate the dynamics of competitive co-evolution and the effects of ontogenetic adaptive changes from the perspective of artificial evolution. The testbed chosen for our experiments is a predator-prey scenario where two mobile robots, each representing an evolving population, compete with each other to – respectively – chase or escape the other robot. The fact of using physical robots constraints us to use only local computation, simple assumptions on the rules of the game, and a very general (simple) fitness function. It will be shown that these "physical constraints" have significant effects on the outcome of the experiments. In order to accelerate the exploration of different experimental conditions and run multiple experiments for statistical analysis, we have resorted to realistic simulations of the physical setup.[1]

We shall show that competitive co-evolution alone (without ontogenetic adaptive changes) can quickly develop efficient chase and evasion strategies in both robot species. A retrospective analysis of the fitness landscape after a co-evolutionary run will give some hints on the incremental aspects of co-evolutionary dynamics. We will also see that using a simple fitness function allows predators to evolve non-trivial behaviors. However, after some time (generations) co-evolutionary dynamics fall into a limit cycle where predators and prey rediscover over and over again the same class of strategies. After explaining the adaptive power of this solution, we will investigate how the introduction of ontogenetic adaptation will affect the co-evolutionary dynamics and show that predators and prey exploit different types of ontogenetic adaptive changes. Finally, we will discuss the role of ontogenetic adaptation in the perspective of co-evolving individuals.

The Red Queen

From the computational perspective of *artificial evolution*, the reciprocal effects of changes induced by one species on the selection pressure of the other species introduce novel complexities with respect to the case of a single species evolved in a static environment. In the latter case (figure 10.1, left), there is a stable relationship between the traits of an organism and its reproduction

---

1 The software allows us to switch between physical and simulated experiments by toggling the value of a single variable.

success. In this case evolution is often seen as a force driving the population towards combinations of traits that maximize reproduction success [369].

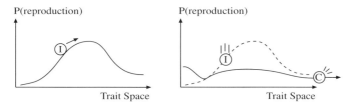

Figure 10.1
Left: Reproduction probability of a single species *I* under evolution in a static environment. Evolution drives the organisms towards zones (combinations of traits) corresponding to higher reproduction success. **Right**: Reproduction probability of species *I* under competitive co-evolution. The reproductive value (fitness) of certain trait combinations can be affected by adaptive changes in the competing species *C*, resulting in a continuous modification of the evolutionary surface. This phenomenon is often called the *Red Queen Effect* [388].

Instead, in competitive co-evolution the relationship between traits and re-productive success of the organism can change over time. Behavioral changes in one species could make some traits of the competing species no longer useful for reproductive success (figure 10.1, right). It might thus happen that progress achieved by one lineage is reduced or eliminated by the competing species. This phenomenon is sometimes referred to as the "Red Queen Effect" [388] (from the imaginary chess figure, invented by novelist Lewis Carroll, who was always running without making any advancement because the land-scape was moving with her).

From a computational perspective, it would be interesting to understand whether the Red Queen Effect can seriously limit the incremental adaptive characteristics of competitive co-evolution. Theoretical models of competitive co-evolution (based on Lotka-Volterra equations [377, 389]) study how popula-tion density (i.e., the number of individuals) varies as a function of pre-defined abilities of the two competing species [380]. These models cannot help us to predict whether artificial competitive co-evolution can be exploited for the pur-pose of evolving increasingly more complex behaviors. Therefore, at the cur-rent stage, experimental work still seems to be a powerful tool to investigate these issues.

Related Work

Prospects of continuous and incremental progress have triggered several attempts to apply competitive co-evolution to difficult problems. Hillis [373] reported a significant improvement in the evolution of sorting programs when parasites (programs deciding the test conditions for the sorting programs) were co-evolved, and similar results were found on co-evolution of players for the Tic-Tac-Toe and Nim games [355, 385]. Recently, Funes et al. [368] have studied co-evolution of machines and humans competing over the Internet and reported strategy improvement in both populations over time.

In the context of adaptive autonomous agents, Koza [374, 375] applied Genetic Programming to the co-evolution of pursuer-evader behaviors, Reynolds [384] observed in a similar scenario that co-evolving populations of pursuers and evaders display increasingly better strategies, and Sims used competitive co-evolution to develop his celebrated artificial creatures [387]. Cliff and Miller realized the potentiality of co-evolution of pursuit-evasion tactics in evolutionary robotics. In a series of papers, they described a 2D simulation of simple robots with evolvable "vision morphology" [379] and proposed a new set of performance and genetic measures in order to describe evolutionary progress which could not be otherwise tracked down due to the Red Queen Effect [356]. Recently, they described some results where simulated agents with evolved eye-morphologies could either evade or pursue their competitors from some hundred generations earlier and proposed some applications of this methodology in the entertainment industry [357]. However, these experiments revealed more difficulties than expected and not all experimental runs produced successful pursuers and evaders. Also other authors have stressed that competitive co-evolution strongly depends on the scoring criterion and can easily degenerate in mediocre solutions [360].

In this article we address the realization of physical mobile robots that co-evolve in competition with each other (figure 10.2). Although the results presented in the following pages are based on both real and simulated experiments, the physical implementation constrains our design in ways that significantly affect the outcome of the experiments and allow us to explore a variety of issues related to the autonomy and adaptation of artificial organisms.

Figure 10.2
Right: The Predator is equipped with the vision module (1D-array of photoreceptors, visual angle of 36°). **Left**: The Prey has a black protuberance which can be detected by the predator everywhere in the environment, but its maximum speed is twice that of the predator. Both Predator and Prey are equipped with 8 infrared proximity sensors.

10.2   Experimental Setup

We employed two Khepera robots, one of which (the *Predator*) was equipped with a vision module while the other (the *Prey*) did not have the vision module, but its maximum speed was set twice that of the predator (figure 10.2).

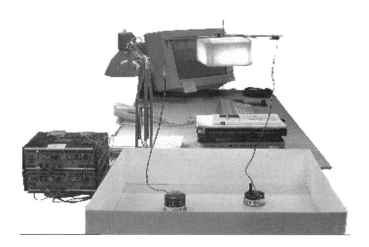

Figure 10.3
Setup to run co-evolutionary experiments on the physical robots. **Top**: the suspended bar with the three rotating contacts and a white box casting light over the arena. **Left**: two voltage transformers for powering the robots and the halogen lamp. **Background**: the workstation on which the two genetic algorithms run. The robots in the arena are equipped with contact detectors and wrapped in white paper to increase the reflection of infrared light.

Both robots were also provided with eight active (emitting-measuring) infrared proximity sensors (six on the front side and two on the back). These sensors could detect a wall at a distance of approximately 3 cm and another robot at a distance of approximately 1 cm because of its smaller reflection surface. The two robots evolved within a square arena of size 47 x 47 cm with high white walls so that the predator could always see the prey (if within the visual angle) as a black spot on a white background (figure 10.3). The two robots were connected to a desktop workstation equipped with two serial ports through a double aerial cable. Aerial cables provided the robots with electric power and data communication to/from the workstation. The two cables ended up in two separate rotating contacts firmly attached to the far ends of a suspended thin bar. Both wires then converged into a single and thicker rotating contact at the center of the bar and ended up in the serial ports of the workstation and in two voltage transformers (on the left of figure 10.3).

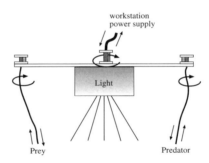

Figure 10.4
The suspended bar with the three rotating contacts and a white box casting light over the arena.

The thick rotating contact allowed the bar to freely rotate around its own center while the remaining two contacts allowed free rotations of the two robots (figure 10.4). Attached under the bar was also a halogen lamp (20 W output) providing illumination over the arena.[2] Both robots were also fitted with a conductive metallic ring around their base to detect collisions. An additional general input/output module provided a digital signal any time the two robots hit each other (but not when they hit the walls). The motor bases of both robots were also wrapped by white paper in order to improve reflection of infrared light emitted by the other robot (figure 10.3).

---

2 No special care was taken to protect the system against external light variations between day and night.

The vision module K213 of Khepera is an additional turret which can be plugged directly on top of the basic platform. It consists of a 1D-array of 64 photoreceptors providing a linear image composed of 64 pixels of 256 gray-levels each, subtending a view-angle of 36°. The optics are designed to bring into focus objects at distances between 5cm and 70cm while an additional sensor of light intensity automatically adapts the scanning speed of the chip to keep the image stable and exploit at best the sensitivity of receptors under a large variety of illumination intensities. However, a reliable image at lower illumination comes at the cost of a slower scanning speed of the 64 receptor values. This means that the image would be updated less frequently, thus giving an advantage to the prey (which indeed exploited it during exploratory experiments). This is the reason why we added the halogen lamp to the rotating bar over the arena. In the simple environment employed for these experiments, the projection of the prey onto the artificial retina of the predator looks like a valley (top of figure 10.5) that indicates the relative position of the prey with respect to the predator.

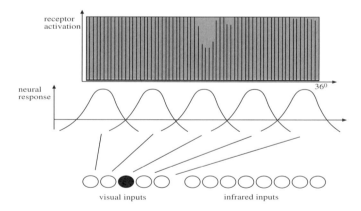

Figure 10.5
Top: A snapshot of the visual field of the predator looking at the prey. The heights of vertical bars represent the activations of the 64 photoreceptors. The black protuberance of the prey looks like a large valley. The small dip on the right of the valley corresponds to the cable. In the illumination conditions of the experiment, the image is refreshed at a rate of approximately 15 Hz. **Bottom**: Visual filtering with five *center/off surround/on* neurons. A neuron is maximally activated when the projection of the prey falls within its receptive field. The most active neuron is set to 1, all the remaining neurons are set to 0 in a Winner-take-All fashion.

Controller Architecture, Evolutionary Algorithm, and Method

Both predator and the prey controllers were simple neural networks of sigmoid neurons. The input signals coming from the eight infrared proximity sensors (and from the vision module for the predator) were fed into two motor neurons with lateral and self-connections. The activation of each output unit was used to update the speed value of the corresponding wheel (forward from 0.5 to 1.0, backward from 0.5 to 0.0). Only the connection strengths were evolved. The maximum speed available for the prey was set to twice that of the predator.

The input layer of the predator was extended to include information coming from the vision module. The activation values of the 64 photoreceptors were fed into a layer of five *center off/surround on* neurons uniformly distributed over the retinal surface (bottom of figure 10.5). The spatial sensitivity of each neuron was approximately $13°$ and the center/surround ratio filtered out low contrast features, such as those generated by weak shadows, the cable of the prey, and other imperfections of the walls. Each neuron generated a binary output of 1 when the prey was within its sensitivity field, and 0 otherwise. These five outputs were fed into the motor neurons along with the signals coming from the infrared sensors.

Given the small size of the neural controllers under co-evolution, we used *direct genetic encoding* of connection strengths. Each connection (including recurrent connections and threshold values of output units) was encoded on five bits, the first bit determining the sign of the synapse and the remaining four bits its strength. Therefore, the genotype of the predator was *5 times [30 synapses + 2 thresholds] = 160* bits long while that of the prey was *5 times[20 synapses + 2 thresholds] = 110* bits long. Two separate populations of N individuals each were co-evolved for g generations. Each individual was tested against the best competitors from k previous generations (a similar procedure was used in [387, 384, 356]) in order to improve co-evolutionary stability. At generation 0, competitors were randomly chosen from the initial population, and later on they were randomly chosen from the pool of best individuals from previous generations (2 at the 3rd generation, 3 at 4th generation, ..., 49 at 50th generation, etc.).

In our previous work (e.g., [362]) both the genetic operators and the robot controllers were run on the workstation and the serial cable was used to exchange sensory and motor information with the robot every 100 ms or longer. This method could not work in the current setup because transmission times and serial processing of the controller states for both robots on the same workstation CPU significantly delayed and disturbed the interaction dynamics between the two robots.

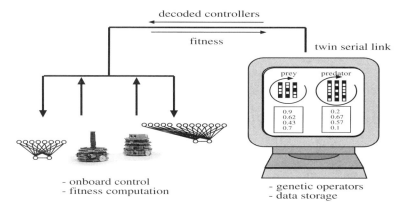

Figure 10.6
The genetic operators run on the main workstation, which also manages data storage and analysis; the neural controllers are automatically downloaded on the microcontrollers of the robots through the serial link. In the predator, an additional microprocessor on the vision module performs visual pre-processing and sends data at 15 Hz frequency to the main microcontroller.

Therefore, we split the computational load by running the genetic operators on the workstation CPU and the neural network on the microcontroller of each Khepera robot, a Motorola MC68331 equipped with 128K ROM and 128K RAM. The speed of the sensorimotor cycles was set to approximately 15 Hz for both prey and predator. For the predator, image acquisition and low-level visual preprocessing were handled by a private 68HC11 processor available on the K213 vision turret (see [365] for more details of this modular architecture).

At the beginning of a co-evolutionary run, the two neurocontrollers, with the connection strengths initialized to zero, were downloaded into the corresponding robots. Two genetic algorithms (with the same parameters in these experiments) were then started on the workstation CPU where each genetic string was decoded into a set of connection strengths and sent through the serial cable to the corresponding robot. Upon receipt of the connection strengths, the internal clock (a cycle counter) of the prey robot was reset to zero and each robot began to move. A tournament ended either when the predator hit the prey or when 500 sensorimotor cycles (corresponding to approximately 35 seconds) were performed by the prey without being hit by the predator. Upon termination, the prey sent back to the workstation CPU the value of the internal clock (ranging between 0 and 499) which was used as fitness measure for both prey and predator. Upon receipt of the prey message, the workstation decoded the next pair of individuals and sent them back to both the predator and prey. In order to reposition the two competitors at the beginning of each tournament, a simple random motion with obstacle avoidance was implemented by both robots for 5 seconds.

The fitness function Φ_i (where i indicates the species) was based only on the average *time to contact* over K tournaments,

$$\Phi_{py} = \frac{1}{K} \sum_{k=1}^{K} \frac{x_k}{500}, \quad \Phi_{pr} = \frac{1}{K} \sum_{k=1}^{K} \left(1 - \frac{x_k}{500}\right),$$

where x_k is the number of sensorimotor cycles performed in tournament k. This value is normalized by the maximum number of sensorimotor cycles available (500) in the case of the prey py, and the complement in the case of the predator pr, and further averaged over the number of tournaments K for both robots. This fitness function rewarded prey capable of resisting longer before being hit by predators, and predators capable of quickly hitting prey. This simple function differs from those used by Cliff and Miller who included distance between the two individuals in order to evolve pursuit and escape behaviors. In our physical setup it was impossible to know the exact distance between the two robots. It will be shown that this subtle difference significantly affects the evolved behaviors.

The fitness values were always between 0 and 1, where 0 means worst. Individuals were ranked after fitness performance in descending order and the best 20% were allowed to reproduce by making an equal number of offspring in order to keep the population size constant. One-point crossover was applied on randomly paired strings with probability $pc = 0.6$, and random mutation (bit switching) was applied to each bit with constant probability $pm = 0.05$.

Software Model

A software model of this physical setup was developed in order to test different experimental conditions and several replications with different random initializations, and to carry out explorations of the fitness landscape. In order to ensure a good match between simulations and physical experiments, we used a sampling technique proposed by Miglino *et al.* [378].

Each robot was positioned close to a wall of the environment and performed a full rotation by steps of $10°$. At every step, all sensor values were recorded and stored in a table. The robot was then positioned 2 mm from the wall and the same procedure was applied again. This technique was repeated every 2 mm up to a distance of 4 cm (more than the maximum sensitivity of the infrared sensors). The final table stored all sensor values for 20 distances from the wall and, at each distance, for 180 uniformly-spaced orientations. Another table was built in the same way by positioning the robot in front of the other robot. Notice that the combination of these two tables is sufficient to represent every possible situation that a robot might encounter in this environment (flat wall, corner, other robot, and combinations of them). These tables were used to retrieve appropriate sensor values from the robot current position in the simulator. The activation of the five vision neurons was computed using trigonometric functions. The main difference between the software model and the physical implementation was that in the former case the initial position of the two robot was always the same (in the center of the arena, 5 cm apart from each other), but at different random orientations, whereas in the latter case the two robots moved randomly for five seconds avoiding obstacles.

In a set of preliminary comparisons, it was found that results obtained with the software model did not differ significantly from the results obtained with physical robots both in terms of co-evolutionary dynamics and in terms of behavioral strategies. More details will be given in the next section.

10.3   Co-Evolutionary Results

An exploratory set of experiments were performed in simulation to understand the influence of various parameters, such as the number of tournaments with opponents from previous generations, crossover and mutation probabilities, replicability of the experiments, etc. A detailed analysis of these data is provided in [366]. Here we provide only a summary of the basic results and compare them to the results obtained with the real robots. Two populations of 100 individuals each were co-evolved for 100 generations. Each individual was tested against the best opponents from the most recent 10 generations. Figure 10.7 shows the average population fitness (left graph) and the fitness of the best individual at each generation. For each generation, the fitness values of the two species do not sum to one because each individual is tested against the best opponents recorded from the previous 10 generations.

As expected, initially the prey score very high, whatever they might do,

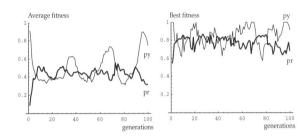

Figure 10.7
Co-evolutionary fitness measured in simulation. **Left**: Average population fitness. **Right**: Fitness
of the best individuals at each generation. `pr`=predator; `py`=prey.

because the predators are not good at catching them. For the same reason, initially the predators score very low. In less than 20 generations a set of counter-phase oscillations emerge in the two populations, as reported by other authors [387, p. 36] too, but we never observed dominance of one population on the other in any of our evolutionary runs (even when continued for 500 generations). However, the fitness of the prey always tended to generate higher peaks than that of the predator due to the position advantage (even in the case of the worst prey and best predator, the latter will always take some time to reach the prey). A similar pattern is observed for the fitness of the best individuals (right graph).

These data are not sufficient to assess whether there is real progress. The only information that they provide is the relative performance of the two species within a (moving) window of ten generations. They indicate that progress in one species is quickly counter-balanced by progress in the competing species, but do not tell us whether evolutionary time generates true progress, or how to choose the best prey and the best predator out of all evolved individuals.

A simple way to learn more about absolute performance of the two species consists of organizing a *Master Tournament* where the best individuals for each generation are tested against the best competitors from all generations. For example, the best prey of generation 1 is tested against 100 best predators and the scores of these tournaments are averaged. If there is true progress, i.e. if a species develops strategies capable of defeating an increasing number of competitors, the Master Fitness should display an ascending trend. However, Master fitness values for these experiments (figure 10.8) indicate that *–in absolute terms–* individuals of later generations are not necessarily better than

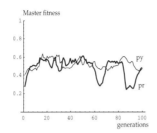

Figure 10.8
Master Fitness for species evolved in simulation. Each data point is the average fitness of all tournaments of the corresponding individual against all the best 100 opponents recorded during co-evolution.

those from previous ones. In other words, individuals of early generations have strategies that can defeat individuals of later generations.

Master Fitness can be used to tell *a)* at which generation we can find the best prey and the best predator; *b)* at which generation we are guaranteed to observe the most interesting tournaments. The first aspect is important for optimization purposes, the latter for pure entertainment. The best individuals are those reporting the highest fitness when also the competitor reports the highest fitness (here the best prey and predators are to be found at generation 20, 50, and 82). Instead, the most entertaining tournaments are those that take place between individuals that report the same fitness level, because these are the situations where both species have the same level of ability to win over the competitor (here the most entertaining tournaments are guaranteed around generation 20 and around generation 50).

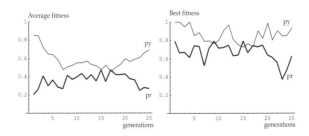

Figure 10.9
Co-evolutionary fitness measured on the real robots. **Left**: Average population fitness. **Right**: Fitness of the best individuals at each generation. pr=predator; py=prey.

The results with the real robot displayed a trend similar to that observed in simulations. Two populations (one for the prey, the other for the predator) of 20 individuals each were co-evolved for 25 generations (P(crossover)=0.6; P(mutation)=0.05 per bit) in approximately 40 hours of continuous operation (time might vary in different replications, depending on the relative performances of the two species). Each individual was tested against the best competitors from the most recent 5 generations. Figure 10.9 shows the average fitness of the population (left graph) and the fitness of the best individual (right graph) along generations for both species. Very quickly the two scores become closer and closer until after generation 15 they diverge again. A similar trend is observed for the fitness of the best individuals at each generation.

25 generations are sufficient to display one oscillatory cycle. Once the relative fitness values of the two species reach the same value, one party improves over the other for some generations until the other counter-adapts (the best predators of the last three generations already show a fitness gain). Figure 10.10 shows the Master Fitness values for the two robot species. The

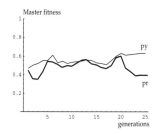

Figure 10.10
Master Fitness for species evolved on the real robots. Each data point is the average fitness of all tournaments of the correponding individual against all the best 25 opponents recorded during co-evolution.

best prey and predators can be found at generation 20 which also hosts the most entertaining tournaments. It can also be noticed that fitness oscillations of the best individuals between generation 9 and 16 (figure 10.9, right) do not show up in the Master Fitness, indicating that they are due to tight interactions between the two competing species which can amplify the effects of small behavioral differences.

The behaviors displayed by the two physical robots at significant points of co-evolution (for example, those corresponding to the overall best individuals and to the most entertaining tournaments) are only a subset of those recorded in simulation. The presence of much larger noise in the real environment filters out brittle solutions that are instead stable in simulations. Nevertheless, *all* strategies displayed by the real robots can be found also in the experiments performed in simulation.[3] Figure 10.11 shows some typical tournaments recorded from individuals at generation 13, 20, and 22. At generation 13 the prey moves quickly around the environment and the predator attacks only when the prey is at a certain distance. Later on, at generation 20, the prey spins in place and, when the predator gets closer, it rapidly avoids it. Prey that move too fast around the environment sometimes cannot avoid an approaching predator because they detect it too late (infrared sensors have lower sensitivity for a small cylindrical object than for a large white flat wall). Therefore, it pays off for the prey to wait for the slower predator and accurately avoid it. However, the predator is smart enough to perform a small circle after having missed the target and re-attack until, by chance, the prey is caught on one of the two sides (where wheels and motors do not leave space for sensors). The drop in per-

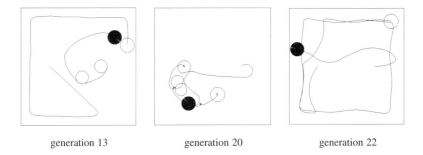

| | generation 13 | generation 20 | generation 22 |

Figure 10.11
Typical strategies of the best predator and prey in the experiments with real robots. Black disk is the predator, white disk is the prey. Trajectories have been plotted running a tournament with simulated individuals who display the same behavioral strategies observed with the real robots.

formance of the predator in the following generations is due to a temporary loss of the ability to avoid walls (which was not needed in the few previous generations because the predator soon localized and approached the prey). At the same time the prey resumes a rapid wall following and obstacle avoidance

---

3 Although individuals *evolved in simulation* do not behave in the same way when *downloaded into the real robots*.

which forces the predator to get closer to walls and collide if the prey is missed (right of figure 10.11). A description of additional behaviors obtained in simulations is given in [366].

Machine Learning and Natural Adaptation

The results described above indicate that co-evolution between competing species with a relatively short generational overlap does not necessarily display the type of monotonic progress over time expected from the optimization-oriented approach that characterizes traditional Machine Learning.

This does not mean that competitive co-evolution is not an viable approach for the purpose of evolving efficient behavioral competencies. In fact, the rapid discovery, variety, and complexity of behaviors observed, together with appropriate methods to pick them out (such as the Master Tournament), hint at the computational advantages of competitive co-evolution. For example, in a companion paper we report results obtained in different environmental conditions where predators evolved against a fixed co-evolved prey (from another run) do not reach the same performance levels obtained when both prey and predators are co-evolved [383]. In other words, under certain circumstances competitive co-evolution can indeed produce more powerful solutions that standard evolution. Furthermore, it has also been shown that, by including all the best opponents evolved so far as test cases for each individual (*Hall of Fame* method), co-evolution displays monotonic progress and becomes very similar to a very robust optimization technique [385, 383]. Finally, other results obtained on variations of the basic physical setup described in this article display ascending trends on the Master Tournaments [383].

However, the basic issue here is to what extent natural evolution should be interpreted as an optimization process (see also [371, 370] for a critical review) and to what extent should we use artificial evolution as an optimization technique in the spirit of traditional Machine Learning. Competitive co-evolution is closer to biological evolution in that the challenges faced by evolving individuals continuously and unpredictably change over time. Under these circumstances, the classic notion of optimal solutions seems inadequate because at every point in time it is impossible to know what the next challenge will be.

With respect to mainstream "evolutionary computation" devoted to searching for peaks on multidimensional and complex, but static, fitness landscapes [369], in a competitive co-evolutionary scenario the landscape continuously changes. Not only one cannot predict the way in which it changes, but very often it will change towards the worst from the point of view of each species (see the right portion of figure 10.1). As a matter of fact, for a co-evolving species there is not a fitness landscape to climb. In other words, at every point in time and space there is not a gradient that can be reliably followed. Therefore, fitness landscapes are useful only for *a posteriori* observations, but are not actually used by a system evolving in unpredictable dynamic environments.

Within this framework, artificial evolution should not be conceived as a method for finding optimal solutions to predefined problems, but as a mechanism for encouraging and developing adaptivity. For example, generation and maintenance of diversity might be an adaptive solution. Another adaptive solution could be that of selecting genotypes whose mutants correspond to different but all equally viable phenotypes. In both cases, the species can quickly respond to environmental changes. Yet another way of evolving adaptivity would be that of encouraging ontogenetic adaptive changes. None of these notions of evolution implies continuous progress as usually defined in the machine learning literature.

Revisiting the experiments described above in this new light, after an initial period during which the two populations settle into a regime of tight interactions (when the two fitness measures become equal), the best individuals of the two populations are always optimal, or almost always, with respect to the environment (competitors) that they are facing. In other words, the optimum is always now.

Exposing the Red Queen

The Red Queen effect illustrated in figure 10.1 is suspected to be the main actor behind the dynamics, complexities, and computational advantages of competitive co-evolution, but how exactly it operates is not known. Capitalizing on the fact that our simple experiment with the robots displayed dynamics similar to those measured in experiments carried out in simulation, we exploited the workstation CPU to study how the fitness landscape of one species is affected by the co-evolving competitor. Let us remember that here the notion of fitness landscape is valid only as an observation metaphor using data collected during a co-evolutionary run.

Given the shorter genotype length of the prey, we analyzed how the its fitness surface changed when the prey was confronted with the best predators saved from successive generations. Let us recall that the genotype of the prey was composed of 5 bits x 22 synapses (see subsection 10.2). Assuming that the most significant bits are those coding the sign of the synapses, we are left with

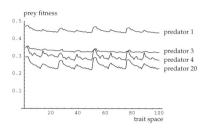

Figure 10.12
The Red Queen in action. Fitness landscape for the prey when tested against the best predators
saved from generation 1, 3, 4, and 20. Each data point is the average over the fitness values
reported by 4,194 prey close on the genotype space.

22 bits.[4] The combination of these 22 genetic traits corresponds to 4,194,304
prey. Each prey was separately tested against the best predators of the first eight
generations and against the best predator of generation 20, yielding a total of
almost 40 million tournaments. In order to facilitate the comparison, at the
beginning of each tournament, both the prey and the predator were positioned
at the same location facing north. The best predators were selected from the
simulation run depicted in figure 10.7. Since there is not enough space on
this page to plot the fitness values of all the prey against each predator, the
4,194,304 fitness values were grouped into 100 bins of 4,194 values each
(discarding remainders) and the average value of each bin was plotted on
figure 10.12.

Despite these approximations, one can see that co-evolution of predators
during initial generations cause a general decrement of the performance of the
prey. However, it should be noticed that these are average values and that for
every bin there are always several prey reporting maximum fitness 1.0. The
Red Queen effect is clearly visible in the temporary and periodic smoothing
of the fitness landscape, as highlighted in figure 10.12. For example, the best
predator of generation 3 causes a redistribution of the fitness values, stretching
out the relative gain of some combinations of traits with respect to others. This
smoothing effect is always temporary and roughly alternates with recovery of
a rough landscape.

It should be noticed that some regions corresponding to better fitness remain relatively better also during periods of stretching, whereas others are

4 The remaining 4 bits for each synapse were set at 0101, a pattern that represents the expected
number of on/off bits per synapse and also codes for the average synaptic strength.

canceled out. That implies that individuals sitting on these latter regions would disappear from the population. If we view these regions as minima or brittle solutions, our data show the potentials of the Red Queen for selecting robust solutions. Furthermore, it can be noticed that the steepness of the surface around the maxima becomes more accentuated along generations. If we assume that steeper regions are more difficult to reach, competitive co-evolution might facilitate progressive development of abilities that would be difficult to achieve in the scenario of a single species evolved in a static environment. In other words, at least during the initial generations, coevolution might spontaneously generate a set of tasks of increasing difficulty, a sort of "pedagogical series of challenges" [385] that might favor fast emergence of complex solutions.

Selection Criteria

In artificial evolution the choice of the selection criterion (fitness function) can make the difference between trivial parameter optimization and generation of creative and "life-like" solutions [361]. From an engineering point of view, it might seem reasonable to pursue an optimization approach by designing a detailed fitness function that attempts to develop behaviors that are partially pre-defined. However, by doing so one might also include wrong assumptions that derive from an insufficient understanding of the environment and/or of the interactions that might arise between the robot and its environment [382]. For example, one might think that a successful predator should aim at the prey and approach it minimizing the distance, whereas the prey should attempt to maximize this distance. Consequently, she would design a fitness function that includes –respectively–distance minimization and maximization for predators and prey, as in [357].

The fitness function employed in our experiments was simply *time to contact*, it is worth asking whether our robots (simulated and real) indirectly optimize this objective. A new set of simulations was run where each individual *was selected* and reproduced according to the usual fitness function described in section 10.2, but was also *evaluated* according to a fitness function based on the *distance* between the two competitors (namely, the *distance* for the prey, and *1 - distance* for the predator).

The fitness values computed according to the two methods (figure 10.13) did not overlap for the predators, but they did for the prey. In other words, predators selected to hit prey in the shortest possible time did not attempt to minimize the distance from the prey, as one might expect. On the other hand, in general prey attempt to maximize the distance. The strategy employed by

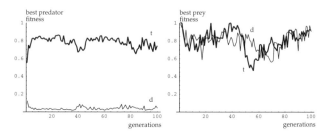

Figure 10.13
Comparisons between fitness of the best individuals measured as *time to contact* (t) and as *distance*. (d). Both species have been evolved using fitness t. **Left**: Best evolved predators do not attempt to minimize distance (predator fitness is 1 - d). **Right**: Best evolved prey attempt to maximize distance (prey fitness is d).

the predators was more subtle. Rather than simply approaching the prey, they tended to "wait for the right moment" and, only then, attack. The behaviors shown in the first two insets of figure 10.11 are an example of this strategy. The best predator of generation 13 attacks only when the prey is within a certain range, and rotates in place in the other cases (neuroethological analyses showed that the predator infers the distance from the prey by observing how fast the prey moves on its own visual field). Similarly, the best predator of generation 20 does not follow the prey once the latter has moved away; rather, it performs one more turn on itself and re-attacks. By doing so, it has higher probability of hitting the prey on the side of the motors where there are no sensors.

These results indicate that competitive co-evolution can discover innovative and unexpected –yet efficient– solutions provided that one does not attempt to force it into pre-defined directions. If a co-evolutionary system in externally channeled in certain directions, it might loose its ability to generate adaptivity and explore unpredictable solutions. We might speculate that to the limit, a strongly constrained co-evolutionary system will converge to trivial solutions, if such a solution exist for the specific architecture evolved, or will degenerate in random search.

10.4   Ontogenetic Adaptive Change

In subsection 10.3 we have mentioned that competitive co-evolution might favor the emergence of ontogenetic adaptive changes (i.e., changes during the "life" of an individual robot) as a way to improve adaptivity. Although most of the co-evolutionary systems described in the literature include some type of

Table 10.1
Genetic encoding of synaptic parameters for each co-evolutionary condition. 1: Genetically-determined controllers; 2: Adaptive-noise controllers; 3: Directional-change controllers.

Condition	Bits for one synapse				
	1	2	3	4	5
1	sign		strength		
2	sign	strength		noise	
3	sign	Hebb rule		rate	

ontogenetic changes in the form of small random changes to the parameters, it is difficult to say whether this form of noise plays an important role on the specific dynamics of co-evolving species. Moreover, all the results presented so far are based on single-run studies and do not include statistical comparisons between different adaptation techniques.

The aim of this section is that of presenting initial results on the effect of ontogenetic adaptive changes in co-evolving competing species. In particular, we want to address the following questions: Does protean behavior affect evolutionary dynamics? Do competing species exploit different types of protean strategies, and how does this affect the competitor's behavior? In the attempt to investigate these issues in very simple settings, we have compared co-evolution of competing species equipped with different types of simple adaptive controllers with results from the experiments described in section 10.3 above. In order to obtained data from multiple runs of the same condition for statistical analysis, all the experiments conducted in this section have been carried out with the software technique described in subsection 10.2.

For sake of comparison, all the neural networks had the same architecture, the same genotype length (5 bits per synapse), and used a comparable encoding technique. We distinguished three evolutionary conditions, each one corresponding to a different type of controller (Table 10.1). In all conditions, the first bit of each synapse coded its sign (whether excitatory or inhibitory).

In the first condition, which is that described in section 10.2 above, the remaining four bits coded the synaptic strength as a value in the range $[0, 1]$. Since no changes take place during the life of the individuals, let us call this condition *genetically-determined controllers*.

In the second condition, only two bits coded the synaptic strength (again, in the range $[0, 1]$), and the remaining two bits coded the level of random noise applied to the synaptic value *at each time step*. Each level corresponded to the lower and upper bounds of a uniform noise distribution: 0.0 (no noise),

± 0.337, ± 0.667, and ± 1.0. For every new sensor reading, each synapse had its own newly-computed noise value added to its strength (with a final check to level out sums below 0.0 or above 1.0). We shall call this condition *adaptive-noise controllers* because each species can evolve the most appropriate noise level for each synapse (including the possibility of not having noise, which corresponds to condition one).

In the third condition, two bits coded four Hebbian rules and the remaining two bits the learning rate (0.0, 0.337, 0.667, and 1.0). Four variations of the Hebb rule were used: "pure Hebb" whereby the synaptic strength can only increase when both presynaptic and postsynaptic units are active, "presynaptic" whereby the synapse changes only when the presynaptic unit is active (strengthened when the postsynaptic unit is active, and weakened when the postsynaptic unit is inactive), "postsynaptic" whereby the synapse changes only when the postsynaptic unit is active (strengthened when the presynaptic unit is active, and weakened when the presynaptic unit is inactive), and "covariance" whereby the synapse is strengthened if the difference between pre- and post-synaptic activations is smaller than a threshold (half the activation level, that is 0.5) and is weakened if the difference is larger than such threshold. After decoding a genotype into the corresponding controller, each synapse was randomly initialized to a value in the range $[0, 1]$ and modified at each time step according to the corresponding Hebbian rule and learning rate. In another article, we have shown that this evolutionary scheme in a single-agent static environment can develop stable controllers which quickly develop navigation strategies starting from small random synaptic strengths [364]; interested readers will find more details in that paper. Flotzinger replicated those results (from a previous preliminary report [363]) and studied in more detail the synaptic dynamics, showing that continuously changing synaptic values reflect to a certain approximation input and output states of the controller [367]. Therefore, let us call this condition *directional-change controllers*, simply indicating that synaptic changes depend on sensory activation and motor actions.

Experimental Results

For each condition, six different evolutionary runs were performed, each starting with a different seed for initializing the computer random functions. A set of pairwise two-tail *t*-tests of the average fitness and best fitness values along generations among all the six runs, performed to check whether different seeds significantly affected the experimental outcomes, gave negative results at significance level 0.05. Therefore, for each condition below, we shall plot only data referring to seed 1 (arbitrarily chosen), but the statistical tests reported will be based on all the runs.

In order to compare the results between the three co-evolutionary conditions, a *relational measure* of performance was developed. It consisted in computing an index of *relative performance* r_i^c by counting how often one species reports higher fitness than the competing species at each generation for each separate run i (where i stands for a replication of the same experiment with a different random seed) in a specific condition c. In our co-evolutionary runs which lasted 100 generations, such index will be in the range $[-100, 100]$, where -100 means that prey always outperformed predators, 0 means that both species were equally better or worse than the competitors, and 100 means that predators always outperformed the prey in 100 generations. As compared to the Master Fitness, this value does not tell us whether there is progress in the population, but it allows us to compare co-evolutionary coupled dynamics between different conditions.

In the condition of genetically-determined controllers $c = 1$ (data given in section 10.3), the average value over six repeated runs is $\overline{R^1} = 16.67$ with standard deviation of the sample mean $\sigma = 38$, indicating that the two species did not significantly differ in the number of wins and losses.

The condition with evolutionary adaptive noise ($c = 2$) displayed an average relative performance $\overline{R^2} = 11.66$ with standard deviation of the sample mean $\sigma = 32.5$ which was not statistically different from that of the condition of genetically-determined controllers (probability value was 0.83 for t-test of the difference of the means between the two conditions, i.e. much bigger than significance level 0.05 typically used for rejecting the equality hypothesis). The oscillatory patterns observed on the fitness values for condition 1 took place in condition 2 too, but were much smoother (figure 10.14, left). Furthermore, in all cases it took roughly twice as many generations –as compared to condition 1– to lock into oscillatory dynamics (marked by the generation when the two fitness lines cross). We then compared between the two species the average noise level used by all individuals in the population and by the best individuals at each generation. Two separate t-tests for measuring differences of average noise level and of noise level of the best individuals both displayed a significant difference ($p \ll 0.1$). Prey clearly used much higher noise levels than predators.

The hypothesis that the prey exploited noise to develop unpredictable controllers (that is, not improving much on initial random controllers) while the predator tried to develop more stable pursuit strategies was reflected by the

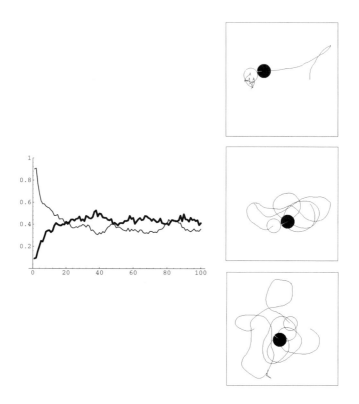

Figure 10.14
Adaptive-noise controllers. **Left**: Average fitness across generations for predator (thick line) and prey (thin line). **Right**: Examples of behaviors (black disk is predator, white disk is prey). Top: generation 20. Center: generation 50. Bottom: generation 80.

behaviors of the two species (figure 10.14, right). Prey displayed unpredictable maneuvers while the predators attempted to track them. The prey trajectory was often changing while retaining sufficient obstacle-avoidance abilities (it sometimes stopped near a wall for a few instants and later moved away). The predator behaviors were more predictable. In general, they were sufficiently good at keeping the prey within the visual field.

Relative performance of the two species in the third condition, (directional-change controllers) significantly differed from condition 1 (and from condition 2). Relative performance was $\overline{R^3} = 72$ with standard deviation of the sample mean $\sigma = 15.39$, $p < 0.01$ for a two-tailed t-test of the difference of the means. In all six repeated runs predators reported higher average and best

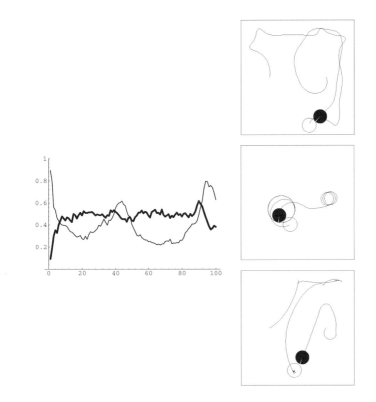

Figure 10.15
Directional-change controllers. **Left**: Average fitness across generations for predator (thick line) and prey (thin line). **Right**: Examples of behaviors (black disk is predator, white disk is prey). Top: generation 20. Center: generation 70. Bottom: generation 95.

fitness values than prey, except for short temporary oscillations (figure 10.15). In all runs, the average fitness of the predator population was more stable than that of prey.

Predators always display very good chasing abilities across generations: once the prey has been locked in its visual field, it quickly accelerates to maximum speed until contact. As a matter of fact, for the predator it is sufficient to get the sign of the synapses right. Then, independently of their initial random values, the synapses from active sensors will be increased causing an acceleration in the right direction. As compared to condition 1, where predators tended to efficiently track only in one direction, here they can turn in both directions at equal speed depending where the prey is. In condition 1 proper tracking in both directions would have required accurate settings of all synaptic strengths from visual inputs. Here, instead, since synapses are temporarily increased depending on active units [363, 367], individual adjustments of synapses take place when and where required depending on current sensory input. The trajectory displayed in the center image of figure 10.15 shows another example of synaptic adjustment. While the prey rotates always around the same circle, the predator performs three turns during which synaptic values from the visual units are gradually increased; at the fourth turn, the synaptic values are sufficiently strong to initiate a straight pursuit (eventually, the prey will try to avoid the predator without success). The temporary drop in performance of the predator after generation 90 is due a more precise tracking combined with a slower motion (bottom image of figure 10.15). Such behavior was probably developed because prey were also slower and more careful in avoiding obstacles (including the predator). Although activity-dependent synaptic change are exploited by the far-sighted predator, not the same happens for the prey. Prey move faster than in conditions 1 and 2, especially when turning near walls (where IR sensors become active and synapses temporarily strengthen), but they cannot increase their behavioral repertoire with respect to condition 1. Not even can they improve it because volatile changes of the synaptic values imply that most of the time they must re-develop on-the-fly appropriate strengths; although this is alright for avoidance of static obstacles, it is a problem when facing a fast-approaching predator.

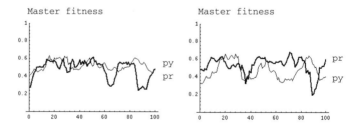

Figure 10.16
Left: Master Tournament between species co-evolved in condition 1 (genetically-determined controllers). **Right**: Master Tournament between predators evolved in condition 3 (directional-change controllers) and prey evolved in condition 1 (right). In the latter case, predators win more often. See text for further implications of these results.

In order to check whether predators' superior performances in condition

3 were due to a real advantage of the predator rather than to some difficulties of the prey to cope with directional-change controllers, we compared Master Fitnesses for predators and prey co-evolved in condition 1 (figure 10.16, left; replicated from figure 10.8 for sake of comparison) with Master Fitnesses for predators evolved in condition 3 against prey evolved in condition 1 (figure 10.16, right). Directional-change predators win more often against genetically-determined prey ($\overline{R} = 42$) than genetically-determined predators do. If the advantage reported by predators co-evolved with directional-change prey had been caused only by difficulties of prey to evolve suitable directional-change controllers, the Master Tournament between species evolved in different conditions (figure 10.16, right) should have not generated differential performances.

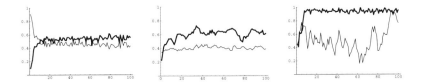

Figure 10.17
Co-evolution of controllers that can exploit either adaptive noise or directional change (thick line = predator; thin line = prey). **Left**: Average population fitness recorded during co-evolution. **Center**: Master Fitness. **Right**: Amount of directional-change synapses in the population. Figures are obtained by counting the number of directional-change synapses per individual (divided by total number of synapses) and further averaging over all individuals in the population.

Finally, we run a new set of experiments where each synapse could decide whether to change according to condition 2 (adaptive noise) or to condition 3 (directional change). The genetic code of all synapses of both species was augmented by one bit. If this bit was on, the previous four bits were interpreted as described for condition 2, otherwise as described for condition 3 (notice that the first bit always codes the sign of the synapses in all conditions). The results clearly indicated that predators always won over the prey (figure 10.17, left) and Master Fitness values even revealed a slightly ascending trend for predators, but not for prey (figure 10.17, center). Analysis of the genotypes showed that all predators consistently evolved directional-change synapses, but prey oscillated between preference for adaptive noise and directional change without any consequence on the outcome of the tournaments that were almost always won by predators.

These results indicate that directional-change provides superior adaptivity with respect to the other two conditions only if coupled with the sensory abilities of the predator. The addition of visual information provides long-range information that is suitable for fast adaptation of chasing strategies. On the other hand, the limited sensory information of the prey cannot capitalize on this form of ontogenetic adaptation. The best the prey can do is to maximize behavioral unpredictability and diversity.

10.5   Conclusive Discussion

The experiments described in this article indicate that competitive co-evolution can generate very quickly efficient chasing and escaping strategies in the two species. Consider for example that a simple chasing strategy (consisting in locating the prey, going towards it, while avoiding the walls) emerged in less than half generations required for evolving a simple obstacle avoidance behavior for the same robot and a similar control architecture in standard evolution (single robot in static environment) [362]. This might be explained by the fact that co-evolution, at least in the initial phases, is analogous to incremental evolution. In other words, competitive co-evolution generates solutions to difficult problems by generating a series of challenges of increasing difficulty. This is reflected by a posteriori analysis of the modification of the fitness landscape described in subsection 10.3. However, after some generations the two populations re-discover old behaviors and endlessly alternate between them. In a companion paper [383] we show that this apparent problem can be solved in two ways: either by testing each individual against best competitors extracted from all previous generations (Hall-of-Fame method), or by making the environment and sensory system of the two species more complex.

The point is that alternating between behavioral strategies is not a problem, but a smart solution for coping with competitors that rapidly change their strategy. The alternative to this result would be to evolve behaviors that display greater and greater generality, i.e. behaviors that can defeat a larger number of opponents. This is possible only if such behaviors exist or are not too rare on the space of all possible behaviors that can be generated with a given control architecture. If such behaviors do not exist, the best that co-evolution can do is to evolve individuals that can quickly re-adopt a previous strategy as soon as the current strategy is no longer successful (because the opponent has changed his behavior). This implies that co-evolution finds individuals that sit on areas of the genotypes characterized by steep peaks, that is individuals whose mutants are significantly different, but still viable and successful. This observation bears analogies with the hypothesis of "life at the edge of chaos" advanced by Langton [376].

We think that it is necessary to reconsider artificial evolution in a new perspective, different from mainstream evolutionary computation oriented towards function optimization (see also [372] for a similar view). In unpredictably changing environments evolution of optimal solutions is not an appropriate approach because optimality cannot be defined a priori. A more suitable metaphor is *evolution of adaptivity*, that is evolution of solutions that can cope with rapidly changing environments. We argue that artificial evolution should strive for evolving adaptive solutions, rather than solution for a fixed set of predefined problems, if we want to evolve and understand artifacts that display life-like properties. In section 10.3 above, we have outlined at least three ways in which artificial evolution could achieve increased adaptivity: *a)* generation and maintenance of diversity (which gives higher probability that some individuals will be able to reproduce in changed environments); *b)* selection of genotypes whose mutant neighbors correspond to different but all equally viable phenotypes (which allows rapid generational switch between different strategies); *c)* exploitation of ontogenetic adaptation (which can quickly cope with environmental changes without requiring genetic changes).

In this research we have explored in more detail the third option (and only given some hints about the second option which is further discussed in another article [383]). Co-evolving predators consistently exploit the possibility of ontogenetic synaptic change with Hebbian rules and report higher performance over the prey in three different conditions: against prey co-evolving under the same directional-change condition, against prey co-evolved under genetically-determined condition, and against prey that are free to evolve under adaptive-noise or directional-change conditions. In all cases ontogenetic adaptation affects co-evolutionary dynamics by reducing the amplitude and frequency of oscillations in fitness values. This suggests that ontogenetic changes can cope with modifications of prey strategies without requiring much philogenetic change. For example, it was shown that rapid synaptic adaptation allows the network to ontogenetically switch between different strategies (chase to the left or chase to the right, depending on the prey behavior) that would otherwise require generational evolution given this specific control architecture.

The prey, given their limited sensory information, did not benefit from the types of ontogenetic changes considered in this research. However, when co-evolved in adaptive-noise conditions, they consistently increased the level of synaptic noise significantly more than predators. This corresponded to unpredictable, rapidly changing, maneuvers. Also in this condition the amplitude and frequency of oscillations of fitness values was decreased. In fact, by displaying a continuously changing behavior, the prey offered the predators a larger set of different behaviors forcing them to adopt more general behavioral solutions. These latter results highlight the strong relationship between physical aspects of the machine and the type of learning system adopted. Ideally, sensory motor morphologies and learning algorithms should be co-evolved.

The experiments described in this article have been carried out (partly) on physical robots and (mostly) on a realistic software model in order to quickly explore different hypotheses and obtain repeated measures for statistical analysis. The fact of having co-developed hardware and software has been a determining factor for several decisions that had to be taken early on during the preparation of the experimental setup. The most important decision regarded the formulation of the fitness function. Considering that our robots could not reliably measure the distance between each other, we resorted to a simpler and more general fitness function based on time to contact. By "simple function" we mean a function that does not force evolution towards predefined behaviors based on human preconceptions derived from a *distal description* of the robot behavior.[5] In this case, we did not ask predators to chase by minimizing distance and prey to escape by maximizing it, as other authors did (e.g., see [357]). This was only one of the possible options that the two co-evolving species could adopt. The analysis described in section 10.3 showed that predators indeed adopted different and more subtle strategies. Whether or not the choice of a selection criterion is so crucial to significantly affect the global co-evolutionary dynamics [360], constraining co-evolution reduces the amount of emergent behaviors that both populations could potentially discover. Within the context of artificial evolution, intended as an open-ended endeavor to develop increased levels of adaptivity, simpler and more intrinsic fitness functions leave more space to autonomous self-organization of intelligent forms of artificial life.

---

5 See [386, 381] for a distinction between proximal and distal descriptions of behavior and its implications for design and analysis of autonomous systems.

Acknowledgments

This chapter has appeared before as an article in the journal *Robotics and Autonomous Systems*. It is reprinted here with permission.

References

[355]P. J. Angeline and J. B. Pollack. Competitive environments evolve better solutions for complex tasks. In S. Forrest, editor, *Proceedings of the Fifth International Conference on Genetic Algorithms*, pages 264–270, San Mateo, CA, 1993. Morgan Kaufmann.

[356]D. Cliff and G. F. Miller. Tracking the Red Queen: Measurements of adaptive progress in co-evolutionary simulations. In F. Morán, A. Moreno, J. J. Merelo, and P. Chacón, editors, *Advances in Artificial Life: Proceedings of the Third European Conference on Artificial Life*, pages 200–218. Springer Verlag, Berlin, 1995.

[357]D. Cliff and G. F. Miller. Co-evolution of Pursuit and Evasion II: Simulation Methods and Results. In P. Maes, M. Matarić, J. Meyer, J. Pollack, H. Roitblat, and S. Wilson, editors, *From Animals to Animats IV: Proceedings of the Fourth International Conference on Simulation of Adaptive Behavior*. MIT Press-Bradford Books, Cambridge, MA, 1996.

[358]R. Dawkins and J. R. Krebs. Arms races between and within species. *Proceedings of the Royal Society London B*, 205:489–511, 1979.

[359]P. Driver and N. Humphries. *Protean behavior: The biology of unpredictability*. Oxford University Press, Oxford, 1988.

[360]S. Ficici and J. Pollack. Coevolving Communicative Behavior in a Linear Pursuer-Evader Game. In R. Pfeifer, B. Blumberg, J. Meyer, and S. Wilson, editors, *From Animals to Animats V: Proceedings of the Fifth International Conference on Simulation of Adaptive Behavior*. MIT Press-Bradford Books, Cambridge, MA, 1998.

[361]D. Floreano. Ago Ergo Sum. In G. Mulhauser, editor, *Evolving Consciousness*. Benjamins Press, New York, To appear.

[362]D. Floreano and F. Mondada. Evolution of homing navigation in a real mobile robot. *IEEE Transactions on Systems, Man, and Cybernetics-Part B*, 26:396–407, 1996.

[363]D. Floreano and F. Mondada. Evolution of plastic neurocontrollers for situated agents. In P. Maes, M. Matarić, J. Meyer, J. Pollack, H. Roitblat, and S. Wilson, editors, *From Animals to Animats IV: Proceedings of the Fourth International Conference on Simulation of Adaptive Behavior*, pages 402–410. MIT Press-Bradford Books, Cambridge, MA, 1996.

[364]D. Floreano and F. Mondada. Evolutionary Neurocontrollers for Autonomous Mobile Robots. *Neural Networks*, 11:1461–1478, 1998.

[365]D. Floreano and F. Mondada. Hardware Solutions for Evolutionary Robotics. In P. Husbands and J. Meyer, editors, *Proceedings of the first European Workshop on Evolutionary Robotics*. Springer Verlag, Berlin, 1998.

[366]D. Floreano and S. Nolfi. God Save the Red Queen! Competition in Co-evolutionary Robotics. In J. Koza, K. Deb, M. Dorigo, D. Fogel, M. Garzon, H. Iba, and R. L. Riolo, editors, *Proceedings of the 2nd International Conference on Genetic Programming*, San Mateo, CA, 1997. Morgan Kaufmann.

[367]D. Flotzinger. Evolving plastic neural network controllers for autonomous robots. Msc dissertation 9580131, COGS, University of Sussex at Brighton, 1996.

[368]P. Funes, E. Sklar, H. Juillè, and J. Pollack. Animal-Animat Coevolution: Using the Animal Population as Fitness Function. In R. Pfeifer, B. Blumberg, J. Meyer, and S. Wilson, editors, *From Animals to Animats V: Proceedings of the Fifth International Conference on Simulation of*

Adaptive Behavior. MIT Press-Bradford Books, Cambridge, MA, 1998.

[369]D. E. Goldberg. *Genetic algorithms in search, optimization and machine learning.* Addison-Wesley, Redwood City, CA, 1989.

[370]J. L. Gould. *Full House: The Spread of Excellence from Plato to Darwin.* Random House (2nd Edition), New York, 1997.

[371]S. J. Gould and R. C. Lewontin. The spandrels of San Marco and the Panglossian paradigm: a critique of the adaptationist program. *Proceedings of the Royal Society London, B*, 205:581–598, 1979.

[372]I. Harvey. Cognition is not computation; evolution is not optimization. In W. Gerstner, A. Germond, M. Hasler, and J. Nicoud, editors, *Artificial Neural Networks - ICANN97*, pages 685–690, Berlin, 1997. Springer Verlag.

[373]W. Hillis. Co-evolving parasites improve simulated evolution as an optimization procedure. *Physica D*, 42:228–234, 1990.

[374]J. R. Koza. Evolution and co-evolution of computer programs to control independently-acting agents. In J. Meyer and S. Wilson, editors, *From Animals to Animats. Proceedings of the First International Conference on Simulation of Adaptive Behavior*. MIT Press, Cambridge, MA, 1991.

[375]J. R. Koza. *Genetic programming: On the programming of computers by means of natural selection.* MIT Press, Cambridge, MA, 1992.

[376]C. G. Langton. Life at the edge of chaos. In C. Langton, J. Farmer, S. Rasmussen, and C. Taylor, editors, *Artificial Life II: Proceedings Volume of Santa Fe Conference*, volume XI. Addison-Wesley: series of the Santa Fe Institute Studies in the Sciences of Complexities, Redwood City, CA, 1992.

[377]A. J. Lotka. *Elements of Physical Biology*. Williams and Wilkins, Baltimore, 1925.

[378]O. Miglino, H. H. Lund, and S. Nolfi. Evolving Mobile Robots in Simulated and Real Environments. *Artificial Life*, 2:417–434, 1996.

[379]G. F. Miller and D. Cliff. Protean behavior in dynamic games: Arguments for the co-evolution of pursuit-evasion tactics. In D. Cliff, P. Husbands, J. Meyer, and S. W. Wilson, editors, *From Animals to Animats III: Proceedings of the Third International Conference on Simulation of Adaptive Behavior*. MIT Press-Bradford Books, Cambridge, MA, 1994.

[380]J. D. Murray. *Mathematical Biology*. Springer Verlag, Berlin, 1993. Second, Corrected Edition.

[381]S. Nolfi. Using emergent modularity to develop control system for mobile robots. *Adaptive Behavior*, 5:343–364, 1997.

[382]S. Nolfi. Evolutionary robotics: Exploiting the full power of self-organization. *Connection Science*, 10:167–183, 1998.

[383]S. Nolfi and D. Floreano. Co-evolving predator and prey robots: Do "arms races" arise in artificial evolution? *Artificial Life*, 4:30–55, 1998. page numbers not exact.

[384]C. W. Reynolds. Competition, Coevolution and the Game of Tag. In R. Brooks and P. Maes, editors, *Proceedings of the Fourth Workshop on Artificial Life*, pages 59–69, Boston, MA, 1994. MIT Press.

[385]C. Rosin and R. Belew. New methods for competitive co-evolution. *Evolutionary Computation*, 5(1):1–29, 1997.

[386]N. E. Sharkey and N. H. Heemskerk. The neural mind and the robot. In A. J. Browne, editor, *Current perspectives in neural computing*. IOP Publishing, London, 1997.

[387]K. Sims. Evolving 3D Morphology and Behavior by Competition. In R. Brooks and P. Maes, editors, *Proceedings of the Fourth Workshop on Artificial Life*, pages 28–39, Boston, MA, 1994. MIT Press.

[388]L. van Valen. A new evolutionary law. *Evolution Theory*, 1:1–30, 1973.

[389]V. Volterra. Variazioni e fluttuazioni del numero di individui in specie animali conviventi. *Memorie dell'Accademia dei Lincei*, 2:31–113, 1926. Variations and fluctuations of the number of individuals in animal species living together. Translation in: R. N. Chapman, Animal Ecology. New York: McGraw Hill 1931, pp. 409–448.

11   Goal Directed Adaptive Behavior in Second-Order Neural Networks: Learning and Evolving in the MAXSON Architecture

Frederick L. Crabbe and Michael G. Dyer

This chapter presents a neural network architecture (MAXSON) based on second-order connections that can learn a multiple goal approach/avoid task using reinforcement from the environment. The paper shows that MAXSON can learn certain spatial navigation tasks much faster than traditional Q-learning, as well as learn goal directed behavior, increasing the agent's chances of long-term survival. The chapter also shows that portions of the *learning rules* can be evolved using genetic algorithms.

11.1   Problem

Agents that reside in complex environments need to be able to meet their survival goals, often when several of these goals simultaneously have high priority. When the environment is dynamic, or when the agents cannot be pre-programmed to meet these goals, they must *learn* to meet them. This chapter presents MAXSON, a flexible neural architecture that: learns faster than traditional reinforcement learning approaches, generates and applies the reinforcement in a neurally plausible manner, and can balance the requirements of multiple simultaneous goals. The chapter also describes two genetic algorithm experiments: 1) evolving the value of constants in the learning rules of the algorithm, and 2) evolving portions of the learning rules themselves.

Environment and Task

In order to evaluate an agent control architecture, it needs both an environment and a task. The environment includes the agent's body (sensors, effectors, and any physiological mechanisms) as well as the external world. The task allows for a metric to measure the relative success of the control architecture.

In this chapter, an agent lives in a two-dimensional, continuous environment, where the objects in the environment are food, water, and poison. To survive, the agent needs to eat the food, drink the water, and avoid the poison. The agent receives goal input in the form of hunger, thirst, and pain [1]. Each goal input is a single value between 0 and 1. As an agent's store of food and water goes down, its hunger and thirst rises. When the agent eats a poison, its pain input rises.

---

1 The goal input corresponds to input coming from within the agent's body, similar to motivational units in [395].

To detect external objects, the agent has a primitive visual system for object detection. The agent can see in a 180 degree field in front of it. Vision is broken up into four input sensors for each type of object the agent can see. Since the world contains three types of external objects, the agent has twelve visual sensors. The agent is bilateral with two visual sensors on each side for each type of object. These sensors perceive the closest object of that type. For instance, the FDL (Food Distance Left) sensor measures the distance to the closest food on the agent's left side, while the FAL (Food Angle Left) sensor measures the angle of this food relative to the direction the agent is facing.

An agent's possible actions are: turn left or right smoothly (up to four degrees), and move forward up to six units, where one unit is one twelfth the agent's size. The agent automatically consumes any object it comes in contact with. Any or all of an agent's actions may be carried out in parallel. For example, if the agent turns right 3.2 degrees, turns left 1.8 degrees, and moves forward 4.6 units, the result is that the agent simultaneously moves forward 4.6 units and turns right 1.4 degrees.

The basic task for an agent is to eat when hungry, drink when thirsty, and always avoid eating the poison. An agent begins knowing nothing about how to approach any of these items, nor which items are suitable for satisfying which goals. The agent must learn to behave appropriately to satisfy these goals.

11.2   MAXSON Architecture

Our agents use an architecture, called MAXSON (figure 11.1) [397], that is made up of two sub-networks: a second-order *policy network*, and a first-order *value network*. The policy network is used to dynamically generate the agent's actions at each time step, while the value network is used to generate and apply reinforcement to the policy network. At each time step the following occurs: (1) the policy network determines the agent's action, (2) the action is performed in the environment, (3) the value network calculates reinforcement for the policy network, (4) the weights on the policy network are adjusted based on that reinforcement, and finally, (5) the weights of the value network are adjusted based on the external reinforcement.

In order to behave intelligently, an agent needs to be able to act based upon its goals, both immediate survival goals such as eating, as well other goals involved in more sophisticated behavior, such as nest construction [398]. This can result in an agent that has multiple possibly conflicting goals that fluctuate

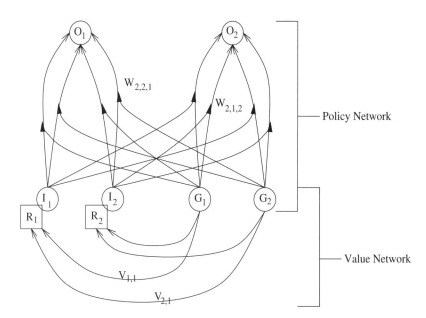

Figure 11.1
A small-scale MAXSON network. I-nodes receive external input. Associated with each I-node is a reinforcement node R. G-nodes receive internal goal input, and O-nodes perform motor actions. Each black triangle (joining two input connections) is a second-order connection with a weight W.

in urgency over time (which is the task environment a MAXSON agent is designed to learn in). The second-order connections in the policy network help the MAXSON agent satisfy these multiple simultaneous goals.

Reinforcement from the external world appears intermittently, upon the satisfaction or failure of some goal. This could require multiple satisfactions of a goal for an agent to learn correctly. The MAXSON agent should be able to learn from a single interaction with an object in the environment, so that an agent needs to eat a poison only once before it begins to avoid poisons. The value network serves this purpose by converting the intermittent reinforcement to reinforcement at each time step for the policy network.

Second-Order Networks

A MAXSON-based agent uses the second-order policy sub-network (figure 11.2) to choose what actions to take at each moment. Second-order connections multiply pairs of inputs to nodes before the inputs are summed [400, 407]. In the policy network, the sensor nodes are broken into two groups: the external input and the internal goal sensors. The set of external input sensors I consist of all the visual sensors (for food, water, and poison objects); the goal sensors G consist of hunger, thirst, and pain. When the agent receives input ($I \cup G$), the associated sensor nodes are activated (activation between 0 and 1). Then, activation from each external input sensor I_i is multiplied with activation from each goal sensor G_g and a weight $W_{i,g,o}$ (weights between 0 and 1), via second-order connections, and then summed at an output node O_o, as shown in Equation 11.1:

$$O_o = \sum_{i \in I, g \in G} I_i G_g W_{i,g,o}. \tag{11.1}$$

If there were 2 external sensors (food_left and food_right), one internal sensor (hunger), one output (turn_left), and two weights:
($W_1 = W_{food\_left, hunger, turn\_left}$ and $W_2 = W_{food\_right, hunger, turn\_left}$)
the activation of turn_left would be:
$O_{turn\_left} = (I_{food\_left} \times G_{hunger} \times W_1 + I_{food\_right} \times G_{hunger} \times W_2).$

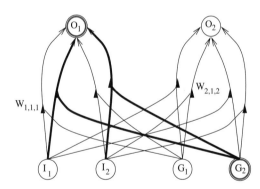

Figure 11.2
A second-order policy sub-network. G-nodes (goals) dynamically modulate the influence of I-nodes on O-nodes (actions) via second-order connections.

Policy Network Weight Adjustment

The agent learns to approach food and water while learning to avoid poison by adjusting the second-order weights based on *immediate distributed reinforcement*. By immediate, we mean that reinforcement is given to the agent at each time step, rather than only when the agent satisfies some goal. By distributed, we mean that each external sensor generates a separate reinforcement signal, rather than having a single reinforcement signal for the whole organism. The reinforcement R_i at external input sensor node I_i is continuously re-calculated by a function of the difference between the activation on I_i at the current time step and the activation on I_i at the previous time step: $R_i = f(I_i^t - I_i^{t-1})$. We describe the neural mechanism that dynamically generates this distributed reinforcement signal in the next section. The second-order weights in the policy network are adjusted as shown in algorithm 1.

---

algorithm 1 : adjusts the second-order policy network weights.

W is the 3D weight matrix,
$\vec{O}$ is the network output vector,
$\vec{R}$ is the reinforcement vector,
$\vec{I}^t$ is the external input sensor vector at the current time step,
$\vec{I}^{t-1}$ is the external input sensor vector at the previous time step and,
$\vec{G}$ is the goal sensor input vector at the current time step.

$$o \leftarrow \arg\max_o \vec{O}$$
$$g \leftarrow \arg\max_g \vec{G}$$

for each i **in** I **do**:
$$w_{i,g,o} \leftarrow w_{i,g,o} + R_i \times O_o \times G_g \times \delta_1, \text{ where:}$$

$$\delta_1 = \begin{cases} 1, & \text{if } |I_i^{t-1} - I_i^t| < \theta_1 \\ 0, & \text{otherwise.} \end{cases}$$

First, the *maximally* responding output node O_o and the *maximally* responding goal sensor node G_g are identified[2] (these are highlighted via dark circles in figure 11.2 as O_1 and G_2). Then the weight on every second-order link from G_g to O_o (dark lines in figure 11.2) is adjusted by the product of the activation of O_o, the activation of G_g, and the reinforcement R_i from the external input sensor node for that weight. Adjustment occurs only if the dif-

---

2 The name MAXSON is an acronym for Max-based Second-Order Network.

ference between the input on the external input sensor node I_i^t and the input at the previous time step on the external input sensor node I_i^{t-1} is less than a constant threshold θ_1.

Reinforcement Calculation by Value Network

In MAXSON, a first-order single layer network (called the *value network*) recalculates the reinforcement for the policy network at each time step. It consists of connections from the goal sensors to the reinforcement nodes associated with the external input sensors (figure 11.3).

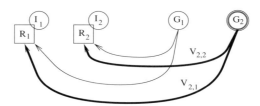

Figure 11.3
A first-order value sub-network. Each R_i node holds the amount of the reinforcement for the adjoining external input sensor node (I_i).

The reinforcement is calculated as shown in algorithm 2. Activation on the *maximal* goal sensor G_g (dark circle G_2 in figure 11.3) is multiplied by the weights $V_{g,i}$ on the links from G_g (dark lines in figure 11.3) and propagated to the reinforcement nodes. Each external input sensor multiplies its input from the value network by the change in its activation over time ($I_i^t - I_i^{t-1}$) to generate the local reinforcement value (R_i).

---

algorithm 2 : calculates reinforcement at each external input sensor node.

V is the 2D weight matrix on the value-network.

$$g \leftarrow \arg\max_g \vec{G}$$

for each i **in** I **do**:
$$R_i \leftarrow (I_i^t - I_i^{t-1}) \times V_{g,i} \times G_g$$

Value Network Weight Adjustment

The value network uses Hebbian style learning [402] to update its weights V based on the temporal difference at the *goal* sensor nodes (algorithm 3).

---

algorithm 3 : adjusts the first-order value network (FOV) weights

---

$i \leftarrow \arg\max_i \vec{I}^{t-1}$

for each g **in** G **do**:
$\quad V_{g,i} \leftarrow V_{g,i} + (I_i^{t-1} \times \delta_2)$, where:

$$\delta_2 = \begin{cases} G_g^{t-1} - G_g^t, & \text{if } |G_g^{t-1} - G_g^t| > \theta_2 \\ 0, & \text{otherwise.} \end{cases}$$

When the change of activation at any goal sensor node G_g is greater than a constant threshold θ_2, then the weight $V_{g,i}$ on the link (dark lines in figure 11.4 from both goal nodes) from that goal sensor node to the external input sensor node (dark circle I_1 in figure 11.4) that was maximally responding at the previous time step I_i^{t-1}, is modified by the difference $(G_g^{t-1} - G_g^t)$ times the activation of the external input sensor node at the previous time step.

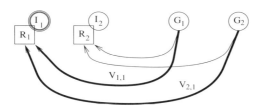

Figure 11.4
Update of weights V in value network.

Architectural Design Features

The unique features of the architecture described above were developed in response to requirements of an efficient neural mechanism for learning the multi-goal task. This section describes these requirements and how they were met.

ON-THE-FLY MANAGEMENT OF MULTIPLE GOALS

The second-order connections (combining the goal and external input sensor input) give a MAXSON agent the ability to properly achieve *multiple* fluctuating goals. The second-order network enables changes in the goal input to radically affect the overall behavior. If a goal changes, a distinct portion of the policy network is given more (or less) control over the output. Using second-order learning (algorithm 1), different sub-networks are modified automatically, one for each goal sensor. When a goal sensor becomes active, the portion of the policy network that meets that goal becomes more active, and when that goal node becomes inactive, the portion of the network that meets that goal is turned off. For example, imagine an agent with moderate hunger, no thirst, food to the left and water to the right. The thirst input is 0, thus turning off the connections from the water sensors to the output nodes that would make the agent move toward the water. Thus the agent moves toward the food. But if the agent suddenly becomes extremely thirsty, the 'approach water' sub-portion of the policy network becomes very active, and, all other things being equal, the agent approaches the water.

CONVERSION OF DELAYED TO IMMEDIATE REINFORCEMENT

The second-order policy network requires *immediate reinforcement* in order to learn. Unfortunately for the agent, reinforcement is only available when an object is eaten or drunk and this lasts for just a single time step. The value network solves this delayed reinforcement problem. The purpose of the value network is to convert short duration delayed reinforcement into the continuous immediate reinforcement used in the second-order learning algorithm. A weight $(V_{g,i})$ on the value network reflects the agent's positive or negative reinforcement attitude toward the external object represented by the external input sensor (I_i) when the goal sensor (G_g) is active. By associating the input that immediately led to a large positive reinforcement with that reinforcement, the agent is able to adjust the value of that object. Later, when the agent moves relative to the object, the value network can generate more appropriate immediate reinforcement. The cross-modal association of one input with another converts the delayed reinforcement into immediate reinforcement.

For example (figure 11.5), when the agent eats poison, the activation

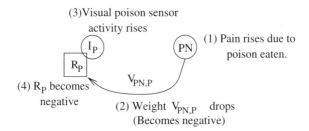

Figure 11.5
A value network example. PN is the pain input node, I_P is the visual node that receives input
about a poison object. R_P is the reinforcement node for I_P.

on the goal pain sensor rises (1). The change in activation on that sensor
triggers the downward weight adjustment (2) between the pain sensor and the
reinforcement node of the external input sensor that detects the poison. Later,
when the agent moves toward a unit of poison, the activation on the poison
visual sensor changes (3) from time $t - 1$ to time t. That temporal difference
combines with the value network $(G \times V)$ to generate an immediate negative
reinforcement (4) at that external input sensor node. The policy network can
now use the resulting immediate vision-based negative reinforcement to learn
how to avoid the poison. Thus an intermittent negative *gustatory* experience
has caused the agent to experience negative reinforcement from more common
visual experiences.

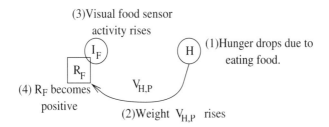

Figure 11.6
Another value network example. H is the hunger goal input node, I_F is the visual node that
receives input about a food object. R_F is the reinforcement node for I_F. The agent has no a priori
knowledge that food satisfies hunger.

In the case when the agent eats food (figure 11.6), the activation on its
goal hunger sensor goes down (1). The change in activation on that sensor

triggers the upward weight adjustment (2) between the hunger sensor and the reinforcement node of the external input sensor that detects the food. Later, when the agent moves toward a unit of food, the activation on the food visual sensor changes over time (3). That temporal difference combines with the value network to dynamically generate an immediate positive reinforcement (4) at that external input sensor node. Thus the intermittent positive gustatory experience has caused the agent to experience a positive reinforcement from more common visual experiences. The policy network can use this immediate visual reinforcement to learn how to approach the food.

USING MAXIMUM NODES FOR FOCUS OF ATTENTION

During second-order learning, attempting to adjust *all* the weights at each sense/act time step resulted in problems in assigning credit to individual weights. Here are two example problems: (1) When an agent outputs a large activation for 'turn_left', and a medium activation for 'turn_right', the agent's resulting action is to turn left. If the agent receives a positive reinforcement, and the algorithm were to adjust weights to *all* the output nodes, then the agent would adjust weights to both 'turn_right' and 'turn_left'. Because the weights are capped at 1 (to prevent unbounded growth), enough of these errors would cause the weights on both links to grow to 1. (2) Suppose that the agent is thirsty but even more hungry; it sees food to the left and turns left, causing the 'food left' sensor to receive positive reinforcement. If the weight between the 'food left' sensor node, the 'thirst' goal node, and the 'turn left' output node were to be adjusted based on the positive reinforcement, then the agent will learn to incorrectly approach food when thirsty. The credit for the positive reinforcement would be improperly given to that link.

Experimentation showed us that in sufficiently complicated environments, these errors occur often and are not compensated for, thus resulting in the agent learning bad policies. In order to focus the attention of the second-order learning algorithm on the appropriate weights, we introduce the idea of only adjusting the weights associated with the *maximum* nodes of a particular group. By only adjusting weights connected to the maximum output node, the credit assignment problem in problem 1 is alleviated. Since the 'turn left' node is the maximum output node, only the weight causing the agent to turn left is the one that is increased. Similarly, by only adjusting the weight connected to the maximum goal sensor, the agent doesn't learn to approach food when thirsty. Since, in this case, hunger is the maximum goal sensor, only the weights on the links emanating from hunger are modified, thus handling problem 2.

TEMPORAL DIFFERENCE BASED SENSOR AND GOAL THRESHOLD

Sometimes an atypical event occurs and it interferes with the agent learning how to behave in the typical case. For example, if an agent that sees food on the left then turns to right, normally it should get a negative reinforcement. But, if while turning to the right a new piece of food happens to come into view then the agent would get a positive reinforcement. In this case, the agent might learn that when there is food on the left, turning to the right is a good idea. The same sort of situation can occur when an occluded object suddenly comes into view.

In order to filter out the effects of these discontinuous events during learning, we use the threshold θ_1 shown in algorithm 1. If the change of input at any sensor is greater than a threshold, no change is made to the weights on the links emanating of that sensor. So, if an object comes into view at some point, the large change in the sensor input causes that data to not be used for learning. Thus θ_1 acts as a filter to disregard non-smooth sensor fluctuations.

Because the reinforcement signal is generated by any large change of an agent's internal goal sensors, the value network must detect when such an event has occurred that should warrant a change in the agent's reinforcement attitude toward some object, and what goal this change is in relation to. To select the appropriate goal to associate with that external reinforcement, we choose a goal G_g whose change is greater than a threshold θ_2. The rationale for this threshold in algorithm 3 is that, when an goal sensor such as hunger changes gradually, it is a part of the normal process of hunger increasing over time, but when it drops suddenly, something special has occurred to satisfy the hunger. It is at these times that the agent should take note of its surroundings and perform cross-modal reinforcement learning.

Both these thresholds are a function of properties outside the MAXSON architecture: i.e. the sensors and physiology of the agent, as well as the physics of the world. We posit that such factors are naturally part of any situated system, and would be set in nature as a product of evolution. We initially found by our own experimentation that given the nature of the simulated environment, both thresholds worked best at 0.02.

11.3 MAXSON Experimental Method

To test our architecture, we ran three experiments (that are in increasing complexity). In the first experiment, the environment contained 10 food units and 10 water units. The task was to gather as much of the food and water as an agent could in 20,000 time steps. A single agent was placed in the environment, and that agent received external visual inputs, but the connections from the goal nodes in the policy network were lesioned, thus the MAXSON policy network became a first-order network. We lesioned these links because agents that were not hungry or thirsty would not eat and drink as fast as possible, and we wanted to measure the agents performance when always eating and drinking. We measured the agent's performance by counting the number of objects the agent ate and drank, giving a maximum score of 20. In the second experiment, the environment contained 10 food units, 10 water units, and 10 poison units, with the goal input still lesioned. The task was still to eat as much food and drink as much water as the agent could, but also to eat as little poison as possible. We measured an agent's performance by subtracting the number of poisons eaten from the total number of food and water eaten. In the third experiment, the environment was the same as in the second experiment, but the links from the goal nodes in the policy network were left intact. In this experiment, an agent should no longer eat and drink as much as it could, but only when it is hungry and thirsty, respectively. The agent should still refrain from eating poison. Each agent was given a maximum food and water storage capacity, and any amount eaten beyond this capacity was lost. We measured an agent's performance by measuring how long it survived in the environment. The maximum time an agent could survive was 60,000 time steps because of the limited amount of food and water.

In each experiment, we compared the MAXSON agent with three other agents: random, table-based Q-learner, and linear function Q-learner. The random agent selected its action from amongst 'turn left', 'move forward', and 'turn right', with equal probability. Q-learning was selected because it is a popular reinforcement learning technique for agents in similar environments. In the Q-learning models, reinforcement of +1 was given for eating food, -1 for eating poison and 0 otherwise.

The table-based Q-learner is based on the $Q(\lambda)$ learner presented in [406]. The continuous input was discretized into a $3 \times m$ table, where m is the number of inputs (12 or 15, depending on experiment) and there are 3 possible discretizations based of the value of each input. Table 11.1 shows an example discretization for an agent with food to the left, poison to the right, low thirst, low pain and high hunger.

The linear function Q-learner uses a linear function of the inputs as an approximation of the Q-function, as suggested in Russell & Norvig, p. 615

Table 11.1
An example discretization to form the table for the table-based Q-learner. P = poison, F= food, A = angle, L = left, R = right, H = hunger, T = thirst, and PN = pain.

	Input value: between 0.0 and .33	between 0.33 and .66	between 0.66 and 1.0
FAL	1	0	0
FAR	0	0	0
FDL	0	1	0
FDR	0	0	0
WAL	0	0	0
WAR	0	0	0
WDL	0	0	0
WDR	0	0	0
PAL	0	0	0
PAR	0	1	0
PDL	0	0	0
PDR	0	0	1
T	1	0	0
H	0	0	1
PN	1	0	0

[404]. There was a separate function for each action a_i, that is, a separate equation to calculate the Q-value for each possible action, such as 'turn left'. The equation is shown in Equation 11.2.

$$2Q(s, a_i) = w_1 E_1 + w_2 E_2 + \ldots + w_{15} I_3. \tag{11.2}$$

The weights were adjusted using gradient descent, as described in Sutton & Barto [406].

The MAXSON agent consisted of the policy and value networks as described in the architecture section above. In the third experiment we ran both a MAXSON agent with the links from its goal nodes in tact, and one with those links lesioned.

For each type of agent, we ran 10 training sessions and report the average of the 10. In each training session, the agent was trained over 180,000 time steps. Periodically, learning was halted and the agent was tested for 20,000 time steps in 10 environments with different starting configurations. One of the random starting configurations is shown in figure 11.7.

We hypothesized that in the first experiment: (a) the table-based Q-learner would not perform well because its simple method of generalizing the input would not adapt to the continuous environment; (b) the linear function Q-learner would learn better; and (c) the MAXSON agent would learn as well as the linear function Q-learner, but do so faster as a result of the conversion

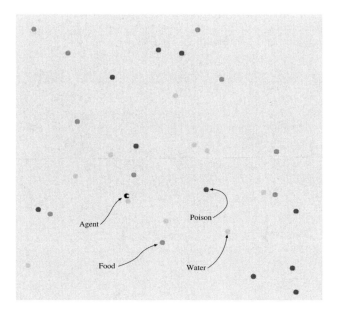

Figure 11.7
One of the random initial positions.

of intermittent gustatory reinforcement to continuous visual reinforcement.

We hypothesized that in the second experiment: (a) the table-based Q-learner would continue to do poorly; (b) the linear function Q-learner would learn the function, but more slowly; and (c) the MAXSON agent would learn at roughly the same speed as before, since learning about the poison happens in parallel with learning about the food and water.

We hypothesized that in the third experiment the MAXSON agent with goal input would out-live all of the other agents because it could conserve food and water while avoiding the poison.

11.4   MAXSON Results

The results of the first experiment (food and water only) are shown in figure 11.8. The MAXSON agents performed the best, converging on a score of nearly 20 by 10,000 time steps. Once a MAXSON agent interacts with all of the different types of objects, it quickly (within a few thousand time steps) learns to consume almost all the food and water. The linear function Q-learner converges in 60,000 time steps to a score around 18, slightly less than the MAXSON agent. The difference between the maximum scores of the linear function Q-learner and the MAXSON agent is statistically significant at 99.92% using an Mann-Whitney U-test. The table-based Q-learner fails to learn any good policy within the experiment time frame. This is most likely because of its inability to generalize the input.

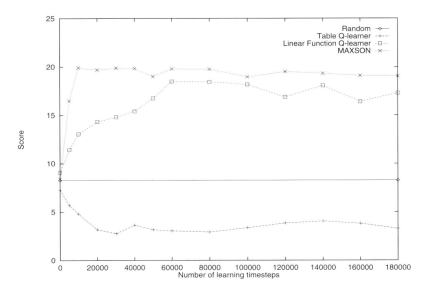

Figure 11.8
Experiment 1. The x-axis is the number of time steps and the y-axis is the score. The MAXSON agents converge six times faster than the linear function Q-learner and obtained a higher score (99.92% significance on a U-test).

Figure 11.9 shows the results for the second experiment (food, water and poison). Again, the MAXSON agents had the best performance, converging to a score of 18 in 20,000 time steps. Much of the extra time taken to learn this task comes from the time it takes the agent to randomly consume all three types of objects. The linear function Q-learner starts well, but peaks at 60,000 time steps with a score of 15.29, and surprisingly begins to drop. The agents begin to move faster toward food and water, but also eat more poison. They eventually converge on a policy that consumes nearly everything in the environment, resulting in a score close to 10. The table-based Q-learner again fails to learn a viable policy in the time given.

Figure 11.10 shows the results for the third experiment (conserve food and water while avoiding poison). The MAXSON agents that take advantage of their goal input have the longest survival time. They are able to approach food and water, but only do so when hungry or thirsty, saving resources for later on. As expected, the MAXSON agent that ignores its goal input does not survive as well. It can eat and drink while avoiding poison, but it consumes all of its resources quickly, and dies by the 15,000th time step. The linear function Q-learner initially learns to perform as well as the MAXSON agent that ignores goal input. It does not improve beyond this because the effect of the goal inputs is small compared to the rest of the Q-function. Then, as it begins to eat more poison, the linear function Q-learning agents poison themselves to death in 10,000 time steps. The table-based Q-learner performs comparatively better in this experiment. While it does not have a policy any different from the previous experiments, its 'strategy' of consuming very little food water or poison performs about as well as a strategy that involves eating lots of poison.

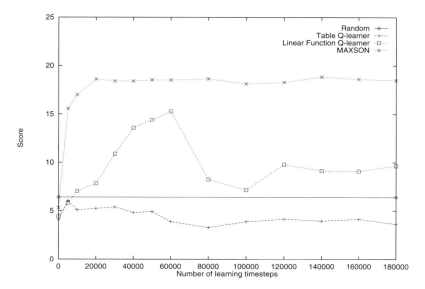

Figure 11.9
Experiment 2. The MAXSON agents converge to a good score (18.4) in 20,000 time steps. The linear function Q-learner reaches 15.29, but eventually converges on a score of 10.

11.5   Learning Discussion

Comparison to Q-learning

Q-learning was developed as a very general method for learning arbitrary functions. Often, general methods do not work as well in a particular domain as methods designed for that domain. Q-learning has been shown to have particular difficulties when the input to the agent is from the agent's point of view, rather than a global location [405]. MAXSON was designed for mobile agents that balance multiple goals in a continuous environment. Because of this, MAXSON has much better performance in our experiments. Not only do the MAXSON agents surpass the Q-learning agents in performance, they also reach the Q-learners' maximum performance an order of magnitude faster.

MAXSON combines six features to give it good performance compared to Q-learning. First, it implicitly takes advantage of the *continuous spatial nature* of this mobile robotic task. The reinforcement at each sensor node generated by the change in input over two time steps is valid because motion in the continuous environment changes the input continuously. This would not be true if the input were an arbitrary function, where moving toward an object could cause the input at a distance sensor node to go down or fluctuate. Second, a MAXSON agent uses credit assignment in the form of *distributed reinforcement* across all the sensors. By distributing the reinforcement, it becomes easier to pick out which part of the network affects the actions with respect to the external objects in view. Third, the weights associated with only the *maximum* nodes are adjusted. By adjusting only the weights associated with the maximum nodes, the system can concentrate on learning one thing at a time and reduce miss-placed credit. By reducing the errors in credit assignment, the network learns more rapidly and avoids learning incorrect associations. Fourth, the *cross-modal association* that occurs in the value network converts a single gustatory reinforcement event, such as eating a unit of food, into immediate visual reinforcement that is active over a period of time. With Q-learning, learning takes place only when the food is eaten, while in MAXSON, after the food is eaten, the agent learns about approaching food during each time step that it is observing food at a distance.

Fifth, the input is separated into goal sensors and external input sensors. By separating out the goal sensors from the external input sensors, the system can treat then differently during learning. Sixth, the second-order connections allow the goals of the agent to have an important major influence over its behavior. An agent does not waste its resources by consuming them when it doesn't need them. This last feature could be incorporated into Q-learning. A function based Q-learner could multiply the goal and external input together as in Equation 11.3.

$$Q(s, a) = w_{1,1}E_1I_1 + w_{1,2}E_1I_2 + w_{1,3}E_1I_3 + ... + w_{12,3}E_{12}I_3. \qquad (11.3)$$

It would, however, be more difficult to incorporate the other features without fundamentally altering the general nature of Q-learning.

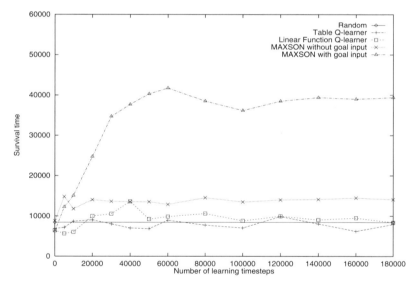

Figure 11.10
Experiment 3. The MAXSON agents that use their goal inputs survive the longest. Here, the y-axis is the survival time in number of time steps. Each data point indicates when an agent died (averaged over 10 trials).

How MAXSON Networks Self-Organize

Figures 11.11,11.12,11.13 illustrate how a typical MAXSON network self-organizes as a result of the multi-goal approach/avoid task. The agent starts out randomly connected and with no knowledge of objects in its environment. The only innate structure (besides the architecture itself) is that eating poison will cause the pain input to increase while eating food/water causes hunger/thirst

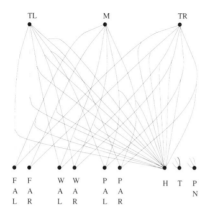

Figure 11.11
Initial policy network architecture with full connectivity and random weights in range of
$[0, 0.01]$. TL = turn-left, TR = turn-right, PN = pain sensed, H/T = hunger/thirst sensed, FAL =
angle to food object sighted on left, PAR = angle to poison object sighted on right, and so on. The
distance visual sensor nodes were left out for clarity. Only connections from the hunger goal
input node are shown.

to diminish. Over time, the MAXSON agent learns the following through
interaction with its environment:

1. It learns which sensory input should control which action output. For instance, it learns that the sensor for food on the left side should drive the 'turn
left' output while poison on the left should drive the 'turn right' output.

2. It learns which goals should modulate which external sensor-to-action connections, via the second-order connections. For instance, it learns that the sensation of Thirst (T) should control connections between the water-sensors and
the motor outputs while the sensation of Pain (PN) should control the connections between the poison-sensors and the motor outputs.

3. Through adjustments in V weights (e.g., due to experiencing pain when
eating poison) it learns to become negatively reinforced merely by the *sight* of
poison at a distance and positively reinforced by the sight of food/water at a
distance.

Figures 11.12 and 11.13b show only the strongest connections. All weights
tend toward extremes: in the policy network, weights are either close to 0, or
close to 1. In the value network, the weights are close to 1, -1, or 0, but not
in-between. Thus, a structured connectionist network self-organizes out of a
distributed fully connected network. The pruning of excessive connections is

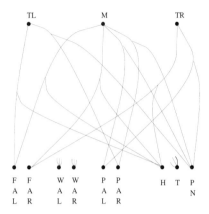

Figure 11.12
Simplified structure of a high-performance policy network after learning. All links from both
hunger and pain with a weight greater than 0.01 are shown to highlight the learned structure. All
links shown have weights greater than 0.5. Connections from thirst are omitted for clarity.

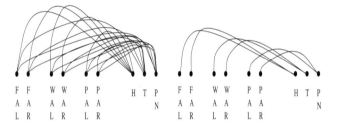

Figure 11.13
Value network before and after learning. Initially it has full connections, but it learns which
sensors are more likely to be related to the achievement of appropriate goals.

common during neural development [403, 399, 396].

11.6   Evolving the Learning Rules

The learning algorithms in MAXSON depend on two threshold parameters
(θ_1 and θ_2) and their relation to the difference over time in the agent's input.
The purpose of these parameters was to exclude certain perceptory inputs
from the learning process. We calculated what we felt were good values that
correctly excluded all of the perceptually misleading events, while minimizing
the number of excluded events. For example, θ_2 was needed to discriminate

between goal meeting events such as eating food, with normal physiological changes, such as hunger rising. The previous sections showed that the learning rules worked with the thresholds set at 0.02. In this section, we discuss Genetic Algorithm (GA) experiments which first evolve the values of the thresholds and then evolve the threshold portion of the rules themselves in order to build them automatically.

In the first experiment we hoped to generate θ_1 and θ_2 with values similar to what we had set by hand. In doing so, the traditional GA model of individually testing each agent to determine if it should be bred in the next generation would take prohibitively long. This is because the agents exist in a continuous environment where actions need to be recalculated more frequently than in a grid-like environment and because, to properly evaluate an agent, the agent must be allowed time to both learn about the environment as well as interact with it to demonstrate the agents's learning. The combination of these factors results in simulations that would run for several months on our hardware. To alleviate this, we hoped to run an entire population together, without explicit evaluation of the agents. At each time step, each agent had a small probability of replicating, resulting in the best agents having more offspring over time.

We ran 50 agents in a 2160 by 2160 environment, with 100 units each of food, water, and poison. When an agent consumed one of the environment objects, it was replaced by one of the same type at a random location. If an agent died, it was replaced by an offspring of a an agent randomly selected from the 15 oldest agents. At each time step, an agent would produce an offspring with probability $p(o) = a \times 10^{-7}$ when the agent's age a is $< 10^4$, and probability 10^{-3} then a is $> 10^4$. The agent genome was two 7-bit numbers, representing the two θs. The θs were calculated from the genome by subtracting 12 and dividing by 100, resulting in a range of -0.12 to 1.11. All values less than zero were treated as zero and all values greater than one were treated as one. This mechanism allowed the use of a binary number genome, while not biasing the thresholds to larger values. The mutation rate ranged from 0.01 to 0.001.

Figure 11.14 shows the average value of θ_2 in the population varying over time in a typical run. Despite varying the density of objects in the environment, as well as the reproduction probabilities, and mutation rates, neither threshold ever converged to useful values. When we examined the longest lived agents in these experiments, we discovered that the majority were performing random walk. The density of the food and water allowed the random walk agents to survive just as well as learning agents, resulting in no selective pressure to evolve the agents. But when the environment was made more challenging by decreasing the density of food and water, while increasing the density of poison, the environment was too difficult for new born agents who have yet to learn how to survive. Despite varying the densities of objects, we were unable to develop a suitable compromise. We felt a better solution was to *increase* the difficulty of the environment as the agents age to increase selectional pressure on agents as they have had a chance to learn.

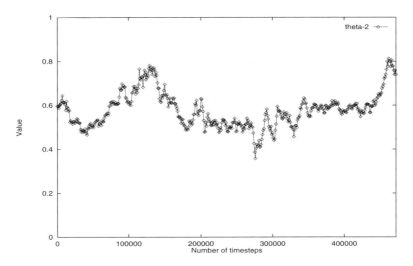

Figure 11.14
Plot of the population average value of θ_2 over time in the first GA experiment.

In order to increase the selectional pressure, we reduced the density of food and water as the agents age. This requires that the simulation synchronize generations so that all members of the next generation begin at the same time. Then by not replacing food and water as it is consumed, the difficulty of the environment automatically increases. After all but the last 15 agents had died, those top 15 agents who lived the longest were used to populate the next generation, using the same parameters as above. Figure 11.15 plots θ_1 and θ_2 in each generation in one of five runs. θ_2 drops quickly to 0.2 and eventually converges to 0.02. Once θ_2 had a reasonable value, θ_1 begins to drop as well, because the agent needs to get reasonable reinforcement from the value network before it can begin to evolve the policy network. θ_1 does not converge to as close a range as θ_2, hovering between 0.18 and 0.3. The other four runs had similar results, with an average time to convergence of 91 generations.

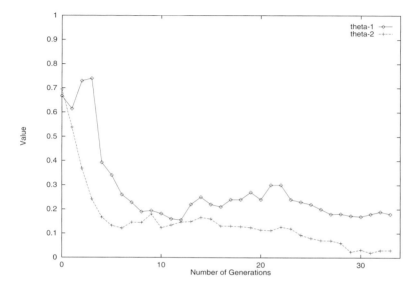

Figure 11.15
Plot of the population average value of θ_1 and θ_2 over the number of generations in the second GA experiment. The average generation length was 23000 time steps.

The evolution of the thresholds introduces the question of what other parts of the learning rules can be evolved. In particular, the learning rule for each network link uses the difference in the activation between 2 time steps of one of the nodes connected to that link and compares this difference to a threshold. We wondered what would happen if a link could compare the temporal difference in the activation of all of the nodes connected to it with a threshold? To investigate this, we changed the learning rules to accommodate more parameters. In the policy network, the learning rule became:

$$w_{i,g,o} \leftarrow w_{i,g,o} + R_i \times O_o \times G_g \times \delta_1 \times \delta_3 \times \delta_4, where:$$

$$\delta_1 = \begin{cases} 1, & \text{if } |I_i^{t-1} - I_i^t| \lessgtr_1 \theta_1 \\ 0, & \text{otherwise.} \end{cases}, \delta_2 = \begin{cases} 1, & \text{if } |G_g^{t-1} - G_g^t| \lessgtr_3 \theta_3 \\ 0, & \text{otherwise.} \end{cases},$$

$$\delta_3 = \begin{cases} 1, & \text{if } |O_o^{t-1} - O_o^t| \lesseqgtr_4 \theta_4 \\ 0, & \text{otherwise.} \end{cases}$$

where θ_1, θ_3, and θ_4 are specified by the genome, as well as $\lesseqgtr_1, \lesseqgtr_3$ and $\lesseqgtr_4$ which determine whether the rule tests for $<$ or for $>$.

The learning rule in the value network became:

$$V_{g,i} \leftarrow V_{g,i} + (I_i^{t-1} \times \delta_2 \times \delta_5)$$

$$\delta_2 = \begin{cases} 1, & \text{if } |G_g^{t-1} - G_g^t| \lesseqgtr_2 \theta_2 \\ 0, & \text{otherwise.} \end{cases}, \delta_4 = \begin{cases} 1, & \text{if } |R_i^{t-1} - R_i^t| \lesseqgtr_5 \theta_5 \\ 0, & \text{otherwise.} \end{cases}$$

where θ_2, θ_5, and each $\lesseqgtr$ are specified by the genome.

The above rules allow temporal difference thresholds on any of the nodes connected to a link to affect the learning on that link.

We expanded the agents' genome to five 7 bit numbers to specify the five thresholds, and 5 more bits to represent whether each $\lesseqgtr$ was $<$ or $>$. We predicted that the rules would evolve to resemble the ones we had designed, such that θ_1 and θ_2 would converge on values similar to the last experiment with $\lesseqgtr_1$ as $<$ and $\lesseqgtr_2$ as $>$, while $\theta_3, \theta_4, \theta_5, \lesseqgtr_3, \lesseqgtr_4$ and $\lesseqgtr_5$ would evolve such that they would have no effect on the learning, in a sense evolving away.

Figure 11.16 shows the value of $\theta_1, \theta_2, \theta_3, \theta_4$ and θ_5 in each generation of one of the runs. θ_1 and θ_2 converge to values similar to the previous experiment, and for every agent in the population, $\lesseqgtr_1$ and $\lesseqgtr_2$ are $<$ and $>$, respectively. θ_3 and θ_4 fall to 0.0, and $\lesseqgtr_3$ and $\lesseqgtr_4$ are $<$, while $\lesseqgtr_5$ rises to 1.0 and $\lesseqgtr_4$ is $>$. As predicted, learning rules evolved to a form where only θ_1 and θ_2 are used in learning. However, in two of the five runs, θ_2 converged to 1.0, with a $\lesseqgtr_2$ being $<$. Essentially, θ_2 evolved away as a threshold as well. All other values converged as expected.

11.7   Evolution Discussion

Because it was the learning rules of the networks being evolved, rather than the weights or structures, it was the learning ability of the agents, rather than their behavior that was being tested. The experiments show that in static environments, it may be difficult to strike a balance between strong selectional pressure, and initial ease of survival. By gradually increasing the selectional pressure on learning agents, they can evolve to learn their tasks. In a more

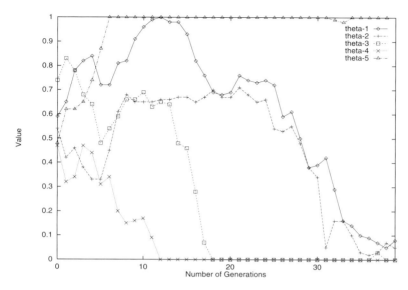

Figure 11.16
Plot of the population average value of θ_1, θ_2, θ_3, and θ_4 over time in the third GA experiment.

natural environment, the absolute level of difficulty of the environment can remain relatively static over an agent's lifetime, however, increasing difficulty can be simulated with social interaction between agents, such as parenting. Parent agents can provide protection to child agents as they learn about the environment, and the parent can gradually lower the amount of protection as the child agent's ability increases, providing the increasing selectional pressure needed for evolution of learning. This implies that in natural evolution, parenting precedes learning; parenting is necessary for learning to come about. This is clearly an area that requires much research.

That θ_1 does not converge to as precise a value as θ_2 implies that the *value* of θ_1 is less important for the success of the agent. There is usually a large difference between the events that θ_1 should include in learning and the set of events that it should exclude. This provides a range of equally valid values for θ_1 to be in.

When the learning rules themselves were allowed to vary, the convergence of the thresholds was not guaranteed, such as when θ_2 unexpectedly evolved away as a threshold. Closer inspection showed that without θ_2, the agents were still able to learn to behave reasonably well. They would incorrectly adjust their value networks based on naturally changing goal input, but the effect on the policy network was such that they were still able to find food and water, if less efficiently. At that point, θ_2 was stuck in a local minimum, because any movement away from 1.0, and the learning rule would begin throwing out data that the agent would otherwise have been using for learning, reducing the agent's fitness.

11.8   Related Work

Work related to MAXSON falls into four categories: second-order networks as agent controllers, neurally based reinforcement learning, neural associative networks, and genetic algorithm techniques.

Second-Order Controller Networks

Braitenberg [393] first showed that an agent with direct connections from left and right sensors to left and right wheels could be made to approach and avoid objects in it's environment. Werner [407] noted that second-order connections combining Braitenberg-like connections with goal input have advantageous properties for controlling agents. He noted that the combination of goal and sensory input enables an agent to pursue goal directed behavior, as well as interrupt such behavior to avoid a danger or take advantage of an opportunity to satisfy a less important goal. Once an agent has begun a consummatory behavior, it persists at it because of the proximity of the object to be consumed dominates the behavior. The agents can prioritize based on the activations of the inputs as well as the weights on the links. Finally, the agents can perform simultaneous actions, and do not need to exclusively choose a single action at each time step.

Werner hand designed the structure of his second-order networks and then used a genetic algorithm to set the weights. MAXSON's learning from fully connected networks results in both a structure (figure 11.12) similar to Werner's hand designed structure and weights that provide the agents with the above desirable properties.

Neural Reinforcement Learning

Often, neural networks are used within a reinforcement learning system as a function approximator for the value, policy, or Q-values function [406]. These networks replace a lookup table of values to scale up to large or continuous problem spaces, while the agent selects the single maximum score action (based on the network output) at each time step. In contrast, MAXSON takes the maximum of input for learning, but can output multiple simultaneous actions. A Q-learning system with an embedded neural network still has all the difficulties of Q-learning described above.

The complementary reinforcement backpropagation algorithm (CBRP) [390] is an example of a neural network that specifies the output directly, making it more similar to MAXSON. CBRP, however, requires that the agent receive immediate reward after each action, as opposed to the delayed reinforcement of the MAXSON environment. CBRP has no way of converting delayed reinforcement to visual immediate reinforcement.

Associative Networks

Billard and Hayes [392] use a technique similar to our value network in a mobile robot (DRAMA) to associate events cross-modally, as well as across time in order to label landmarks, and to learn series of perceptions. In DRAMA, event recognition systems (made up of feed forward networks) identify sensory events that are fed into an associative module. This fully connected module associates events that co-occur or occur in similar time frames by increasing the weights on the links between the nodes representing each event. They also applied DRAMA to social imitation learning [391]. A mechanism external to the architecture enabled the robotic agent to imitate the actions of another robot. By associating auditory input with imitated motor actions, the agents could learn a simple language. While DRAMA does learn about its environment, it neither contains an action selection mechanism such as MAXSON's policy network, nor does it use the output of the associator to generate reinforcement.

Genetic Algorithm Techniques

Cecconi, Menczer and Belew [394] used genetic algorithms to evolve neural networks that learned from parental example. They found that prolonging immaturity of agents was selected for when agents had the ability to learn from their parents.

Gomez and Miikkulainen [401] discuss making an environment incrementally more difficult because the final environment would be too difficult for the initial agents to start off in.

11.9   Conclusion

When agents need to learn about their environment to survive, it is important that they do so quickly and accurately. They should take advantage of the sort of environment they live in to maximize their chances of success. Our architecture uses second-order connections between goal and external input sensors, converts delayed discrete reinforcement to immediate continuous reinforcement across sensory modalities, applies max-based credit assignment strategies, and makes effective use of the spatial continuous nature of the task. As a result, the MAXSON neural network architecture is able to learn to approach food and water, while learning to avoid poison. It learns to achieve these multiple simultaneous goals much faster and more flexibly than the more general Q-learning techniques.

Genetic Algorithms can be used not only to evolve constants in the learning rules of MAXSON, but they can also evolve portions of the rules themselves. This technique can confirm both the sufficiency, as well as the necessity of aspects of the learning rules, helping to clarify the nature of the learning algorithm. It also can provider insight on the nature of learning and the role it plays among social agents.

Acknowledgments

This work is supported in part by an Intel University Research Program grant to the second author. The model runs Pentium II based computers, also donated by the Intel Corporation.

References

[390]D. Ackley and M. Littman. Generalization and scaling in reinforcement learning. In *Advances in Neural Information Processing Systems 2*, 1990.

[391]A. Billard and G. Hayes. Learning to communicate through imitation in autonomous robots. In *Proceedings of the International Conference on Artificial Neural Networks*, 1997.

[392]A. Billard and G. Hayes. Drama: A connectionist architecture for control and learning in autonomous robots. *Adaptive Behavior*, 7(1), 1999.

[393]V. Braitenberg. *Vehicles: Experiments in Synthetic Psychology*. MIT Press, Cambridge, MA, USA, 1984.

[394]F. Cecconi, F. Menczer, and R. Belew. Maturation and the evolution of imitative learning in artificial organisms. *Adaptive Behavior*, 4(1), 1996.

[395]F. Cecconi and D. Parisi. Neural networks with motivational units. In *From animals to animats: Proceedings of the Second International Conference on Simulation of Adaptive*

Behavior, pages 346–355, 1993.

[396]P. S. Churchland and T. J. Sejnowski. *The Computational Brain*. Bradford Book/MIT Press, Cambridge, MA, 1992.

[397]F. L. Crabbe and M. G. Dyer. Maxson: Max-based second-order neural network reinforcement learner for mobile agents in continuous environments. Technical Report CSD-900009, UCLA, 1999.

[398]F. L. Crabbe and M. G. Dyer. Second-order networks for wall-building agents. In *Proceedings of the International Joint Conference on Neural Networks*, Washington D.C., July 1999.

[399]G. M. Edelman. *Neural Darwinism*. Basic Books, New York, 1987.

[400]C. L. Giles and T. Maxwell. Learning, invariance, and generalization in high-order neural networks. *Applied Optics*, 26(23):4972–4978, 1987.

[401]F. Gomez and R. Miikkulainen. Incremental evolution of complex general behavior. *Adaptive Behavior*, 5(3-4):317–347, 1997.

[402]D. O. Hebb. *The Organization of Behavior*. Wiley, NewYork, 1949.

[403]R. W. Oppenheim. Naturally occuring cell death during neural development. *Trends in Neurosciences*, 8:487–493, 1985.

[404]S. Russell and P. Norvig. *Artificial Intelligence. A Modern Approach*. MIT Press, Cambridge, MA, 1995.

[405]R. Sun and T. Peterson. Partitioning in reinforcement learning. In *Proceedings of the International Joint Conference on Neural Networks*, 1999.

[406]R. S. Sutton and A. G. Barto. *Reinforcement Learning*. MIT Press, Cambridge, MA, 1998.

[407]G. M. Werner. Using second order neural connection for motivation of behavioral choices. In *From animals to animats3: Proceedings of the Third International Conference on Simulation of Adaptive Behavior*, 1994.

12 Evolving Heterogeneous Neural Agents by Local Selection

Filippo Menczer, W. Nick Street, and Melania Degeratu

Evolutionary algorithms have been applied to the synthesis of neural architectures, but they normally lead to uniform populations. Homogeneous solutions, however, are inadequate for certain applications and models. For these cases, *local selection* may produce the desired heterogeneity in the evolving neural networks. This chapter describes algorithms based on local selection, and discusses the main differences distinguishing them from standard evolutionary algorithms. The use of local selection to evolve neural networks is illustrated by surveying previous work in three domains (simulations of adaptive behavior, realistic ecological models, and browsing information agents), as well as reporting on new results in feature selection for classification.

12.1 Introduction

The synthesis of neural architectures has been among the earliest applications of evolutionary computation [467, 408, 457, 420]. Evolutionary algorithms have been used to adjust the weights of neural networks without supervision [458, 453], to design neural architectures [456, 435, 427, 455], and to find learning rules [412].

Evolutionary algorithms, however, typically lead to uniform populations. This was appropriate in the above applications, since some optimal solution was assumed to exist. However, homogeneous solutions — neural or otherwise — are inadequate for certain applications and models, such as those requiring *cover* [421, 443] or *Pareto* [465, 431] optimization. Typical examples stem from expensive or multi-criteria fitness functions; in these cases, an evolutionary algorithm can be used to quickly find a set of alternative solutions using a simplified fitness function. Some other method is then charged with comparing these solutions.

Selection schemes have emerged as the aspect of evolutionary computation that most directly affects heterogeneity in evolutionary algorithms. In fact, selective pressure determines how fast the population converges to a uniform solution. The *exploration-exploitation* dilemma is commonly invoked to explain the delicate tension between an algorithm's efficiency and its tendency to prematurely converge to a suboptimal solution.

Parallel evolutionary algorithms often impose geographic constraints on evolutionary search to assist in the formation of diverse subpopulations [426,

415]. The motivation is in avoiding the communication overhead imposed by standard selection schemes; different processors are allocated to subpopulations to minimize inter-process dependencies and thus improve efficiency. The poor match between parallel implementations and the standard notion of optimization by convergence is noted for example by McInerney [443], who distinguishes between *convergence* — all individuals converging on the best solution — and *cover* — all good solutions being represented in the population — as measures of successful termination. Parallel evolutionary algorithms are more amenable to cover optimization than to standard convergence criteria, due to the limited communication inherent in most parallel implementations.

The problem of ill-convergence exhibited by traditional selection schemes is related to the issue of *niching*. In a niched evolutionary algorithm, according to Goldberg [421], stable subpopulations would ultimately form around each of the local fitness optima. Individual solutions in such subpopulations would be allocated in proportion to the magnitude of the fitness peaks.

Although there is a well-developed biological literature in niching [429], its transfer to artificial evolutionary search has been limited [421]. Standard evolutionary algorithms are ineffective for niching, due to high selective pressure and premature convergence [419]. Several methods have been devised to deal with this problem by maintaining diversity. One example for proportional selection is to tune the selective pressure adaptively, by a nonlinear scaling of the fitness function [454]. Different selection methods of course impose varying degrees of selection pressure. For example, tournament selection is known to converge slowly and to have niching effects [422].

The most notable selection variations explicitly aimed at niching are *crowding* [416, 438] and *fitness sharing* [424, 430, 439]. In both of these methods, selection is somehow altered to take into account some measure of similarity among individuals. Shortcomings of both methods are problem-dependency and inefficiency; if p is the population size, selection with sharing or crowding has time complexity $O(p)$ rather than $O(1)$ *per individual*. The slowdown can be important for practical cases with large populations, and computing similarity imposes a large communication overhead for parallel implementations. Moreover, even assuming that the number of niches H is known a priori, it is estimated that the population size required to maintain the population across niches grows rapidly with H [440]. The role of selection for multi-criteria and parallel optimization remains an active area of research in the evolutionary computation community [428, 441, 431].

This chapter discusses the *locality* of a selection scheme and its effects on an evolutionary algorithm's behavior with respect to convergence. We can loosely define *local selection* (LS) as a selection scheme that minimizes interactions among individuals. Locality in selection schemes has been a persistent theme in the evolutionary computation community [423, 425, 417, 441].

The chapter is organized as follows. Section 12.2 describes ELSA, an evolutionary algorithm based on a local selection scheme, which lends itself naturally to maintaining heterogeneous populations for cover optimization and multi-criteria applications. We illustrate the algorithm and outline its main distinctions from other evolutionary algorithms. Sections 12.3 and 12.4 demonstrate the problems and advantages of local selection by discussing its application in four neural domains, for cover and Pareto optimization, respectively. We show that although local selection is not a panacea, it may produce heterogeneous populations of neural networks when such diverse solutions are called for. Finally, in section 12.5 we summarize our conclusions and consider directions for further applications of local selection.

12.2   Evolution by Local Selection

Our original motivation for considering local selection in evolutionary algorithms stemmed from an interest in ecological modeling [448, 447]. Local selection is a more realistic reproduction scheme in an evolutionary model of real populations of organisms. In such a model, an agent's fitness must result from individual interactions with the environment, which contains shared resources along with other agents, rather than from global interactions across the population.

The Algorithm

We can best characterize local selection and succinctly describe its differences from global schemes by casting the evolutionary algorithm into an ecological framework. The resulting algorithm, which we call ELSA (Evolutionary Local Selection Algorithm), is illustrated at a high level of abstraction in figure 12.1.

Each agent (candidate solution) in the population is first initialized with some random solution and an initial reservoir of *energy*. If the algorithm is implemented sequentially, parallel execution of agents can be simulated with randomization of call order.

In each iteration of the algorithm, an agent explores a candidate solution (possibly including an action) similar to itself. The agent is taxed with E_{cost}

```
initialize population of p₀ agents, each with energy θ/2
while there are alive agents
    for each agent a
        a' ← perturb(a)
        ΔE ← e(Fitness(a'), E_envt)
        E_envt ← E_envt − ΔE
        E_a ← E_a + ΔE
        E_a ← E_a − E_cost
        if (E_a > θ)
            new(a')
            E_a' ← E_a/2
            E_a ← E_a − E_a'
        else if (E_a < 0)
            die(a)
        end
    end
    E_envt ← E_envt + E_replenish
end
```

Figure 12.1
ELSA pseudo-code.

for this action and collects ΔE from the environment. In the applications illustrated in this chapter, E_{cost} for any action is a constant unless otherwise stated. The net energy intake of an agent, expressed by the function $e()$, depends both on its fitness and on the state of the environment, i.e., on the number of other agents considering similar solutions (either in search or in criteria space, depending on the application). This is equivalent to a sort of environment-mediated crowding. Actions result in energetic benefits only inasmuch as the environment has sufficient energetic resources; if these are depleted, no benefits are available until the environmental resources are replenished.

In the selection part of the algorithm, an agent compares its current energy level with a threshold θ. If its energy is higher than θ, the agent reproduces. The mutated clone that was just evaluated becomes part of the population, with half of its parent's energy. When an agent runs out of energy, it is killed.

The environment acts as a data structure that keeps track of the net effects of the rest of the population. This way, direct communications between individuals (such as comparisons, ranking, or averaging of fitness values) become unnecessary, and the only interactions consist in the indirect competition for the finite environmental resources.

If we want to maintain the population average around some fixed value p_0 irrespective of problem size, we can let

$$E_{replenish} = p_0 \cdot E_{cost}. \qquad (12.1)$$

In fact, since energy is conserved, the average amount of energy that leaves the system per unit time (through costs) has to be equal to the amount of energy that enters the system per unit time (through replenishment):

$$\langle pE_{cost} \rangle = E_{replenish}$$
$$\langle p \rangle E_{cost} = p_0 E_{cost}$$
$$\langle p \rangle = p_0$$

where $\langle \cdot \rangle$ indicates time average.

In an implementation based on the pseudo-code of figure 12.1, some other details must be filled in. In particular, for neural agents, a solution can be represented by the weight vector of the neural net. If crossover is to be used, a candidate network can be recombined with another member of the population before being evaluated or before being inserted into the population, in case the parent is selected for reproduction. There has been ample discussion in the literature about the feasibility of recombination in the evolution of neural networks (see, e.g., [454, 453]), but such discussion is outside the scope of this chapter. Mutation is the only genetic operator used in the domains discussed in this chapter. The mutation operator provides evolving neural nets with a local search step, and the details of its dynamics are discussed for each task-specific application.

Local Versus Global Selection

Selection is the central point where this algorithm differs from most other evolutionary algorithms. Here an agent may die, reproduce, or neither (corresponding to the solution being eliminated from the pool, duplicated, or maintained). Energy is always conserved. The selection threshold θ is a constant independent of the rest of the population — hence selection is *local*. This fact reduces communication among agent processes to a minimum and has several positive consequences.

First, two agents compete for shared resources only if they are situated in the same portion of the environment (i.e., of the search or criteria space, depending on the application). It is the environment that drives this competition and the consequent selective pressure. No centralized decision must be made about how long an agent should live, how frequently it should reproduce, or when it should die. The search is biased directly by the environment.

Second, LS is an implicitly niched scheme and therefore it naturally enforces the maintenance of population diversity. This makes the search algorithm more amenable to cover and multi-modal optimization than to standard convergence criteria. The bias is to exploit all resources in the environment, rather than to locate the single best resource.

Third, the size of the population, rather than being determined a priori, emerges from the *carrying capacity* of the environment. This is determined by (i) the costs incurred by any action, and (ii) the replenishment of resources. Both of these factors are independent of the population.

Finally, the removal of selection's centralized bottleneck makes the algorithm parallelizable and therefore amenable to distributed implementations. ELSA is therefore an ideal candidate to study the potential speedup achievable by running agents on multiple remote hosts.

Local selection of course has disadvantages and limitations as well. Imagine a population of agents who can execute code on remote servers in a distributed environment, but have to look up data on a central machine for every action they perform. A typical example of such a situation would be a distributed information retrieval task in which agents share a centralized page cache. Because of communication overhead and synchronization issues, the parallel speedup achievable in this case would be seriously hindered. As this scenario indicates, the feasibility of distributed implementations of evolutionary algorithms based on local selection requires that the environment can be used as a data structure. Like natural organisms, agents must be able to "mark" the environment so that local interactions can take advantage of previous experience.

Local selection algorithms cannot immediately be applied to any arbitrary problem. First, a problem space may not lend itself to being used as a data structure. For example, marking the environment in continuous function optimization with arbitrary precision might hinder discretization and thus compromise the feasibility of local data structures. Second, it may be difficult to devise an isomorphism of the problem such that the environmental resource model could be applied successfully. For example, associating environmental resources to partial solutions of a combinatorial optimization problem may require a decomposition property that the problem is not known to possess.

In a multi-criteria or distributed task, the environment models the problem space and the resources that are locally available to individual solutions. It is in such cases that the distinction between local and global interactions among individuals becomes important; the selection mechanism and environmental resource model capture the nature of such interactions. In a standard evolutionary algorithm, an individual is selected for reproduction based on how its fitness

Table 12.1
Schematic comparison between local and global selection schemes. r-selection and K-selection refer to population models commonly used in ecology, which assume infinite and bounded resources, respectively.

Feature	Global selection	Local selection
reproduction threshold	$\theta = f(E_1, \ldots, E_{pop})$	$\theta = const$
search bias	exploitation	exploration
adaptive landscape	single-criterion	multi-criteria
convergence goal	single-point	cover
solution quality	best (fragile)	good (robust)
biological equivalent	r-selection	K-selection

compares with the rest of the population. For example, proportional selection can be modeled by a selection threshold $\langle E \rangle$, where $\langle \cdot \rangle$ indicates population average, for both reproduction (in place of θ) and death (in place of 0). Likewise, binary tournament selection can be modeled by a selection threshold E_r where the subscript r indicates a randomly picked individual. In local selection schemes, θ is independent of the rest of the population and the computations that determine whether an individual should die or reproduce can be carried out without need of direct comparisons with other individuals. Table 12.1 illustrates schematically the main features that differentiate the two classes of selection schemes.

12.3   Heterogeneous Neural Agents for Cover Optimization

We refer to neural agents here to mean evolving agents whose genetic representation is, or is associated with, a neural network. Many applications have been tackled with neural systems, and when examples are not available to supervise the training of the neural network, evolutionary algorithms represent one way to train the network in an unsupervised fashion — provided an evaluation function is available to compute fitness.

In this section we summarize previous work done in three different domains. In each case, a local selection algorithm similar to ELSA was used to evolve a population of neural agents for a distinct task. Each of the following subsections describe one such domain, motivates the use of the evolutionary local selection algorithm, and draws some observations based on the main results.

Coevolving Sensors and Behaviors in Toy Environments

The first domain we consider is an artificial life model simulating environments constructed *ad-hoc* to study the evolution of sensory systems.

Sensors represent a crucial link between the evolutionary forces shaping a species' relationship with its environment, and the individual's cognitive abilities to behave and learn. We used *latent energy environments* (LEE) models to define environments of carefully controlled complexity, which allowed us to state bounds for random and optimal behaviors, independent of strategies for achieving the behaviors. A description of the LEE framework is outside the scope of this chapter, and the interested reader is referred to [448, 447].

LEE provided us with an analytic basis for constructing the environments, a population of neural networks to represent individual behaviors, and an evolutionary local selection algorithm to model an adaptive process shaping the neural nets, in particular their input (sensory) system and their connection weights [446]. The experiments considered different types of sensors, and different sets of environmental resources that such sensors would detect. The idea was to study the conditions under which *efficient* (informative) sensory systems could be found by evolutionary synthesis.

The optimal sensory system was known by design, given the task faced by the LEE agents. Each agent had sensors providing perceptual information about its external (local) environment and sensors providing memory information about its internal ("gut") environment. The task involved navigating in a grid world and eating appropriate combinations of resources: if the gut contained a *dark* resource element, then the agent would gain energy by eating a *light* element, and vice versa. Combining two elements of the same resource would result in a loss of energy. The situation is illustrated in figure 12.2.

Evolving the weights of neural agents with optimal sensors resulted in behaviors corresponding to a carrying capacity approximately 3.5 times that of populations of random walkers (agents with "blind" sensors). However, evolving both neural network weights and sensory systems together yielded significant subpopulations with suboptimal sensors, and high variability of emerging behaviors caused by genetic drift. Optimal sensor configurations were not robust in the face of mutations, because they required finely tuned neural net weights. Conversely, many suboptimal sensory systems were robust because they could share weights, and the corresponding behaviors would not be necessarily disrupted by sensor mutations.

The genetic drift effect was overcome by allowing the neural nets to learn

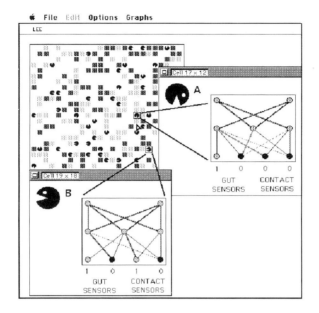

Figure 12.2
Two agents in similar circumstances but different sensory systems. Both agents have a light
element in their gut and one in front of them. The right move would be to veer away. Agent A has
inefficient sensors, because both of its contact sensors only detect dark elements in the cell facing
the agent. So the light element is not detected, and the agent might lose energy by going forward
and eating it. Agent B has an efficient sensory system. Its contact sensors detect the light element
in front of it, and the agent will be able to perform the right action.

via reinforcement learning during an agent's life. The weight changes due to
learning were not inherited by offspring, however, so that learning was non-
Lamarckian. This indirect interaction between learning and evolution was an
example of the so-called *Baldwin effect* [409]. This phenomenon provided the
neural agents with significantly more efficient sensory systems, as illustrated
in figure 12.3.

An important observation can be drawn from these experiments regarding
the use of evolutionary local selection algorithms with neural agents. Heterogeneity is not always a good thing: for this task, the selective pressure was insufficient to evolve both informative sensory systems and connection weights
that could exploit the sensory information. Evolutionary local selection algorithms are appropriate when we want to maintain a diverse population of local,
possibly suboptimal solutions, not when we are trying to converge to some

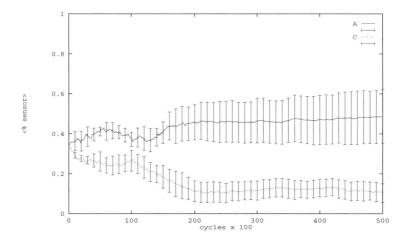

Figure 12.3
Percentages of efficient sensors (A) versus inefficient sensors (C) evolved in simulations with
non-Lamarckian reinforcement learning during life. (Reprinted from [446] with permission.)

optimal solution.

Foraging Efficiently in Marine Environments

Our second domain is a somewhat more realistic model of ecological environment, in which we study the evolution of behaviors and compare the predictions of the model with actual field data.

Tropical oceanic fishes, such as tunas, billfishes, and sharks, live together
in the same environment — the pelagic open ocean. *In situ* experiments have
been developed to observe horizontal and vertical movements of individuals of
different pelagic predator species, but there is a need for models that explain
the evolutionary origin of such movement behaviors, and their relationships
with these fishes' shared biotic environment or with other constraints, e.g.,
physiological ones.

We proposed a minimal model the explore the hypothesis that movement
behaviors are driven entirely by prey distributions and dynamics, and tested
the predictive power of this model with simulations based on the LEE framework [413]. In these experiments, the behaviors of an evolving population of
artificial fishes adapted in a three-dimensional environment. Spatial distribu-

tions, energetic values, and temporal dynamics (depth versus time of day) of two types of prey were based on data from observations of the open ocean in French Polynesia.

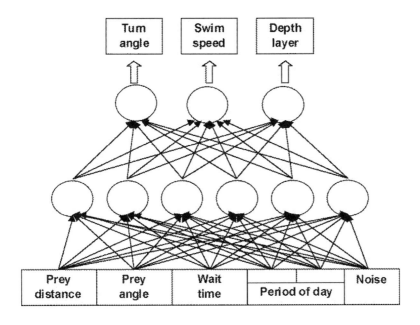

Figure 12.4
Architecture of the neural networks used to model the behaviors of tropical oceanic pelagic predator fishes.

Individuals were represented by simple neural agents as illustrated in figure 12.4. Agents could sense prey from the closest patch, without discerning prey types. They also had sensors indicating the time elapsed since the last eaten prey and the time of day. The energy spent swimming was a function of the swimming speed.

The evolutionary local selection algorithm was used to evolve a heterogeneous set of agents. At reproduction, mutations would add random noise (drawn from a uniform distribution between -1 and $+1$) to approximately 2% of the weights, randomly selected. All weights were bounded to the interval $[-5, +5]$.

The movement behaviors of evolved neural agents across ten simulations

Table 12.2
Correspondence between the most frequent vertical swimming patterns as predicted by the evolutionary model based on local selection and as observed in the most common tropical oceanic predator species. (Data from [413].)

Model fre-quency rank	Nighttime layer	Daytime layer	Species
1	surface	intermediate	Albacore tuna
2	surface	surface	Skipjack tuna, Striped marlin, Pacific blue marlin
2	surface	intermediate, surface	Yellowfin tuna
4	surface	intermediate, deep	Blue shark
5	surface	deep	Bigeye tuna, Swordfish

were analyzed and classified into patterns, then compared with those observed in real fishes (four species of tunas, three species of billfish, and one species of shark), mostly by acoustic telemetry. Beyond our expectations, most of the artificial individuals evolved vertical patterns virtually identical to those exhibited by fishes in the wild. The agreement between this simple computational model and ethological data, illustrated in table 12.2, validated the use of minimal assumption models for the study of behaviors in multi-species ecosystems.

From the viewpoint of the evolutionary synthesis of these neural agents, the main observation we draw from this work is that local selection allowed for the concurrent evolution of many heterogeneous behaviors to model this co-adapted multi-species system. Had a standard evolutionary algorithm been applied to this model, the population would have likely converged to one of the observed patterns. Given that the purpose of the experiment was not to search for one "optimal" behavior, but rather to identify a set of behaviors that could be compared with those of actual species, local selection was key in achieving this goal.

Browsing Adaptively in Information Environments

The third domain in which we have applied evolutionary local selection algorithms is the search for relevant information in documents across the Internet. Distributed information retrieval is an lively area of research due to the popularity of the Web and the scalability limitations of search engine technology [444, 437]. We tested the feasibility of local selection algorithms for distributed information retrieval problems by building artificial graphs to model different aspects of Web-like search environments [449, 445].

In each experiment we constructed a large graph, where each node was associated with some payoff. Nodes, edges, and payoffs modeled hypertext documents, hyperlinks, and relevance, respectively. The population of agents visited the graph as agents traversed its edges. The idea was to maximize the collective payoff of visited nodes, given that there would be only time to visit a fraction of the nodes in the graph. Since the modeled search graph is typically distributed across remote servers, agents were charged costs for traversing edges and evaluating nodes' payoff. Each link l was also associated with a feature vector with components $f_1^l, \ldots, f_{N_f}^l \in [0, 1]$. These features modeled environmental cues, such as word frequencies, that could guide a browsing neural agent toward relevant nodes.

Each agent's genotype comprised a single-layer neural net or perceptron, i.e., a weight vector with components $w_1, \ldots, w_{N_f+1} \in R$. Link feature vectors were used as inputs by these neural agents. Node payoffs and link feature vectors were constructed in such a way as to guarantee the existence of a set of weights that, if used by a neural agent, would yield an "accurate" prediction of the payoff of the node pointed to by the input link. The prediction accuracy of such optimal weight vector was a user-defined parameter.

The agent's representation also specified the node on which the agent was currently situated. Therefore an action consisted, first of all, of evaluating each outlink from the current node. The outputs of the neural net would represent the agent's predictions of the payoffs of the nodes reachable from the current node. The agent then followed a link picked by a stochastic selector. As for the other applications, some fraction of the weights were mutated by additive uniform noise at reproduction.

The energetic benefit of an action was the payoff of the newly visited node, provided it had not been previously visited by any agent. Nodes were therefore "marked" to keep track of used resources (no replenishment). A constant energy cost was charged for any node visited. The goal was to evolve agents with optimal genotypes, enabling them to follow the best links and thus achieve maximum payoff intake.

To gauge the performance of ELSA in the graph search problem, we compared local selection with a traditional evolutionary algorithm. To this end we replaced local selection by binary tournament selection because the latter scheme was "traditional" (i.e., global) and yet it did not require operations such as averaging, and thus it fit naturally within the steady-state framework of ELSA. Basically the same algorithm of figure 12.1 was used, with the difference that the energy level of a randomly chosen member of the population was used in place of both θ for reproduction and 0 for death.

We ran a set of experiments on random graphs with 1000 nodes, an average fanout of 5 links, and 16 features per link. Nodes with payoff above some threshold were considered "good." The algorithm was stopped when 50% of all the nodes had been visited. Then the fraction of good nodes found by the population up to that point (*recall*) was recorded. The random graphs were generated according to several distinct parameterizations. Across all such parameterizations, ELSA significantly and consistently outperformed tournament selection. Local selection populations continued to discover a constant rate of good nodes, while tournament populations tended to converge prematurely. The improvement depended on the graph parameters, but was generally between two- and ten-fold.

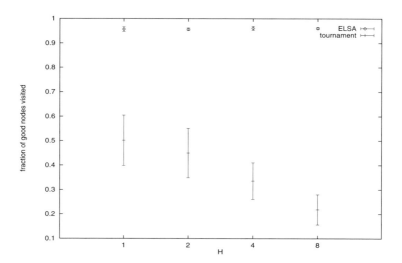

Figure 12.5
Performance of ELSA and tournament selection on graph search problems with various values of H. (Data from [449].)

An example of this performance is shown in figure 12.5. Here, the algorithms were tested on graphs with various values of H, the number of "good clusters." Good nodes were clustered in the sense that they had a higher probability to be linked to other nodes in the same cluster than to nodes in other clusters or to "bad" nodes. Increasing H made the problem multi-modal, and therefore tournament selection degraded in performance due to premature convergence.

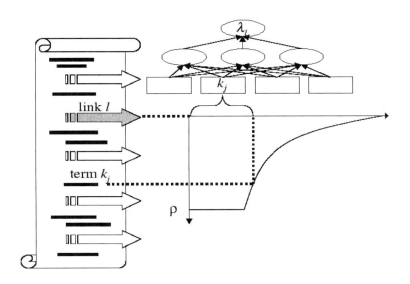

Figure 12.6
How an *InfoSpider* estimates each link from the current document. An agent genotype comprises both a neural net and a vector of terms, one per input. For each link in the document, each input of the neural net is computed by counting the document words matching the keyword corresponding to that input, with weights that decay with distance from the link. (Reprinted from [450] with permission.)

A more sophisticated representation of neural agents, called *InfoSpiders*, is shown in figure 12.6. These agents adapt to user preferences and to local context through both reinforcement learning and an evolutionary local selection algorithm. Evolution is used also to select word features, which determine the inputs of the neural net. Reinforcement learning is used to adjust the connection weights and improve link estimation during an agent's life. *InfoSpiders* have been used to search through actual Web data with very promising preliminary results [452, 450]. For example, figure 12.7 shows the result of a comparison in performance between *InfoSpiders* and best-first-search, on a hypertext collection from Encyclopedia Britannica Online [445]. *InfoSpiders* had a significant advantage when the relevant set was not too many links away from the starting page. These results point to the need for hybrid systems that use search engines to provide good starting points and *InfoSpiders* to search for recent information.

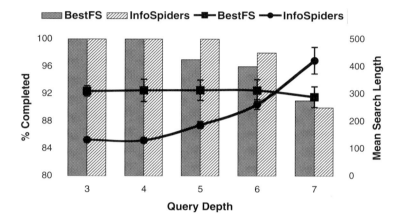

Figure 12.7
Performance of *InfoSpiders* versus best-first-search. Completed queries (bars) were those for which the search algorithms could locate 10% of the relevant documents before running out of time. For these queries we recorded *search length* (lines), the number of non relevant pages visited, averaged over queries whose relevant sets were at the same distance (*depth*) from the starting page. (Data from [445].)

The same algorithmic observation made for the ecological modeling domain applies to applications in the information search domain. Here, cover optimization is necessary because we want the agents to locate as many relevant documents as possible, rather than one "most relevant" document. Local selection algorithms make this objective evolutionarily achievable.

12.4   Heterogeneous Neural Agents for Pareto Optimization

In these experiments we consider the problem of feature subset selection in inductive or similarity-based machine learning. Given two disjoint sets A_1 and A_2 of feature vectors in some n-dimensional space, the problem is to construct a separating surface that allows future examples to be correctly classified as being members of either A_1 or A_2. Here we use neural networks as the classification method, and limit ourselves to two-class problems.

In order to construct classifiers that generalize well to unseen points, it is important to control the complexity of the model. In many domains, biasing the learning system toward simpler models results in better accuracy, as well as more interpretable models. One way to control complexity is through the selection of an appropriate subset of the predictive features for model building. There is a trade-off between training accuracy and model complexity; it is difficult to determine, for a given problem, the relative importance of these two competing objectives.

The feature selection problem is an example of multi-criteria or Pareto optimization, in which more than one objective is optimized at the same time [462, 465]. In the general case, when faced with a multi-criteria problem, the decision maker does not know how the various objectives should be combined. Therefore, the goal of the solver is to find the set of solutions that represents the best compromises between conflicting criteria. This set is called the *Pareto front*. The ELSA framework is particularly well-suited for Pareto optimization because it maintains populations of heterogeneous solutions. By mapping different criteria to different environmental resources, we can create the conditions for agents exploiting different regions of the Pareto space to coexist [451]. Competition occurs along the shared resources, i.e., orthogonally to the Pareto front.

Feature Selection

From a data mining perspective, the problem of determining which predictive features contribute the most to the accuracy of the model is often an important goal in its own right. This is particularly true in medical domains, where a particular feature may be the result of a diagnostic test that can be time-consuming, costly, or dangerous. We examine one such domain in our experiments.

The combinatorial feature selection problem has been studied extensively in the machine learning and statistics literature. Heuristic search methods such as forward selection and backward elimination have long been used in contexts such as regression [418]. Exact solutions may be found using integer programming [460] if one assumes that the error metric is monotonic, which is not the case when estimating out-of-sample error. John [433] makes the distinction between *wrapper* models, which choose feature subsets in the context of the classification algorithm, and *filter* models, such as Relief [434],

which choose a subset before applying the classification method. Bradley *et al.*
[411] build feature minimization directly into the classification objective, and
solve using parametric optimization.

The method described here uses the evolutionary algorithm to search
through the space of possible subsets, estimating generalization accuracy for
each examined subset. A similar approach, along with a thorough overview of
the field, can be found in [469]. Feature selection in neural networks can be
seen as a more specific instance of the architecture selection problem; see for
instance [461]. Other recent surveys of the feature selection problem may be
found in [436] and [414].

Algorithmic Details

In order to isolate the effect of feature selection, the architecture of each
neural network is set in such a way to keep the complexity of the networks
approximately constant. We use the heuristic that the number of weights in the
network should be no more than some small fraction of the number of training
cases [459]. For example, for a training set with 500 instances, a network with
5 input features would require 3 hidden units, while a network with 10 input
features would have only 2 hidden units.

Training of the individual neural networks is performed using standard
backpropagation [463]. Note that this is in contrast to the applications of
section 12.3, in which evolution was used to adjust the weights and biases in
the networks. Here, the evolutionary algorithm is used solely to search through
the space of possible feature subsets.

$$\Delta E \leftarrow e(Fitness(a'), E_{envt})$$
$$E_{envt} \leftarrow E_{envt} - \Delta E$$
$$E_a \leftarrow E_a + \Delta E$$

for each energy source k
$$\Delta E \leftarrow \min(Fitness(a', k), E^k_{envt})$$
$$E^k_{envt} \leftarrow E^k_{envt} - \Delta E$$
$$E_a \leftarrow E_a + \Delta E$$
end

Figure 12.8
Original ELSA pseudo-code (left, cf. figure 12.1) and the version adapted for multi-criteria
optimization (right).

The ELSA algorithm in figure 12.1 was slightly modified to account for the
multiple environmental resources corresponding to the fitness criteria [451].
The change is illustrated in figure 12.8. The environment corresponds to the
set of possible values (or intervals) for each of the criteria being optimized. We

imagine an energy source for each criterion, divided into bins corresponding to its values. So, for criterion F_k and value v, the environment keeps track of the energy $E_{envt}^k(v)$ corresponding to the value $F_k = v$. Further, the environment keeps a count of the number of agents $P_k(v)$ having $F_k = v$. The energy corresponding to an action (alternative solution) a for criterion F_k is given by

$$Fitness(a, k) = \frac{F_k(a)}{P_k(F_k(a))}. \tag{12.2}$$

```
E_replenish  ←  E_bin · B
for each  energy source  k
    for each  bin  v
        δE  ←  min(E_replenish, E_bin − E_envt^k(v))
        E_replenish  ←  E_replenish − δE
        E_envt^k(v)  ←  E_envt^k(v) + δE
    end
end
```

Figure 12.9
ELSA energy replenishment pseudo-code for multi-criteria optimization.

Figure 12.9 shows how the environment is replenished at each time step. The quantity E_{bin} is typically a constant (cf. $E_{replenish}$ in equation 12.1). The idea is to fill each bin to E_{bin}. B is the total number of values taken by all criteria, or bins into which the values of continuous criteria are discretized. Thus the total amount of replenishment energy could depend on the size of the problem. However, in order to maintain the population average around some fixed value irrespective of the problem size, we can set

$$E_{bin} = \frac{E_{replenish}}{B} = \frac{p_0 \cdot E_{cost}}{B}. \tag{12.3}$$

In this application the genotype of a neural agent is a bit string s with length equal to the dimensionality of the feature space, N. Each bit is set to 1 if the feature is to be used, and 0 otherwise. We thus measure the complexity of the classifier as simply the fraction of features being used. Each time an agent is evaluated, 2/3 of the examples in the data set are randomly chosen as a training set for a newly constructed neural net (using the features selected by the genotype as inputs). Online backpropagation is applied until the training error converges. Then the remaining 1/3 of the examples is used as a test set and the generalization error is used to compute the prediction accuracy of the

Table 12.3
Parameter values used with ELSA in the feature selection problem. Note that mutation consists of flipping one random bit.

Parameter	Value
E_{cost}	0.3
θ	0.2
p_0	100
B	$(N+1) + 20$
$\Pr(mutation)$	1

trained neural agent. Our criteria to be maximized are therefore

$$F_{complexity}(s) \quad = \quad \frac{\text{number of zeros in } s}{N} \tag{12.4}$$

$$F_{accuracy}(s) \quad = \quad \text{generalization accuracy using feature vector } s. \tag{12.5}$$

The application of ELSA to this problem is a straightforward implementation of the algorithm in figure 12.1, with the change of figure 12.8 and equation 12.2, and the two criteria of equations 12.4 and 12.5. Bins are created in correspondence to each of the possible values of the criteria. While $F_{complexity}$ has $N+1$ discrete values (between 0 and 1), $F_{accuracy}$ takes continues values and thus must be discretized into bins. We use 20 bins for the accuracy criterion. The values of the various algorithm parameters are shown in table 12.3. Some of the parameters are preliminarily tuned. Replenishment takes place as shown in figure 12.9, with E_{bin} determined according to Equation 12.3. [1]

For these experiments we compare the performance of ELSA with a well-known multi-criteria evolutionary algorithm, the Niched Pareto Genetic Algorithm (NPGA) [432, 431]. In NPGA, Pareto domination tournament selection is used in conjunction with fitness sharing. Pareto domination tournaments are binary tournaments in which the domination of each candidate is assessed with respect to a randomly chosen sample of the population. If a candidate dominates the whole sample and the other candidate does not, then the dominant candidate wins the tournament. If both or neither candidates dominate the whole sample, then the tournament is won by the candidate with the lower niche count. The latter is, roughly, a weighted count of individuals within distance σ_{share} in criteria space. The size of the sample, t_{dom}, is used to regulate

---

1 In this experiment only about half of the available energy is used by the ELSA population, so that the actual population size oscillates around $p_0/2$.

Table 12.4
Parameter values used with NPGA in the feature selection problem. As for ELSA, mutation consists of flipping one random bit.

Parameter	Value
σ_{share}	14.0
t_{dom}	16
p	100
$\Pr(mutation)$	1

the selective pressure. NPGA has proven very successful in Pareto optimization over a range of problems. The various parameters used for NPGA are shown in table 12.4. Several of the parameter values are the result of preliminary parameter tuning. For example, the performance of NPGA was deteriorated by the use of crossover in this setting, and therefore the recombination operator was eliminated.

Data Sets

Experiments were performed on two data sets, both of which are available at the UC-Irvine Machine Learning Repository [410].

Wisconsin Prognostic Breast Cancer (WPBC) data: The predictive problem in the WPBC [442] data is to determine whether a particular breast cancer patient can be expected to have a recurrence of the disease within 5 years after surgery. The examples in the each contain $N = 33$ predictive features. They include morphometry information on the individual cell nuclei taken from a cytology slide, along with traditional prognostic factors such as tumor size and metastatic status of local lymph nodes. There are 62 positive examples and 166 negative examples.

Ionosphere data: The task in the Ionosphere data [464] is to discriminate "good" (structured) vs. "bad" (unstructured) antenna returns from free electrons in the ionosphere. The examples consist of $N = 34$ continuous attributes. There are 351 examples, divided between 225 good and 126 bad returns.

Experimental Results

In the feature subset selection problem, the evaluation of the criteria appears as a black box to the evolutionary algorithms. The accuracy computation is expensive and completely dominates the time complexities of the algorithms. Therefore the only operations that contribute to the measured time complexity of the algorithms are the accuracy criterion computations, and time is measured in number of $F_{accuracy}$ evaluations.

We ran the two algorithms for 100,000 function evaluations. Each run, on a dedicated 400 MHz P2 Linux workstation, took approximately 5 minutes for the WPBC data set and 47 minutes for the Ionosphere data set.

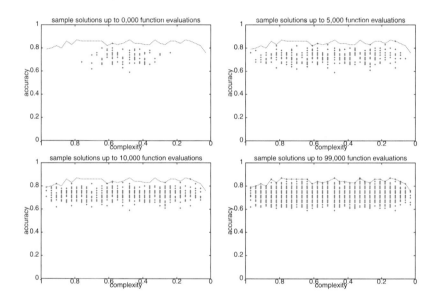

Figure 12.10
Cumulative ELSA populations in Pareto phase-space for the WPBC data set. The x-axis labels indicate the fraction of features used. The snapshots plot samples of the neural agents up to 0, 5, 10, and 99 thousand function evaluations. The convex hull of the sampled populations up to 99,000 evaluations is also shown; the actual Pareto front is unknown.

Figure 12.10 pictures the population dynamics of the ELSA algorithm for the WPBC data set in Pareto phase-space, i.e., the space where the criteria values are used as coordinates. The Pareto front is unknown, so we can only observe the populations and qualitatively assess their progress relative to one another. Since we want to maximize accuracy and minimize complexity, we know that a solution represented as a point in Pareto phase-space is dominated by solutions above it (more accurate) or to its right-hand side (less complex).

The estimated Pareto front in figure 12.10 is nearly flat, reflecting the fact that the complexity of the neural networks was held nearly constant. Still, we see that using only one or two features is insufficient to learn the concept, and using nearly all of them leads to overfitting. The apparent best agent used five input features, reflecting a mix of nuclear size (area, radius) and nuclear shape (symmetry, concavity) features. Interestingly, it did not use lymph node status, a traditional prognostic factor. Removal of these lymph nodes is an extra surgical procedure, performed purely for prognosis, that leaves the patient vulnerable to infection and lymphedema, a painful swelling of the arm. This result supports previous evidence that detailed nuclear morphometry is equal or superior to lymph status as a prognostic measure [466, 468].

ELSA is able to cover the entire range of feature vector complexities. A quantitative measure of coverage can be obtained by measuring the "area" of Pareto space covered by the population of algorithm X at time t:

$$S_X(t) = \sum_{c=0}^{1} \max_{a \in P_X(t)} \left(F_{accuracy}(a) | F_{complexity}(a) = c \right)$$

where $P_X(t)$ is the population of algorithm X at time t. Figure 12.11 plots the areas S_{ELSA} and S_{NPGA} versus time, for each data set. NPGA eventually converges to a subpopulation with inferior coverage of the Pareto front, and ELSA achieves significantly better performance.

12.5   Conclusion

This chapter discussed a particular type of evolutionary algorithms, those using local selection, and their use in the synthesis of neural architectures. We have shown that local selection can be feasible, efficient, and effective in evolving populations of heterogeneous neural agents. This is necessary when *cover* or *Pareto* optimization are more desirable than convergence to a single (global or local) optimum.

As demonstrated in section 12.3, there are certainly many cases when a strong selective pressure is necessary, and local selection is inappropriate. We have found this to be the case when we applied ELSA to NP-complete combinatorial optimization problems such as SAT and TSP [449]. The only selective pressure that ELSA can apply comes from the sharing of resources. Therefore the way in which environmental resources are coupled with the problem space in a particular application of ELSA is crucial to its success.

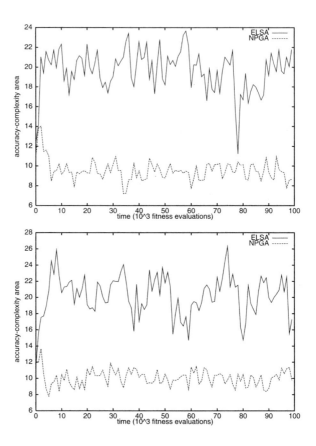

Figure 12.11
Plots of the areas covered in Pareto phase-space by the ELSA and NPGA populations over time, for the WPBC (top) and Ionosphere (bottom) data sets.

One limitation of ELSA is in the fact that the appropriate mapping of a problem onto an environmental model may be hard to determine.

However, there are many applications where we need to maintain a diverse population of alternative solutions. Section 12.3 illustrated two such examples from the domains of ecological modeling and autonomous information agents. Furthermore, heterogeneous neural architectures are required for multi-criteria problems in which the goal is to maintain a population that approximates the Pareto front. Section 12.4 discussed two examples of real-world classification tasks, where the evolutionary local selection algorithm was used to select important features, allowing neural networks to be trained as both parsimonious and accurate predictors.

LS algorithms can be used whenever the fitness function is evaluated by an external environment, in the sense that the environment provides appropriate data structures for maintaining the shared resources associated with fitness. Consider, for example, evaluating a robot in a physical environment: the environment itself holds information about its state. The robot prompts for some of this information through its sensors, and storing such information may be less efficient than simply prompting for the same information again as needed. It may be impossible to store *all* relevant observations about a distributed, dynamic environment. The environment therefore takes the role of a data structure, to be queried inexpensively for current environmental state.

At a minimum, in order for LS to be feasible, an environment must allow for "marking" so that resources may be shared and in finite quantities. In the graph search domain, we have seen that visited nodes are marked so that the same node does not yield payoff multiple times. If InfoSpiders were implemented with mobile agents, this would create a problem of distributed caching. If marking is allowed and performed in constant time, LS also has constant time complexity per individual. This is a big win over the selection schemes of alternative niched evolutionary algorithms, such as fitness sharing and Pareto domination tournaments, whose complexity scales linearly with the population size [431].

Evolutionary local selection algorithms can be extended and applied in many ways. One extension that we have not discussed is the use of recombination operators in ELSA. As stated in section 12.2, crossover is not used in evolving any of the neural agents described in this chapter. Actually, we ran the experiments described in section 12.4 using crossover as well. For ELSA, the mate was a randomly chosen agent. Since we did not expect any correlation across features in these classification tasks, uniform crossover was applied: each bit for whose value the parents disagreed was set to 0 or 1 with equal probability. As it turned out, the performance with crossover was inferior. These results and, more in general, the interactions between local selection and recombination, in particular with local rather than panmictic mating, deserve further analysis in the future.

The application to inductive learning discussed in this chapter can be extended to perform wrapper-model feature subset selection. Local selection can be applied as in the experiments described in section 12.4 to identify promising feature subsets of various sizes. The best of these can then be subjected to a more thorough and costly analysis such as cross-validation to obtain a more reliable estimate of generalization accuracy. This approach would be particularly attractive in an "any-time learning" context, in which little overhead would be required to maintain a record of the best individual encountered so far. Note that the measure of complexity can easily be adapted to other predictive models such as decision trees or linear classifiers [451]. We are also using ELSA for Pareto optimization in clustering problems, where the number of clusters can be used as a third fitness criterion.

Local selection can also serve as a framework for experiments with ensemble classifiers. By extending the environmental model to associate resources with features, in addition to criteria values, we can encourage individual classifiers to specialize in particular regions of the feature space. The predictions of these "orthogonal" classifiers can then be combined (say, by voting) to produce a single classification system that is more accurate than any of the individuals working alone.

Finally, distributed robotics is another application area for which evolutionary local selection algorithms may prove feasible. For example, populations of robots may be faced with unknown, heterogeneous environments in which it is important to pay attention to many sensory cues and maintain a wide range of behaviors to be deployed depending on local conditions.

Acknowledgments

The authors are most grateful to Rik Belew, Laurent Dagorn, and Alvaro Monge, who collaborated on the research reported in section 12.3. The work described in this chapter was supported in part by a travel grant from the University of Iowa, Apple Computers, Encyclopedia Britannica, University of Iowa CIFRE grant 50254180, NSF grant IIS 99-96044, and the University of Iowa College of Business Summer Grant Program.

References

[408]R. Albrecht, C. Reeves, and N. Steele, editors. *Proc. International Conference on Artificial Neural Networks and Genetic Algorithms.* Springer-Verlag, 1993.

[409]R. Belew and M. Mitchell, editors. *Adaptive Individuals in Evolving Populations: Models and Algorithms.* Santa Fe Institute Studies in the Sciences of Complexity. Addison Wesley, Reading, MA, 1996.

[410]C. L. Blake and C. J. Merz. UCI repository of machine learning databases [http://www.ics.uci.edu/~mlearn/MLRepository.html], 1998. University of California, Irvine,

Department of Information and Computer Sciences.

[411]P. S. Bradley, O. L. Mangasarian, and W. N. Street. Feature selection via mathematical programming. *INFORMS Journal on Computing*, 10(2):209–217, 1998.

[412]D. Chalmers. The evolution of learning: an experiment in genetic connectionism. In *Proc. 1990 Connectionist Models Summer School*, 1990.

[413]L. Dagorn, F. Menczer, P. Bach, and R. Olson. Co-evolution of movement behaviors by tropical pelagic predatory fishes in response to prey environment: A simulation model. Submitted to Ecological Modeling.

[414]M. Dash and H. Liu. Feature selectin for classification. *Intelligent Data Analysis*, 1(3):131–156, 1997.

[415]Y. Davidor. A naturally occurring niche and species phenomenon: The model and first results. In R. Belew and L. Booker, editors, *Proceedings of the 4th International Conference on Genetic Algorithms*, 1991.

[416]K. De Jong. *An analysis of the behavior of a class of genetic adaptive systems*. PhD thesis, University of Michigan, 1975.

[417]K. De Jong and J. Sarma. On decentralizing selection algorithms. In *Proc. 6th ICGA*, 1995.

[418]N. R. Draper. *Applied Regression Analysis*. John Wiley and Sons, New York, 3rd edition, 1998.

[419]L. Eshelman and J. Schaffer. Crossover's niche. In *Proceedings of the 5th International Conference on Genetic Algorithms*, 1993.

[420]D. Fogel. *Evolutionary Computation: The fossil record*, chapter 17, pages 481–484. IEEE Press, 1989.

[421]D. Goldberg. *Genetic Algorithms in Search, Optimization, and Machine Learning*, pages 185–197. Addison-Wesley, Reading, MA, 1989.

[422]D. Goldberg. A note on Boltzmann tournament selection for genetic algorithms and population-oriented simulated annealing. *Complex Sustems*, 4:445–460, 1990.

[423]D. Goldberg and K. Deb. A comparative analysis of selection schemes used in genetic algorithms. In G. Rawlings, editor, *Foundations of Genetic Algorithms*. Morgan Kaufmann, 1991.

[424]D. Goldberg and J. Richardson. Genetic algorithms with sharing for multimodal function optimization. In *Proceedings of the 2nd International Conference on Genetic Algorithms*, 1987.

[425]V. Gordon and D. Whitley. Serial and parallel genetic algorithms as function optimizers. In *Proceedings of the 5th International Conference on Genetic Algorithms*, 1993.

[426]P. Grosso. *Computer Simulation of Genetic Adaptation: Parallel Subcomponent Interaction in a Multilocus Model*. PhD thesis, University of Michigan, 1985.

[427]F. Gruau. Genetic synthesis of boolean neural networks with a cell rewriting developmental process. In *COGANN-92: International Workshop on Combinations of Genetic Algorithms and Neural Networks*, 1992.

[428]G. Harik. Finding multimodal solutions using restricted tournament selection. In *Proceedings of the 6th International Conference on Genetic Algorithms*, 1995.

[429]D. Hartl and A. Clarke. *Principles of Population Genetics*. Sinauer Associates, 1989.

[430]J. Horn. Finite markov chain analysis of genetic algorithms with niching. In *Proc. 5th ICGA*, 1993.

[431]J. Horn. Multicriteria decision making and evolutionary computation. In *Handbook of Evolutionary Computation*. Institute of Physics Publishing, 1997.

[432]J. Horn, N. Nafpliotis, and D. Goldberg. A niched pareto genetic algorithm for multiobjective optimization. In *Proc. 1st IEEE Conf. on Evolutionary Computation*, 1994.

[433]G. H. John, R. Kohavi, and K. Pfleger. Irrelevant features and the subset selection problem. In *Proceedings of the 11th International Conference on Machine Learning*, San Mateo, CA,

1994. Morgan Kaufmann.

[434]K. Kira and L. Rendell. The feature selection problem: Traditional methods and a new algorithm. In *Proceedings of the Tenth National Conference on Artificial Intelligence*, pages 129–134, San Mateo, CA, 1992. Morgan Kaufmann.

[435]H. Kitano. Designing neural networks using genetic algorithms with graph generation system. *Complex Systems*, 4:461–476, 1990.

[436]P. Langley. Selection of relevant features in machine learning. In *Proceedings of the AAAI Fall Symposium on Relevance*, pages 1–5. AAAI Press, 1994.

[437]S. Lawrence and C. Giles. Searching the world wide web. *Science*, 280:98–100, 1998.

[438]S. Mahfoud. Crowding and preselection revisited. In *Parallel Problem Solving from Nature 2*, 1992.

[439]S. Mahfoud. Simple analytical models of genetic algorithms for multimodal function optimization. In *Proc. 5th ICGA*, 1993.

[440]S. Mahfoud. Population sizing for sharing methods. In *Foundations of Genetic Algorithms 3*, 1994.

[441]S. Mahfoud. A comparison of parallel and sequential niching methods. In *Proc. 6th ICGA*, 1995.

[442]O. L. Mangasarian, W. N. Street, and W. H. Wolberg. Breast cancer diagnosis and prognosis via linear programming. *Operations Research*, 43(4):570–577, July-August 1995.

[443]J. McInerney. *Biologically Influenced Algorithms and Parallelism in Non-Linear Optimization*. PhD thesis, University of California, San Diego, 1992.

[444]F. Menczer. ARACHNID: Adaptive retrieval agents choosing heuristic neighborhoods for information discovery. In *Proc. 14th Intl. Conf. on Machine Learning*, 1997.

[445]F. Menczer. *Life-like agents: Internalizing local cues for reinforcement learning and evolution*. PhD thesis, University of California, San Diego, 1998.

[446]F. Menczer and R. Belew. Evolving sensors in environments of controlled complexity. In R. Brooks and P. Maes, editors, *Artificial Life IV*, Cambridge, MA, 1994. MIT Press.

[447]F. Menczer and R. Belew. From complex environments to complex behaviors. *Adaptive Behavior*, 4:317–363, 1996.

[448]F. Menczer and R. Belew. Latent energy environments. In *Adaptive Individuals in Evolving Populations: Models and Algorithms*. Addison Wesley, 1996.

[449]F. Menczer and R. Belew. Local selection. In *Proc. 7th Annual Conference on Evolutionary Programming*, San Diego, CA, 1998.

[450]F. Menczer and R. Belew. Adaptive retrieval agents: Internalizing local context and scaling up to the web. *Machine Learning*, 1999. Forthcoming.

[451]F. Menczer, M. Degeratu, and W. Street. Efficient and scalable pareto optimization by evolutionary local selection algorithms. Submitted to Evolutionary Computation Journal.

[452]F. Menczer and A. Monge. Scalable web search by adaptive online agents: An InfoSpiders case study. In M. Klusch, editor, *Intelligent Information Agents: Agent-Based Information Discovery and Management on the Internet*. Springer, 1999.

[453]F. Menczer and D. Parisi. Evidence of hyperplanes in the genetic learning of neural networks. *Biological Cybernetics*, 66:283–289, 1992.

[454]F. Menczer and D. Parisi. Recombination and unsupervised learning: Effects of crossover in the genetic optimization of neural networks. *Network*, 3:423–442, 1992.

[455]O. Miglino, S. Nolfi, and D. Parisi. Discontinuity in evolution: How different levels of organization imply preadaptation. In *Adaptive Individuals in Evolving Populations: Models and Algorithms*. Addison Wesley, 1996.

[456]G. Miller, P. Todd, and S. Hedge. Designing neural networks using genetic algorithms. In *Proc. 3rd International Conf. on Genetic Algorithms*, 1989.

[457]M. Mitchell. *An introduction to genetic algorithms.* MIT Press, 1996.

[458]D. Montana and L. Davis. Training feedforward networks using genetic algorithms. In *Proc. Internationsl Joint Conf. on Artificial Intelligence*, 1989.

[459]J. Moody. The effective number of parameters: An analysis of generalization and regularization in nonlinear learning systems. In *Advances in Neural Information Processing Systems 4*, 1992.

[460]P. M. Narendra and K. Fukunaga. A branch and bound algorithm for feature subset selection. *IEEE Transactions on Computers*, C-26(9):917–922, September 1977.

[461]D. W. Opitz and J. W. Shavlik. Connectionist theory refinement: Genetically searching the space of network topologies. *Journal of Artificial Intelligence Research*, 6(1):177–209, 1997.

[462]V. Pareto. *Manual of political economy.* Kelley, New York, 1971.

[463]D. E. Rumelhart, G. E. Hinton, and R. J. Williams. Learning internal representations by error propagation. In D. E. Rumelhart and J. L. McClelland, editors, *Parallel Distributed Processing*, volume 1, chapter 8. MIT Press, Cambridge, MA, 1986.

[464]V. G. Sigillito, S. P. Wing, L. V. Hutton, and K. B. Baker. Classification of radar returns from the ionosphere using neural networks. *Johns Hopkins APL Technical Digest*, 10:262–266, 1989.

[465]R. E. Steuer. *Multiple Criteria Optimization: Theory, Computation, and Application.* John Wiley and Sons, 1986.

[466]W. N. Street. A neural network model for prognostic prediction. In J. Shavlik, editor, *Machine Learning: Proceedings of the Fifteenth International Conference*, pages 540–546, San Francisco, CA, 1998. Morgan Kaufmann.

[467]L. Whitley and J. Schaffer, editors. *COGANN-92: International Workshop on Combinations of Genetic Algorithms and Neural Networks.* IEEE Computer Society Press, 1992.

[468]W. H. Wolberg, W. N. Street, and O. L. Mangasarian. A comparison of computer-based nuclear analysis versus lymph node status for staging breast cancer. *Clinical Cancer Research*, 1999. Forthcoming.

[469]J. Yang and V. Honavar. Feature subset selection using a genetic algorithm. In H. Motoda and H. Liu, editors, *Feature Extraction, Construction, and Subset Selection: A Data Mining Perspective.* Kluwer, New York, NY, 1998.

13 Learning Sequential Decision Tasks through Symbiotic Evolution of Neural Networks

David E. Moriarty and Risto Miikkulainen

This chapter presents an approach called SANE for learning and performing sequential decision tasks. Compared to problem-general heuristics, SANE forms more effective decision strategies because it learns to utilize domain-specific information. SANE evolves neural networks through a genetic algorithm and can learn in a wide range of domains with minimal reinforcement. SANE's genetic algorithm, called symbiotic evolution, is more powerful than standard genetic algorithms because diversity pressures are inherent in the task of each individual. SANE is shown to be effective in two sequential decision tasks. As a value-ordering method in constraint satisfaction search, SANE required only 1/3 of the backtracks of a problem-general heuristic. As a filter for minimax search, SANE formed a network capable of focusing the search away from misinformation, creating stronger play.

13.1 Introduction

Sequential decision tasks [472, 474] can be characterized by the following scenario: An agent observes a state of a dynamic system and chooses from a finite set of actions. The system then enters a new state upon which the agent must select another action. The system may return a payoff after each decision made or after a sequence of decisions. The objective is to select the sequence of actions that return the highest cumulative payoff. Often the best strategy is not to maximize each individual payoff, because some actions may produce high immediate payoffs but may enter states from which high later payoffs are impossible. Developing good strategies involves assigning credit to individual decisions based on the overall payoff, which is a difficult problem in machine learning known as the *credit assignment problem.*

Sequential decision tasks appear in many practical real-world problems including control, game playing, scheduling, and resource allocation. In many current applications decisions are based on simple heuristics or "rule of thumb" strategies. These strategies are normally problem-general and do not take advantage of domain-specific information. For example, in a communication network, packet routing is normally decided by a shortest-path algorithm, which is a problem-general policy. However, Littman and Boyan have shown that better routing policies can be achieved by incorporating more domain-specific knowledge such as network topology and reliability of local information [483].

Similarly, in most high-rise buildings, better elevator dispatching systems are being built by incorporating knowledge of the specific traffic patterns on each floor. Therefore, it appears that a learning mechanism to automatically develop such domain-specific strategies could be of great benefit in a wide range of tasks.

This paper describes a new approach called SANE (Symbiotic, Adaptive Neuro-Evolution) that combines genetic algorithms and neural networks to learn and perform sequential decision tasks. Neural networks have proven very effective in pattern recognition and pattern association tasks and have been shown to generalize well to unseen situations. Genetic algorithms provide a general training tool in which few assumptions about the domain are necessary. Since genetic algorithms only require a single fitness evaluation over the entire (possibly multi-step) task, they can be applied to domains with very sparse reinforcement, which makes them particularly well-suited for evaluating performance in sequential decision tasks.

SANE was implemented in two sequential decision tasks in the field of artificial intelligence. In the first task, SANE evolved a network to perform value ordering in a constraint satisfaction problem. The SANE network required 1/30 of the backtracks of random value ordering and 1/3 of the backtracks of the commonly-used maximization of future options heuristic. In the second task, SANE was implemented to focus a minimax search in the game of Othello. In this task, SANE formed a network to decide which moves from a given board situation are promising enough to evaluate. Using the powerful evaluation function from the Bill program [482], SANE was able to generate better play while examining 33% fewer board positions than normal, full-width minimax search. SANE's performance in these domains demonstrates both its effectiveness and applicability to a broad range of tasks.

The body of this paper is organized as follows. In the next section, the basic steps in SANE are described along with details of the current implementation. Sections 3 and 4 present the empirical results in the tasks of value ordering and focusing a minimax search. Future research directions are outlined in section 5, which include applications to non-Markovian tasks and domains with multiple decision tasks.

13.2   Symbiotic, Adaptive Neuro-Evolution

Recently there has been much interest in combining genetic algorithms and neural networks. Genetic algorithms are global search techniques patterned after Darwin's theory of natural evolution. Numerous potential solutions are encoded in strings called *chromosomes* and evaluated in a task. Substrings, or *genes*, of the best solutions are combined to form new solutions, which are inserted into the population. Each iteration of the genetic algorithm consists of solution evaluation and recombination and is called a *generation*. The idea is that structures that led to good solutions in previous generations can be combined to form better solutions in subsequent generations.

In neuro-evolution, the solutions take the form of neural networks. Most approaches to neuro-evolution operate on a population of complete neural networks that are encoded in separate chromosomes [473, 480, 490]. By evolving full solutions to the problem (i.e. complete neural networks), the algorithm typically converges the population towards a single dominant individual. Such concentration is desirable if it occurs at the global optimum, however, often populations *prematurely converge* to a local optimum. Once the population has converged,the search becomes a random walk using the mutation operator.

The problem of premature convergence is not unique to neuro-evolution, but is an open research issue in the genetic algorithms community as well. To prevent premature convergence, the population must remain diverse. Diversity will disperse individuals throughout the search space giving the population a more global view of the space of solutions. As a result, convergence at suboptimal solutions is much more unlikely.

SANE incorporates the idea of diversity into neuro-evolution. SANE evolves a population of neurons, where the fitness of each neuron is determined by how well it cooperates with other neurons in the population. To evolve a network capable of performing a task, the neurons must optimize different aspects of the network and form a mutualistic symbiotic relationship. Neurons will evolve into several *specializations* that search different areas of the solution space. Premature convergence is thus avoided and the population can discover better solutions to more difficult problems.

SANE evolves a population of hidden neurons for a given type of architecture such as a 2-layer-feedforward network (2 layers of weights). The basic steps in one generation of SANE are as follows (table 13.1): During the evaluation stage, random subpopulations of size ζ are selected and combined to form a neural network. The network is evaluated in the task and assigned a score,

Table 13.1
The basic steps in one generation of SANE.

1.	Clear all fitness values from each neuron.
2.	Select ζ neurons randomly from the population.
3.	Create a neural network from the selected neurons.
4.	Evaluate the network in the given task.
5.	Add the network's score to each selected neuron's fitness value.
6.	Repeat steps 2-5 a sufficient number of times.
7.	Get the neurons' average fitness scores by dividing their total fitness values by the number of networks they were implemented in.
8.	Perform crossover operations on the population based on the average fitness value of each neuron.

which is subsequently added to each selected neuron's fitness variable. The process continues until each neuron has participated in a sufficient number of networks. The average fitness of each neuron is then computed by dividing the sum of its fitness scores by the number of networks in which it participated. The neurons with high average fitness have cooperated well with other neurons in the population. Neurons that do not cooperate and are detrimental to the networks that they form receive low fitness scores and are selected against.

Once each neuron has a fitness value, crossover operations are used to combine the chromosomes of the best-performing neurons. Mutation is employed at low levels to introduce new genetic material. In this sense, mutation is only used as an insurance policy against missing key genetic material, not as a mechanism to create diversity.

Each neuron is defined in a bitwise chromosome that encodes a series of connection definitions, each consisting of an 8-bit label field and a 16-bit weight field. The absolute value of the label determines where the connection is to be made. The neurons only connect to the input and the output layer. If the decimal value of the label, D, is greater than 127, then the connection is made to output unit $D \bmod O$, where O is the total number of output units. Similarly, if D is less than or equal to 127, then the connection is made to input unit $D \bmod I$, where I is the total number of input units. The weight field encodes a floating point weight for the connection. Figure 13.1 shows how a neural network is formed from three sample hidden neuron definitions.

Once each neuron has participated in a sufficient number of networks, the population is ranked according to the average fitness values. A mate is selected for each neuron in the top quarter of the population by choosing a neuron with an equal or higher average fitness value. A one-point crossover operator is

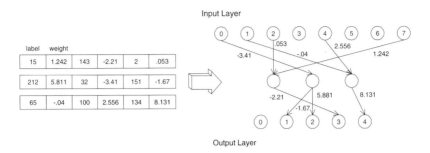

label	weight				
15	1.242	143	-2.21	2	.053
212	5.811	32	-3.41	151	-1.67
65	-.04	100	2.556	134	8.131

Figure 13.1
Forming a simple 8 input, 3 hidden, 5 output unit neural network from three hidden neuron definitions. The chromosomes of the hidden neurons are shown to the left and the corresponding network to the right. In this example, each hidden neuron has 3 connections.

used to mate two neurons creating two offspring per mating. The two offspring replace the worst-performing neurons (according to the rank) in the population. Mutation at the rate of 1% is performed on the entire population as the last step in each generation.

The implementation of SANE outlined above has performed well, however, SANE could be implemented with a variety of different neuron encodings and even with network architectures that allow recurrency. More advanced encodings and evolutionary strategies may enhance both the search efficiency and generalization ability. Extensions to the current implementation will be a subject of future research.

An empirical evaluation of SANE was performed in the standard reinforcement learning benchmark of balancing a pole on a cart [488]. The learning speed and generalization ability of SANE was compared to those of the best-known reinforcement learning approaches to this problem: the single-layer Adaptive Heuristic Critic (AHC) [471], the two-layer Adaptive Heuristic Critic [470] and the GENITOR neuro-evolution system [490]. SANE was found to be considerably faster (in CPU time) and more efficient (in training episodes) than the two-layer AHC and GENITOR implementations. Compared to the single-layer AHC, SANE was an order of magnitude faster even though it required more training episodes. The generalization capabilities of the four methods were comparable. An analysis of the final populations verifies that SANE finds solutions in diverse, unconverged populations and can maintain diversity in prolonged evolution.

The purpose of this paper is to show how SANE can be applied to existing and novel sequential decision tasks. The first task, value ordering in constraint satisfaction problems, was selected because it is an important problem where general solutions have performed inconsistently. The second task, focusing minimax search, was selected to demonstrate how SANE can be applied to existing problems previously unrealized as sequential decision tasks.

13.3   CSP Value Ordering

Constraint satisfaction problems (CSP) are common in many areas of computer science such as machine vision, scheduling, and planning. A number of variables must be assigned values such that none of the constraints among them are violated. CSPs are usually solved through depth-first search: the variables are chosen for instantiation one at a time, and their different legal values are tried one at a time. The order in which variables and values are considered determines how soon a solution is found, and therefore, choosing the variable and value bindings wisely can significantly reduce search time.

Most CSP applications use the first-fail method [476] for ordering the variable bindings. At each level of the search, the variable with the smallest number of possible values is chosen for instantiation. However, deciding the order in which the values are assigned is much more difficult, partly because good value-ordering heuristics are highly problem specific [481]. Learning the domain-specific heuristic information to build an effective value-ordering policy would therefore be a significant demonstration of SANE in an important sequential decision task.

The Car Sequencing Problem

Car sequencing is an instance of the job-shop scheduling problem [489]. In an automobile factory, a continuously moving assembly line is used to put options such as power windows on cars. When a car enters an option station, the workers walk along with the car until the option has been installed. The capacity of the option station is indicated by "r out of s": For example, an option station with a capacity of 2 out of 5 can handle a maximum of 2 cars for every 5 that pass on the assembly line. If 3 cars require that option, the option station will be overdriven. Different classes of cars require different options. The problem is to find an ordering on the assembly line such that no option station becomes overdriven.

Table 13.2 shows a particular car sequencing problem taken from [489]. The number of classes, number of options, capacities of the option stations,

Table 13.2
The car-sequencing problem with 6 classes and 5 option stations. The options required by each class are indicated with a +. The capacities of the option stations are shown in the form r/s.

Classes	1	2	3	4	5	6	Capacity (r/s)
Option 1	+	-	-	-	+	+	1/2
Option 2	-	-	+	+	-	+	2/3
Option 3	+	-	-	-	+	-	1/3
Option 4	+	+	-	+	-	-	2/5
Option 5	-	-	+	-	-	-	1/5

and options required by each class were fixed. The number of cars in each class and total number of cars to schedule were varied in different instances of the problem. In a constraint satisfaction formulation, the slots on the assembly line represent the variables and the classes represent the possible values for the variables. In our experiments, the first-fail heuristic was used for variable ordering, which results in always assigning each slot in the order they appear on the assembly line [485]. A good strategy for value ordering was left to be developed by SANE.

Evolving a Value-ordering Neural Network

A 2-layer neural network was evolved using SANE to decide which car class to place in the next slot on the assembly line. Networks were evaluated by implementing them as part of a chronological backtrack search program. At each level of the search, the network received a window of the previous 12 slot assignments as input (figure 13.2). Each slot was represented by six input units (one for each class). Initially, all the input units would be 0, because no assignments have been made. Since the neural network needs some activation in the input layer to produce output, an extra (bias) input unit that was always 1 was included to allow the network to generate initial choices. The entire input layer, thus, consisted of 73 units. Figure 13.2 shows an example instantiation of the assembly line and the input the network receives.

The output layer consisted of six units, one for each class. The activation of each output unit (computed as a weighted sum of its input activations) indicates how strongly the network suggests assigning that class to the next slot. The output layer, thus, represents a ranking of the classes and determines the order in which classes are assigned to the slots during search, unless the choice violates either of the following two constraints: (1) there must be a car of that class remaining to be assigned, and (2) the assignment must not violate

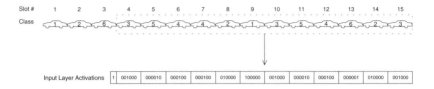

Figure 13.2
A partial sequence instantiation and the corresponding input to the network. The network
receives the previous 12 assignments as input. For example, a car of class 3 has been assigned to
slot 4. The first input unit is always 1 to allow the network to make initial choices. The next slot
to be scheduled is slot 16.

any option station's capacity.

The network has no knowledge of the number and types of cars to schedule. Its output layer merely represents the order in which values should be
tried given the current slot assignments. If there are no cars left of the highest
ranked class or the assignment would cause an option station to be overdriven,
the class with the next highest output unit is tried, unless it too violates one
of the two constraints. Implementing these two simple constraints outside the
network serves to *essentialize* the problem and relieve it of much of the trivial
overhead. The primary task is to differentiate between good and bad choices.
By not requiring the network to identify which classes are valid, it can more
easily learn the value-ordering task. This is analogous to removing the require-
ment of legal move identification from a move-evaluating network in game
playing, which also proved to be a good strategy [487].

A simple forward-checking algorithm was also implemented to prune the
search space early. For each option station, the total number of cars requiring
that option was counted. If the number exceeded the capacity of the option
station over all remaining slots, the search path was terminated.

The population consisted of 800 linear threshold neurons with each threshold set at 0. The subpopulation size ζ was 100, and 40 networks were formed
per generation of neurons. Each neuron thus participated in an average of 5
networks per generation. Each neuron was encoded a 240-bit chromosome that
contained ten 24-bit connection definitions.

The evaluation consisted of selecting 5 scheduling problems from a
database of 1000 problem instances and using the network to order the classes
in a chronological backtrack search. The problem instances contained between
10 to 25 cars, and the option requirements and station capacities were the same
as in table 13.2. The score of each network was determined by the total number

of backtracks incurred, which creates a challenging credit assignment problem for the individual value-ordering decisions.

Value-ordering Results

The population was evolved for 100 generations requiring approximately 40 minutes on an IBM RS6000 25T. The best network in each generation was evaluated using a 50 problem validation set. As the final result, the best network over all generations was selected and tested on a different 50 problem test set. For comparison, random value ordering and the maximization of future options heuristic [477, 481] were also run on the test set. The maximization of future options heuristic was implemented to prefer the class that leaves the most option stations free.

The average number of backtracks per problem in the test set were 781 for random value ordering, 85 for the maximization of future options heuristic, and 26 for the SANE network. While the problem-general heuristic did reduce the number of backtracks significantly over random ordering, it required 3 times more backtracks than the SANE network.

The SANE network appeared to take a first-fail approach to value ordering by preferring classes that place the most demand on the system. This approach is most obvious in the case of class 1, and constitutes the largest difference between the network's ordering and that of the maximization of future options heuristic. The network always preferred to schedule cars of class 1 as soon as possible, whereas the maximization of future options heuristic normally tried them last. Intuitively, cars of class 1 should be difficult to schedule, because they require the most options. Thus, it seems sensible that if a car of class 1 needs to be scheduled and it can fit without causing any immediate conflicts, it should be placed in the next slot. The maximization of future options heuristic, however, will not schedule it because it will limit the remaining options available to future cars. This approach delays the scheduling of class 1 cars and can incur large backtracks if they cannot fit later.

The maximization of future options is considered a good problem-general approach because it directs the search toward areas in the search space with high solution densities [477]. Using a similar heuristic, Kale was able to solve an order of magnitude larger instances of the n-queens problem than with the standard left-right column ordering. In this particular case, however, SANE discovered a better ordering through domain-specific knowledge. It is the attainment of this domain-specific knowledge that separates SANE from other more problem-general approaches and should allow SANE to be effective in a broad range of problems.

13.4   Focusing Minimax Search

Value-ordering provided a well-studied decision task where problem-general approaches have performed poorly. SANE, however, requires no pre-existing knowledge of the decision task but instead learns its decision policies through direct interaction with the domain. In other words, since SANE can learn in domains with very sparse reinforcement, decision tasks that previously received little attention because they were either too hard to learn or analyze may be optimized by SANE networks. This section presents an application of SANE to such a novel decision task.

Almost all current game programs rely on the minimax search algorithm to return the best move. Because of time and space constraints, searching to the end of the game is not feasible for most games. Heuristic evaluation functions, therefore, are used to approximate the payoff of a state. However, heuristics create errors that propagate up the search tree, and can greatly diminish the effectiveness of minimax [478]. Minimax also does not promote risk taking, assuming that the opponent will always make the best move. Often in losing situations the best move may not be towards the highest min/max value, especially if it will still result in a loss. Knowledge of move probabilities could guide the search towards a more aggressive approach and take advantage of possible mistakes by the opponent.

Most game programs overcome weak evaluation functions by searching deeper in the tree. Presumably, as the search frontier gets closer to the goal, the evaluations become more accurate. While this may be true, there is no guarantee that deeper searches will provide frontier nodes closer to the goal states. Hansson and Mayer showed that without a sound inference mechanism, deeper searches can actually cause more error in the frontier nodes [475]. A more directed search, therefore, seems necessary. Using SANE to focus minimax away from misinformation and towards more effective moves is an important, novel application to game playing and further demonstrates SANE's ability to incorporate domain-specific knowledge (In this case, weaknesses of minimax and the evaluation function) to form an effective decision strategy.

Creating a Focus Window

In earlier work [486], we showed how standard neuro-evolution methods can evolve a focus network in the game of Othello to decide which moves in a

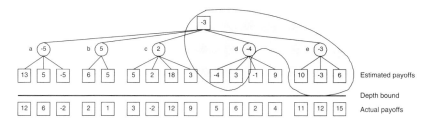

Figure 13.3
A minimax search to level 2. Min (circles) selects the lowest payoff and max (squares) the highest of min's choices. A full-width search considers all possible moves, while a focused search considers only those moves in the focus window (shown by the shaded region). The value for the root node is shown for a focused search. The full-width search would select move b, although move e is max's best choice. The focused search does not consider move b and selects move e.

given board situation are to be explored. In this paper, the SANE method was applied to the same task with significantly stronger results. In the search focus task, the network sees the updated board and evaluates each move at each level of minimax search. Only those moves that are better than a threshold value will be further explored. The search continues until a fixed depth bound is reached. An evaluation function is applied to the leaf states, and the values are propagated up the tree using the standard minimax method. The α-β pruning algorithm is used as in a full-width search to prune irrelevant states.

Restricting the number of moves explored has two key advantages: (1) the branching factor is reduced, which greatly speeds up the search. As a result, searches can proceed deeper on more promising paths. (2) The focus networks are forced to decide which moves the minimax search should evaluate, and in order to play well, they must develop an understanding of the minimax algorithm. It is possible that they will also discover limitations of minimax and the evaluation function, and learn to compensate by not allowing minimax to evaluate certain moves.

Figure 13.3 illustrates the focused search process. The player has a choice of 5 moves (a through e) and is searching 2 moves ahead. The leaf states are evaluated according to a static evaluation function. The actual payoff value of each leaf is shown below the depth bound. The difference between these values is the error or misinformation generated by the evaluation function. Move e is the strongest move since it will generate an actual payoff of at least 11. Because of the misinformation, which evaluates move e at -3, a full-width search would select move b, since it returns a payoff of at least 5. The focused search, however, is able to select move e by excluding move b from

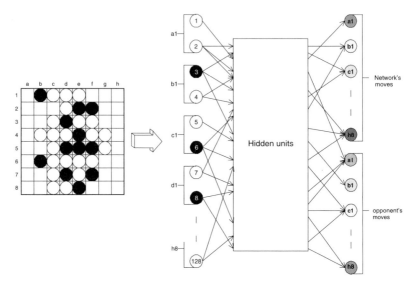

Figure 13.4
The architecture of the focus networks for Othello. Two inputs are used to encode each position
on the board. The encoding of the first four spaces (a1, b1, c1, d1) for the given board with the
network playing black are shown in the input layer. The activation of the output layer is shown by
the shading. The corners (such as a1 and h8) have high activations since corners are almost
always good moves.

consideration.

Implementation of Focus Networks in Othello

Two input units were used to represent the type of piece in each board space
(figure 13.4). If the space contains the network's piece, the first input unit is
turned on (value = 1). If the space contains the opponent's piece, the second
input unit is turned on. If the space is empty, neither input unit is activated. The
two input units are never both on.

Each output unit corresponded directly to a space on the board. The activation of an output unit determined whether a move was to be considered or
not. If the activation was greater than or equal to 0, the move was included
in the focus window. Separate output units were used for the two players to
allow offensive and defensive strategies to develop. Thus, the ranking for the
network's moves may differ from the ranking of the opponent's moves.

To evaluate a network, it was inserted into an α-β search program and
played against a full-width, fixed-depth minimax-α-β search. The number of

Table 13.3
The winning percentage of SANE and the average number of states examined per game for each depth bound.

Level	1	2	3	4	5	6
% of games won by SANE	54	54	62	49	53	51
Avg. states for SANE	198	931	5808	30964	166911	939999
Avg. states for full-width	207	977	6305	35932	212285	1217801

wins over ten games played determined the network's score. To create different games, an initial state was selected randomly among the 244 possible board positions after four moves. Both players were allowed to search through the second level and used the evaluation function from the Bill program [482], which is composed of large Bayes-optimized lookup tables gathered from expert games.[1] Bill was at one time the world-champion program and is still believed to be one of the best in the world. Any improvement over the current Bill evaluation function would thus be a significant result.

Focused Search Results

The SANE neurons were evolved for 200 generations, which took about 11 hours of CPU time on an IBM RS6000 25T. After evolution, the best network of each generation was tested against another full-width search in each of the 244 initial games, however, this time each player was allowed to search through level 3. The network with the highest winning percentage over these tests was selected as the best network.

Table 13.3 shows the best focus network's performance over various search levels against the full-width opponent. The results show that the focus network was playing a comparable and in most cases better game than Bill. Most remarkably, the focus networks won while looking at only a subset of the states as the full-width search. Of all available moves to level 6, only 77% were included in the focus network's window. Since the full-width search is looking at the same moves as the focused search plus additional moves, there must be some misinformation in the additional moves that are causing it to select poor moves. Since the focused search employs the same evaluation function to the same depth and yet is selecting better moves, it appears that the focus network is shielding the root from this misinformation.

The results indicate that SANE can evolve better and more efficient game

---

1 Thanks to Richard Korf and Kai-Fu Lee for providing Bill's evaluation function.

play through more selective search. SANE is able to tailor the minimax search to make the best use out of the information the evaluation function provides. SANE can optimize even highly sophisticated evaluation functions, like that of the Bill program. This is a significant improvement over the standard neuro-evolution approach used in [486], which could improve play with a weak heuristic, but could not extend to Bill's evaluation function in deeper searches.

More generally, the simulations demonstrate SANE's ability to form effective decision policies in novel decision tasks. Whereas most research has improved game-playing through optimization of the evaluation function [475, 482] or altering the minimax algorithm [479, 484], SANE attacks misinformation by making search-level decisions that can overcome deficiencies in minimax and the evaluation function. Such a novel approach to game-tree search, which is one of the most-studied fields in artificial intelligence, illustrates how SANE, through its generality and ability to learn with sparse reinforcement, may uncover previously unrealizable sequential decision tasks.

13.5   Future Work

Each of the decision tasks described in this paper were Markovian decision problems, where the future behavior of the system depended only on the current state and future inputs. While many interesting tasks can be formulated as Markov problems, in many real-world applications, factors outside the current observable state may also influence system behavior. For example in chess, move decisions are often based not only on the current board configuration, but also on the opponent's apparent strategy up to that point. SANE can be applied to such tasks with the addition of recurrent connections. A recurrent network maintains an internal representation in its hidden layer and it can be used to identify historical factors that affect system performance. Since forming recurrent connections requires little additional computation in SANE, SANE should be able to efficiently evolve recurrent networks for non-Markovian tasks.

Future work on SANE also includes applying it to larger real-world domains with multiple decision tasks. One such domain is local area networks (LAN), where possible tasks include packet routing, resource allocation, congestion control, and priority queuing. While standard methods for LAN control exist, SANE's domain-specific knowledge, attained through direct interaction with the LAN, should produce more effective decision policies. Other possible domains include elevator control, air and automobile traffic control, and robot control. Since SANE makes few domain assumptions, it should be applicable in each of these domains as well as many others.

An important question to be explored in future research is: Can SANE simultaneously evolve networks for separate decision tasks? For example, can neurons involved in priority queueing be evolved with neurons involved in packet routing? Evolving neurons for many different networks at once should not be very different from evolving them for a single network, because in any case SANE must develop neurons that specialize and serve very different roles. The input layers and output layers of each network could be concatenated to form a single, multi-task network. Since a hidden neuron can establish connections to any input or output unit, it can specialize its connections to a single decision task or form connections between sub-networks that perform different tasks. Such inter-network connections could produce interesting interactions between decision strategies, which is an issue that to our knowledge has not been studied before.

13.6   Conclusion

SANE provides a new mechanism for learning and performing sequential decision tasks. SANE's neural networks provide effective pattern recognition and generalization, while the genetic algorithm allows SANE to learn under sparse reinforcement. The value ordering and minimax tasks illustrate how SANE can outperform problem-general heuristics by incorporating domain-specific information such as the option capacities of an assembly line or the weaknesses of an evaluation function. SANE's few domain assumptions and ability to learn in tasks with sparse reinforcement should make it applicable to a broad range of decision tasks.

References

[470]C. W. Anderson. Learning to control an inverted pendulum using neural networks. *IEEE Control Systems Magazine*, 9:31–37, 1989.

[471]A. G. Barto, R. S. Sutton, and C. W. Anderson. Neuronlike adaptive elements that can solve difficult learning control problems. *IEEE Transactions on Systems, Man, and Cybernetics*, SMC-13:834–846, 1983.

[472]A. G. Barto, R. S. Sutton, and C. J. C. H. Watkins. Learning and sequential decision making. In M. Gabriel and J. W. Moore, editors, *Learning and Computational Neuroscience*. MIT Press, Cambridge, MA, 1990.

[473]R. K. Belew, J. McInerney, and N. N. Schraudolph. Evolving networks: Using the genetic algorithms with connectionist learning. In J. D. Farmer, C. Langton, S. Rasmussen, and

C. Taylor, editors, *Artificial Life II*, pages 511–547, Reading, MA, 1991. Addison-Wesley.

[474]J. J. Grefenstette, C. Ramsey, and A. C. Schultz. Learning sequential decision rules using simulation models and competition. *Machine Learning*, 5:355–381, 1990.

[475]O. Hansson and A. Mayer. Probabilistic heuristic estimates. *Annals of Mathematics and Artificial Intelligence*, 2:209–220, 1990.

[476]R. Haralick and G. Elliot. Increasing tree search efficiency for constraint satisfaction problems. *Artificial Intelligence*, 14(3):263–313, 1980.

[477]L. V. Kale. A perfect heuristic for the n non-attacking queens problem. *Information Processing Letters*, 34(4):173–178, 1990.

[478]R. E. Korf. Search: A survey of recent results. In H. E. Shrobe, editor, *Exploring Artificial Intelligence*. Morgan Kaufmann, San Mateo, California, 1988.

[479]R. E. Korf and D. M. Chickering. Best-first minimax search: Othello results. In *AAAI-94*, 1994.

[480]J. R. Koza and J. P. Rice. Genetic generalization of both the weights and architecture for a neural network. In *International Joint Conference on Neural Networks*, volume 2, pages 397–404, New York, NY, 1991. IEEE.

[481]V. Kumar. Algorithms for constraint satisfaction problems: A survey. *AI Magazine*, 13:32–44, 1992.

[482]K. Lee and S. Mahajan. The development of a world class Othello program. *Artificial Intelligence*, 43:21–36, 1990.

[483]M. L. Littman and J. A. Boyan. A distributed reinforcement learning scheme for network routing. Technical Report CMU-CS-93-165, School of Computer Science, Carnegie Mellon University, 1993.

[484]D. A. McAllester. Conspiracy numbers for min-max search. *Artificial Intelligence*, 35:287–310, 1988.

[485]D. E. Moriarty and R. Miikkulainen. Evolutionary neural networks for value ordering in constraint satisfaction problems. Technical Report AI94-218, Department of Computer Sciences, The University of Texas at Austin, 1994.

[486]D. E. Moriarty and R. Miikkulainen. Evolving neural networks to focus minimax search. In *Proceedings of the Twelfth National Conference on Artificial Intelligence (AAAI-94)*, pages 1371–1377, Seattle, WA, 1994. MIT Press.

[487]D. E. Moriarty and R. Miikkulainen. Discovering complex Othello strategies through evolutionary neural networks. *Connection Science*, 7(3):195–209, 1995.

[488]D. E. Moriarty and R. Miikkulainen. Efficient reinforcement learning through symbiotic evolution. *Machine Learning*, 22:11–32, 1996.

[489]P. Van Hentenryck, H. Simonis, and M. Dincbas. Constraint satisfaction using constraint logic programming. *Artificial Intelligence*, 58:113, 1992.

[490]D. Whitley, S. Dominic, R. Das, and C. W. Anderson. Genetic reinforcement learning for neurocontrol problems. *Machine Learning*, 13:259–284, 1993.

14 From Evolving a Single Neural Network to Evolving Neural Network Ensembles

Xin Yao and Yong Liu

Evolutionary artificial neural networks (EANNs) refer to a special class of artificial neural networks (ANNs) in which evolution is another fundamental form of adaptation in addition to learning. The evolution in EANNs is often simulated by an evolutionary algorithm. This chapter describes an evolutionary programming-based EANNs which learn both their weights and architectures simultaneously using a hybrid algorithm. A nonlinear ranking scheme and five mutation operators are used in our algorithm. These five mutation operators are applied sequentially and selectively to each individual in a population. Such sequential application encourages the evolution of smaller ANNs with fewer hidden nodes and connections. We have tested our evolutionary programming-based EANNs on a wide range of problems, include parity problems of various size, the two-spiral problem, four different medical diagnosis problems, the Australian credit card problem, and a couple of time-series prediction problems. Very good results have been achieved.

While the evolutionary approach to ANN design and training has produced some of the best results for many test problems, there are rooms for further improvements. For example, most evolutionary approaches to ANN design and training use an evolutionary algorithm to minimize certain error function. The best individual in a population gets most attention and is used as the final output from the evolutionary system. The rest of the population is discarded. We argue in this chapter that a population contains more useful information than the best individual. Such information can be used to improve the performance of evolved ANNs. In essence, we can regard a population of ANNs as an ANN ensemble and combine outputs from different individuals using various techniques, such as voting and averaging. Experimental studies will be presented to show the advantages of exploiting the population information.

14.1 Introduction

Artificial neural networks (ANNs) have been used widely in many application areas in recent years. Most applications use feedforward ANNs and the back-propagation (BP) training algorithm. There are numerous variants of the classical BP algorithm and other training algorithms. All these training algorithms assume a fixed ANN architecture. They only train weights in the fixed architecture that includes both connectivity and node transfer functions. The problem of designing a near optimal ANN architecture for an application remains unsolved. However, this is an important issue because there are strong biological and engineering evidences to support that the function, i.e., the information processing capability of an ANN is determined by its architecture.

There have been many attempts in designing ANN architectures (especially connectivity[1]) automatically, such as various constructive and pruning algorithms [503, 530, 497, 540, 535]. Roughly speaking, a constructive algorithm starts with a minimal network (i.e., a network with a minimal number of hidden layers, nodes, and connections) and adds new layers, nodes, and connections if necessary during training, while a pruning algorithm does the opposite, i.e., deletes unnecessary layers, nodes, and connections during training. However, "such *structural hill climbing* methods are susceptible to becoming trapped at structural local optima." [493] In addition, they "only investigate restricted topological subsets rather than the complete class of network architectures." [493]

Design of a near optimal ANN architecture can be formulated as a search problem in the architecture space where each point represents an architecture. Given some performance (optimality) criteria, e.g., minimum error, fastest learning, lowest complexity, etc., about architectures, the performance level of all architectures forms a surface in the space. The optimal architecture design is equivalent to finding the highest point on this surface. There are several characteristics with such a surface, as indicated by Miller *et al.* [526], which make evolutionary algorithms better candidates for searching the surface than those constructive and pruning algorithms mentioned above.

This chapter describes a new evolutionary system, i.e., EPNet, for evolving feedforward ANNs [561]. It combines the architectural evolution with the weight learning. The evolutionary algorithm used to evolve ANNs is based on evolutionary programming (EP) [507]. It is argued in this chapter that EP is a better candidate than genetic algorithms (GAs) for evolving ANNs. EP's emphasis on the behavioral link between parents and offspring can increase the efficiency of ANN's evolution.

EPNet is different from previous work on evolving ANNs on a number of aspects. First, EPNet emphasizes the evolution of ANN behaviours [557] and uses a number of techniques, such as partial training after each architectural mutation and node splitting, to maintain the behavioral link between

---

1 This chapter is only concerned with connectivity and will use architecture and connectivity interchangeably. The work on evolving both connectivity and node transfer functions was reported elsewhere [515].

a parent and its offspring effectively. While some of previous EP systems [509, 524, 493, 523, 506, 507], acknowledged the importance of evolving behaviours, few techniques have been developed to maintain the behavioral link between parents and their offspring. The common practice in architectural mutations was to add or delete hidden nodes or connections uniformly at random. In particular, a hidden node was usually added to a hidden layer with full connections. Random initial weights were attached to these connections. Such an approach tends to destroy the behaviour already learned by the parent and create poor behavioral link between the parent and its offspring.

Second, EPNet encourages parsimony of evolved ANNs by attempting different mutations sequentially. That is, node or connection deletion is always attempted before addition. If a deletion is "successful", no other mutations will be made. Hence, a parsimonious ANN is always preferred. This approach is quite different from existing ones which add a network complexity (regularization) term in the fitness function to penalize large ANNs (i.e., the fitness function would look like $f = f_{error} + \alpha f_{complexity}$). The difficulty in using such a function in practice lies in the selection of suitable coefficient α, which often involves tedious trial-and-error experiments. Evolving parsimonious ANNs by sequentially applying different mutations provides a novel and simple alternative which avoids the problem. The effectiveness of the approach has been demonstrated by the experimental results presented in this chapter.

Third, EPNet has been tested on a number of benchmark problems [561, 516], including the parity problem of various sizes, the Australian credit card accessment problem, four medical diagnosis problems (breast cancer, diabetes, heart disease, and thyroid), and the MacKey-Glass time series prediction problem. It was also tested on the two-spiral problem [563]. Few evolutionary systems have been tested on a similar range of benchmark problems. The experimental results obtained by EPNet are better than those obtained by other systems in terms of generalization and the size of ANNs.

Although there have been many studies on how to evolve ANNs more effectively and efficiently [552, 555, 556, 558], including the EPNet work, the issue of how to best use population information has been overlooked [559, 564]. Few attempts have been made to exploit the population information. We argue in this chapter that learning is different from optimization. The difference between learning and optimization can be exploited in evolutionary computation where both learning and optimization are population-based. It is shown that a population contains more information than any single individual in the population. Such information can be used to improve generalization of learned systems. Four simple methods for combining different individuals in a population are described in this chapter [562]. Although the idea of combining different individuals in an ensemble has been studied in the ANN field and statistics [512, 532], few attempts have been made in evolutionary learning to use population information to generate better systems.

The rest of this chapter is organized as follows: Section 14.2 discusses different approaches to evolving ANN architectures and indicates potential problems with the existing approaches; Section 14.3 describes EPNet in detail and gives motivations and ideas behind various design choices; Section 14.4 presents experimental results on EPNet and some discussions; Section 14.5 discusses the difference between evolutionary learning and optimization and the opportunity of exploiting such difference in population-based learning; Section 14.6 gives the four combination methods we used in our studies. The purpose here is not to find the best combination method, but to demonstrate the effectiveness of our approach even with some simple methods; and finally Section 14.7 concludes with a summary of the chapter and a few remarks.

14.2   Evolving Artificial Neural Network Architectures

There are two major approaches to evolving ANN architectures [552, 558]. One is the evolution of "pure" architectures (i.e., architectures without weights). Connection weights will be trained after a near optimal architecture has been found. The other is the simultaneous evolution of both architectures and weights.

The Evolution of Pure Architectures

One major issue in evolving pure architectures is to decide how much information about an architecture should be encoded into a chromosome (genotype). At one extreme, all the detail, i.e., every connection and node of an architecture can be specified by the genotype, e.g., by some binary bits. This kind of representation schemes is called the *direct encoding scheme* or the *strong specification scheme*. At the other extreme, only the most important parameters of an architecture, such as the number of hidden layers and hidden nodes in each layer are encoded. Other detail about the architecture is either pre-defined or left to the training process to decide. This kind of representation schemes is called the *indirect encoding scheme* or the *weak specification scheme*. Figure 14.1 [554, 556] shows the evolution of pure architectures under either a direct or an indirect encoding scheme.

---

1. Decode each individual (i.e., chromosome) in the current generation into an architecture. If the indirect encoding scheme is used, further detail of the architecture is specified by some developmental rules or a training process.

2. Train each neural network with the decoded architecture by a pre-defined learning rule/algorithm (some parameters of the learning rule could be learned during training) starting from different sets of random initial weights and, if any, learning parameters.

3. Define the fitness of each individual (encoded architecture) according to the above training result and other performance criteria such as the complexity of the architecture.

4. Reproduce a number of children for each individual in the current generation based on its fitness.

5. Apply genetic operators to the children generated above and obtain the next generation.

Figure 14.1
A typical cycle of the evolution of architectures.

It is worth pointing out that genotypes in figure 14.1 do not contain any weight information. In order to evaluate them, they have to be trained from a random set of initial weights using a training algorithm like BP. Unfortunately, such fitness evaluation of the genotypes is very noisy because a phenotype's fitness is used to represent the genotype's fitness. There are two major sources of noise:

1. The first source is the random initialization of the weights. Different random initial weights may produce different training results. Hence, the same genotype may have quite different fitness due to different random initial weights used by the phenotypes.

2. The second source is the training algorithm. Different training algorithms may produce different training results even from the same set of initial weights. This is especially true for multimodal error functions. For example, a BP may reduce an ANN's error to 0.05 through training, but an EP could reduce the error to 0.001 due to its global search capability.

Such noise can mislead the evolution because of the fact that the fitness of a phenotype generated from genotype G_1 is higher than that generated from genotype G_2 does not mean that G_1 has higher fitness than G_2. In order to reduce such noise, an architecture usually has to be trained many times from different random initial weights. The average results will then be used to estimate the genotype's fitness. This method increases the computation time for fitness evaluation dramatically. It is one of the major reasons why only small ANNs were evolved in previous studies [549, 550].

In essence, the noise identified in this chapter is caused by the one to many mapping from genotypes to phenotypes. Angeline *et al.* [493] and Fogel [507, 508] have provided a more general discussion on the mapping between genotypes and phenotypes. It is clear that the evolution of pure architectures has difficulties in evaluating fitness accurately. As a result, the evolution would be very inefficient.

The Simultaneous Evolution of Both Architectures and Weights

One way to alleviate the noisy fitness evaluation problem is to have a one to one mapping between genotypes and phenotypes. That is, both architecture and weight information are encoded in individuals and are evolved simultaneously. Although the idea of evolving both architectures and weights is not new [493, 521, 524, 507], few have explained why it is important in terms of accurate fitness evaluation. The simultaneous evolution of both architectures and weights can be summarized by figure 14.2.

---

1. Evaluate each individual based on its error and/or other performance criteria such as its complexity.
2. Select individuals for reproduction and genetic operation.
3. Apply genetic operators, such as crossover and mutation, to the ANN's architectures and weights, and obtain the next generation.

Figure 14.2
A typical cycle of the evolution of both architectures and weights. The word "genetic" used above is rather loose and should not be interpreted in the strict biological sense. Genetic operators are just search operators.

The evolution of ANN architectures in general suffers from the permutation problem [495] or called competing conventions problem. It is caused by the many to one mapping from genotypes to phenotypes since two ANNs which order their hidden nodes differently may have different genotypes but are behaviorally (i.e., phenotypically) equivalent. This problem not only makes the evolution inefficient, but also makes crossover operators more difficult to produce highly fit offspring. It is unclear what building blocks actually are in this situation.

Some Related Work

There is some related work to evolving ANN architectures. For example, Smalz and Conrad [542] proposed a novel approach to assigning credits and fitness to neurons (i.e., nodes) in an ANN, rather than the ANN itself. This is quite different from all other methods which only evaluate a complete ANN without going inside it. The idea is to identify those neurons which "are most compatible with all of the network contexts associated with the best performance on any of the inputs" [542]. Starting from a population of redundant, identically structured networks that vary only with respect to individual neuron parameters, their evolutionary method first evaluates neurons and then copies with mutation the parameters of those neurons that have high fitness values to other neurons in the same class. In other words, it tries to put all fit neurons together to generate a hopefully fit network. However, Smalz and Conrad's evolutionary method does not change the network architecture, which is fixed [542]. The appropriateness of assigning credit/fitness to individual neurons also needs further investigation. It is well-known that ANNs use distributed representation. It is difficult to identify a single neuron for the good or poor performance of a network. Putting a group of "good" neurons from different ANNs together may not produce a better ANN unless a local representation is used. It appears that Smalz and Conrad's method [542] is best suited to ANNs such as radial basis function (RBF) networks.

Odri *et al.* [531] proposed a non-population-based learning algorithm which could change ANN architectures. It uses the idea of evolutional development. The algorithm is based on BP. During training, a new neuron may be added to the existing ANN through "cell division" if an existing neuron generates a non-zero error [531]. A connection may be deleted if it does not change very much in previous training steps. A neuron is deleted only when all of its incoming or all of its outgoing connections have been deleted. There is no obvious way to add a single connection [531]. The algorithm was only tested on the XOR problem to illustrate its ideas [531]. One major disadvantage of this algorithm is its tendency to generate larger-than-necessary ANN and overfit training data. It can only deal with strictly layered ANNs.

14.3   EPNet[561]

In order to reduce the detrimental effect of the permutation problem, an EP algorithm, which does not use crossover, is adopted in EPNet. EP's emphasis on the behavioral link between parents and their offspring also matches well with the emphasis on evolving ANN behaviours, not just circuitry. In its current implementation, EPNet is used to evolve feedforward ANNs with sigmoid transfer functions. However, this is not an inherent constraint. In fact, EPNet has minimal constraint on the type of ANNs which may be evolved. The feedforward ANNs do not have to be strictly layered or fully connected between adjacent layers. They may also contain hidden nodes with different transfer functions [515].

The major steps of EPNet can be described by figure 14.3, which are explained further as follows [561, 563]:

1. Generate an initial population of M networks at random. The number of hidden nodes and the initial connection density for each network are uniformly generated at random within certain ranges. The random initial weights are uniformly distributed inside a small range.

2. Partially train each network in the population on the training set for a certain number of epochs using a modified BP (MBP) with adaptive learning rates. The number of epochs, K_0, is specified by the user. The error value E of each network on the validation set is checked after partial training. If E has not been significantly reduced, then the assumption is that the network is trapped in a local minimum and the network is marked with 'failure'. Otherwise the network is marked with 'success'.

3. Rank the networks in the population according to their error values, from the best to the worst.

4. If the best network found is acceptable or the maximum number of generations has been reached, stop the evolutionary process and go to step 11. Otherwise continue.

5. Use the rank-based selection to choose one parent network from the population. If its mark is 'success', go to step 6, or else go to step 7.

6. Partially train the parent network for K_1 epochs using the MBP to obtain an offspring network and mark it in the same way as in step 2, where K_1 is a user specified parameter. Replace the parent network with the offspring in the current population and go to step 3.

7. Train the parent network with a simulated annealing (SA) algorithm to obtain an offspring network. If the SA algorithm reduces the error E of the parent network significantly, mark the offspring with 'success', replace its parent by it in the current population, and then go to step 3. Otherwise discard

this offspring and go to step 8.

8. First decide the number of hidden nodes N_{hidden} to be deleted by generating a uniformly distributed random number between 1 and a user-specified maximum number. N_{hidden} is normally very small in the experiments, no more than 3 in most cases. Then delete N_{hidden} hidden nodes from the parent network uniformly at random. Partially train the pruned network by the MBP to obtain an offspring network. If the offspring network is better than the worst network in the current population, replace the worst by the offspring and go to step 3. Otherwise discard this offspring and go to step 9.

9. Calculate the approximate importance of each connection in the parent network using the nonconvergent method. Decide the number of connections to be deleted in the same way as that described in step 8. Randomly delete the connections from the parent network according to the calculated importance. Partially train the pruned network by the MBP to obtain an offspring network. If the offspring network is better than the worst network in the current population, replace the worst by the offspring and go to step 3. Otherwise discard this offspring and go to step 10.

10. Decide the number of connections and nodes to be added in the same way as that described in step 8. Calculate the approximate importance of each virtual connection with zero weight. Randomly add the connections to the parent network to obtain *Offspring 1* according to their importance. Addition of each node is implemented by splitting a randomly selected hidden node in the parent network. The new grown network after adding all nodes is *Offspring 2*. Partially train *Offspring 1* and *Offspring 2* by the MBP to obtain a survival offspring. Replace the worst network in the current population by the offspring and go to step 3.

11. After the evolutionary process, train the best network further on the combined training and validation set until it "converges".

The above evolutionary process appears to be rather complex, but its essence is an EP algorithm with five mutations: hybrid training, node deletion, connection deletion, connection addition and node addition. Details about each component of EPNet are given in the following subsections.

Encoding Scheme for Feedforward Artificial Neural Networks

The feedforward ANNs considered by EPNet are generalized multilayer perceptrons [546] (pp.272-273). The architecture of such networks is shown in

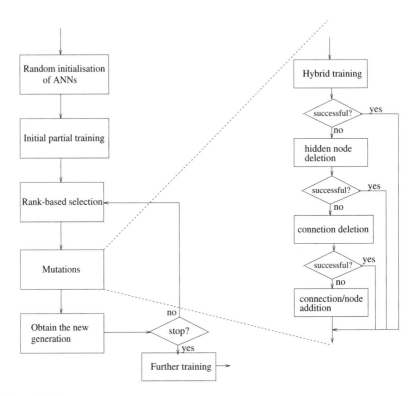

Figure 14.3
Major steps of EPNet.

figure 14.4, where **X** and **Y** are inputs and outputs respectively.

$$x_i = X_i, \ 1 \le i \le m$$

$$net_i = \sum_{j=1}^{i-1} w_{ij}x_j, \ m < i \le m + N + n$$

$$x_j = f(net_j), \ m < j \le m + N + n$$

$$Y_i = x_{i+m+N}, \ 1 \le i \le n$$

where f is the following sigmoid function:

$$f(z) = \frac{1}{1 + e^{-z}}$$

m and n are the number of inputs and outputs respectively, N is the number of hidden nodes.

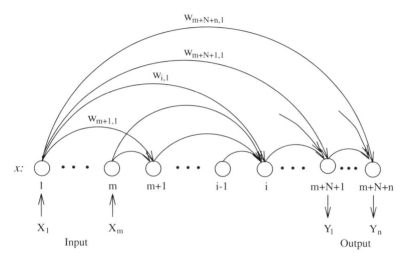

Figure 14.4
A fully-connected feedforward artificial neural network [546] (pp.273).

In figure 14.4, there are $m + N + n$ circles, representing all of the nodes in the network, including the input nodes. The first m circles are really just copies of the inputs $X_1, \ldots, X_m$. Every other node in the network, such as node number i, which calculates net_i and x_i, takes inputs from every node that precedes it in the network. Even the last output node (the $(m + N + n)$th), which generates Y_n, takes input from other output nodes, such as the one which outputs Y_{n-1}.

The direct encoding scheme is used in EPNet to represent ANN architectures and connection weights (including biases). This is necessary because EPNet evolves ANN architectures and weights simultaneously and needs information about every connection in an ANN. Two equal size matrices and one vector are used to specify an ANN in EPNet. The dimension of the vector is determined by a user-specified upper limit N, which is the maximum number of hidden nodes allowable in the ANN. The size of the two matrices is $(m + N + n) \times (m + N + n)$, where m and n are the number of input and output nodes respectively. One matrix is the connectivity matrix of the ANN, whose entries can only be 0 or 1. The other is the corresponding weight matrix whose entries are real numbers. Using two matrices rather than one is purely implementation-driven. The entries in the hidden node vector can be either 1, i.e., the node exists, or 0, i.e., the node does not exist. Since this chapter is only concerned with feedforward ANNs, only the upper triangle will be considered in the two matrices.

Fitness Evaluation and Selection Mechanism

The fitness of each individual in EPNet is solely determined by the inverse of an error value defined by Eq.(14.1) [533] over a *validation* set containing T patterns:

$$E = 100 \cdot \frac{o_{max} - o_{min}}{T \cdot n} \sum_{t=1}^{T} \sum_{i=1}^{n} (Y_i(t) - Z_i(t))^2 \qquad (14.1)$$

where o_{max} and o_{min} are the maximum and minimum values of output coefficients in the problem representation, n is the number of output nodes, $Y_i(t)$ and $Z_i(t)$ are actual and desired outputs of node i for pattern t.

Eq.(14.1) was suggested by Prechelt [533] to make the error measure less dependent on the size of the validation set and the number of output nodes. Hence a mean squared error percentage was adopted. o_{max} and o_{min} were the maximum and minimum values of outputs [533].

The fitness evaluation in EPNet is different from previous work in EANNs since it is determined through a validation set which does not overlap with the training set. Such use of a validation set in an evolutionary learning system improves the generalization ability of evolved ANNs and introduces little overhead in computation time.

The selection mechanism used in EPNet is rank based. Let M sorted individuals be numbered as $0, 1, \ldots, M - 1$, with the 0th being the fittest. Then the $(M - j)$th individual is selected with probability [553]

$$p(M - j) = \frac{j}{\sum_{k=1}^{M} k}$$

The selected individual is then modified by the five mutations. In EPNet, error E is used to sort individuals directly rather than to compute $f = 1/E$ and use f to sort them.

Replacement Strategy and Generation Gap

The replacement strategy used in EPNet reflects the emphasis on evolving ANN behaviours and maintaining behavioral links between parents and their offspring. It also reflects that EPNet actually emulates a kind of Lamarckian rather than Darwinian evolution. There is an on-going debate on whether Lamarckian evolution or Baldwin effect is more efficient in simulated evolution [491, 547]. Ackley and Littman [491] have presented a case for Lamarckian evolution. The experimental results of EPNet seem to support their view.

In EPNet, if an offspring is obtained through further BP partial training, it always replaces its parent. If an offspring is obtained through SA training, it replaces its parent only when it reduces its error significantly. If an offspring is obtained through deleting nodes/connections, it replaces the worst individual in the population only when it is better than the worst. If an offspring is obtained through adding nodes/connections, it always replaces the worst individual in the population since an ANN with more nodes/connections is more powerful although it's current performance may not be very good due to incomplete training.

The generation gap in EPNet is minimal. That is, a new generation starts immediately after the above replacement. This is very similar to the steady-state GA [548, 544] and continuous EP [510], although the replacement strategy used in EPNet is different.

Hybrid Training

The only mutation for modifying ANN's weights in EPNet is implemented by a hybrid training algorithm consisting of an MBP and a simplified SA algorithm.

The classical BP algorithm [538] is notorious for its slow convergence and convergence to local minima. Hence it is modified in order to alleviate these two problems. A simple heuristic is used to adjust the learning rate for each ANN in the population. Different ANNs may have different learning rates. During BP training, the error E is checked after every k epochs, where k is a parameter determined by the user. If E decreases, the learning rate is increased by a predefined amount. Otherwise, the learning rate is reduced. In the later case the new weights and error are discarded.

In order to deal with the local optimum problem suffered by the classical BP algorithm, an extra training stage is introduced when BP training cannot improve an ANN anymore. The extra training is performed by an SA algorithm. When the SA algorithm also fails to improve the ANN, the four mutations will be used to change the ANN architecture. It is important in EPNet to train an ANN first without modifying its architecture. This reflects the emphasis on a close behavioral link between the parent and its offspring.

The hybrid training algorithm used in EPNet is not a critical choice in the whole system. Its main purpose is to discourage architectural mutations if training, which often introduces smaller behavioral changes in comparison with architectural mutations, can produce a satisfactory ANN. Other training algorithms which are faster and can avoid poor local minima can also be used [560, 565]. The investigation of the best training algorithm is outside the scope of this chapter.

Architecture Mutations

In EPNet, only when the hybrid training fails to reduce the error of an ANN will architectural mutations take place. For architectural mutations, node or connection deletions are always attempted before connection or node additions in order to encourage the evolution of small ANNs. Connection or node additions will be tried only after node or connection deletions fail to produce a good offspring. Using the order of mutations to encourage parsimony of evolved ANNs represents a dramatically different approach from using a complexity (regularization) term in the fitness function. It avoids the time-consuming trial-and-error process of selecting a suitable coefficient for the regularization term.

HIDDEN NODE DELETION

Certain hidden nodes are first deleted uniformly at random from a parent ANN. The maximum number of hidden nodes that can be deleted is set by a user-specified parameter. Then the mutated ANN is partially trained by the MBP. This extra training process can reduce the sudden behavioral change caused by the node deletion. If this trained ANN is better than the worst ANN in the population, the worst ANN will be replaced by the trained one and no further mutation will take place. Otherwise connection deletion will be attempted.

CONNECTION DELETION

Certain connections are selected probabilistically for deletion according to their importance. The maximum number of connections that can be deleted is set by a user-specified parameter. The importance is defined by a significance test for the weight's deviation from zero in the weight update process [505]. Denote the weight update $\Delta w_{ij}(w) = -\eta[\partial L_t / \partial w_{ij}]$ by the local gradient of the linear error function L ($L = \sum_{t=1}^{T} \sum_{i=1}^{n} |Y_i(t) - Z_i(t)|$) with respect to example t and weight w_{ij}, the significance of the deviation of w_{ij} from zero is defined by the test variable [505]

$$test(w_{ij}) = \frac{\sum_{t=1}^{T} \xi_{ij}^t}{\sqrt{\sum_{t=1}^{T}(\xi_{ij}^t - \overline{\xi}_{ij})^2}} \qquad (14.2)$$

where $\xi_{ij}^t = w_{ij} + \Delta w_{ij}^t(w)$, $\overline{\xi}_{ij}$ denotes the average over the set ξ_{ij}^t, $t = 1, \ldots, T$. A large value of test variable $test(w_{ij})$ indicates higher importance of the connection with weight w_{ij}.

The advantage of the above nonconvergent method [505] over others is that it does not require the training process to converge in order to test connections. It does not require any extra parameters either. For example, Odri et al.'s method needs to "guess" values for four additional parameters. The idea behind the test variable (14.2) is to test the significance of the deviation of w_{ij} from zero [505]. Eq.(14.2) can also be used for connections whose weights are zero, and thus can be used to determine which connections should be added in the addition phase.

Similar to the case of node deletion, the ANN will be partially trained by the MBP after certain connections have been deleted from it. If the trained ANN is better than the worst ANN in the population, the worst ANN will be replaced by the trained one and no further mutation will take place. Otherwise node/connection addition will be attempted.

CONNECTION AND NODE ADDITION

As mentioned before, certain connections are added to a parent network probabilistically according to Eq.(14.2). They are selected from those connections with zero weights. The added connections are initialized with small random weights. The new ANN will be partially trained by the MBP and denoted as *Offspring 1*.

Node addition is implemented through splitting an existing hidden node, a process called "cell division" by Odri et al. [531]. In addition to reasons given by Odri et al. [531], growing an ANN by splitting existing ones can preserve the behavioral link between the parent and its offspring better than by adding random nodes. The nodes for splitting are selected uniformly at random among all hidden nodes. Two nodes obtained by splitting an existing node i have the same connections as the existing node. The weights of these new nodes have the following values [531]:

$$w_{ij}^1 = w_{ij}^2 = w_{ij}, \; i \geq j$$

$$w_{ki}^1 = (1 + \alpha)w_{ki}, \ i < k$$

$$w_{ki}^2 = -\alpha w_{ki}, \ i < k$$

where $\mathbf{w}$ is the weight vector of the existing node i, $\mathbf{w}^1$ and $\mathbf{w}^2$ are the weight vectors of the new nodes, and α is a mutation parameter which may take either a fixed or random value. The split weights imply that the offspring maintains a strong behavioral link with the parent. For training examples which were learned correctly by the parent, the offspring needs little adjustment of its inherited weights during partial training.

The new ANN produced by node splitting is denoted as *Offspring 2*. After it is generated, it will also be partially trained by the MBP. Then it has to compete with *Offspring 1* for survival. The survived one will replace the worst ANN in the population.

Further Training After Evolution

One of the most important goal for ANNs is to have a good generalization ability. In EPNet, a training set is used for the MBP and a validation set for fitness evaluation in the evolutionary process. After the simulated evolution, the best evolved ANN is further trained using the MBP on the combined training and validation set. Then this further trained ANN is tested on an unseen testing set to evaluate its performance.

Alternatively, all the ANNs in the final population can be trained using the MBP and the one which has the best performance on a second validation set is selected as EPNet's final output. This method is more time-consuming, but it considers all the information in the final population rather than just the best individual. The importance of making use of the information in a population has recently been demonstrated by evolving both ANNs [559, 564] and rule-based systems [500, 564]. The use of a second validation set also helps to prevent ANNs from overfitting the combined training and the first validation set. Experiments using either one or two validation sets will be described in the following section.

14.4   Experimental Studies

The Parity Problems

EPNet was first tested on the N parity problem where $N = 4 - 8$ [516]. The results obtained by EPNet [561] are quite competitive in comparison with those obtained by other algorithms. Table 14.1 compares EPNet's best results with those of cascade-correlation algorithm (CCA) [503], the perceptron cascade algorithm (PCA) [497], the tower algorithm (TA) [530], and the FNNCA [540]. All these algorithms except for the FNNCA can produce networks with short cut connections. Two observations can be made from this table. First, EPNet can evolve very compact networks. In fact, it generated the smallest ANN among the five algorithms compared here. Second, the size of the network evolved by EPNet seems to grow slower than that produced by other algorithms when the size of the problem (i.e., N) increases. That is, EPNet seems to perform even better for large problems in terms of the number of hidden nodes. Since CCA, PCA and TA are all fully connected, the number of connections in EPNet-evolved ANNs is smaller as well.

Table 14.1
Comparison between EPNet and other algorithms in terms of the minimal number of hidden nodes in the best network generated. The 5-tuples in the table represent the number of hidden nodes for the 4, 5, 6, 7, and 8 parity problem respectively. "-" means no result is available.

Algorithm	EPNet	CCA	PCA	TA	FNNCA
Number of hidden nodes	2,2,3,3,3	2,2,3,4,5	2,2,3,3,4	2,2,3,3,4	3,4,5,5,-

Figure 14.5 shows the best network evolved by EPNet for the 8 parity problem. Table 14.2 gives its weights. It is rather surprising that a 3 hidden node network can be found by EPNet for the 8 parity problem. This demonstrates an important point made by many evolutionary algorithm researchers — an evolutionary algorithm can often discover novel solutions which are very difficult to find by human beings.

Although there is a report on a 2 hidden node ANN which can solve the N parity problem [543], their network was hand-crafted and used a very special node transfer function, rather than the usual sigmoid one.

The Medical Diagnosis Problems

Since the training set was the same as the testing set in the experiments with the N parity problem, EPNet was only tested for its ability to evolve ANNs that learn well but not necessarily generalize well. In order to evaluate EPNet's ability in evolving ANNs that generalize well, EPNet was applied to four real-world problems in the medical domain, i.e., the breast cancer problem,

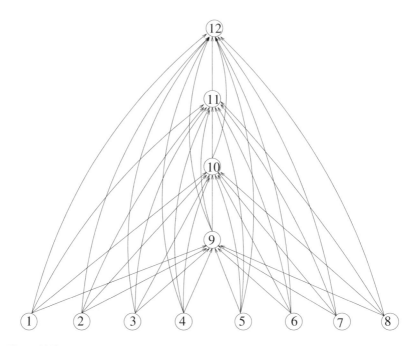

Figure 14.5
The best network evolved by EPNet for the 8 parity problem.

the diabetes problem, the heart disease problem, and the thyroid problem. All
date sets were obtained from the UCI machine learning benchmark repository.
These medical diagnosis problems have the following common characteristics
[533]:

• The input attributes used are similar to those a human expert would use in
order to solve the same problem.

• The outputs represent either the classification of a number of understandable
classes or the prediction of a set of understandable quantities.

• In practice, all these problems are solved by human experts.

• Examples are expensive to get. This has the consequence that the training
sets are not very large.

• There are missing attribute values in the data sets.

These data sets represent some of the most challenging problems in the ANN
and machine learning field. They have a small sample size of noisy data.

Table 14.2
Connection weights and biases (represented by T) for the network in figure 14.5.

	T	1	2	3	4	5
9	−12.4	25.2	27.7	−29.4	−28.9	−29.7
10	−40.4	19.6	18.9	−18.1	−19.1	−18.5
11	−48.1	16.0	16.1	−15.9	−16.3	−15.8
12	45.7	−10.0	−11.0	10.0	9.9	9.4

	6	7	8	9	10	11
9	−25.4	−28.5	27.8	0	0	0
10	−17.3	−18.8	20.4	−67.6	0	0
11	−15.9	−15.8	16.7	−55.0	−26.7	0
12	10.0	9.6	−11.4	6.8	2.3	76.3

THE BREAST CANCER DATA SET

The purpose of the data set is to classify a tumor as either benign or malignant based on cell descriptions gathered by microscopic examination. The data set contains 9 attributes and 699 examples of which 458 are benign examples and 241 are malignant examples.

THE DIABETES DATA SET

The problem posed here is to predict whether a patient would test positive for diabetes according to World Health Organization criteria given a number of physiological measurements and medical test results.

This is a two class problem with class value 1 interpreted as "tested positive for diabetes". There are 500 examples of class 1 and 268 of class 2. There are 8 attributes for each example. The data set is rather difficult to classify. The so-called "class" value is really a binarized form of another attribute which is itself highly indicative of certain types of diabetes but does not have a one to one correspondence with the medical condition of being diabetic.

THE HEART DISEASE DATA SET

The purpose of the data set is to predict the presence or absence of heart disease given the results of various medical tests carried out on a patient. This database contains 13 attributes, which have been extracted from a larger set of 75. The database originally contained 303 examples but 6 of these contained missing class values and so were discarded leaving 297. 27 of these were retained in case of dispute, leaving a final total of 270. There are two classes: presence and absence (of heart disease). This is a reduction of the number of classes in the original data set in which there were four different degrees of heart disease.

THE THYROID DATA SET

This data set comes from the "ann" version of the "thyroid disease" data set from the UCI machine learning repository. Two files were provided. "ann-train.data" contains 3772 learning examples. "ann-test.data" contains 3428 testing examples. There are 21 attributes for each example.

The purpose of the data set is to determine whether a patient referred to the clinic is hypothyroid. Therefore three classes are built: normal (not hypothyroid), hyperfunction and subnormal functioning. Because 92 percent of the patients are not hyperthyroid, a good classifier must be significantly better than 92%.

EXPERIMENTAL SETUP

All the data sets used by EPNet were partitioned into three sets: a training set, a validation set, and a testing set. The training set was used to train ANNs by MBP, the validation set was used to evaluate the fitness of the ANNs. The best ANN evolved by EPNet was further trained on the combined training and validation set before it was applied to the testing set.

As indicated by Prechelt [533, 534], it is insufficient to indicate only the number of examples for each set in the above partition, because the experimental results may vary significantly for different partitions even when the numbers in each set are the same. An imprecise specification of the partition of a known data set into the three sets is one of the most frequent obstacles to reproduce and compare published neural network learning results. In the following experiments, each data set was partitioned as follows:

• For the breast cancer data set, the first 349 examples were used for the training set, the following 175 examples for the validation set, and the final 175 examples for the testing set.

• For the diabetes data set, the first 384 examples were used for the training set, the following 192 examples for the validation set, the final 192 examples for the testing set.

• For the heart disease data set, the first 134 examples were used for the training set, the following 68 examples for the validation set, and the final 68 examples for the testing set.

• For the thyroid data set, the first 2514 examples in "ann-train.data" were used for the training set, the rest in "ann-train.data" for the validation set, and the whole "ann-test.data" for the testing set.

The input attributes of the diabetes data set and heart disease data set were rescaled to between 0.0 and 1.0 by a linear function. The output attributes of all the problems were encoded using a 1-of-m output representation for m classes. The winner-takes-all method was used in EPNet, i.e., the output with the highest activation designates the class.

There are some control parameters in EPNet which need to be specified by the user. It is however unnecessary to tune all these parameters for each problem because EPNet is not very sensitive to them. Most parameters used in the experiments were set to be the same: the population size (20), the initial connection density (1.0), the initial learning rate (0.25), the range of learning rate (0.1 to 0.75), the number of epochs for the learning rate adaptation (5), the number of mutated hidden nodes (1), the number of mutated connections (1 to 3), the number of temperatures in SA (5), and the number of iterations at each temperature (100). The different parameters were the number of hidden nodes of each individual in the initial population and the number of epochs for MBP's partial training. The number of hidden nodes for each individual in the initial population was chosen from a uniform distribution within certain ranges: 1 to 3 hidden nodes for the breast cancer problem; 2 to 8 for the diabetes problem; 3 to 5 for the heart disease problem; and 6 to 15 for the thyroid problem.

The number of epochs (K_0) for training each individual in the initial population is determined by two user-specified parameters: the "stage" size and the number of stages. A stage includes a certain number of epochs for MBP's training. The two parameters mean that an ANN is first trained for one stage. If the error of the network reduces, then another stage is executed, or else the training finishes. This step can repeat up to *the-number-of-stages* times. This simple method balances fairly well between the training time and the accuracy. For the breast cancer problem and the diabetes problem, the two parameters were 400 and 2. For the heart disease problem, they were 500 and 2. For the thyroid problem, they were 350 and 3.

The number of epochs for each partial training during evolution (i.e., K_1) was determined in the same way as the above. The two parameters were 50 and 3 for the thyroid problem, 100 and 2 for the other problems. The number of epochs for training the best individual on the combined training and testing data set was set to be the same (1000) for all four problems. A run of EPNet was terminated if the average error of the population had not decreased by more than a threshold value ϵ after consecutive G_0 generations or a maximum number of generations was reached. The same maximum number of generations (500) and the same G_0 (10) were used for all four problems. The threshold value ϵ was set to 0.1 for the thyroid problem, and 0.01 for the other three. These parameters were chosen after some limited preliminary experiments. They were not meant to be optimal.

EXPERIMENTAL RESULTS

Tables 14.3 and 14.4 show EPNet's results over 30 runs. The *error* in the tables refers to the error defined by Eq.(14.1). The *error rate* refers to the percentage of wrong classifications produced by the evolved ANNs.

It is clear from the two tables that the evolved ANNs have very small sizes, i.e., a small number of hidden nodes and connections, as well as low error rates. For example, an evolved ANN with just one hidden node can achieve an error rate of 19.794% on the testing set for the diabetes problem. Another evolved ANN with just three hidden nodes can achieve an error rate of 1.925% on the testing set for the thyroid problem.

Table 14.3
Architectures of evolved artificial neural networks.

		Number of connections	Number of hidden nodes	Number of generations
Breast	Mean	41.0	2.0	137.3
Cancer	SD	14.7	1.1	37.7
Data	Min	15	0	100
Set	Max	84	5	240
Diabetes	Mean	52.3	3.4	132.2
Data	SD	16.1	1.3	48.7
Set	Min	27	1	100
	Max	87	6	280
Heart	Mean	92.6	4.1	193.3
Disease	SD	40.8	2.1	60.3
Data	Min	34	1	120
Set	Max	213	10	320
Thyroid	Mean	219.6	5.9	45.0
Data	SD	74.36	2.4	12.5
Set	Min	128	3	10
	Max	417	12	70

Table 14.4
Accuracies of evolved artificial neural networks.

		Training set		Validation set		Test set	
		error	error rate	error	error rate	error	error rate
Breast	Mean	3.246	0.03773	0.644	0.00590	1.421	0.01376
Cancer	SD	0.589	0.00694	0.213	0.00236	0.729	0.00938
Data	Min	1.544	0.01719	0.056	0.00000	0.192	0.00000
Set	Max	3.890	0.04585	1.058	0.01143	3.608	0.04000
Diabetes	Mean	16.674	0.24054	13.308	0.18854	15.330	0.22379
Data	SD	0.294	0.00009	0.437	0.00008	0.300	0.00014
Set	Min	16.092	0.21875	12.574	0.16667	14.704	0.19271
	Max	17.160	0.26042	14.151	0.20313	15.837	0.25000
Heart	Mean	10.708	0.13632	13.348	0.17304	12.270	0.16765
Disease	SD	0.748	0.01517	0.595	0.01995	0.724	0.02029
Data	Min	8.848	0.09702	12.388	0.13235	10.795	0.13235
Set	Max	12.344	0.16418	14.540	0.20588	14.139	0.19118
Thyroid	Mean	0.470	0.00823	0.689	0.01174	1.157	0.02115
Data	SD	0.091	0.00146	0.127	0.00235	0.098	0.00220
Set	Min	0.336	0.00517	0.469	0.00636	0.887	0.01634
	Max	0.706	0.01154	1.066	0.01749	1.328	0.02625

COMPARISONS WITH OTHER WORK

Direct comparison with other evolutionary approaches to designing ANNs is very difficult due to the lack of such results. Instead, the best and latest results available in the literature, regardless of whether the algorithm used was an evolutionary, a BP or a statistical one, were used in the comparison. It is possible that some papers which should have been compared with were overlooked. However, the aim here is not to compare EPNet exhaustively with all other algorithms but to present ideas.

The Breast Cancer Problem: Setiono and Hui [540] have recently published a new ANN constructive algorithm called FNNCA. Prechelt [533] also reported results on manually constructed ANNs. He tested a number of different ANN architectures for the breast cancer problem. The *best* results produced by FNNCA [540] and by hand-designed ANNs (denoted as HDANNs) [533] are compared to the *average* results produced by EPNet in table 14.5.

Although EPNet can evolve very compact ANNs which generalize well, they come with the cost of additional computation time in order to perform search. The total time used by EPNet could be estimated by adding the initial

Table 14.5
Comparison among FNNCA [540], a hand-designed ANN [533], and EPNet on the breast cancer problem. ANNs designed manually and by FNNCA have more connections than those evolved by EPNet, even when the number of hidden nodes is the same since EPNet can generate sparsely connected ANNs. Only the average results from EPNet are shown here. EPNet's best results are clearly superior, as indicated by table 14.4.

	Best Results by FNNCA in 50 Runs	Best Results by HDANNS by Trial-and-Error	Average Results by EPNet Over 30 Runs
# Hidden Nodes	2	6	2.0
Testing Error Rate	$0.0145^{\dagger}$	0.01149	0.01376

This minimum error rate was achieved when the number of hidden nodes was 3. The testing error rate was 0.0152 when the number of hidden nodes was 2.

training time ($400 \times 20 = 8000$ epochs), the evolving time (approximately 200 epochs per generation for maximally 500 generations), and the final training time (1000 epochs) together. That is, it could require roughly 109000 epochs for a single run. The actual time was less since few runs reached the maximal number of generations. Similar estimations can be applied to other problems tested in this chapter. For many applications, the training time is less important than generalization. Section 14.1 has explained why the evolutionary approach is necessary and better than constructive algorithms for such applications.

The Diabetes Problem: The diabetes problem is one of the most challenging problems in ANN and machine learning due to its relatively small data set and high noise level. In the medical domain, data are often very costly to obtain. It would be unreasonable if an algorithm relies on more training data to improve its generalization.

Table 14.6 compares EPNet's result with those produced by a number of other algorithms [525]. It is worth pointing out that the other results were obtained by 12-fold cross validation [525]. They represented the best 11 out of 23 algorithms tested [525].

In terms of best results produced, Prechelt [533] tried different ANNs manually for the problem and found an 8 hidden node ANN which achieved the testing error rate of 0.2135 (21.35%), while EPNet achieved the testing error rate of 0.1927 (19.27%). The largest ANN evolved by EPNet among 30 runs had only 6 hidden nodes. The average was 3.4.

The Heart Disease Problem: Table 14.7 shows results from EPNet and other neural and non-neural algorithms. The GM algorithm [537] is used to construct RBF networks. It produced a RBF network of 24 Gaussians with 18.18% testing error. Bennet and Mangasarian [496] reported a testing error

Table 14.6
Comparison between EPNet and others [525] in terms of the average testing error rate on the diabetes problem.

Algorithm	EPNet	Logdisc	DIPOL92	Discrim	SMART	RBF
Testing Error Rate	0.224	0.223	0.224	0.225	0.232	0.243
Algorithm	ITrule	BP	Cal5	CART	CASTLE	Quadisc
Testing Error Rate	0.245	0.248	0.250	0.255	0.258	0.262

rate of 16.53% with their MSM1 method, 25.92% with their MSM method, and about 25% with BP, which is much worse than the worst ANN evolved by EPNet. The best manually designed ANN achieved 14.78% testing error [533], which is worse than the best result of EPNet, 13.235%.

Table 14.7
Comparison among MSM1 [496], a hand-designed ANN [533], and EPNet on the heart disease problem. The smallest error rate achieved by EPNet was 0.13235. '-' in the table means 'not available'.

	Results by MSM1	Best Results by HDANNS by Trial-and-Error	Average Results by EPNet Over 30 Runs
# Hidden Nodes	-	4	4.1
Testing Error Rate	0.1653	0.1478	0.16767

The Thyroid Problem: Schiffmann *et al.* [539] tried this problem using a 21-20-3 network. They found that several thousand learning passes were necessary to achieve a testing error rate of 2.6% for this network. They also used their genetic algorithm to train multilayer ANNs on the reduced training data set containing 713 examples. They obtained a network with 50 hidden nodes and 278 connections, which had testing error rate 2.5%. These results are even worse than those generated by the worst ANN evolved by EPNet. However, the best manually designed ANN [533] has a testing error rate of 1.278%, which is better than EPNet's best result, 1.634%. This is the only case where the best manually designed ANN [533] outperforms EPNet's best. Table 14.8 summarizes the above results.

Table 14.8
Comparison among Schiffmann *et al.*'s best results [496], a hand-designed ANN [533], and EPNet on the thyroid problem. The smallest error rate achieved by EPNet was 0.01634.

	Results by Schiffmann	Best Results by HDANNS by Trial-and-Error	Average Results by EPNet Over 30 Runs
# Hidden Nodes	50	12	5.9
Testing Error Rate	0.025	0.01278	0.02115

The Australian Credit Card Assessment Problem

One of things which have often been overlooked in evolutionary algorithms is the information contained in the final population of the evolution. Most people just use the best individual in the population without thinking of exploring possible useful information in the rest of the population. In EPNet, simulated evolution is driven by an EP algorithm without any recombination operator. Due to the many to many mapping between genotypes and phenotypes [508], different individuals in the final population may have similar error rates but quite different architectures and weights. Some of them may have overfitted the training and/or validation set, and some may not. In order to avoid overfitting and achieve better generalization, a second validation set has been proposed to stop training in the last step of EPNet.

In the following experiment, the original validation set was divided into two equal subsets; the first (V-set 1) was used in the fitness evaluation and the second (V-set 2) was used in the last step of EPNet. In the last step, *all* individuals in the final population were first trained by the MBP on the combined training set and V-set 1. Then the one which produced the minimum error rate on V-set 2 was chosen as the final output from EPNet and tested on the testing set. Ties were broken in favor of the network with the minimum number of connections. If there was still a tie, it was broken at random.

The effectiveness of using a second validation set in EPNet was tested on another difficult problem — the Australian credit card assessment problem. The problem is to assess applications for credit cards based on a number of attributes. There are 690 cases in total. The output has two classes. The 14 attributes include 6 numeric values and 8 discrete ones, the latter having from 2 to 14 possible values. This data set was also obtained from the UCI machine learning repository. The input attributes used for ANNs are rescaled to between 0.0 and 1.0 by a linear function.

EXPERIMENTAL RESULTS AND COMPARISONS

The whole data set was first randomly partitioned into training data (518 cases) and testing data (172 cases). The training data was then further partitioned into three subsets: (1) the training subset (346 cases); (2) validation set 1 (86 cases); and (3) validation set 2 (86 cases).

The experiments used the same parameters as those for the diabetes problem except for the maximum number of generations which was set at 100. The average results over 30 runs are summarized in tables 14.9–14.10. Very good results have been achieved by EPNet. For example, an ANN with only 2 hidden nodes and 43 connections could achieve an error rate of 10.47% on the testing set. Table 14.11 compares EPNet's results with those produced by other algorithms [525]. It is worth pointing out that the other results were obtained by 10-fold cross validation [525]. They represented the best 11 out of 23 algorithms tested [525]. It is clear that EPNet performed much better than others even though they used 10-fold cross validation.

Table 14.9
Architectures of evolved ANNs for the Australian credit card data set.

	Mean	Std Dev	Min	Max
Number of connections	88.03	24.70	43	127
Number of hidden nodes	4.83	1.62	2	7

Table 14.10
Accuracy of evolved ANNs for the Australian credit card data set.

	Training set error	error rate	Validation set 1 error	error rate	Validation set 2 error	error rate	Test set error	error rate
Mean	9.69	0.111	6.84	0.074	9.84	0.091	10.17	0.115
SD	2.05	0.021	1.47	0.022	2.31	0.024	1.55	0.019
Min	6.86	0.081	4.01	0.035	5.83	0.047	7.73	0.081
Max	15.63	0.173	9.94	0.105	14.46	0.140	14.08	0.157

The MacKey-Glass Chaotic Time Series Prediction Problem

This section describes EPNet's application to a time series prediction problem. The problem is different from previous ones in that its output is continuous. It

Table 14.11
Comparison between EPNet and others [525] in terms of the average testing error rate.

Algorithm	EPNet	Cal5	ITrule	DIPOL92	Discrim	Logdisc
Testing Error Rate	0.115	0.131	0.137	0.141	0.141	0.141
Algorithm	CART	RBF	CASTLE	NaiveBay	IndCART	BP
Testing Error Rate	0.145	0.145	0.148	0.151	0.152	0.154

is not a classification problem. This problem is used to illustrate that EPNet is applicable to a wide range of problems since it does not assume any *a priori* knowledge of the problem domain. The only part of EPNet which needs changing in order to deal with the continuous output is the fitness evaluation module.

The MacKey-Glass time series investigated here is generated by the following differential equation

$$\dot{x}(t) = \beta x(t) + \frac{\alpha x(t - \tau)}{1 + x^{10}(t - \tau)} \qquad (14.3)$$

where $\alpha = 0.2$, $\beta = -0.1$, $\tau = 17$ [504, 520]. As mentioned by Martinetz *et al.* [522], $x(t)$ is quasi-periodic and chaotic with a fractal attractor dimension 2.1 for the above parameters.

The input to an ANN consists of four past data points, $x(t)$, $x(t - 6)$, $x(t - 12)$ and $x(t - 18)$. The output is $x(t + 6)$. In order to make multiple step prediction (i.e., $\Delta t = 90$) during testing, iterative predictions of $x(t + 6)$, $x(t+12)$, ..., $x(t+90)$ will be made. During training, the true value of $x(t+6)$ was used as the target value. Such experimental setup is the same as that used by Martinetz *et al.* [522].

In the following experiments, the data for the MacKey-Glass time series was obtained by applying the fourth-order Runge-Kutta method to Eq.(14.3) with initial condition $x(0) = 1.2$, $x(t - \tau) = 0$ for $0 \le t < \tau$, and the time step is 1. The training data consisted of point 118 to 617 (i.e., 500 training patterns). The following 500 data points (starting from point 618) were used as testing data. The values of training and testing data were rescaled linearly to between 0.1 and 0.9. No validation sets were used in the experiments. Such experimental setup was adopted in order to facilitate comparison with other existing work.

The normalized root-mean-square (RMS) error E was used to evaluate the performance of EPNet, which is determined by the RMS value of the absolute prediction error for $\Delta t = 6$, divided by the standard deviation of $x(t)$ [504, 522],

$$E = \frac{\langle [x_{pred}(t, \Delta t) - x(t + \Delta t)]^2 \rangle^{\frac{1}{2}}}{\langle (x - \langle x \rangle)^2 \rangle^{\frac{1}{2}}}$$

where $x_{pred}(t, \Delta t)$ is the prediction of $x(t + \Delta t)$ from the current state $x(t)$ and $\langle x \rangle$ represents the expectation of x. As indicated by Farmer and Sidorowich[504], "If $E = 0$, the predictions are perfect; $E = 1$ indicates that the performance is no better than a constant predictor $x_{pred}(t, \Delta t) = \langle x \rangle$."

The following parameters were used in the experiments: the maximum number of generations (200), the number of hidden nodes for each individual in the initial population (8 to 16), the initial learning rate (0.1), the range of learning rate (0.1 to 0.75), the number of mutated hidden nodes (1), the two parameters for training each individual in the initial population (1000 and 5), and the two parameters for each partial training during evolution (200 and 5). All other parameters were the same as those for the medical diagnosis problems.

EXPERIMENTAL RESULTS AND COMPARISONS

Table 14.12 shows the average results of EPNet over 30 runs. The *error* in the table refers to the error defined by Eq.(14.1). Table 14.13 compares EPNet's results with those produced by BP and the cascade-correlation (CC) learning [498]. EPNet evolved much compact ANNs than the cascade-correlation networks, which are more than 6 times larger than the EPNet-evolved ANNs. EPNet-evolved ANNs also generalize better than the cascade-correlation networks. Compared with the networks produced by BP, the EPNet-evolved ANNs used only 103 connections (the median size) and achieved comparable results.

For a large time span $\Delta t = 90$, EPNet's results also compare favorably with those produced by Martinetz *et al.* [522] which had been shown to be better than Moody and Darken [528]. The average number of connections (weights) in an EPNet-evolved ANN is 103.33, while the smallest "neural-gas" network has about 200 connections (weights) [522], which is almost twice as large as the average size of EPNet-evolved ANN. To achieve a prediction error of 0.05, a "neural-gas" network had to use 1000 training data points and a size about 500 connections (weights) [522]. The smallest prediction error among 30

EPNet runs was 0.049, while the average prediction error was 0.065. For the
same training set size of 500 data points, the smallest prediction error achieved
by "neural-gas" networks was about 0.06. The network achieving the smallest
prediction error had 1800 connections (200 hidden nodes), which is more than
10 times larger than the largest EPNet-evolved ANN.

Table 14.12
The average results produced by EPNet over 30 runs for the MacKey-Glass time-series prediction
problem.

	Mean	Std Dev	Min	Max
Number of Connections	103.33	24.63	66	149
Number of Hidden Nodes	10.87	1.78	8	14
Error on Training Set	0.0188	0.0024	0.0142	0.0237
Error on Testing Set ($\Delta = 6$)	0.0205	0.0028	0.0152	0.0265
Error on Testing Set ($\Delta = 90$)	0.0646	0.0103	0.0487	0.0921

Table 14.13
Generalization results comparison among EPNet, BP, and CC learning for the MacKey-Glass
time-series prediction problem.

Method	Number of Connections	Testing Error $\Delta t = 6$	$\Delta t = 84$
EPNet	103	0.02	0.06
BP	540	0.02	0.05
CC Learning	693	0.06	0.32

14.5   Evolutionary Learning and Optimization

Learning is often formulated as an optimization problem in the machine learning field. For example, back-propagation (BP) is often used to train feed-
forward ANNs [538]. This training process is also called the *learning* process
of ANNs. BP is known as one of the most widely used *learning* algorithms.
However, BP is in essence a gradient-based *optimization* algorithm which is
used to minimize an error function (often a mean square error) of ANNs. The
so-called learning problem here is a typical optimization problem in numerical analysis. Many improvements on the ANN learning algorithm are actually

improvements over optimization algorithms [513], such as conjugate gradient methods [514, 527].

Learning is different from optimization in practice because we want the learned system to have best generalization, which is different from minimizing an error function. The ANN with the minimum error does not necessarily mean that it has best generalization unless there is an equivalence between generalization and the error function. Unfortunately, measuring generalization exactly and accurately is almost impossible in practice [551], although there are many theories and criteria on generalization, such as the minimum description length (MDL) [536], Akaike information criteria (AIC) [492], and minimum message length (MML) [545]. In practice, these criteria are often used to define better error functions in the hope that minimizing the functions will maximize generalization. While better error functions often lead to better generalization of learned systems, there is no guarantee. Regardless of the error functions used, BP or other more advanced learning algorithms are still used as *optimization* algorithms. They just optimize different error functions. The nature of the problem is unchanged.

Similar situations occur with other machine learning methods, where an "error" function has to be defined. A "learning" algorithm then tries to *minimize* the function. However, no error functions can guarantee that they correspond to the true generalization [551]. This is a problem faced by most inductive learning methods. There is no way in practice one can get around this except for using a good empirical function which might not correspond to the true generalization. Hence, formulating learning as optimization in this situation is justified.

Evolutionary learning is a population-based learning method. Most people use an evolutionary algorithm to maximize a fitness function or minimize an error function, and thus face the same problem as that described above. Maximizing a fitness function is different from maximizing generalization. The evolutionary algorithm is actually used as an optimization, not learning, algorithm. While little can be done for traditional non-population-based learning, there are opportunities for improving population-based learning, e.g., evolutionary learning.

Since the maximum fitness is not equivalent to best generalization in evolutionary learning, the best individual with the maximum fitness in a population may not be the one we want. Other individuals in the population may contain some useful information that will help to improve generalization of learned systems. It is thus beneficial to make use of the whole population rather than any single individual. A population always contains at least as much information as any single individual. Hence, combining different individuals in the last generation to form an integrated system is expected to produce better results.

14.6   A Population of EANNs as an Ensemble

As discussed in Section 14.5, the previous implementation of EPNet actually used EP as an optimization algorithm to minimize ANN's error rate on a validation set. The best individual was always chosen as the final output. The rest of the population was discarded. However, an individual with the minimum error rate on a validation set might not have the minimum error rate on a unseen testing set. The rest of the population may contain some useful information for improving generalization of EANNs. In order to integrate useful information in different individuals in the last generation, we can treat each individual as a module and linearly combine them together [562]. We will call this combined system as an ensemble of EANNs. The reason we consider linear combination is its simplicity. The purpose here is not to find the best combination method, but to show the importance of using population information and the advantage of combining EANNs. Better results would be expected if we had used nonlinear combination methods.

Majority Voting

The simplest linear combination method is majority voting. That is, the output of the most number of EANNs will be the output of the ensemble. If there is a tie, the output of the EANN (among those in the tie) with the lowest error rate on V-set 2 will be selected as the ensemble output. The ensemble in this case is the whole population. All individuals in the last generation participate in voting and are treated equally.

The results of majority voting on the three problems are given in Table 14.14. The majority voting method outperformed the single best individual on two out of three problems. This is rather surprising since majority voting did not consider the difference among different individuals. It performed worse than the best individual on the heart disease problem probably because it treated all individuals in the population equally. However, not all individuals are equally important. Some may perform poorly due to a mutation in the previous generation. The greatest advantage of majority voting is its simplicity. It requires virtually no extra computational cost.

Table 14.15 shows the results of the t-test comparing the best individual to

Table 14.14
Accuracies of the ensemble formed by majority voting. The results were averaged over 30 runs.

			Error rate		
		Train	V-set 1	V-set 2	Test
Card	Mean	0.128	0.048	0.133	0.095
	SD	0.013	0.015	0.016	0.012
	Min	0.101	0.023	0.105	0.076
	Max	0.150	0.081	0.151	0.122
Diabetes	Mean	0.218	0.175	0.169	0.222
	SD	0.020	0.024	0.020	0.022
	Min	0.177	0.135	0.115	0.172
	Max	0.276	0.240	0.208	0.255
Heart	Mean	0.083	0.002	0.057	0.167
	SD	0.025	0.011	0.017	0.024
	Min	0.052	0.000	0.029	0.132
	Max	0.157	0.059	0.088	0.235

the ensemble formed by majority voting. At the 0.05 level of significance, the ensemble is better than the best individual for the Australian credit card and diabetes problems and worse for the heart disease problem.

Table 14.15
t-test values comparing the best individual to the ensemble formed by majority voting. The values were calculated based on 30 runs.

		t-test value	
	Card	Diabetes	Heart
$Ensemble - Individual$	-1.8024	-2.7186	2.5362

Rank-Based Linear Combination

One way to consider differences among individuals without involving much extra computational cost is to use the fitness information to compute a weight for each individual. In particular, we can use EANN's ranking to generate weights for each EANN in combining the ensemble output. That is, given N sorted EANNs with an increasing error rate on V-set 2, where N is the population size, and their outputs $o_1, o_2, \ldots, o_N$. Then the weight for the ith

EANN is

$$w_i = \frac{\exp\left(\beta(N + 1 - i)\right)}{\sum_{j=1}^{N} \exp\left(\beta j\right)} \tag{14.4}$$

where β is a scaling factor. It was set as 0.75, 0.5, and 0.75 for the Australian credit card, diabetes and heart disease problem, respectively. These numbers were selected after modest preliminary experiments with $\beta = 0.1, 0.25, 0.5$ and 0.75. The ensemble output is

$$O = \sum_{j=1}^{N} w_j o_j \tag{14.5}$$

The results of the rank-based linear combination method are given in Table 14.16. In this case, the results produced by the ensemble are either better than or as good as those produced by the best individual.

Table 14.16
Accuracies of the ensemble formed by the rank-based linear combination method. The results were averaged over 30 runs.

			Error rate		
		Train	V-set 1	V-set 2	Test
Card	Mean	0.112	0.063	0.123	0.095
	SD	0.017	0.019	0.014	0.012
	Min	0.081	0.035	0.093	0.070
	Max	0.156	0.105	0.151	0.116
Diabetes	Mean	0.213	0.185	0.171	0.225
	SD	0.020	0.030	0.021	0.023
	Min	0.172	0.125	0.125	0.172
	Max	0.245	0.260	0.198	0.271
Heart	Mean	0.057	0.003	0.044	0.154
	SD	0.023	0.009	0.022	0.031
	Min	0.007	0.000	0.000	0.088
	Max	0.119	0.029	0.088	0.235

Table 14.17 shows the results of the t-test comparing the best individual to the ensemble formed by the rank-based linear combination. The ensemble is better than the best individual for the Australian credit card and diabetes problems at the 0.05 level of significance. It also outperforms the best individual for the heart disease problem (no statistical significance though).

Table 14.17
t-test values comparing the best individual to the ensemble formed by the rank-based linear combination. The values were calculated based on 30 runs.

	t-test value		
	Card	Diabetes	Heart
$Ensemble - Individual$	-2.3000	-3.4077	-0.1708

Linear Combination by the RLS Algorithm

One of the well-known algorithms for learning linear combination weights (i.e., one-layer linear networks) is the RLS algorithm [529](pp.31–33). It is used to find the weights that minimize the mean square error

$$E = \sum_{i=1}^{M} \left(d(i) - \sum_{j=1}^{N} w_j o_j(i) \right)^2 \tag{14.6}$$

where M is the number of training examples and $d(i)$ is the desired output for example i. (There should have another summation over all the outputs of the ensemble on the right-hand side of Eq.(14.6). We omitted it in our discussion for convenience sake.) Minimizing the error E with respect to weight w_k yields

$$\frac{\partial E}{\partial w_k} = -2 \sum_{i=1}^{M} \left(d(i) - \sum_{j=1}^{N} w_j o_j(i) \right) o_k(i) = 0 \tag{14.7}$$

Eq. (14.7) can be expressed in matrix form

$$\mathbf{r}_{oo}\mathbf{w} = \mathbf{r}_{od} \tag{14.8}$$

where

$$\mathbf{r}_{oo} = \sum_{i=1}^{M} \mathbf{o}(i)\mathbf{o}^T(i) \tag{14.9}$$

and

$$\mathbf{r}_{od} = \sum_{i=1}^{M} d(i)\mathbf{o}(i) \tag{14.10}$$

A unique solution to Eq. (14.8) exists if the correlation matrix $\mathbf{r}_{oo}$ is non-singular. The weight vector $\mathbf{w}$ could be found by inverting $\mathbf{r}_{oo}$ and multiplying it by $\mathbf{r}_{od}$ according to Eq. (14.8). However, this method is time-consuming because whenever a new training example becomes available it requires inversion and multiplication of matrices. The RLS algorithm [529](pp.31–33) uses a different method to determine the weights.

From Eq. (14.9) and Eq. (14.10) we can get

$$\mathbf{r}_{oo}(i) = \mathbf{r}_{oo}(i-1) + \mathbf{o}(i)\mathbf{o}^T(i) \tag{14.11}$$

and

$$\mathbf{r}_{od}(i) = \mathbf{r}_{od}(i-1) + d(i)\mathbf{o}(i) \tag{14.12}$$

Using Eqs. (14.8), (14.11) and (14.12), we can get

$$\mathbf{w}(i) = \mathbf{w}(i-1) + \mathbf{k}(i)e(i) \tag{14.13}$$

where

$$e(i) = d(i) - \mathbf{w}^T(i-1)\mathbf{o}(i) \tag{14.14}$$

and

$$\mathbf{k}(i) = \mathbf{r}_{oo}^{-1}(i)\mathbf{o}(i) \tag{14.15}$$

A recursion for $\mathbf{r}_{oo}^{-1}(i)$ is given by [529]

$$\mathbf{r}_{oo}^{-1}(i) = \mathbf{r}_{oo}^{-1}(i-1) - \frac{\mathbf{r}_{oo}^{-1}(i-1)\mathbf{o}(i)\mathbf{o}^T(i)\mathbf{r}_{oo}^{-1}(i-1)}{1 + \mathbf{o}^T(i)\mathbf{r}_{oo}^{-1}(i-1)\mathbf{o}(i)} \tag{14.16}$$

In our implementation of the above RLS algorithm, three runs were always performed with different initial $\mathbf{r}_{oo}^{-1}(0)$ and weights $\mathbf{w}(0)$. The initial weights were generated at random in $[-0.1, 0.1]$.

$$\mathbf{r}_{oo}^{-1}(0) = \alpha \mathbf{I}_N$$

where $\alpha = 0.1, 0.2$ and 0.3, and $\mathbf{I}_N$ is an $N \times N$ unit matrix. The best result out of the three runs was chosen as the output from the RLS algorithm.

The results of the ensemble formed by the RLS algorithm are given in Table 14.18. It is clear that the ensemble performed better than the best individual for all three problems. The results also indicate that a better combination method can produce better ensembles. In fact, the RLS algorithm is one of the recommended algorithms for performing linear combinations [512, 532]. However, other algorithms [494] can also be used.

Table 14.19 shows the results of the t-test comparing the best individual to the ensemble formed by the RLS algorithm. The ensemble is better than the best individual at the 0.05 level of significance for the Australian credit card

Table 14.18
Accuracies of the ensemble formed by the RLS algorithm. The results were averaged over 30 runs.

			Error rate		
		Train	V-set 1	V-set 2	Test
Card	Mean	0.114	0.042	0.125	0.093
	SD	0.018	0.012	0.014	0.011
	Min	0.087	0.023	0.093	0.076
	Max	0.147	0.070	0.163	0.116
Diabetes	Mean	0.211	0.159	0.171	0.226
	SD	0.024	0.025	0.017	0.021
	Min	0.169	0.104	0.115	0.193
	Max	0.255	0.208	0.208	0.260
Heart	Mean	0.058	0.000	0.039	0.151
	SD	0.027	0.000	0.021	0.033
	Min	0.015	0.000	0.000	0.088
	Max	0.119	0.000	0.088	0.221

and diabetes problems, and better at the 0.25 level of significance for the heart disease problem.

Table 14.19
t-test values comparing the best individual to the ensemble formed by the RLS algorithm. The values were calculated based on 30 runs.

	t-test value		
	Card	Diabetes	Heart
$Ensemble - Individual$	-2.7882	-1.9046	-0.7862

Using a Subset of the Population as an Ensemble

For the previous three combination methods, all the individuals in the last generation were used in the ensembles. It is interesting to investigate whether we can reduce the size of the ensembles without too much increase in testing error rates. Such investigation can provide some hints on whether all the individuals in the last generation will contain some useful information and shed some lights on the importance of a population in evolutionary learning.

As the space of possible subsets is very large ($2^N - 1$) for a population of size N, it is impractical to use exhaustive search to find an optimal subset.

Instead, we used a genetic algorithm (GA) [511] to search for a near optimal subset. The weights for each EANN in each subset were determined by the same RLS algorithm as that described in Section 14.6. The GA used the following parameters: population size (50), maximum number of generations (50), crossover rate (0.6), mutation rate (0.01), two-point crossover and bit-string length (20). These parameters were chosen somewhat arbitrarily. They might not be the best implementation. Elitism was used in the GA. The major steps of the GA can be summarized by Figure 14.6.

---

1. Initialize the population at random.
2. Train each individual by the RLS algorithm and use the result to define the individual's fitness.
3. Reproduce a number of children for each individual in the current generation based on a nonlinear ranking scheme [553].
4. Apply crossover and mutation to the children generated above and obtain the next generation.

Figure 14.6
Major steps of the evolution of ensemble structures.

The results of the ensemble formed by a subset of the last generation are given in Table 14.20. The same GA as described above was used to search for near optimal subsets for all three problems. Table 14.21 gives the sizes of the subsets evolved. It is clear that the sizes have been reduced by 50% on average. Table 14.22 shows t-test values comparing the accuracies of the best individual to those of the ensemble. The ensemble is better than the best individual for the Australian credit card and diabetes problems at the 0.10 and 0.005 level of significance, respectively. It is worse than the best individual for the heart disease problem at the 0.05 level of significance. This worse result might be caused by the small number of generations (only 50) we used in our experiments. A large number could probably produce better results, but would increase the search time. We let the GA run for 100 generations for the heart disease problem. The average testing error rate over 30 runs was improved from 0.164 to 0.159. A t-test revealed that the ensemble was only worse than the best individual at the 0.10 level of significance for the heart disease problem.

Table 14.20
Accuracies of the ensemble formed by a near optimal subset of the last generation. The results were averaged over 30 runs.

			Error rate		
		Train	V-set 1	V-set 2	Test
Card	Mean	0.117	0.036	0.106	0.095
	SD	0.018	0.007	0.012	0.012
	Min	0.087	0.023	0.081	0.070
	Max	0.159	0.058	0.128	0.116
Diabetes	Mean	0.219	0.129	0.160	0.222
	SD	0.025	0.024	0.016	0.023
	Min	0.174	0.094	0.125	0.182
	Max	0.268	0.167	0.188	0.260
Heart	Mean	0.068	0.000	0.017	0.164
	SD	0.028	0.000	0.017	0.030
	Min	0.022	0.000	0.000	0.118
	Max	0.134	0.000	0.059	0.221

Table 14.21
The ensemble size found by the GA. The results are average over 30 runs.

	Card	Diabetes	Heart
Mean	10.5	8.4	10.3
SD	3.78	2.14	4.56
Min	3	5	1
Max	20	12	19

14.7   Conclusions

This chapter describes an evolutionary system, i.e., EPNet, for designing and training ANNs. The idea behind EPNet is to put more emphasis on evolving ANN behaviours, rather than its circuitry. A number of techniques have been adopted in EPNet to maintain a close behavioral link between parents and their offspring. For example, partial training is always employed after each architectural mutation in order to reduce the behavioral disruption to an individual. The training mutation is always attempted first before any architectural mutation since it causes less behavioral disruption. A hidden node is not added to an existing ANN at random, but through splitting an existing node.

It was observed in our experiments that the performance of evolved ANNs

Table 14.22
t-test values comparing the best individual to the ensemble formed by a subset of the last generation. The values were calculated based on 30 runs.

	t-test value		
	Card	Diabetes	Heart
$Ensemble - Individual$	-1.6247	-2.7904	1.7250

deteriorates when the number of epochs and steps in partial training was lower than certain value. That is, a weak behavioral link between the parent and its offspring will have a negative impact on the system's performance.

In order to reduce the noise in fitness evaluation, EPNet evolves ANN architectures and weights simultaneously. Each individual in a population evolved by EPNet is an ANN with weights. The evolution simulated by EPNet is closer to the Lamarckian evolution than to the Darwinian one. Learned weights and architectures in one generation are inherited by the next generation. This is quite different from most genetic approaches where only architectures not weights are passed to the next generation.

EPNet encourages parsimony of evolved ANNs by ordering its mutations, rather than using a complexity (regularization) term in the fitness function. It avoids the tedious trial-and-error process to determine the coefficient for the complexity term. The effectiveness of the method has been shown by the compact ANNs evolved by EPNet, which have very good generalization ability.

EPNet has been tested on a number of benchmark problems, including the N parity problem, the two-spiral problem, the medical diagnosis problems, the Australian credit card assessment problem, and the MacKey-Glass time series prediction problem. Very competitive results have been produced by EPNet in comparison with other algorithms. EPNet imposes very few constraints on feasible ANN architectures, and thus faces a huge search space of different ANNs. It can escape from structural local minima due to its global search capability. The experimental results have shown that EPNet can explore the ANN space effectively. It can discover novel ANNs which would be very difficult to design by human beings.

It is emphasized in this chapter that learning is different from optimization *in practice* although learning problems are often formulated as optimization ones. Population-based learning, and evolutionary learning in particular, should exploit such difference by making use of the information in a *popula-*

tion. This chapter shows that a population contains more information than any individual in it. Such information can be used effectively to improve generalization of the learning systems.

The four methods introduced here are all linear combinations. The first two involve little extra computational cost. In particular, the rank-based combination method makes use of the fitness information readily available from EPNet to compute weights and achieves good results. This method fits evolutionary learning well due to its simplicity and effectiveness. The other two combination methods are based on the well-known RLS algorithm. They require a little more computational time, but produce good results. If computation time is not of primary concern, other linear [494] or nonlinear methods can also be used.

This chapter shows one way to evolve an ANN ensemble, where individuals try to solve a complex problem collectively and cooperatively. However, no special considerations were made in the evolution of ANNs to encourage such cooperation. One of our future work is to encourage the evolution of cooperating individuals in a population through techniques such as fitness sharing [502, 499, 501] and negative correlation [517, 518, 519].

Acknowledgments

This work was partially supported by the Australian Research Council through its small grant scheme.

References

[491]D. H. Ackley and M. S. Littman. A case for Lamarckian evolution. In C. G. Langton, editor, *Artificial Life III, SFI Studies in the Sciences of Complexity, Vol. XVIII*, pages 487–509, Reading, MA, 1994. Addison-Wesley.

[492]H. Akaike. A new look at the statistical model identification. *IEEE Trans. Automatic Control*, AC-19(6):716–723, December 1974.

[493]P. J. Angeline, G. M. Sauders, and J. B. Pollack. An evolutionary algorithm that constructs recurrent neural networks. *IEEE Trans. on Neural Networks*, 5(1):54–65, 1994.

[494]P. F. Baldi and K. Hornik. Learning in linear neural networks: a survey. *IEEE Trans. on Neural Networks*, 6(4):837–858, 1995.

[495]R. K. Belew, J. McInerney, and N. N. Schraudolph. Evolving networks: using genetic algorithm with connectionist learning. Technical Report #CS90-174 (Revised), Computer Science & Engr. Dept. (C-014), Univ. of California at San Diego, La Jolla, CA 92093, USA, February 1991.

[496]K. P. Bennett and O. L. Mangasarian. Robust linear programming discrimination of two linearly inseparable sets. *Optimization Methods and Software*, 1:23–34, 1992.

[497]N. Burgess. A constructive algorithm that converges for real-valued input patterns.

International Journal of Neural Systems, 5(1):59–66, 1994.

[498]R. S. Crowder. Predicting the Mackey-Glass timeseries with cascade-correlation learning. In D. S. Touretzky, G. E. Hinton, and T. J. Sejnowski, editors, *Proc. of the 1990 Connectionist Models Summer School*, pages 117–123. Carnegie Mellon University, 1990.

[499]P. Darwen and X. Yao. A dilemma for fitness sharing with a scaling function. In *Proc. of the 1995 IEEE Int'l Conf. on Evolutionary Computation (ICEC'95), Perth, Australia*, pages 166–171. IEEE Press, New York, NY 10017-2394, 1995.

[500]P. Darwen and X. Yao. Automatic modularization by speciation. In *Proc. of the 1996 IEEE Int'l Conf. on Evolutionary Computation (ICEC'96), Nagoya, Japan*, pages 88–93. IEEE Press, New York, NY 10017-2394, 1996.

[501]P. Darwen and X. Yao. Every niching method has its niche: fitness sharing and implicit sharing compared. In H.-M. Voigt, W. Ebeling, I. Rechenberg, and H.-P. Schwefel, editors, *Parallel Problem Solving from Nature (PPSN) IV*, volume 1141 of *Lecture Notes in Computer Science*, pages 398–407, Berlin, 1996. Springer-Verlag.

[502]P. J. Darwen and X. Yao. Speciation as automatic categorical modularization. *IEEE Transactions on Evolutionary Computation*, 1(2):101–108, 1997.

[503]S. E. Fahlman and C. Lebiere. The cascade-correlation learning architecture. In D. S. Touretzky, editor, *Advances in Neural Information Processing Systems 2*, pages 524–532. Morgan Kaufmann, San Mateo, CA, 1990.

[504]J. D. Farmer and J. J. Sidorowich. Predicting chaotic time series. *Physical Review Letters*, 59(8):845–847, 1987.

[505]W. Finnoff, F. Hergent, and H. G. Zimmermann. Improving model selection by nonconvergent methods. *Neural Networks*, 6:771–783, 1993.

[506]D. B. Fogel. Using evolutionary programming to create neural networks that are capable of playing tic-tac-toe. In *Proc. of the 1993 Int'l Joint Conf. on Neural Networks (IJCNN'93)*, pages 875–880. IEEE Press, New York, NY 10017-2394, 1993.

[507]D. B. Fogel. *Evolutionary Computation: Towards a New Philosophy of Machine Intelligence*. IEEE Press, New York, NY, 1995.

[508]D. B. Fogel. Phenotypes, genotypes, and operators in evolutionary computation. In *Proc. of the 1995 IEEE Int'l Conf. on Evolutionary Computation (ICEC'95), Perth, Australia*, pages 193–198. IEEE Press, New York, NY 10017-2394, 1995.

[509]D. B. Fogel, L. J. Fogel, and V. W. Porto. Evolving neural networks. *Biological Cybernetics*, 63:487–493, 1990.

[510]G. B. Fogel and D. B. Fogel. Continuous evolutionary programming: analysis and experiments. *Cybernetics and Systems*, 26:79–90, 1995.

[511]D. E. Goldberg. *Genetic Algorithms in Search, Optimization, and Machine Learning*. Addison-Wesley, Reading, MA, 1989.

[512]S. Hashem. *Optimal Linear Combinations of Neural Networks*. PhD thesis, School of Industrial Engineering, Purdue University, December 1993.

[513]D. R. Hush and B. G. Horne. Progress in supervised neural networks. *IEEE Signal Processing Magazine*, 10(1):8–39, January 1993.

[514]E. M. Johansson, F. U. Dowla, and D. M. Goodman. Backpropagation learning for multi-layer feed-forward neural networks using the conjugate gradient method. *Int'l J. of Neural Systems*, 2(4):291–301, 1991.

[515]Y. Liu and X. Yao. Evolutionary design of artificial neural networks with different nodes. In *Proc. of the 1996 IEEE Int'l Conf. on Evolutionary Computation (ICEC'96), Nagoya, Japan*, pages 670–675. IEEE Press, New York, NY 10017-2394, 1996.

[516]Y. Liu and X. Yao. A population-based learning algorithm which learns both architectures and weights of neural networks. *Chinese Journal of Advanced Software Research (Allerton Press, Inc., New York, NY 10011)*, 3(1):54–65, 1996.

[517]Y. Liu and X. Yao. Negatively correlated neural networks can produce best ensembles. *Australian Journal of Intelligent Information Processing Systems*, 4(3/4):176–185, 1997.

[518]Y. Liu and X. Yao. Ensemble learning via negative correlation. *Neural Networks*, 12(10), December 1999.

[519]Y. Liu and X. Yao. Simultaneous training of negatively correlated neural networks in an ensemble. *IEEE Trans. on Systems, Man, and Cybernetics, Part B: Cybernetics*, 29(6):716-725, December 1999.

[520]M. Mackey and L. Glass. Oscillation and chaos in physiological control systems. *Science*, 197:287, 1977.

[521]V. Maniezzo. Genetic evolution of the topology and weight distribution of neural networks. *IEEE Trans. on Neural Networks*, 5(1):39–53, 1994.

[522]T. M. Martinetz, S. G. Berkovich, and K. J. Schulten. "neural-gas" network for vector quantization and its application to time-series prediction. *IEEE Trans. on Neural Networks*, 4(4):558–569, 1993.

[523]J. R. McDonnell and D. Waagen. Neural network structure design by evolutionary programming. In D. B. Fogel and W. Atmar, editors, *Proc. of the Second Annual Conference on Evolutionary Programming*, pages 79–89. Evolutionary Programming Society, La Jolla, CA, 1993.

[524]J. R. McDonnell and D. Waagen. Evolving recurrent perceptrons for time-series modeling. *IEEE Trans. on Neural Networks*, 5(1):24–38, 1994.

[525]D. Michie, D. J. Spiegelhalter, and C. C. Taylor. *Machine Learning, Neural and Statistical Classification*. Ellis Horwood Limited, London, 1994.

[526]G. F. Miller, P. M. Todd, and S. U. Hegde. Designing neural networks using genetic algorithms. In J. D. Schaffer, editor, *Proc. of the Third Int'l Conf. on Genetic Algorithms and Their Applications*, pages 379–384. Morgan Kaufmann, San Mateo, CA, 1989.

[527]M. F. Møller. A scaled conjugate gradient algorithm for fast supervised learning. *Neural Networks*, 6(4):525–533, June 1993.

[528]J. Moody and C. J. Darken. Fast learning in networks of locally-tuned processing units. *Neural Computation*, 1:281–294, 1989.

[529]B. Mulgrew and C. F. N. Cowan. *Adaptive Filters and Equalisers*. Kluwer Academic Publ., Boston, 1988.

[530]J.-P. Nadal. Study of a growth algorithm for a feedforward network. *International Journal of Neural Systems*, 1:55–59, 1989.

[531]S. V. Odri, D. P. Petrovacki, and G. A. Krstonosic. Evolutional development of a multilevel neural network. *Neural Networks*, 6(4):583–595, 1993.

[532]M. P. Perrone. *Improving Regression Estimation: Averaging Methods for Variance Reduction with Extensions to General Convex Measure Optimization*. PhD thesis, Department of Physics, Brown University, May 1993.

[533]L. Prechelt. Proben1 — a set of neural network benchmark problems and benchmarking rules. Technical Report 21/94, Fakultät für Informatik, Universität Karlsruhe, 76128 Karlsruhe, Germany, September 1994.

[534]L. Prechelt. Some notes on neural learning algorithm benchmarking. *Neurocomputing*, 9(3):343–347, 1995.

[535]R. Reed. Pruning algorithms — a survey. *IEEE Trans. on Neural Networks*, 4(5):740–747, 1993.

[536]J. Rissanen. Modeling by shortest data description. *Automatica*, 14(5):465–471, September 1978.

[537]A. Roy, S. Govil, and R. Miranda. An algorithm to generate radial basis function (RBF)-like nets for classification problems. *Neural Networks*, 8:179–201, 1995.

[538]D. E. Rumelhart, G. E. Hinton, and R. J. Williams. Learning internal representations by error propagation. In D. E. Rumelhart and J. L. McClelland, editors, *Parallel Distributed Processing: Explorations in the Microstructures of Cognition, Vol. I*, pages 318–362. MIT Press, Cambridge, MA, 1986.

[539]W. Schiffmann, M. Joost, and R. Werner. Synthesis and performance analysis of multilayer neural network architectures. Technical Report 16/1992, University of Koblenz, Institute für Physics, Rheinau 3-4, D-5400 Koblenz, 1992.

[540]R. Setiono and L. C. K. Hui. Use of a quasi-newton method in a feedforward neural network construction algorithm. *IEEE Trans. on Neural Networks*, 6(1):273–277, 1995.

[541]Y. Shang and B. Wah. Global optimization for neural network training. *IEEE Computer*, 29(3):45–54, 1996.

[542]R. Smalz and M. Conrad. Combining evolution with credit apportionment: a new learning algorithm for neural nets. *Neural Networks*, 7(2):341–351, 1994.

[543]D. Stork and J. Allen. How to solve the N-bit parity problem with two hidden units. *Neural Networks*, 5(6):923–926, 1992.

[544]G. Syswerda. A study of reproduction in generational and steady state genetic algorithms. In G. J. E. Rawlins, editor, *Foundations of Genetic Algorithms*, pages 94–101. Morgan Kaufmann, San Mateo, CA, 1991.

[545]C. S. Wallace and J. D. Patrick. Coding decision trees. Technical Report 91/153, Dept. of Computer Science, Monash University, Clayton, Victoria 3168, Australia, August 1991.

[546]P. J. Werbos. *The Roots of Backpropagation: From Ordered Derivatives to Neural Networks and Political Forecasting*. John Wiley & Sons, New York, NY 10158-0012, 1994.

[547]D. Whitley, S. Gordon, and K. Mathias. Lamarkian evolution, the Baldwin effect and function optimization. In Y. Davidor, H.-P. Schwefel, and R. Männer, editors, *Parallel Problem Solving from Nature (PPSN) III*, pages 6–15. Springer-Verlag, Berlin, 1994.

[548]D. Whitley and T. Starkweather. GENITOR II: a distributed genetic algorithm. *Journal of Experimental and Theoretical Artificial Intelligence*, 2:189–214, 1990.

[549]D. Whitley and T. Starkweather. Optimizing small neural networks using a distributed genetic algorithm. In *Proc. of Int'l Joint Conf. on Neural Networks, Vol. I*, pages 206–209, Washington, DC, 1990. Lawrence Erlbaum Associates, Hillsdale, NJ.

[550]X. Yao and Y. Shi. A preliminary study on designing artificial neural networks using co-evolution. In *Proc. of the IEEE Singapore Intl Conf on Intelligent Control and Instrumentation*, pages 149–154, IEEE Singapore Section, Singapore, June 1995.

[551]D. H. Wolpert. A mathematical theory of generalization. *Complex Systems*, 4(2):151–249, 1990.

[552]X. Yao. Evolution of connectionist networks. In T. Dartnall, editor, *Preprints of the Int'l Symp. on AI, Reasoning & Creativity*, pages 49–52, Queensland, Australia, 1991. Griffith University.

[553]X. Yao. An empirical study of genetic operators in genetic algorithms. *Microprocessing and Microprogramming*, 38(1-5):707–714, September 1993.

[554]X. Yao. Evolutionary artificial neural networks. *International Journal of Neural Systems*, 4(3):203-222, 1993.

[555]X. Yao. A review of evolutionary artificial neural networks. *International Journal of Intelligent Systems*, 8(4):539–567, 1993.

[556]X. Yao. Evolutionary artificial neural networks. In A. Kent and J. G. Williams, editors, *Encyclopedia of Computer Science and Technology*, volume 33, pages 137–170. Marcel Dekker Inc., New York, NY 10016, 1995.

[557]X. Yao. The importance of maintaining behavioural link between parents and offspring. In *Proc. of the 1997 IEEE Int'l Conf. on Evolutionary Computation (ICEC'97), Indianapolis, USA*, pages 629–633. IEEE Press, New York, NY, April 1997.

[558]X. Yao. Evolving artificial neural networks. *Proceedings of the IEEE*, 87(9):1423–1447, September 1999.

[559]X. Yao and Y. Liu. Ensemble structure of evolutionary artificial neural networks. In *Proc. of the 1996 IEEE Int'l Conf. on Evolutionary Computation (ICEC'96), Nagoya, Japan*, pages 659–664. IEEE Press, New York, NY 10017-2394, 1996.

[560]X. Yao and Y. Liu. Fast evolutionary programming. In L. J. Fogel, P. J. Angeline, and T. Bäck, editors, *Evolutionary Programming V: Proc. of the Fifth Annual Conference on Evolutionary Programming*, pages 451–460, Cambridge, MA, 1996. The MIT Press.

[561]X. Yao and Y. Liu. A new evolutionary system for evolving artificial neural networks. *IEEE Transactions on Neural Networks*, 8(3):694–713, 1997.

[562]X. Yao and Y. Liu. Making use of population information in evolutionary artificial neural networks. *IEEE Trans. on Systems, Man, and Cybernetics, Part B: Cybernetics*, 28(3):417–425, 1998.

[563]X. Yao and Y. Liu. Towards designing artificial neural networks by evolution. *Applied Mathematics and Computation*, 91(1):83–90, 1998.

[564]X. Yao, Y. Liu, and P. Darwen. How to make best use of evolutionary learning. In R. Stocker, H. Jelinek, and B. Durnota, editors, *Complex Systems: From Local Interactions to Global Phenomena*, pages 229–242, Amsterdam, 1996. IOS Press.

[565]X. Yao, Y. Liu, and G. Lin. Evolutionary programming made faster. *IEEE Transactions on Evolutionary Computation*, 3(2):82–102, July 1999.

15 Evolutionary Synthesis of Bayesian Networks for Optimization

Heinz Mühlenbein and Thilo Mahnig

We shortly review our theoretical analysis of genetic algorithms and provide some new results. The theory has lead to the design of three different algorithms, all based on probability distributions instead of recombination of strings. In order to be numerically tractable, the probability distribution has to be factored into a small number of factors. Each factor should depend on a small number of variables only. For certain applications the factorization can be explicitly determined. In general it has to be determined from the search points used for the optimization. Computing the factorization from the data leads to learning Bayesian networks. The problem of finding a minimal structure which explains the data is discussed in detail. It is shown that the Bayesian Information Criterion is a good score for this problem. The algorithms are extended to probabilistic prototype trees used for synthesizing programs.

15.1   Introduction

Simulating evolution as seen in nature has been identified as one of the key computing paradigms for the next decade. Today evolutionary algorithms have been successfully used in a number of applications. These include discrete and continuous optimization problems, synthesis of neural networks, synthesis of computer programs from examples (also called genetic programming) and even evolvable hardware. But in all application areas problems have been encountered where evolutionary algorithms performed badly. Therefore a mathematical theory of evolutionary algorithms is urgently needed. Theoretical research has evolved from two opposite ends – from the theoretical approach there are theories emerging that are getting closer to practice; from the applied side ad hoc theories have arisen that often lack theoretical justification.

Evolutionary algorithms for optimization are the easiest for theoretical analysis. Here results from classical population genetics and statistics can be used. In our theoretical analysis we have approximated the dynamics of genetic algorithms by probability distributions. Subsequently this analysis has lead to a new algorithm called the *Univariate Marginal Distribution Algorithm* UMDA. It uses search distributions instead of the usual recombination/crossover of genetic strings [574].

The outline of the paper is as follows. First the theory to analyze genetic algorithms and UMDA is introduced. Then UMDA is extended to the *Factorized*

Distribution Algorithm FDA. It uses a general factorization of the probability distribution. FDA optimizes problems where UMDA and genetic algorithms perform badly [573]. FDA needs a valid factorization as input. For some problems this cannot be done. The factorization has to be determined from the data. This problem is solved by mapping probability distributions to Bayesian networks. To find a good Bayesian network structure explaining the data is called *learning*. The corresponding algorithm *Learning Factorized Distribution Algorithm* LFDA is discussed with several numerical examples.

We then investigate if the theory can be applied to other problems in evolutionary computation. The first example is synthesis of programs by a probabilistic tree. The second example is the synthesis of neural trees.

The paper summarizes popular approaches for synthesizing networks or programs. It analyzes the approaches with a common theoretical framework. In addition it formulates open research issues.

15.2   From Recombination to Distributions

For notational simplicity we restrict the discussion to binary variables $x_i \in \{0, 1\}$. We use the following conventions. Capital letters X_i denote variables, small letters x_i assignments. Let $\mathbf{x} = (x_1, \ldots, x_n)$ denote a binary vector. Let a function $f : \mathbf{X} \to R^{\geq 0}$ be given. We consider the optimization problem $\mathbf{x}_{opt} = \mathrm{argmax} f(\mathbf{x})$.

Definition Let $p(\mathbf{x}, t)$ denote the probability of $\mathbf{x}$ in the population at generation t. Then $p(x_i, t) = \sum_{\mathbf{x}, X_i = x_i} p(\mathbf{x}, t)$ defines the univariate marginal distributions.

Mühlenbein [574] has shown that any genetic algorithm can be approximated by an algorithm using univariate marginal distributions only.

UMDA

- **STEP 0:** Set $t \Leftarrow 1$. Generate $N \gg 0$ points randomly.
- **STEP 1:** Select $M \leq N$ points according to a selection method. Compute the marginal frequencies $p_i^s(x_i, t)$ of the selected set.
- **STEP 2:** Generate N new points according to the distribution $p(\mathbf{x}, t + 1) = \prod_{i=1}^{n} p_i^s(x_i, t)$. Set $t \Leftarrow t + 1$.
- **STEP 3:** If termination criteria are not met, go to STEP 1.

The simple genetic algorithm uses fitness proportionate selection [568]. In this case the probabilities of the selected points are given by $p^s(\mathbf{x}, t) = p(\mathbf{x}, t) f(\mathbf{x}) / \bar{f}(t)$ where $\bar{f}(t) = \sum_{\mathbf{x}} p(\mathbf{x}, t) f(\mathbf{x})$ denotes the average fitness of the population.

For theoretical analysis we consider $\bar{f}(t)$ as depending on $p(x_i, t)$. In order to emphasize this dependency we write

$$W(p(X_1 = 0, t), p(X1 = 1, t), \ldots, p(X_n = 1, t)) := \bar{f}(t) \qquad (15.1)$$

For infinite populations the dynamics of UMDA leads to a deterministic difference equations for $p(x_i, t)$ [574].

$$p(x_i, t + 1) = p(x_i, t) \frac{\bar{f}_i(t)}{W} \qquad (15.2)$$

where $\bar{f}_i(t) = \sum_{\mathbf{x}, X_i = x_i} f(\mathbf{x}) \prod_{j \neq i}^n p(x_j, t)$. These equations can be written as

$$p(x_i, t + 1) = p(x_i, t) \frac{\frac{\partial W}{\partial p(x_i)}}{W(t)} \qquad (15.3)$$

Equation 15.3 shows that UMDA performs a gradient ascent in the landscape given by W. Despite its simplicity UMDA can optimize difficult multi-modal functions. We take as first example the function BigJump. It is defined as follows, with $|\mathbf{x}|_1 = \sum x_i$ equal to the number of 1-bits:

$$\text{BigJump}(n, m, k, \mathbf{x}) := \begin{cases} |\mathbf{x}|_1 & 0 \leq |\mathbf{x}|_1 \leq n - m \\ 0 & n - m < |\mathbf{x}|_1 < n \\ k \cdot n & |\mathbf{x}|_1 = n \end{cases} \qquad (15.4)$$

The bigger m, the wider the valley. k can be increased to give bigger weight to the maximum. For $m = 1$ we obtain the popular OneMax function defined by $OneMax(n) = |x|_1$.

BigJump depends only on the number of bits on. To simplify the analysis we assume that all $p(x_i = 1)$ are identical to a single value denoted as $p(t)$. Then W depends only on one parameter, p. $W(p)$ is shown for $m = 30$ and $k = 20$ in figure 15.1. In contrast to the BigJump function $W(p)$ looks fairly smooth. The open circles are the values of $p(t)$ determined by an UMDA rum, setting $p(t) := 1/n \sum_i p(x_i, t)$. Note how closely the simulation follows the theoretical curve. Furthermore the probability $p(t)$ changes little over time

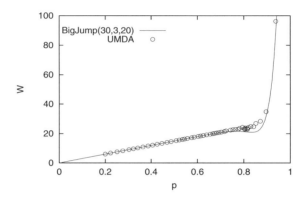

Figure 15.1
BigJump(30,3,20), UMDA, p versus average fitness, Popsize=2000

when W increases only slightly.

This simple example demonstrates in a nutshell the results of our theory. It can be formulated as follows: *Evolutionary algorithms transform the original fitness landscape given by $f(\mathbf{x})$ into a fitness landscape defined by $W(\mathbf{p})$. This transformation smoothes the rugged fitness landscape $f(\mathbf{x})$. There exist difficult fitness landscapes $f(\mathbf{x})$ like $BigJump$ which are transformed into simple landscapes $W(p)$. In these landscapes simple evolutionary algorithms will find the global optimum.*

A still more spectacular example is the Saw landscape. The definition of the function can be extrapolated from figure 15.2. In $\text{Saw}(n, m, k)$, n denotes the number of bits and $2m$ the distance from one peak to the next. The highest peak is multiplied by k (with $k \leq 1$), the second highest by k^2, then k^3 and so on. The landscape is very rugged. In order to get from one local optimum to another one, one has to cross a deep valley.

But again the transformed landscape $W(p)$ is fairly smooth. An example is shown in figure 15.3. Whereas $f(x)$ has 5 isolated peaks, $W(p)$ has three plateaus, a local peak and the global peak. Therefore we expect that UMDA should be able to cross the plateaus and terminate at the local peak. This behavior can indeed be observed in figure 15.3. Furthermore, as predicted by equation 15.3 the progress of UMDA slows down on the plateaus.

These two examples show that UMDA can solve difficult multi-modal optimization problems. But there are many optimization problems where UMDA is misled. UMDA will converge to local optima, because it cannot explore cor-

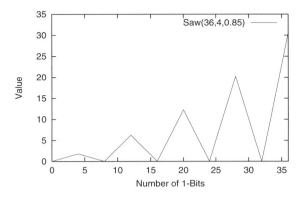

Figure 15.2
Definition of Saw(36,4,0.85)

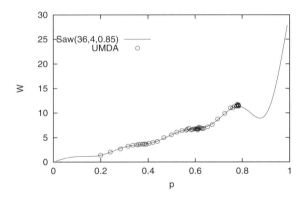

Figure 15.3
Saw(36,4,0.85), UMDA, p versus average fitness, Popsize=2000

relations between the variables. The first example is a deceptive function. We use the definition

$$\text{Decep}(\mathbf{x}, k) := \begin{cases} k - 1 - |\mathbf{x}|_1 & 0 \le |\mathbf{x}|_1 < k \\ k & |\mathbf{x}|_1 = k \end{cases} \tag{15.5}$$

The global maximum is isolated at $x = (1, \dots 1)$. A deceptive function of order k is a needle in a haystack problem. This is far too difficult to optimize.

We simplify the optimization problem by adding l distinct $Decep(k)$-functions to give a fitness function of size $n = l * k$. This function is also deceptive. The local optimum $x = (0, \ldots, 0)$ is surrounded by good fitness values, whereas the global optimum is isolated.

$$\text{Decep}(n, k) = \sum_{i=1, k+1, \ldots}^{n} \text{Decep}\big((x_i, x_{i+1}, \ldots, x_{i+k-1}), k\big) \qquad (15.6)$$

In figure 15.4 we show the average fitness $W(p)$ and an actual UMDA run. Starting at $p(0) = 0.5$ UMDA converges to the local optimum $\mathbf{x} = (0, \ldots, 0)$. UMDA will converge to the global optimum if it starts near to the optimum, e.g. $p(0) \geq 0.6$. Also shown is a curve which arises from an algorithm using fourth order marginal distributions. This algorithm converges to the global optimum, even when the initial population is generated randomly. But also for this algorithm $p(t)$ decreases first. The algorithm is discussed in section 15.3.

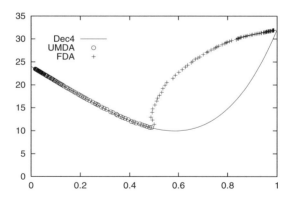

Figure 15.4
Average fitness $W(p)$ for UMDA and FDA for Decep(36,4)

The next example is a modified BigJump. The peak is now shifted away from the corner $\mathbf{x} = (1, \ldots, 1)$. It is defined as follows

$$\text{S-Peak}(n, m, k) \quad = \quad \left(\sum_{i=1}^{n} x_i \right) +$$
$$k \cdot (m + 1) \big((1 - x_1) \cdots (1 - x_m) x_{m+1} \cdots x_n \big)$$

This function is difficult to optimize, because the global optimum at $(0, \ldots, 0, 1, \ldots, 1)$ is now in competition with a local optimum at $x = (1, \ldots, 1)$. We discuss in more detail the function S-Peak(30,3). For the presentation we assume that the first three univariate marginal distributions are equal, e.g. $p(x_1) = p(x_2) = p(x_3) := a$ and the remaining ones are equal to b. This means that W depends on two parameters. In order to generate the global optimum a has to approach 0 and b has to approach 1. In figure 15.5 iso-lines of $W(a, b)$ are shown as well as trajectories for UMDA runs starting at different initial positions. The trajectories are almost vertical to the iso-lines, as predicted by the gradient ascent.

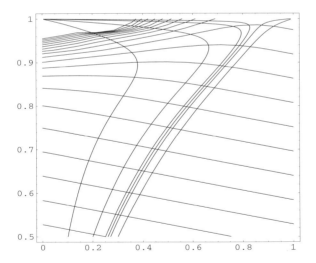

Figure 15.5
Trajectories of UMDA for S-Peak(30,3)

In all runs the initial b was set to 0.5, a varied from 0.1 to 0.3. For $0 < a(0) < 0.26$ UMDA will converge to the global optimum, for $a \geq 0.26$ UMDA will converge to the local optimum.

Selection

Proportionate selection allows a mathematical analysis. The equations for the univariate marginal distributions can be explicitly given. Proportionate selection is therefore also popular in population genetics. It is considered to be a model for *natural selection*.

But proportionate selection has a drawback in practice. It strongly depends on the fitness values. When the population approaches an optimum, selection gets weaker and weaker, because the fitness values are similar. Therefore breeders of livestock have used other selection methods. For large populations they mainly apply *truncation selection*. It works as follows. A truncation threshold τ is fixed. Then the τN best individuals are selected as parents for the next generation. These parents are then randomly mated.

We use mainly truncation selection in our algorithms. Another popular scheme is *tournament selection*. In tournament selection of size k, k individuals are randomly chosen. The best individual is taken as parent. Unfortunately the mathematics for both selection methods is more difficult. Analytical results for tournament selection have been obtained in [574].

We model binary tournament selection as a game. Two individuals with genotype $\mathbf{x}$ and $\mathbf{y}$ "play" against each other. The one with the larger fitness gets a payoff of 2. If the fitness values are equal, both will win half of the games. This gives a payoff of 1. The game is defined by a *payoff matrix* with coefficients

$$
a_{xy} = \begin{cases} 2 & f(\mathbf{x}) > f(\mathbf{y}) \\ 1 & f(\mathbf{x}) = f(\mathbf{y}) \\ 0 & f(\mathbf{x}) < f(\mathbf{y}) \end{cases}
$$

With some effort one can show that

$$
\sum_{\mathbf{x}} \sum_{\mathbf{y}} p(\mathbf{x}, t) a_{xy} p(\mathbf{y}, t) = 1 \tag{15.7}
$$

After a round of tournaments the genotype frequencies are given by

$$
p^s(\mathbf{x}, t+1) = p(\mathbf{x}, t) \sum_{\mathbf{y}} a_{xy} p(\mathbf{y}, t). \tag{15.8}
$$

If we set

$$
b(\mathbf{x}, t) = \sum_{\mathbf{y}} a_{xy} p(\mathbf{y}, t),
$$

then the above equation is similar to proportionate selection using the function $b(\mathbf{x}, t)$. But b depends on the genotype frequencies. Furthermore the average $\bar{b}(t) = \sum p(\mathbf{x}, t) b(\mathbf{x}, t)$ remains constant, $\bar{b}(t) \equiv 1$.

The difference equations for the univariate marginal frequencies can be derived in the same manner as for proportionate selection. They are given by

$$p(x_i, t + 1) = p(x_i, t) \cdot \bar{B}_i(t) \tag{15.9}$$

$$\bar{B}_i(t) = \sum_{\mathbf{x}|x_i=1} b(\mathbf{x}, t) \prod_{\substack{j=1 \\ j \neq i}}^{n} p_j(x_j, t) - 1 \tag{15.10}$$

Tournament selection uses only the order relation of the fitness values. The fitness values themselves do not change the outcome of a tournament. Therefore the evolution of the univariate marginal frequencies depends on the order relation only. Tournament selection does not perform gradient ascent on the average fitness of the population.

The different selection schemes are shown in figure 15.6 for OneMax(128).

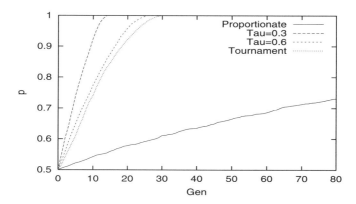

Figure 15.6
Comparison of selection methods for OneMax(128)

For OneMax proportionate selection is very weak. It takes the population a long time to approach the optimum. In contrast, truncation selection and tournament selection lead to a much faster convergence. p increases almost linearly until near the optimum. Truncation selection with $\tau = 0.6$ behaves very similarly to tournament selection.

A more complicated problem is the multi-modal function Saw$(36, 4, 0.85)$ displayed in figure 15.7. From figure 15.3 we recall that there are two plateaus at $p = 0.4$ and $p = 0.6$ and a local optimum at about $p = 0.78$. This structure is reflected both for truncation selection and proportionate selection. But truncation selection converges much faster. Both selection methods end on the local optimum $p = 0.78$.

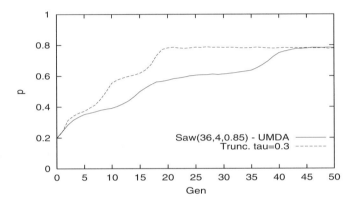

Figure 15.7
Comparison of selection methods for Saw(36,4,0.85)

The main conclusion of the theory remains valid for all selection schemes. *Evolution is mainly driven by the fitness landscape defined by* $W(p)$. For proportionate selection this can be theoretically shown. For the other selection methods an approximate analysis gives the same result. The analysis is based on the *response to selection* equation

$$W(p(t+1)) - W(p(t)) \approx b \cdot I_\tau(\sigma(W(p(t)))) \qquad (15.11)$$

The response $W(p(t+1)) - W(p(t))$ is determined by the fitness distribution, not the fitness values. In a first approximation it is assumed that the fitness distribution is normally distributed and can be characterized by the standard deviation $\sigma(W(p(t)))$. $b(t)$ is called realized heritability and I_τ the selection intensity corresponding to truncation threshold τ.

This equation and the selection problem is discussed in detail in [574]. It has been used to determine an analytical solution for OneMax.

UMDA solves many difficult multi-modal functions. But it can easily be deceived by a simple function like the deceptive function. The deception problem can be solved by using exact factorizations of the probability. This is discussed next.

15.3   FDA – The Factorized Distribution Algorithm

For the mathematical analysis we will assume Boltzmann selection. Boltzmann selection can be seen as proportionate selection applied to the transformed function $F(\mathbf{x}) = \exp(\beta f(\mathbf{x}))$.

Definition: *For Boltzmann selection the distribution after selection is given by*

$$p^s(\mathbf{x}, t) = p(x, t) \frac{e^{\beta f(x)}}{W_\beta} \tag{15.12}$$

where $\beta > 0$ is a parameter, also called the inverse temperature, and $W_\beta = \sum p(\mathbf{x}, t) e^{\beta f(x)}$ is the weighted average of the population.

For Boltzmann distributions we have proven a factorization theorem for the distribution $p(\mathbf{x}, t)$ and convergence for an algorithm using this factorization [575]. The proof is simple, because if $p(x, t)$ is a Boltzmann distribution with factor β_1 and Boltzmann selection is done with factor β_2, then $p(\mathbf{x}, t + 1) = p(\mathbf{x}, t)$ is a Boltzmann distribution with factor $\beta = \beta_1 + \beta_2$.

THEOREM 15.1:   Let $p(\mathbf{x}, 0)$ be randomly distributed. Let $\beta_1, \ldots, \beta_{t-1}$ be the schedule of the inverse temperature for Boltzmann selection. Then the distribution is given by

$$p(\mathbf{x}, t) = \frac{e^{\beta f(\mathbf{x})}}{Z_\beta} \tag{15.13}$$

where $\beta = \sum_{i=1}^{t-1} \beta_i$. Z_β is the partition function $Z_\beta = \sum_{\mathbf{x}} e^{\beta f(\mathbf{x})}$.

Equation 15.13 is a complete analytical solution of the dynamics. But it cannot be used for an algorithm. $p(\mathbf{x}, t)$ consists of $2^n - 1$ variables. Therefore the amount of computation is exponential. But there are many cases where the distribution can be factored into conditional marginal distributions each depending only on a small number of parameters. We recall the definition of conditional probability.

Definition *The conditional probability* $p(\mathbf{x}|\mathbf{y})$ *is defined as*

$$p(\mathbf{x}|\mathbf{y}) = \frac{p(\mathbf{x}, \mathbf{y})}{p(\mathbf{y})} \tag{15.14}$$

From this definition the following theorem easily follows.

THEOREM 15.2 BAYESIAN FACTORIZATION: Each probability can be factored into

$$p(\mathbf{x}) = p(x_1) \prod_{i=2}^{n} p(x_i|pa_i) \tag{15.15}$$

Proof: By definition of conditional probabilities we have

$$p(\mathbf{x}) = p(x_1) \prod_{i=2}^{n} p(x_i|x_1, \cdots, x_{i-1}) \tag{15.16}$$

Let $pa_i \subset \{x_1, \cdots, x_{i-1}\}$. If x_i and $\{x_1, \cdots, x_{i-1}\} \setminus pa_i$ are conditionally independent given pa_i, we can simplify $p(x_i|x_1, \cdots, x_{i-1}) = p(x_i|pa_i)$. ∎

PA_i are called the parents of variable X_i. This factorization defines a directed graph. In the context of graphical models the graph and the conditional probabilities are called a Bayesian network [570, 567]. The factorization is used by the Factorized Distribution Algorithm FDA.

FDA

- **STEP 0:** Set $t \Leftarrow 0$. Generate $N \gg 0$ points randomly.
- **STEP 1:** Selection
- **STEP 2:** Compute the conditional probabilities $p^s(x_i|pa_i, t)$ using the selected points.
- **STEP 3:** Generate a new population according to

$$p(x, t+1) = \prod_{i=1}^{n} p^s(x_i|pa_i, t)$$

- **STEP 4:** If termination criteria is met, FINISH.
- **STEP 5:** Set $t \Leftarrow t + 1$. Go to STEP 2.

FDA can be used with an exact or an approximate factorization. It is not restricted to Bayesian factorization. FDA uses *finite samples* of points to estimate the conditional distributions. Convergence of FDA to the optimum will depend on the size of the samples.

If the factorization does not contain conditional marginal distributions, but only marginal distributions, FDA can be theoretically analyzed. The difference equations of the marginal distributions are of the form given in equation 15.3 [572].

The amount of computation of FDA depends on the size of the population (N) and the number of variables used for the factors. There exist many problems where the size of the factors is bounded by k independent from n. In this case FDA is very efficient [573]. But for the function BigJump an exact factorization needs a factor of size n. Then the amount of computation of FDA is exponential in n. We have seen before that for BigJump UMDA will already find the global optimum. Thus an exact factorization is not a necessary condition for convergence. But it is necessary if we want to be sure that the optimum is found.

Approximation of the Distribution

The FDA theory needs an exact factorization. In order to use approximate distributions one can try to formulate the problem as an approximation problem of distributions. Given a target distribution (the Boltzmann distribution) and a family of probability models: What is the best approximation of the target distribution and how can the best approximation be found?

We restrict the discussion to distributions defined by the product of univariate marginal distributions.

Approximation Problem: Given a Boltzmann distribution

$$p(\mathbf{x}, t) = \frac{e^{\beta f(\mathbf{x})}}{Z_\beta} \qquad (15.17)$$

with $\beta > 0$. Given approximations $\tilde{p}(\mathbf{x}, t) = \prod \tilde{p}(x_i, t)$: Which set of $\tilde{p}(x_i, t)$ minimizes some distance to the Boltzmann distribution?

A popular measure for estimating the approximation error between distributions is the *entropy distance* proposed by Kullback and Leibler [571].

Definition: The Kullback Leibler divergence between two distributions is defined by

$$KL(\tilde{p}, p) = \sum_{\mathbf{x}} \tilde{p}(\mathbf{x}) \cdot \log \frac{\tilde{p}(\mathbf{x})}{p(x)} \qquad (15.18)$$

The KL measure has the following properties

- $KL(\tilde{p}, p) \geq 0$
- $KL(\tilde{p}, p) = 0$ iff $\tilde{p} = p$

The entropy distance is not symmetric, i.e. $KL(\tilde{p}, p) \neq KL(p, \tilde{p})$. The entropy distance depends on how close p and $\tilde{p}$ are to the boundary. To see this, note that the term $(x + \epsilon) \log((x + \epsilon)/x)$ grows to infinity when x goes to 0. Thus the entropy distance can be arbitrarily large while p and $\tilde{p}$ differ by ϵ. More generally, the entropy distance is extremely sensitive to small deviations close to the boundary of the probability simplex.

The above argument indicates that convergence in terms of entropy distance is harder than convergence in some L^p norm. This raises the question why we should use this measure. A discussion is outside the scope of this paper.

The best approximation minimizes $KL(\tilde{p}, p)$. The computation of the best approximation is very difficult. The topic is still under study. In practice a different approach is now popular. The approach is based on the theory of Bayesian networks.

15.4   LFDA - Learning a Bayesian Factorization

Computing the structure of a Bayesian network from data is called learning. Learning gives an answer to the question: *Given a population of selected points* $M(t)$, *what is a good Bayesian factorization fitting the data?* The most difficult part of the problem is to define a quality measure also called scoring measure.

A Bayesian network with more arcs fits the data better than one with less arcs. Therefore a scoring metric should give the best score to the minimal Bayesian network which fits the data. It is outside the scope of this paper to discuss this problem in more detail. The interested reader is referred to the two papers by Heckerman and Friedman et al. in [570].

For Bayesian networks two quality measures are most frequently used - the *Bayes Dirichlet* (BDe) score and the *Minimal Description Length* (MDL) score. We concentrate on the MDL principle. This principle is motivated by universal coding. Suppose we are given a set D of instances, which we would like to store. Naturally, we would like to conserve space and save a compressed version of D. One way of compressing the data is to find a suitable model for D that the encoder can use to produce a compact version of D. In order to recover D we must also store the model used by the encoder to compress D. Thus the total description length is defined as the sum of the length of the compressed version of D and the length of the description of the model. The MDL principle postulates that the optimal model is the one that minimizes the total description length.

In the context of learning Bayesian networks, the model is a network B describing a probability distribution p over the instances appearing in the data. Several authors have approximately computed the MDL score. Let $M = |D|$ denote the size of the data set. Then MDL is approximately given by

$$MDL(B, D) = -\text{ld}(P(B)) + M \cdot H(B, D) + \frac{1}{2} PA \cdot \text{ld}(M) \quad (15.19)$$

with $\text{ld}(x) := \log_2(x)$. $P(B)$ denotes the prior probability of network B, $PA = \sum_i 2^{|pa_i|}$ gives the total number of probabilities to compute. $H(B, D)$ is defined by

$$H(B, D) = -\sum_{i=1}^{n} \sum_{pa_i} \sum_{x_i} \frac{m(x_i, pa_i)}{M} \text{ld} \frac{m(x_i, pa_i)}{m(pa_i)} \quad (15.20)$$

where $m(x_i, pa_i)$ denotes the number of occurrences of x_i given configuration pa_i. $m(pa_i) = \sum_{x_i} m(x_i, pa_i)$. If $pa_i = \emptyset$, then $m(x_i, \emptyset)$ is set to the number of occurrences of x_i in D.

The formula has an interpretation which can be easily understood. If no prior information is available, $P(B)$ is identical for all possible networks. For minimizing, this term can be left out. $0.5 PA \cdot \text{ld}(M)$ is the length required to code the parameter of the model with precision $1/M$. Normally one would need $PA \cdot \text{ld}(M)$ bits to encode the parameters. However, the central limit theorem says that these frequencies are roughly normally distributed with a variance of $M^{-1/2}$. Hence, the higher $0.5\text{ld}(M)$ bits are not very useful and can be left out. $-M \cdot H(B, D)$ has two interpretations. First, it is identical to the logarithm of the maximum likelihood ($\text{ld}(L(B|D))$). Thus we arrive at the following principle:

Choose the model which maximizes $ld(L(B|D)) - \frac{1}{2} PA \cdot ld(M)$.

The second interpretation arises from the observation that H(B,D) is the conditional entropy of the network structure B, defined by PA_i, and the data D. The above principle is appealing, because it has no parameter to be tuned. But the formula has been derived under many simplifications. In practice, one needs more control about the quality vs. complexity tradeoff. Therefore we use a weight factor α. Our measure to be maximized is called BIC.

$$BIC(B, D, \alpha) = -M \cdot H(B, D) - \alpha PA \cdot \text{ld}(M) \qquad (15.21)$$

This measure with $\alpha = 0.5$ has been first derived by Schwarz [578] as *Bayesian Information Criterion.*

To compute a network B^* which maximizes BIC requires a search through the space of all Bayesian networks. Such a search is more expensive than to search for the optima of the function. Therefore the following greedy algorithm has been used. k_{max} is the maximum number of incoming edges allowed.

$\mathbf{BN(\alpha, k_{max})}$

- **STEP 0:** Start with an arc-less network.
- **STEP 1:** Add the arc (x_i, x_j) which gives the maximum increase of BIC(α) if $|PA_j| \leq k_{max}$ and adding the arc does not introduce a cycle.
- **STEP 2:** Stop if no arc is found.

Checking whether an arc would introduce a cycle can be easily done by maintaining for each node a list of parents and ancestors, i.e. parents of parents etc. Then $(x_i \rightarrow x_j)$ introduces a cycle if x_j is ancestor of x_i.

The BOA algorithm of Pelikan [576] uses the BDe score. This measure has the following drawback. It is more sensitive to coincidental correlations implied by the data than the MDL measure. As a consequence, the BDe measure will prefer network structures with more arcs over simpler networks [566]. The BIC measure with $\alpha = 1$ has also been proposed by Harik [569]. But Harik allows only factorizations without conditional distributions. This distribution is only correct for separable functions.

Given the BIC score we have several options to extend FDA to LFDA which learns a factorization. Due to limitations of space we can only show results of an algorithm which computes a Bayesian network at each generation using algorithm $BN(0.5, k_{max})$. FDA and LFDA should behave fairly sim-

Table 15.1
Numerical results for different algorithms, LFDA with $BN(\alpha, 8)$

Function	n	α	N	τ	Succ.%	SDev
OneMax	30	UMDA	30	0.3	75	4.3
	30	0.25	100	0.3	2	1.4
	30	0.5	100	0.3	38	4.9
	30	0.75	100	0.3	80	4.0
	30	0.25	200	0.3	71	4.5
BigJump(30,3,1)	30	UMDA	200	0.3	100	0.0
	30	0.25	200	0.3	58	4.9
	30	0.5	200	0.3	96	2.0
	30	0.75	200	0.3	100	0.0
	30	0.25	400	0.3	100	0.0
Saw(32,2,0.5)	32	UMDA	50	0.5	71	4.5
	32	UMDA	200	0.5	100	0.0
	32	0.25	200	0.5	41	2.2
	32	0.5	200	0.5	83	1.7
	32	0.75	200	0.5	96	0.9
	32	0.25	400	0.5	84	3.7
Deceptive-4	32	UMDA	800	0.3	0	0.0
	32	FDA	100	0.3	81	3.9
	32	0.25	800	0.3	92	2.7
	32	0.5	800	0.3	72	4.5
	32	0.75	800	0.3	12	3.2
S-Peak(15,3,15)	15	UMDA	1000	0.5	75	4.3
	15	0.25	1000	0.5	77	4.2
	15	0.5	1000	0.5	70	4.6
	15	0.75	1000	0.5	76	4.3

ilarly, if LFDA computes factorizations which are in probability terms very similar to the FDA factorization. FDA uses the same factorization for all generations, whereas LFDA computes a new factorization at each step which depends on the given data M.

We have applied LFDA to many problems [573]. The results are encouraging. Here we only discuss the functions introduced in Section 15.2. We recall that UMDA finds the optimum of BigJump, Saw and small instances of S-Peak. UMDA uses univariate marginal distributions only. Therefore its Bayesian network has no arcs.

Table 15.1 summarizes the results. For LFDA we used three different values of α, namely $\alpha = 0.25, 0.5, 0.75$. The smaller α, the less penalty for the size of the structure. Let us discuss the results in more detail. $\alpha = 0.25$ gives by far the best results when a network with many arcs is needed. This is the case for Deceptive-4. Here a Bayesian network with three parents is optimal. $\alpha = 0.25$ performs bad on problems where a network with no arcs defines a good search distribution. For the linear function OneMax $BIC(0.25)$ has only a success rate of 2%. The success rate can be improved if a larger population size N is used. The reason is as follows. $BIC(0.25)$ allows denser networks. But if a small population is used, spurious correlations may arise. These correlations have a negative impact for the search distribution. The problem can be solved by using a larger population. Increasing the value from $N = 100$ to $N = 200$ increases the success rate from 2% to 71% for OneMax.

For Bigjump, Saw and S-Peak a Bayesian network with no arcs is able to generate the optimum. An exact factorization requires a factor with n parameters. We used the heuristic BN with $k_{max} = 8$. Therefore the exact factorization cannot be found. In all these cases $\alpha = 0.75$ gives the best results. $BIC(0.75)$ enforces smaller networks. But $BIC(0.75)$ performs very bad on Deceptive-4. Taking all results together $BIC(0.5)$ gives good results. This numerical results supports the theoretical estimate.

The numerical result indicates that control of the weight factor α can substantially reduce the amount of computation. For Bayesian network we have not yet experimented with control strategies. We have intensively studied the problem in the context of neural networks [580]. The method will be discussed in section 15.6.

Network Equivalence and Optimality

Many Bayesian networks represent the same probability. These networks are called *equivalent*. Let us discuss a simple example.

$$p(x) = p(x_1)p(x_2|x_1)p(x_3|x_2, x_1)p(x_4|x_3) \qquad (15.22)$$

The independence structure is shown in figure 15.8.

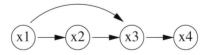

Figure 15.8
Structure of a Bayesian network

It can be proven that the following factorizations describe the same probability distribution.

$$p(x) = p(x_2)p(x_3|x_2)p(x_1|x_2,x_3)p(x_4|x_3) \qquad (15.23)$$

$$p(x) = p(x_3)p(x_4|x_3)p(x_2|x_3)p(x_1|x_2,x_3) \qquad (15.24)$$

$$p(x) = p(x_4)p(x_3|x_4)p(x_2|x_3)p(x_1|x_2,x_3) \qquad (15.25)$$

Furthermore all Bayesian factorizations which contain one of the above factorizations also generate the true distribution. We say that B_1 *is contained in* B_2 *if all arcs of* B_1 *are also arcs in* B_2.

THEOREM 15.3: Let B^* be a Bayesian network which generates the data and has the minimal number of arcs. The MDL score, as well as the BDe score has the following characteristics.

- As $M \to \infty$ the true structure B^* maximizes the scores.
- As $M \to \infty$ the maximal scoring structures are equivalent.

Proof: The proof is technically difficult, we just give an outline. Suppose network B has an arc not contained in B^*, then for $M \to \infty$

$$-M \cdot H(B, D) \quad \to \quad -M \cdot H(B^*, D) - e \cdot M$$

where e depends on B. Therefore

$$BIC(B^*, D, \alpha) - BIC(B, D, \alpha) \to e \cdot M - \alpha \cdot log(M) \cdot (dim(B^*) - dim(B))$$

Because $M/log(M) \to \infty$ the score of B^* is much larger than the score of B. This proves the first part of the theorem. Now let us assume that B^* has an arc not contained in B. As $M \to \infty$ we have $-M \cdot H(B, D) \to -M \cdot H(B^*, D)$. Therefore

$$BIC(B, D, \alpha) - BIC(B^*, D, \alpha) \to \alpha \cdot log(M) \cdot (dim(B^*) - dim(B)) \qquad (15.26)$$

But if $dim(B) > dim(B^*)$ then $BIC(B, D, \alpha)$ cannot be maximal. ∎
The above theorem is true for all values of $\alpha > 0$. For the proof only the term $log(M)$ is needed. We can now ask if our search algorithm $BN(\alpha, k)$ is able to find an optimal structure, given enough data. Unfortunately the following result shows that this cannot be proven in general [566].

Let a probability distribution be given. Then the problem of finding a Bayesian network with a minimum number of arcs is NP-hard for $k > 1$. If only trees are allowed, there exists a polynomial algorithm (in the number of *variables).*

Bayesian Networks

In this paper we have used Bayesian networks in a new context: to find good search distributions for an optimization problem. Normally Bayesian networks are used in a different context: to provide a formalism for reasoning about partial beliefs under conditions of uncertainty. Therefore Bayesian networks are also called *belief networks*. The nodes represent random variables. The arcs signify the existence of direct causal influences between the variables. Ultimately the belief network represents a probability distribution over X having the Bayesian product form.

The following problems are defined over belief networks with fixed structure:

Belief updating: Given a set of observations, compute the posterior probability of each proposition.

Missing values: Given some observed variables, find a maximum probability assignment to the rest of the variables.

Creating hypothesis: Given some evidence, find an assignment to a subset of hypothesis variables that maximizes their probability.

In general these tasks are NP-hard. But they permit a polynomial propagation algorithm for tree networks. The above tasks will be discussed in the context of neural networks in section 15.6. Next we will investigate genetic programming.

15.5 Synthesis of Programs

Salustewicz and Schmidhuber [577] have proposed a method for the synthesis of programs bases on probabilities. This method is very similar to the methods discussed in this paper. Therefore we summarize the major concepts of the method. In their method programs are generated according to a probabilistic prototype tree (PPT).

A program contains instructions chosen from a set of functions $F = \{f_1, f_2, \ldots, f_k\}$ and a terminal set $T = \{t_1, t_2, \ldots t_l\}$. Functions have one or more arguments, terminals have no argument. The terminal set consists of input variables x_i and a generic random constant $R \in [0; 1)$ which will be changed during the run.

Programs are encoded in m-ary trees with m being the maximum number of function arguments. Each non-leaf node encodes a function from F and each leaf node a terminal from T. The number of subtrees that each node has corresponds to the number of arguments for its function. The Probabilistic Prototype Tree (PPT) is generally a complete m-ary tree. At each node $N_{d,w}$ it contains a probability vector $p_{d,w}$ and a random constant $R_{d,w}$. d denotes the depth of the node and w defines the node's horizontal position. PPT is parsed from top to bottom and left to right. The probability vector $p_{d,w}$ has $i = l + k$ elements. Each element $p_{d,w}(I)$ denotes the probability of choosing instruction $I \in F \cup T$ at $N_{d,w}$.

A program PROG is generated from PPT in the following way. An instruction I_{prog} at node $N_{d,w}$ is selected with probability $p_{d,w}(I_{prog})$. If $I_{prog} \in F$, a subtree is created for each argument of I_{prog}. If $I_{prog} \in T$ the selected input variable or a constant is put at the program tree. Therefore a program is generated with probability

$$p(PROG) = \prod_{d,w} p_{d,w}(I_{prog}) \qquad (15.27)$$

Thus the algorithm uses univariate marginal distributions. I_{prog} is not a binary variable, but has i distinct values. Therefore our theory developed in the first sections can be applied. We have yet to define a fitness. Normally the program gets only examples $(\mathbf{x}_j, \mathbf{y}_j)$. A measure of the goodness of a program is given by

$$score(PROG) = \sum_j |\mathbf{y}_j - PROG(\mathbf{x}_j)| \qquad (15.28)$$

The quadratic score popular with neural networks can be used instead.

The presented model is very similar to UMDA. The only extension is the usage of a probabilistic tree instead of a probabilistic string. Each probabilistic variable has $l + k$ elements. Using only univariate marginal distributions is obviously a very crude approximation for the problem domain considered. An extension to conditional marginal distributions seems necessary. In a first approximation each node at layer $k + 1$ can be conditioned on its parent node at layer k. For tree networks very efficient algorithms exist which determine the optimal structure. This proposal needs further study.

15.6   Neural Trees

Bayesian networks are founded on probability theory. The problem of determining the optimal parameters of a Bayesian network given the data is solved by probability theory. The optimal parameter are just the empirical frequencies of the conditional marginal distributions. There also exist powerful heuristics like $BN(\alpha)$ which change the structure of a Bayesian network to better fit the data.

For general neural networks like the famous multilayer perceptron the situation is much more difficult. The determination of the optimal parameters (called weights) is difficult. Special algorithms have been developed for this problem. In addition there exist no heuristics backed up by theory which adapt the structure.

In principle Bayesian networks can also be used in the domain of neural networks: to learn a function $\mathbf{x} \rightarrow \mathbf{y} = f(\mathbf{x})$. The mapping $(\mathbf{x}, \mathbf{y})$ can be represented by a conditional probability distribution $p(\mathbf{y}|\mathbf{x})$. But during the training $\mathbf{y}$ will depend on all variables of $\mathbf{x}$ or of the variables of a hidden layer. This means that the number of parents used for Bayesian factorization is n. Thus the amount of computation is of order $O(2^n)$ making this approach obsolete.

Currently two paths are followed to attack this problem. The first path restricts the class of neural networks. There exist a subclass of neural networks called *sigmoid belief networks* which allow a probabilistic interpretation. The interconnection structure of the belief networks has to be restricted to trees in order that the algorithms invented for Bayesian networks can be applied.

We have experimented with neural trees. Here the neurons are complex, but the structure is restricted to trees. Because the neurons are complex, we do not yet have a probabilistic interpretation of neural trees. Therefore we are faced with two problems: to determine the optimal weights for a structure and to find the optimal structure.

Let $\mathcal{NT}(d, b)$ denote the set of all possible trees of maximum depth d and maximum number of branches for each node b. The nonterminal nodes represent (formal) neurons and the neuron type is an element of the basis function set $\mathcal{F} = \{\text{neuron types}\}$. Each terminal node is labeled with an element from the terminal set $\mathcal{T} = \{x_1, x_2, \ldots, x_n\}$, where x_i is the ith component of the external input $\mathbf{x}$. Each link (i, j) represents a directed connection from node i to node j and is associated with a value $w_{i,j}$, called synaptic weight. The members of $\mathcal{NT}(d, b)$ are referred to as neural trees. The root node is also called the output unit and the terminal nodes are called input units. The rest are hidden units. The layer of a node is defined as the longest path length among the paths to the terminal nodes of its subtree.

Different neuron types compute different net inputs. For the evolution of higher-order networks, we consider two types of units. The sigma units compute the sum of weighted inputs from the lower layer:

$$net_i = \sum_j w_{ij} y_j \qquad (15.29)$$

where y_j are the inputs to the ith neuron. The pi units compute the product of weighted inputs from the lower layer:

$$net_i = \prod_j w_{ij} y_j \qquad (15.30)$$

where y_j are the inputs to i. The output of the neurons is computed either by the threshold response function

$$y_i = \sigma(net_i) = \left\{ \begin{array}{ccc} 1 & : & net_i \geq 0 \\ -1 & : & net_i < 0 \end{array} \right. \qquad (15.31)$$

or the sigmoid transfer function

$$y_i = f(net_i) = \frac{1}{1 + e^{-net_i}} \qquad (15.32)$$

where net_i is the net input to the unit.

A higher-order network with m output units can be represented by a list of m neural trees. That is, the genotype A_i of ith individual in our evolutionary framework consists of m sigma-pi neural trees:

$$A_i = (A_{i,1}, A_{i,2}, \ldots, A_{i,m}) \quad \forall k \in \{1, \ldots, m\}, \ A_{i,k} \in \mathcal{NT}(d, b) \qquad (15.33)$$

These neural networks are called *sigma-pi neural trees*. The neural tree representation does not restrict the functionality since any feed-forward network can be represented with a forest of neural trees. The connections between input units to arbitrary units in the network is also possible since input units can appear more than once in the neural tree representation. The output of one unit can be used as input to more than one unit in the upper layers by using them more than once.

Searching for the Best Structure

The structural adaptations alter the topology, size, depth, and shape of neural networks: the first three are changed by crossover and the last by mutations.

As with other genetic programming methods, the crossover operation is in essence performed by exchanging subtrees of parent individuals. Because of the uniformity of the neural tree representation, no syntactic restriction is necessary in choosing the crossover points. Instead of producing two offspring, we create only one, which allows a guided crossover by subtree evaluation. From two parent individuals A and B, the offspring C is generated by the following procedure:

1. Select a subtree a of A at random or one that has poor local fitness value.
2. Select a subtree b of B at random or one that has good local fitness value.
3. Produce an offspring C by copying A and replacing a with b.

The local fitness is measured by a combination of the error and size of the subtrees. Other criteria for subtree evaluation proposed in the literature include the error of the subtree, error difference, frequency of subtrees, use of the average fitness of population, correlation-based selection, combination of frequency and error difference [580]. Mutation and adding of library functions is also discussed there.

15.7 MDL-Based Fitness Function

The goal is to find a neural tree or model A whose evaluation $f_A(\mathbf{x})$ best approximates the unknown relation $\mathbf{y} = f(\mathbf{x})$ given an input $\mathbf{x}$. The goodness of the program for the dataset D is measured by the quadratic error

$$E(A|D) \;=\; \frac{1}{N} \sum_{c=1}^{N} (\mathbf{y}_c - f_A(\mathbf{x}_c))^2 , \tag{15.34}$$

where N is the number of training examples.

We can now apply the MDL principle as before. The data consists of examples $(\mathbf{x}, \mathbf{y})$. In general, however, the distribution of the examples is unknown and the exact formula for the fitness function is impossible to obtain. Therefore we propose to approximate MDL by

$$MDL(A, D) = E(A|D) + \alpha C(A), \tag{15.35}$$

where the parameter α controls the trade-off between complexity $C(A)$ and fitting error $E(D|A)$ of the neural tree.

Now we describe a heuristic that controls α. Care must be taken in applying the MDL principle to neural trees so that redundant structures should be pruned as much as possible, but at the same time premature convergence should be avoided. Avoiding the loss of diversity is especially important in the early stages, while strong pruning is desirable to get parsimonious solutions and improve generalization performance in the final stage.

To balance the parsimony with accuracy dynamically, we fix the error factor at each generation and change the complexity factor adaptively with respect to the error. Each individual of our population consists of a neural tree. Let $E_i(t)$ and $C_i(t)$ denote the error and complexity of ith individual at generation t. The complexity of neural trees can be measured as the sum of the units, weights, and layers. The fitness of an individual i at generation t is defined as follows:

$$F_i(t) \quad = \quad E_i(t) + \alpha(t)C_i(t), \tag{15.36}$$

where $0 \leq E_i(t) \leq 1$ and $C_i(t) > 0$ is assumed.

We control $\alpha(t)$ as follows

$$\alpha(t) = \begin{cases} \frac{1}{N^2}\frac{E_{best}(t-1)}{\hat{C}_{best}(t)} & \text{if } E_{best}(t-1) > \epsilon \\ \frac{1}{N^2}\frac{1}{E_{best}(t-1)\cdot\hat{C}_{best}(t)} & \text{otherwise,} \end{cases} \tag{15.37}$$

where N is the size of the training set. User-defined constant ϵ specifies the maximum training error allowed for the final solution.

Note that $\alpha(t)$ depends on $E_{best}(t-1)$ and $\hat{C}_{best}(t)$. $E_{best}(t-1)$ is the error value of the program which had the smallest (best) fitness value at generation $t-1$. $\hat{C}_{best}(t)$ is the size of the best program at generation t estimated at generation $t-1$. It is computed as follows

$$\hat{C}_{best}(t) = C_{best}(t-1) + \Delta C_{sum}(t-1) \tag{15.38}$$

where ΔC_{sum} is a moving average that keeps track of the difference in the complexity between the best individual of one generation and the best individual of the next:

$$\Delta C_{sum}(t) = 0.5\big(C_{best}(t) - C_{best}(t-1) + \Delta C_{sum}(t-1)\big) \tag{15.39}$$

with $\Delta C_{sum}(0) = 0$ (see [579] for more details). $\hat{C}_{best}(t)$ is used for the normalization of the complexity factor. In essence, two adaptation phases are distinguished. When $E_{best}(t-1) > \epsilon$, $\alpha(t)$ decreases as the training error falls since $E_{best}(t-1) \leq 1$ is multiplied. This encourages fast error reduction at the early stages of evolution. For $E_{best}(t-1) \leq \epsilon$, in contrast, as $E_{best}(t)$ approaches 0 the relative importance of complexity increases due to the division by a small value $E_{best}(t-1) \ll 1$. This encourages stronger complexity reduction at the final stages to obtain parsimonious solutions. Numerical results of this method can be found in [580].

15.8   Conclusion

Our theory of evolutionary algorithms has shown that their dynamic behavior can best be explained by the fitness distribution defined by $p(\mathbf{x})$ and not by the fitness landscape $f(\mathbf{x})$. Many evolutionary algorithms are doing gradient ascent on the landscape defined by the average fitness $W(p)$. We have shown that genetic algorithms can be approximated by evolutionary algorithms using probability distributions. The theory leads to a synthesis problem: finding a good factorization for the search distribution. This problem lies in the center of probability theory. For Bayesian networks numerical efficient algorithms have been developed. We have discussed the algorithm LFDA in detail, which computes a Bayesian network by minimizing the Bayesian Information Criterion.

We have outlined how the theory might be used to synthesize programs from probabilistic prototype trees. The advantage of this approach is its backup by a solid theory. In order to be numerical efficient, additional research is necessary.

Synthesis of complex neural networks is still outside this theory. Here two solutions seem possible: either Bayesian networks are extended to the application domain of neural networks or the structure of neural networks is restricted so that it can be handled in a Bayesian framework.

References

[566]R. Bouckaert. Properties of bayesian network learning algorithms. In R. L. de Mantaras and D. Poole, editors, *Proc. Tenth Conference on Uncertainty in Artificial Intelligence*, pages 102–109, San Francisco, 1994. Morgan Kaufmann.

[567]B. Frey. *Graphical Models for Machine Learning and Digital Communication*. MIT Press, Cambrigde, 1998.

[568]D. Goldberg. *Genetic Algorithms in Search, Optimization and Machine Learning*. Addison-Wesley, Reading, 1989.

[569]G. Harik. Linkage learning via probabilistic modeling in the ecga. Technical Report IlliGal 99010, University of Illinois, Urbana-Champaign, 1999.

[570]M. Jordan. *Learning in Graphical Models*. MIT Press, Cambrigde, 1999.

[571]S. Kullback and Leibler. On information and suffiency. *Annals of Mathematical Statistics*, 22:76–86, 1951.

[572]H. Mühleinbein and T. Mahnig. Convergence theory and applications of the factorized distribution algorithm. *Journal of Computing and Information Technology*, 7:19–32, 1999.

[573]H. Mühleinbein and T. Mahnig. Fda – a scalable evolutionary algorithm for the optimization of additively decomposed functions. *Evolutionary Computation*, 1999. to be published.

[574]H. Mühlenbein. The equation for the response to selection and its use for prediction. *Evolutionary Computation*, 5(3):303–346, 1997.

[575]H. Mühlenbein, T. Mahnig, and A. R. Ochoa. Schemata, distributions and graphical models in evolutionary optimization. *Journal of Heuristics*, 5:215–247, 1999.

[576]M. Pelikan, D. Goldberg, and E. Cantu-Paz. Boa: The bayesian optimization algorithm. Technical Report IlliGal 99003, University of Illinois, Urbana-Champaign, 1999.

[577]R. Salustewicz and J. Schmidhuber. Probabilistic incremental program evolution. *Evolutionary Computation*, 5:123–143, 1997.

[578]G. Schwarz. Estimating the dimension of a model. *Annals of Statistics*, 7:461–464, 1978.

[579]B.-T. Zhang and H. Mühlenbein. Balancing accuracy and parsimony in genetic programming. *Evolutionary Computation*, 3:17–38, 1995.

[580]B.-T. Zhang, P. Ohm, and H. Mühlenbein. Evolutionary induction of sparse neural trees. *Evolutionary Computation*, 5:213–236, 1997.

Index